A Grammar of Saramaccan Creole

Mouton Grammar Library
56

Editors
Georg Bossong
Bernard Comrie
Matthew Dryer

De Gruyter Mouton

A Grammar of Saramaccan Creole

by
John H. McWhorter
Jeff Good

De Gruyter Mouton

ISBN 978-3-11-099540-4
e-ISBN 978-3-11-027826-2
ISSN 0933-7636

Library of Congress Cataloging-in-Publication Data

A CIP catalog record for this book has been applied for at the Library of Congress.

Bibliographic information published by the Deutsche Nationalbibliothek

The Deutsche Nationalbibliothek lists this publication in the Deutsche Nationalbibliografie; detailed bibliographic data are available in the Internet at http://dnb.dnb.de.

© 2022 Walter de Gruyter GmbH & Co. KG, Berlin/Boston
This volume is text- and page-identical with the hardback published in 2012.

Printing: Hubert & Co. GmbH & Co. KG, Göttingen
Printed on acid-free paper

Printed in Germany

www.degruyter.com

Table of contents

Abbreviations — xi
Introduction — xiii

1 Segmental phonology — 1
- 1.1. Segment inventory — 1
- 1.1.1. Introduction — 1
- 1.1.2. Consonants — 2
- 1.1.2.1. Oral stops — 2
- 1.1.2.2. Plain nasals and prenasalized stops — 7
- 1.1.2.3. Fricatives — 10
- 1.1.2.4. Approximants — 12
- 1.1.3. Vowels — 15
- 1.1.3.1. Basic vowel qualities — 15
- 1.1.3.2. Nasal vowels — 17
- 1.1.3.3. Long vowels and vowel combinations — 18
- 1.2. Phonotactics — 24
- 1.2.1. Syllable structure and epenthetic vowels — 24
- 1.2.2. Co-occurrence restrictions and related kinds of patterns — 25
- 1.2.3. Ideophones — 27
- 1.3. Lexical strata — 28
- 1.4. Sporadic alternations — 29

2 Prosodic phonology — 30
- 2.1. Introduction — 30
- 2.2. Word-level prosody — 30
- 2.2.1. Introduction — 30
- 2.2.2. Accentual words — 32
- 2.2.2.1. Words with high tones and TBU's unspecified for tone — 32
- 2.2.2.2. Accented words with short syllables — 33
- 2.2.2.3. Accented words with "heavy" syllables — 35
- 2.2.2.4. Manifestations of stress and possible foot structures — 36
- 2.2.2.5. Minimal pairs — 39
- 2.2.3. Tonal words — 39
- 2.2.3.1. High tones and low tones — 39
- 2.2.3.2. Indeterminacy in determining if a word is marked for tone or accent — 41
- 2.2.3.3. Minimal pairs and tonal features of morphological processes — 42
- 2.2.3.4. Lack of evidence for stress — 43
- 2.2.3.5. Ideophones — 44
- 2.2.4. Word-level prosody: Exceptions — 44
- 2.3. Phrasal prosody — 45
- 2.3.1. Tonal plateauing — 46
- 2.3.1.1. Compounds and regular reduplication — 46
- 2.3.1.2. Noun phrases — 47
- 2.3.1.3. Adpositional phrases — 49
- 2.3.1.4. Tones in the verbal complex — 50

2.3.1.5.	Simple clauses	50
2.3.1.6.	Adverbial expressions	51
2.3.1.7.	Interaction between intonational processes and plateauing	52
2.3.2.	Tones in serial verb constructions	53
2.4.	Intonational processes	57
2.4.1.	Overview	57
2.4.2.	Utterance-final lowering	57
2.4.3.	Negative lowering	58
2.4.4.	Emphasis within a clause	60
2.4.5.	Yes/no questions	61
2.5.	Notes on tonal and intonational phonetics and problems of analysis	62

3 Morphology and morphophonemics — 63

3.1.	Derivational morphology	63
3.1.1.	Reduplication	63
3.1.1.1.	Deverbal resultatives	63
3.1.1.2.	Intensification	64
3.1.1.3.	X-like	64
3.1.1.4.	Aggregate plural	64
3.1.1.5.	Nominalization	65
3.1.1.6.	Tone plateauing in reduplicated words	65
3.1.2.	The nominalizers *-ma* and *-wǎ*	66
3.1.3.	An incipient derivational affix?	66
3.2.	Inflectional morphology	67
3.2.1.	Imperfective *tá* with *gó* 'to go'	67
3.2.2.	Tonal marking of verb serialization	67
3.2.3.	Nominal marker *a-*?	68
3.3.	Morphophonemics	68
3.3.1.	Possessive *(f)u*	68
3.3.2.	Other morphophonemic processes with *fu*	69
3.3.3.	Negation and pronouns	69
3.3.4.	Third-person singular *ɛ̃*	69
3.3.4.1.	After a verb	69
3.3.4.2.	With locative marker *a*	70
3.3.4.3.	With negator *ná*	71
3.3.4.4.	With copula *da*	71
3.3.4.5.	With *njǎ* 'eat' and *fő* 'beat'	71
3.3.5.	Locative *(n)a*	71
3.3.6.	Hortative verb *bé*	72
3.4.	Compounding	72
3.5.	Rapid speech phenomena	74

4 The noun phrase — 76

4.1.	Determiners	76
4.2.	Demonstratives	79
4.3.	Possession	80
4.4.	Relative clauses	85
4.4.1.	The accessibility hierarchy	85
4.5.	Quantifiers	88

	4.6.	Coordination	92
	4.7.	Gerunds	92
	4.8.	Adjective + *wá* 'one'	93
5	**Personal pronouns**		94
	5.1.	Pronominal inventory	94
	5.2.	Clitic status	95
	5.2.1.	Third-person singular oblique *ɛ̃*	95
	5.2.2.	First-person singular *m*	96
	5.3.	Second-person singular *ju*	97
	5.4.	Pleonastic pronoun	97
	5.5.	Reflexives	97
	5.6.	Reciprocals	99
6	**Adjectives**		100
	6.1.	Definition of adjectival class	100
	6.2.	Adjectives and reduplication	102
	6.3.	Irregularities in reduplication of property items	103
	6.4.	Resultative adjectives	106
	6.5.	Comparative constructions	108
	6.5.1.	Positive comparison	108
	6.5.2.	Degree of comparison	110
	6.5.3.	Equal comparison	110
	6.5.4.	Negative comparison	110
	6.5.5.	Superlatives	111
	6.5.6.	Excessives	111
	6.6.	Color terms	112
7	**Core predicate phrase modifiers: Negators, tense, aspect, and modals**		113
	7.1.	Negation	113
	7.1.1.	Predicate negation	113
	7.1.2.	Irregularity in surface manifestation of negative marking	115
	7.1.3.	Negative quantifiers	116
	7.2.	Tense markers	117
	7.2.1.	Past marker *bi*	117
	7.2.2.	Future marker *ó*	121
	7.3.	Aspect markers	121
	7.3.1.	Imperfective marker *tá*	121
	7.3.2.	Grammatical status of *bi*, *ó*, and *tá*	123
	7.3.3.	Habitual marker *ló*	123
	7.3.4.	Past habitual marker *náa*	124
	7.3.5.	Durativity	125
	7.3.6.	Completive marker *kaa*	125
	7.3.7.	*Kó* as completive marker	128
	7.3.8.	Continuative marker *gó dóu*	128
	7.4.	Modal markers	129
	7.4.1.	Deontic	129
	7.4.2.	Epistemic	131
	7.4.2.1.	Probability	131

	7.4.2.2.	Ability	132
	7.4.2.3.	Possibility	133
	7.5.	Order of occurrence	135
8	**Verb serialization**	137
	8.1.	Diagnostic issues	137
	8.1.1.	Taxonomy	137
	8.1.2.	Constraints on argument sharing	138
	8.2.	Directional serials	139
	8.3.	Serials encoding core grammatical distinctions	141
	8.3.1.	*Dá* 'give'	141
	8.3.2.	Degree	142
	8.3.3.	Repetition	143
	8.3.4.	Complementation	143
	8.3.5.	Hortative marker	144
	8.4.	Serials with moderately grammaticalized meaning	145
	8.5.	Verbs used serially without change in meaning	147
	8.5.1.	*Kabá* 'finish'	147
	8.5.2.	Other verbs	147
	8.5.3.	*Téi* 'take' as "instrumental"?	148
	8.6.	Verb serialization as *Sprachgefühl*	149
9	**Coordination and subordination**	150
	9.1.	Coordination	150
	9.1.1.	Conjunction	150
	9.1.2.	Disjunction	151
	9.1.3.	Exclusion	151
	9.2.	Subordination	152
	9.2.1.	Finite complements	152
	9.2.1.1.	Factive complements	152
	9.2.1.2.	Hortative complements	152
	9.2.1.3.	Complements of perception and causation verbs	152
	9.2.2.	Nonfinite complements	154
	9.2.2.1.	Control verbs	154
	9.2.2.2.	Small clauses	155
	9.2.2.3.	Gerund complements	156
	9.2.3.	Subordination: Adverbial complement clauses	157
	9.2.3.1.	Temporal complements	157
	9.2.3.2.	Purpose complements	158
	9.2.3.3.	Locational complements	160
	9.2.3.4.	Manner complements	160
	9.2.3.5.	Causal complements	160
	9.2.3.6.	Conditional complements	161
	9.2.3.7.	Concessive complements	162
	9.2.3.8.	Substitutive complements	163
10	**Passive and imperative**	164
	10.1.	Valence-decreasing operations	164
	10.1.1.	Passive voice	164

	10.1.2.	Middle voice	167
	10.1.3.	Object omission	168
	10.2.	Valence-increasing operations	168
	10.2.1.	Ditransitives	168
	10.2.2.	Causatives	170
	10.3.	The imperative mood	171
11	**Questions**		173
	11.1.	Yes/no questions	173
	11.2.	Information questions	175
	11.3.	Indirect questions	176
12	**Nonverbal predication and *be*-verbs**		178
	12.1.	Identificational equative predicates: *Da*	178
	12.1.1.	Basic traits	178
	12.1.2.	Irregularities	178
	12.1.3.	Omission	180
	12.1.4.	Allomorphy	181
	12.1.5.	*Da* as sentential presentative	182
	12.2.	Class equative predicates: *Dé* or *da*	182
	12.3.	Locative and other predicates: *Dé*	183
	12.4.	Existential predicates	184
13	**Position, direction, and time**		186
	13.1.	Spatial indicators	186
	13.2.	Deictic adverbials	188
	13.3.	Direction	190
	13.3.1.	Some directional verbs	190
	13.3.2.	Allative and ablative movement	190
	13.3.2.1.	Ablative	190
	13.3.2.2.	Allative	192
	13.4.	Time expressions	193
	13.4.1.	Units of time	193
	13.4.2.	Timeline placement of events	194
14	**Adverbial modification**		196
	14.1.	Intensifiers	196
	14.2.	Time adverbials	197
	14.3.	Adverbs of quantity	199
	14.4.	Adverbs of manner	200
	14.5.	Adverbs of frequency	201
	14.6.	The evidential adverbial construction	202
	14.7.	Ideophones	202
	14.8.	Placement of adverbs	204
15	**Information structure**		205
	15.1.	Contrastive focus	205
	15.1.1.	Impressionistic prominence	205
	15.1.2.	Contrastive focus on verbs	205

	15.1.3.	Contrastive focus on arguments and adjuncts	206
	15.1.3.1.	Fronting	206
	15.1.3.2.	Contrastive focus marker *wɛ*	206
	15.1.3.3.	Contrastive focus marking with *hɛ́*	208
	15.1.3.4.	Focus marker *hɛ́ da*	209
	15.1.3.5.	Reduplicated pronouns?	209
	15.2.	Pragmatic markers	209
	15.2.1.	Given-information marking	209
	15.2.2.	New-information marking: *Nɔ́ɔ* and *hɛ́*	210
	15.2.2.1.	Position of *nɔ́ɔ*	211
	15.2.2.2.	*Nɔ́ɔ* and adverbial complements	212
	15.2.2.3.	New information versus focus-marking	213
	15.2.2.4.	*Hɛ́* as new-information marker in the bounded past	214
	15.3.	Combinations of focus and pragmatic markers	214
	15.4.	Pragmatic-marking adverbs	216
	15.4.1.	*Nɔ́ɔ* 'just, only'	216
	15.4.2.	*Nɔ́ɔmɔ* 'indeed'	216
	15.4.3.	*Seéi*	217
	15.4.4.	*Awáa* 'at last'	218
	15.4.5.	Interjection *é*	220
	15.4.6.	Interjection *o*	220
16	**Numerals and other time expressions**		**221**
	16.1.	Cardinal numbers	221
	16.2.	Ordinal numbers	221
	16.3.	Distribution	222
	16.4.	Fraction	222
	16.5.	Time by the clock	222
	16.6.	Days of the week	223
	16.7.	Months	223
17	**Lexical variation**		**224**
	17.1.	Dialects	224
	17.2.	Free variation	224

Word list 226
Folktale transcription 228
Conversational passage 232
References 235
Index 239

Abbreviations

AG: agentive marker
COMP: complementizer
CPLT: completive
DEF: definite determiner
FOC: focus marker
FUT: future
HAB: habitual
HORT: hortative
IDEO: ideophone
IMF: imperfective
INDF: indefinite determiner
INJ: interjection
INT: interrogative marker
LOC: locative
NEG: negator
NF: nonfinite marker
NI: new information marker
PL: plural
POSS: possessive marker
RD: reduplicated
REL: relative marker
UFUT: uncertain future
1P: first-person plural pronoun (subject or object)
1S: first-person singular pronoun (subject or object)
2P: second-person plural subject pronoun
2PO: second-person plural oblique pronoun
2S: second-person singular pronoun (subject or object)
3P: third-person plural pronoun (subject or object)
3S: third-person singular subject pronoun
3SO: third-person singular oblique pronoun
3ST: third-person singular tonic pronoun

Introduction

Saramaccan is a language only a few centuries old, spoken in Surinam by about 50,000 people. Most live in rain forest villages and camps along the Suriname River, while speakers of one dialect live along the Saramacca River. Almost 15,000, however, live in the adjacent country French Guiana, in the wake of a civil war in Surinam (1986–1992) involving aggression from government forces. Also, some several hundred emigrants live mostly in the Netherlands and the United States. Its speakers are descendants of African slaves who escaped from plantations near the coast of Surinam in the late seventeenth and early eighteenth centuries.

These slaves created a language that is neither European nor African, but a new hybrid language. Saramaccan's lexicon is composed primarily of English and Portuguese-derived lexical items. On the 200-word Swadesh list, 54% of the words are English and 37% are Portuguese (Voorhoeve 1973). Surinam was a Dutch colony from 1665 to 1975, and thus of the remaining words, about half are from Dutch. The Dutch lexical contribution is adstratal, especially prominent in terms introduced from the world outside of the villages, but not limited to this (e.g. the word for 'day' is *dáka* from Dutch *dag*).

The rest of the lexicon is derived from West African languages of the Niger-Congo family spoken by the slaves who created the language. Fongbe (of the Kwa subfamily) and Kikongo (a Bantu language) are the main contributors, both contributing about 130 words (Smith 1987a, Daeleman 1972). There are also some words from the Kwa language Twi as well as a small number from Amerindian languages such as Tirió spoken by the indigenous inhabitants of the Surinamese rain forest. The West African items are especially prominent in the "cultural" realm, such as names of animals and plants, and also furnish ideophones, as central to adverbial expression in Saramaccan as in many African languages. However, West African languages also furnished terms for a number of core concepts such as 'side' (*bandja*) and 'father' (*tatá*) (from Kikongo), as well as central grammatical items such as *andí* 'what,' *ambé* 'who,' and focus marker *wɛ* (from Fongbe).

Despite this lexical hybridity, Saramaccan is fundamentally an English-based creole, diachronically related to several varieties of what can be termed Atlantic English-based Creole. This term refers to creoles comprising variations on a common lexical and grammatical template, including creoles of Surinam, English-based New World creoles such as Jamaican, Guyanese, and Gullah, and West African varieties such as Sierra Leone Krio, Nigerian "Pidgin" English, and Cameroonian Pidgin English.

Grammatically, these languages are roughly as akin as German dialects, such that there is mutual intelligibility between many; for example, a Sierra Leone Krio speaker can manage a conversation with a speaker of Gullah Creole spoken in South Carolina in the United States. Researchers who have studied closely the relationship between these varieties largely concur that they all trace to a single ancestor. Most suppose this ancestor arose in the Caribbean, such as on St. Kitts or Barbados; some place the origin on the West African coast. In either case, Saramaccan can be seen as one of several sister descendants of an ancestral Atlantic English-based pidgin or creole variety of seventeenth-century provenance.

Saramaccan is unusual among these creoles, for one, in its heavy amount of Portuguese vocabulary. However, this is predominantly lexical: only 16% of its grammatical items have Portuguese sources (Smith 1987b: 145). Saramaccan's grammar is also deeply permeated by that of Fongbe, to an extent that renders it the most African-influenced (or, as it has been put, "deepest" or "most radical") of the Atlantic English-based creoles. Saramaccan has phonemic tone as a systematic feature extending to a modestly substantial number of minimal-pair contrasts, syntactic uses for reduplication, ample verb serialization, heavy use of ideophones, postposed nominals as spatial markers, and many other parallels with Fongbe (Kikongo's contribution was only lexical).

Beyond these substratally derived features, in terms of typology Saramaccan has SVO word order, with a mild degree of topic-prominence, and is mostly a head-initial language. However, the genitive construction can contravene this: *Ámba tatá* 'Amba's father,' although there is an alternate genitive construction, equally prevalent, that does not: *dí hási u de* 'their horse' (lit. 'the horse of them'). Also, compounds are head-final: *tjá-bóto-ma* 'boat carrier' (lit. 'carry boat -er').

Saramaccan's history begins with its sister creole in Surinam, Sranan, today the vernacular lingua franca of the country. Surinam was one of the English's first New World colonies, settled in 1651. The slaves who worked these early plantations developed Sranan, a creole with a predominantly English core lexicon and, like Saramaccan, strong grammatical influence from Fongbe.

In 1665, Portuguese-speaking Jewish plantation owners migrated to Surinam from Brazil via today's French Guiana (eastwardly adjacent to Surinam). Two years later in 1667, according to the Treaty of Breda the Dutch gave their New Amsterdam colony to the English in exchange for Surinam. New Amsterdam became New York, while Surinam was now under Dutch rule. When the English plantation owners departed, they took many slaves with them but left many behind. The Portuguese Jews bought many of these slaves to work their plantations.

As a result of this last, on the Portuguese plantations a new creole developed: a variety of Sranan with heavy relexification by Portuguese. When Moravian missionary C. L. Schumann compiled a Sranan dictionary in the late 1700s, speakers differentiated certain words as from a separate "Dju-tongo" (Jew-language) spoken on the Portuguese-owned plantations. The "Dju-tongo" words are clearly what we now know as Saramaccan. However, by that time, this alternate creole was spoken not only on the Portuguese plantations, but in the rain forest communities established by slaves who had escaped from them, starting in about 1690 according to most estimates. It would appear, then, that the language now known as Saramaccan emerged on Portuguese plantations in the 1670s and 1680s.

Formerly it was proposed that Saramaccan began as a Portuguese creole, derived from a Portuguese pidgin thought to have been the source of all of the New World plantation creoles (cf. Voorhoeve 1973). This idea incorporated Saramaccan into the Monogenesis Hypothesis of the origin of most of the world's plantation creoles, according to which African slaves had learned a Portuguese pidgin on the West African coast before being brought to plantations, and relexified it with words from the language of the colony their plantation was in. Thus it was thought that Saramaccan resulted when this Portuguese pidgin was partially relexified by English, the dominant language of Surinam's first colonizers.

However, although the Monogenesis Hypothesis continues to be cited in many treatises on creoles as one of many schools of thought on creole genesis, no working creolist subscribes to it today (research over the past few decades has refuted it, although it was a reasonable hypothesis based on the data available before this). As such, while the idea that Saramaccan began as a Portuguese pidgin is still cited in sources written by laymen to the particulars of the subject, this idea is obsolete among scholars who study Saramaccan and its history (Goodman 1987 is a useful summary of the fundamental findings on the issue).

Because of its history, Saramaccan is, as noted previously, one of the creoles most unlike the European languages that provided its words. Saramaccan's progenitor creole Sranan only co-existed with its lexifier, English, for a mere sixteen years, 1651 to 1667. After this, the language of the masters was Dutch. Thus the Sranan that slaves brought to Portuguese plantations was not a language reflecting the effects of long-term diglossia with English, like Jamaican patois does today, with its continuum of dialects ranging from the "deepest" patois to standard English. It was, rather, a language that had used English as a lexical source but had not been occasioned by social history to be pulled towards English's grammar any further than it initially was.

Then, spoken in the interior apart from Europeans, Saramaccan was especially impacted by the African languages native to escapees from the plantations (the plantation "Dju-tongo" progenitor of Saramaccan eventually went extinct; there is no modern-day indigenous coastal variety of Saramaccan). For this reason, not only is Saramaccan's lexicon permeated more deeply by African languages than most creoles, but its grammar parallels that of Fongbe in particular to a degree that even Sranan, ever influenced on the coast by Dutch, does not.

For further information on the history of the Saramaka people, the authoritative sources are Price (1976) and especially Price (1983), which documents Saramaka history as recounted by the Saramaka themselves.

Saramaccan is one of three closely related creoles of Surinam; namely, Saramaccan, Sranan, and Ndjuka.

Sranan was the progenitor creole of the two others. The other creole is known by the generic term Ndjuka, and is spoken by descendants of slaves who escaped from plantations owned by the Dutch where Sranan was spoken. Ndjuka exists in four dialects. Paramaccan and the dialect called, itself, Ndjuka are spoken in eastern Surinam. Aluku (alternately Boni) is spoken mostly in neighboring French Guiana, while Kwinti is spoken westward of Saramaccan dialects, on the Coppename River. Ndjuka (in the generic sense) is essentially a dialect of Sranan, about as similar to it as Swedish is to Norwegian. Ndjuka retains a CVCV phonological template to a greater degree than Sranan, as well as a degree of phonemic tone and other Fongbe-derived features that are absent in Sranan. These features likely reflect an earlier stage of Sranan, which has become somewhat less akin to Fongbe over the centuries because of contact with Dutch. Nevertheless, Fongbe influence is even stronger in Saramaccan than in the Ndjuka varieties.

There are three dialects of Saramaccan. The Upper River (*líbase*) dialect (despite the initial appearance of the terminology, actually the dialect spoken further *south* in the interior) contrasts with the Lower River (*básuse*) dialect most prominently in certain shibboleths, such as that in the Upper River dialect, the predicate negator is *â* rather than the Lower River's *á*, and that the portmanteau morpheme combining the first-person singular pronoun and the negator is *má* in the Upper River dialect and *mé* in the Lower River one.

The other dialect is Matawai, spoken by about a thousand people on the Saramacca River. At present Matawai is barely studied. However, data from it in Hancock (1987) shows that it has the Upper River dialect's phonetically conservative *â* negator, and that its descendants of European etyma are overall more phonetically conservative than in the other two Saramaccan dialects, retaining *baála* rather than *baáa* for 'brother,' *dẽ / dẽ́* rather than *de / dé* for 'they, their,' *jéti* rather than *éti* for 'still, yet,' *kabá* rather than *kaa* as a completive marker, *éfu* rather than *ée* for 'if,' and so on, suggesting in these respects a language intermediate between Saramaccan and Ndjuka, whose English-derived lexicon is less phonetically evolved from the English etyma than Saramaccan's.

Overall, the three creoles share a common grammar as Swedish, Danish, and Norwegian, or Russian, Ukrainian, and Belorussian, do, with Saramaccan's being the most influenced by Fongbe although all three grammars are to a considerable extent. There is a high degree of mutual intelligibility between Sranan and Ndjuka. However, Saramaccan's Portuguese lexical component renders it only fitfully intelligible to Sranan and Ndjuka speakers.

Although this is the first full-length grammar of Saramaccan, the language has been rather extensively studied. Historical documents in the language begin with missionaries' work in the late eighteenth century, and include a dictionary and New Testament Bible translation compiled at this time (cf. Schuchardt 1914; also, Arends and Perl 1995 collects other early Saramaccan documents). The Summer Institute of Linguistics has published a brief grammatical sketch (Rountree 1992), a self-teaching book (Rountree and Glock 1977), a lengthy wordlist (Rountree, Asodanoe, and Glock 2000), a rich corpus of sundry materials, and various scholarly articles. A number of academic scholars have specialized in Saramaccan to varying extents, starting with Jan Voorhoeve in the 1960s, and continuing from the 1980s and afterward with Enoch Aboh, Mervyn Alleyne, Peter Bakker, Derek Bickerton, Frank Byrne, Jeff Good, Marvin Kramer, Claire

Lefebvre, Norval Smith, Tonjes Veenstra, and myself, such that the bibliography on the language's grammar now numbers several dozen articles and several dissertations, some of which have been subsequently published as books (e.g. Byrne 1987, Veenstra 1996). Anton DeGroot's dictionaries (1977, 1981) provide an invaluable corpus of copious idiomatic examples; Rountree and Glock's pedagogical grammar (1977) is similar in this respect.

This grammar is intended as a theory-neutral description of the main features of Saramaccan, as would be considered as such by all linguists regardless of the schools of thought they work in. Our main goal has been to provide a description that will be of use to as wide a spectrum of linguists as possible, and still be of use to linguists in, for example, fifty years and beyond.

Moreover, this grammar is not intended as focusing on issues most of interest within creole studies, but as a description of one of the 6000 languages of the world. As such, this grammar does not address arguments as to whether Saramaccan constructions are based on West African sources, the extent to which Saramaccan's grammar exhibits complexity, or the claim (addressed mainly in the eighties) that Saramaccan is uniquely suited to shed light on the nature of generativists' conceptions of Universal Grammar. These issues are amply engaged in the scholarly literature, and I regard them as unrelated to the project of compiling a description of the language, although certainly the description could be used as a basis for further examination of such issues.

Our corpus consists primarily of elicited sentences, along with folktales and transcribed passages of conversation between informants, and a great many sentences spontaneously uttered by informants during elicitation sessions or elsewhere. Our principal informants have been speakers of the Lower River dialect, and therefore this grammar describes that dialect.

It must be stated forthrightly, however, that this grammar is founded upon a deficiency: almost all of the corpus was collected from emigrants in Amsterdam, the Bay Area of California, and New York City. Certainly, an ideal grammar of Saramaccan would be composed on the basis of my or my co-author's having lived for a year or more in a Saramaka village, hearing and speaking the language in living context on a daily basis.

However, we have put the utmost effort into compensating for this lapse as much as possible. Elicitation sentences were posed, as much as possible, within copious background context-setting; e.g. "Your brother has swallowed a mouse with a string attached to it, and then you yank on the string and pull the mouse out of him. How would you say what you did?" to elicit serial verb constructions encoding the ablative, or "Someone got bitten by a dog and holds you responsible even though you don't even have a dog – what would you say?" to examine the occurrence of indefinite articles with negation. The goal in such cases was to occasion sidebar comments that would constitute as many alternate renditions of a given construction as possible (often, fortuitously of aspects of grammar that were not being investigated at the time). In this light, it is germane that I have learned to speak and understand the language to a modest but functional extent. This has allowed comprehending and taking down phrases and usages that informants use on the fly, and with some informants, elicitation sessions themselves have been largely in Saramaccan.

None of this can entirely compensate for an extended stay in a Saramaka village. However, between 1) checking this grammar against depictions of the living language in sources such as DeGroot (1977, 1981), Rountree and Glock (1977), and Aboikoni and Glock (1997), and 2) listening to our informants as they have spoken to me and to one another, I believe that we have, at the least, captured the essence of the grammatical structure of the language, although certainly any number of our judgments will be subject to counterproposals or revisions.

An unavoidable gap under the circumstances, however, is sociolinguistic information. Much work remains to be done on charting dialectal and regional differences in Saramaccan, as well as aspects of language use such as greetings, ritual and play language, musical lyrics, and the diglossic relationship between Saramaccan and Sranan, as well as between Saramaccan and

Dutch. This grammar cannot be one that includes significant amounts of information of this kind. However, for some elucidation on such issues, Price and Price (1991), intimately depicting the Saramakas' group story-telling style with ample selections in Saramaccan itself, is useful.

Nevertheless, it can generally be stated that because of the intimate relationship between Sranan and Saramaccan, with a great deal of bilingualism between the two having apparently existed since the seventeenth century, a "pure" Saramaccan is an abstract idealization rather than a reality. Sranan influence is considerable upon the spoken language (cf. section 5.3. and the folktale transcription, e.g.), and it is a regular feature of elicitation sessions for discussions to arise as to whether a feature is Saramaccan or Sranan. In many cases, it is clear that features are, essentially, both.

Our data was collected primarily by myself and Jeff Good, with the assistance of Marvin Kramer (on certain constructions relevant to his dissertation), Heiko Narrog (on modality), Suzanne Wilhite (on possessive constructions), Irina Galichenko (on phonetics), and Susanne Stadlbauer.

Chapters 1 and 2 were written by Jeff Good. The others were written by me, enhanced by what from Jeff Good I could, in the formal sense, term as feedback, but which was just as often, more precisely, counsel. My presentation of this grammar would be distinctly lesser if not submitted to Jeff's razor-sharp eyes, and if he had written the entire grammar by himself, it would have been of equal or greater quality. Special mention is also due to Adam Sposato, who served as a copy editor for the final draft of the grammar. Here is where the custom is to say that "his attention to detail and sharp eye for inconsistencies have improved the book you see here considerably." However, here, it is an understatement indeed: Adam's attention and eye were nothing short of extraordinary.

I am grateful to the Hellman Family Faculty Fund Grant at the University of California, Berkeley, which funded the informant work and a summer's stay in Surinam by Marvin Kramer. Thanks also to Paula Floro of the UC Berkeley linguistics department, for administering the Hellman grant funds under a noisomely variegated range of circumstances. Jeff Good's work was additionally supported by research funds from the University at Buffalo.

To this day I am slightly baffled as to the generosity and patience of my informants over the years, but can only offer deepest thanks to Rudi Amsdorf, Oti Josefson, Henry Leisberger, Gerda Menig, Oscar Pika, Ardina Rensch, the late Hermanus Rensch, Mrs. L. Van Throo, Frans Vorswijk, and Berry Vrede.

I owe special thanks to Gerda Menig and Oscar Pika for letting me visit their home on countless Sunday afternoons to put them through elicitations on sentences that must have seemed hopelessly trivial ("The pencil rolled off of the table," "I have a dog, not a cat," and so on). And thanks to Oscar for the drives back to the train station, and to him and Gerda for warming me with the courteous fiction that I "really" speak Saramaccan.

Superlative acknowledgment is due to Rohit Paulus, who worked with me and Jeff Good the most, and also connected me to my New York informants. Rohit has been a godsend for the American linguist interested in Saramaccan, as someone who is fluent in English and Saramaccan as well as Dutch and Sranan, and is, besides, what linguists know as one of those "good informants," naturally understanding what we mean in asking whether a sentence is "good," "bad," or questionable (classic Rohit is "Well, if you said that, people in Surinam would understand, but..."). For several years he has been ever available for questions from people who, to him, are bizarrely obsessed with how to say in Saramaccan things like "He painted the house red" and "No, ask *me* the question!" Well Rohit, *Awáa u kabá dí búku – nɔ́ɔ gáátǎngi fii!*

John H. McWhorter
New York, NY
March 2012

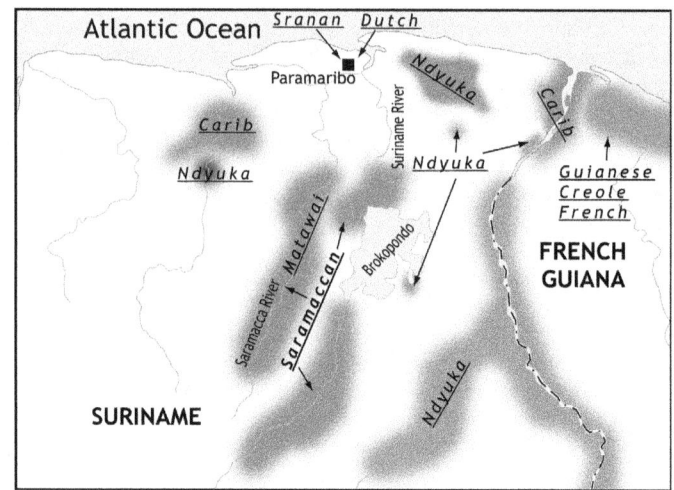

Location of Saramaccan and other creole languages of Surinam

The authors thank Eva-Maria Schmortte for designing this map of Surinam.

Chapter 1
Segmental phonology

1.1. Segment inventory

1.1.1. Introduction

The consonant inventory of Saramaccan, following the transcription system used in this grammar, is given in Table 1, and the vowel inventory is given in Table 2. As will be discussed in section 1.1.3., all Saramaccan vowels can appear with distinctive nasalization, and there is also a distinction between short and long vowels, as well as a wide range of vowel combinations. Symbols in parentheses indicate possible marginal distinctions which may be present in the language, and the relevant facts will be discussed in sections covering the consonants preceding the parenthesized elements. The tilde indicates sounds which are in dialectal or free variation with one another. In cases where the phonetic characterization of a sound may not be obvious from its transcriptional representation, it is indicated using a broad IPA transcription in square brackets.

Table 1. Saramaccan consonant inventory

	LABIAL	ALVEOLAR	PALATAL	VELAR	LAB-VEL	GLOTTAL
VL. STOPS	p	t	tj [tʃ]	k	kp~kw	
VD. STOPS	b (ɓ)	d (ɗ)	dj [d͡ʒ]	g	gb~gw	
PRENASAL. STOPS	mb [mᵇ]	nd [nᵈ]	ndj [nʲ]	ng [ŋᵍ]		
NASALS	m	n	nj [ɲ]			
VL. FRICATIVES	f	s				h
VD. FRICATIVES	v	z				
APPROXIMANTS		l	j		w (hw [ʍ])	

2 *Segmental phonology*

Table 2. Saramaccan vowel inventory

	FRONT	CENTRAL	BACK
HIGH	i		u
UPPER MID	e		o
LOWER MID	ɛ		ɔ
LOW		a	

The transcription system used here differs from those used in Saramaccan orthographic systems in two important ways. First, it represents the lower mid vowels as ɛ and ɔ, instead of as è and ò, as found in work such as Voorhoeve (1959), or as ë and ö, which is probably the most common convention and is typical of work produced under the auspices of SIL International (see, for example, Rountree, Asodanoe, and Glock 2000). Second, it represents nasalization by means of a tilde over a vowel, where orthographic systems instead use "silent" word-final or preconsonantal nasals (comparable to what is found in French orthography).

Saramaccan consonants and vowels are discussed in detail in sections 1.1.2. and 1.1.3. The description given here is based on observations and recordings of our consultants as well as published sources, with a particular reliance on Rountree, Asodanoe, and Glock's (2000) Saramaccan–English wordlist, which, due to its availability in electronic form, was quite valuable for locating minimal pairs and detecting and verifying distributional restrictions. In some cases, the recordings were informally analyzed instrumentally using Praat (Boersma and Weenink 2009), though no systematic instrumental analysis was undertaken here. Thus, phonetic aspects of the description are largely impressionistic in nature.

1.1.2. Consonants

1.1.2.1. Oral stops

The consonant *p*

The Saramaccan consonant *p* has a comparable phonetic realization to English *p*, though often with less aspiration, and has no known significant distributional restrictions. Examples of words containing *p* include: *páa* 'pair,' *peé* 'play,' *píki* 'answer,' *hópo* 'stand up,' *hípi* 'pile,' and *saápu* 'sharp.' Some minimal pairs for *p* with similar consonants include: *pái* 'father-in-law' vs. *bái* 'warn' vs. *kpái/kwái* 'tree type'; and *písi* 'piece' vs. *bísi* 'sand' vs. *físi* 'fish.'

The consonant *b* (*ɓ*)

Most descriptions of Saramaccan recognize only two voiced bilabial stops, a plain *b* and a prenasalized *mb*. However, it has been recently noted (see Smith and Haabo 2007) that the language also appears to make use of an implosive bilabial stop *ɓ* (see also the discussion of the alveolar implosive *ɗ* in the section on *d* below). (Smith and Haabo's 2007 claims regarding implosives are completely distinct from Voorhoeve's [1959: 440] treatment of the Saramaccan labial-velar stops as implosive.) No minimal pairs across the plain/implosive distinction have been reported, rendering the phonemic status of the b/ɓ distinction unclear. The distinction has not been represented in any orthographic system for the language, and we maintain the convention of using only b here.

An attempt to elicit the distinction with two consultants based on three words in Smith and Haabo (2007), *bebé* 'drink,' *bása* 'bastard,' and *báta* 'bottle,' suggested that the first two words contained implosive stops and the last a plain stop, though Smith and Haabo (2007) only found the first to contain implosives. (See also the section on *d* for a case where the distinction appeared to be found in the speech of the same two consultants but with a different distribution than what was reported in Smith and Haabo 2007.) Given that it is known that there is dialectal variation in the pronunciation of another class of stops, the labial-velars, it seems likely to be the case that dialectal differences are relevant here as well, presumably explaining the variation between the forms we encountered and what was previously reported.

The phonetic realization of plain *b* is largely comparable to English *b*, except that it is more consistently voiced, even in initial position. There are no known significant distributional restrictions on the appearance of what is transcribed here as *b*. However, further study may reveal important distributional differences between *b* and *ɓ*.

Some minimal pairs for consonants similar to b/ɓ include: *bái* 'warn' vs. *pái* 'father-in-law' vs. *mái* 'mother-in-law'; *bíi* 'beer' vs. *píi* 'pick' vs. *mbíi* 'mill'; *bebé* 'drink' vs. *gbegbé* 'tree type'; and the near-minimal pair *bítju* 'worm' vs. *vítjɛ* 'monkey type.'

The consonant *t*

The Saramaccan consonant *t* has a comparable realization to English *t*, except with a more dental articulation and less aspiration, and has no known significant distributional restrictions. Examples of words containing *t* include: *tái* 'tie,' *túu* 'all,' *teɛmé* 'tremble,' *wáta* 'water,' and *kɔ́tɔ* 'cold.' Some minimal pairs for *t* with similar consonants include: *tíi* 'steer' vs. *díi* 'dear' vs. *síi* 'seed'; *téni* 'ten' vs. *tjéni* 'cane'; and *paatí* 'separate' vs. *paandí* 'plant.'

The consonant *d (ɗ)*

Most descriptions of Saramaccan recognize only two voiced alveolar stops, a plain *d* (with a more dental articulation than English *d*) and a prenasalized stop *nd*. However, as was discussed in more detail in the description of the consonant *b*, it has been recently argued that the language exhibits a distinction between implosive and plain stops for labials and alveolars. Still, as discussed above, no minimal pairs across the plain/implosive distinction have been found for any place of articulation, rendering the phonemic status of this opposition unclear.

In the speech of our primary consultant, some recorded instances of *d* in the third-person plural pronoun *de* appeared to have an implosive quality while others did not. Smith and Haabo (2007: 109) report this as a word with a consistently implosive pronunciation. In addition, when the words *disá* 'leave' and *diíngi* 'drink' (the first of which is reported to begin with an implosive stop) were elicited from two other consultants, the speakers did report a distinction in the initial sound which was consistent with impressionistic evidence and could be characterized along implosive/plain lines. At the same time, the word *duumí* 'sleep' appeared to begin with the same sound as *disá*, implying it, too, contained an implosive *d*, though this word is reported to have a plain *d* by Smith and Haabo (2007). As mentioned in the discussion of b/ɓ, it is probably the case that dialectal factors are at play here.

The phonetic realization of plain *d* is largely comparable to English *d*, except with a more dental articulation. It is also more consistently voiced in initial position. There are no known significant distributional restrictions on the appearance of what is transcribed here as *d*. However, further study may reveal important distributional differences between *d* and *ɗ*.

Some minimal pairs for consonants similar to d/ɗ include: díi 'dear' vs. tíi 'steer'; dómbo 'lump' vs. djómbo 'jump'; dé '3P' (tonic form) vs. zé 'sea'; káda 'snake type' vs. kánda 'candle'; and dúsu 'thousand' vs. núsu 'nose' vs. lúsu 'loosen.'

The consonant *tj*

The Saramaccan consonant *tj*, at least for our consultants, is phonetically affricated along the lines of [t͡ʃ], with a relatively dental articulation at the beginning as compared to the English alveopalatal affricate and often with less frication than in English. It is presented here with the stops following earlier descriptions, and the transcription of this sound as *tj* is standard – indeed, it is found in Schumann's (1778) word list. However, most sources say little about the phonetic interpretation of this transcription. The inventory given in Smith and Haabo (2004: 529) is in accord with our own observations in treating this sound as an affricate rather than a stop. However, Voorhoeve (1959: 440) phonetically transcribes this sound as [c], implying that he observed it as a voiceless palatal stop (and he offered a comparable transcription for *dj*, as will be discussed below). As seen in Table 1, *tj* forms part of a larger palatal series parallel to the labial and alveolar series (except for the lack of any palatal fricatives). It shows no known significant distributional restrictions.

Examples of words containing *tj* include: *tjá* 'carry,' *tjiká* 'suffice,' *tjúba* 'rain,' and *matjáu* 'axe.' Some minimal pairs for *tj* with similar consonants include: *tjéni* 'cane' vs. *téni* 'ten'; *fitjá* 'overgrown' vs. *fiká* 'remain'; and the near minimal pairs *tjumá* 'burn' vs. *djulá* 'swear' and *tjubí* 'hide' vs. *djú béɛ* 'immediate family.' Neither *tj* nor *dj* are among the more frequent consonants in Saramaccan, presumably explaining the difficulty in finding a true minimal pair between the two.

There are a handful of lexical doublets in Saramaccan involving alternations between *tj* and *k*. Examples include *tjína/kína* 'taboo' and *lémíki/lémítji* 'lime tree.' However, there is no indication that this reflects an allophonic relationship among these sounds in the language, and, at least in the second case, a ready explanation for the presence of this doublet is that it reflects borrowing of variant Sranan forms, which shows free allophonic palatalization of velars before *i* (see Smith and Haabo [2004: 559]).

The consonant *dj*

Like *tj*, the Saramaccan consonant *dj*, for our consultants, is phonetically affricated to [d͡ʒ], though we present it here with the stops following earlier practice. As with *tj*, while the transcription of this consonant as *dj* is standard, most sources say little about its phonetic realization. Smith and Haabo (2004: 529) also give its phonetic realization as an alveopalatal affricate, but Voorhoeve (1959: 440) phonetically transcribes this sound as [ɟ], indicating that he observed the sound as a voiced palatal stop. Whatever the reasons for this discrepancy, it is clear from all sources that only a single consonant is involved, and it can be placed in a palatal series in opposition to *tj*. It shows no known significant distributional restrictions.

Examples of words containing *dj* include: *djómbo* 'jump,' *djái* 'yard,' *bódjéɛ* 'sly,' and *fiidjí* 'fry.' Some minimal pairs for *dj* with similar consonants include: *djómbo* 'jump' vs. *dómbo* 'lump'; *djú* 'Jew' vs. *ndjú* 'peanut type' (though our consultants are not familiar with this latter word); the near minimal pair *djǔsu* 'soon' vs. *gũũsi* 'wine red'; the near minimal set *kódjo* 'cudgel' vs. *gogó* 'rear' vs. *djodjo* 'rag'; and the near minimal pairs *tjumá* 'burn' vs. *djulá* 'swear' and *tjubí* 'hide' vs. *djú béɛ* 'immediate family.' The consonant *dj* is not particularly frequent in Saramaccan, presumably explaining the difficulty in finding more true minimal pairs.

Donicie and Voorhoeve (1963) give at least one *dj/g* doublet of the kind discussed above for *tj/k* in the word *djéi/géi* 'seem,' which other sources give solely as *djéi*. As with *tj/k* alternations, there is no evidence for any kind of allophonic relationship between *dj* and *g* in Saramaccan.

The consonant *k*

The Saramaccan consonant *k* has a comparable realization to English *k*, though with less aspiration, and has no known significant distributional restrictions. Examples of words containing *k* include: *kákísa* 'skin,' *kɛtekú* 'beads,' and *kɔ́tɔ* 'cold.' Some minimal pairs for *k* with similar consonants include: *kó* 'come' vs. *gó* 'go'; *fíká* 'remain' vs. *fítjá* 'overgrown'; and *kái* 'call' vs. *kpái/kwái* 'tree type.' As discussed in the section on *tj*, there are a handful of lexical doublets where *k* alternates with *tj*, but there is no evidence of a synchronic phonological relationship between the two consonants.

The consonant *g*

The Saramaccan consonant *g* has a comparable realization to English *g*, though it seems to have more voicing in initial position, and has no known significant distributional restrictions. Unlike *b* and *d*, no voiced velar implosives have been reported for Saramaccan. Some examples of words containing *g* include: *gãã́* 'big,' *gíí* 'stingy,' and *lɛgɛdɛ* 'lie.' Some minimal pairs for *g* with similar consonants include: *gó* 'go' vs. *kó* 'come'; *lági* 'inferior' vs. *lángi* 'depend'; *agó* 'knot' vs. *agbó* 'leaf type'; the near minimal pair *gũũsi* 'wine red' vs. *djũsu* 'soon'; and the near minimal set *gogó* 'rear' vs. *kódjo* 'cudgel' vs. *djodjo* 'rag.'

The consonant *kp~kw*

It appears to be the case that Saramaccan can be described as contrasting voiceless labial-velar and labialized velar stops, i.e. *kp* vs. *kw*, though there are also words where these consonants can alternate with each other and we are not aware of any minimal pairs for them, which is why they are treated together here. To the extent that there may be a phonemic distinction between labial-velars and labialized velars, as well as an additional possible contrast between plain and implosive stops, the language would appear to have a particularly rich stop inventory.

The factors conditioning the alternation between labial-velars and labialized velars have not been thoroughly studied, but they appear to be primarily sociolinguistic and lexical, as opposed to phonological. Voorhoeve (1959: 436) does not indicate the existence of this alternation at all, nor do early sources like Schumann (1778), but the former only includes *kp/gb* in the phonemic inventory of the language while the latter only transcribes *kw/gw*. Rountree (1972b) suggests that the *kp~kw* and *gb~gw* alternation is the result of allophonic free variation, and Smith and Haabo (2004: 529) indicate that some dialects of the language actually distinguish between labial-velars and labialized velars while others have these two segments in free variation. Finally, Rountree and Glock (1977: 68) specify that, while there is free variation between labial-velars and labialized velars in many words, there are some which only ever appear with labial-velars, with two examples for voiceless labial-velars that we have verified with two consultants being *akpó* 'arrow type' and *akpósokpa* 'trowel type.' The same consultants also appeared to favor *kw* in two words that were examined which Rountree, Asodanoe, and Glock (2000) indicate as showing variable pronunciation, *kwái* 'tree type' and *kwáliki* 'quarter,' while viewing both *kpáta* and *kwáta* 'monkey type' as apparently equally acceptable variants of that word and being split on the most acceptable pronunciations for *kpátíwójo/kwátíwójo* 'opossum' and *kpéi/kwéi* 'square off' (despite both being from the same village).

Coming to a fuller understanding of the nature of these alternations would clearly require a detailed sociolinguistic and lexical study, and it seems likely that some of the complications may be due to dialect mixture. In any event, while there do not appear to be any minimal pairs distinguishing labial-velars from labialized velars, the possibility that, for a given speaker, there are some words not allowing labial-velars to alternate with labialized velars suggests that the distinction is at least marginally phonemic.

6   *Segmental phonology*

While the presence of labial-velars in Saramaccan, much like the presence of prenasalized stops, can be connected to substrate influence, it is not the case that words with labial-velars have a consistently West African origin. In fact, one finds that words showing a phonetic *kw* sequence in a European source language can appear in some Saramaccan varieties with a *kp*. This is the case, for example, with the reported variation in forms like *kpéi/kwéi* 'square off' whose source is English *square*, *kpáliki/kwáliki* 'quarter (coin)' whose source is the Sranan word *kwarki* of the same meaning (which, in turn, ultimately derives from Dutch *kwartje*), and *kpátíwójo/kwátíwójo* 'opossum' which is ultimately (though not synchronically) derived from a compound based on two Portuguese words, *quatro* 'four' and *olho* 'eye' (the exact form of the first element in the compound is not completely clear, but that it began with a *kw* sequence is secure).

Voorhoeve (1959: 440) places both the voiceless and voiced labial-velars under the heading "implosive" (though transcribing them using labial-velar sequences). However, no other sources use this particular label and while, impressionistically, there can be an implosive quality to the voiced labial-velar *gb*, this is not found for *kp*, and Voorhoeve's label would not appear to reflect a contemporary usage of the term.

Some minimal pairs for *kp~kw* with similar consonants include (indication of *kp~kw* variation follows Rountree, Asodanoe, and Glock 2000): *kpái/kwái* 'tree type' vs. *pái* 'father-in-law' vs. *kái* 'call' vs. *wái* 'happy'; and the near minimal set *akpó* 'arrow type' vs. *agba* 'chin' vs. *agbó* 'leaf type.'

In this grammar, in words which alternate in pronunciation between *kp* and *kw*, the transcription simply follows which variant form of the word was used when the relevant example was collected or, in the case of examples drawn from other sources, the transcription given there.

The consonant *gb~gw*

For discussion of the general status of labial-velars and the alternation between labial-velars and labialized velars, see the section on *kp~kw* above. The same basic issues arise for understanding observed alternations between the voiced pair *gb~gw* as the voiceless pair *kp~kw*. The main difference between the presence of *gb~gw* versus *kp~kw* in Saramaccan is that we have not identified any words of non-African origin with an original *gw* sequence appearing in Saramaccan with a *gb* sequence. However, this is probably due to the accidental fact that words containing *gw* sequences in European languages are not as frequent as words containing *kw* sequences, making the *gw* sequence less likely to have entered Saramaccan via that route.

Rountree and Glock (1977: 68) give two words *agbagó* 'shrub type' and *agbã́* 'pot type' as not permitting the *gb~gw* alternation. This pattern for these words was verified with two consultants and was also found for the word *agba* 'chin.' The same speakers appeared to have *gwamba* 'meat' as the dominant form for that word, though they recognized *gbamba* as a possible variant, with a similar pattern for *dagwé* 'snake type' holding for one of these speakers. As with the case of comparable words containing *kp*, examples like these indicate that the distinction between *gb* and *gw* may be marginally phonemic, at least for some speakers.

Some near minimal pairs/sets for *gb~gw* with similar consonants include (indication of *gb~gw* variation follows Rountree, Asodanoe, and Glock 2000): *gbegú/gwegú* 'turtle' vs. *bégi* 'request' vs. *wégi* 'weigh'; *dagbé/dagwé* 'snake type' vs. *dágu* 'dog'; and *agba* 'chin' and *agbó* 'leaf type' vs. *akpó* 'arrow type.' There is a relative lack of words containing *gb~gw* in Saramaccan, which would seem to largely explain the difficulties in finding true minimal pairs. Furthermore, many of the words containing *gb* are ideophones (see section 1.2.3.), which we have generally excluded when looking for minimal pairs because of special phonological properties they exhibit distinguishing them from other lexical classes. This makes unclear the extent to which minimal pairs involving comparisons between ideophones and non-ideophones should be considered clear demonstrations of phonemic oppositions.

In this grammar, in words which alternate in pronunciation between *gb* and *gw*, the transcription simply follows which variant form was used when the relevant example was collected or, in the case of examples drawn from other sources, the transcription given there.

Rountree, Asodanoe, and Glock (2000) provide two forms, *seéngba* 'ant type' and *sɛngbé* 'without handle,' containing orthographic *ngb* sequences suggesting the possibility of a prenasalized labial-velar stop. When these words were elicited from two consultants, however, variant forms *sémba* and *sénge* were produced, respectively. So, we are unable to comment on the phonetics of the variants of these words recorded in that source. However, if they did turn out to include something along the lines of a prenasalized labial-velar, this would almost certainly represent a very marginal sound in the relevant varieties, and it seems likely that the nasals in those transcriptions are actually representing vowel nasalization rather than prenasalized labial-velars.

1.1.2.2. Plain nasals and prenasalized stops

The consonant *m*

The Saramaccan consonant *m* has a comparable realization to English *m* and no known significant distributional restrictions, except for a possible gap involving its presence before the mid tense vowels *e* and *o* and a poor attestation before or after nasalized vowels, both to be discussed below in section 1.2.2. As discussed in the section on *mb*, for certain speakers, some of the words given as containing an *mb* in some sources may be realized with *m* instead, in particular when *mb* would be expected word-initially. Some examples of words containing *m* include: *máta* 'mattress,' *míti* 'meet,' and *paamúsi* 'promise.' A minimal set for *m* with similar consonants is *míi* 'child' vs. *mbíi* 'mill' vs. *bíi* 'beer.'

In limited cases, *m* can be syllabic. When this happens, it is always associated with vowel reduction from a full form. This is most frequently encountered with a reduced form of the first-person singular tonic pronoun *mí* (cf. section 5.1.) and is also found in a reduced form of *mamá* 'mother,' *m'má*, that is used in isolation as a term for address and is also found in some compounds, for example, *m'máfóu* 'bush hen' (variant of *mamáfóu*).

Except for a few possible exceptions discussed in section 1.2.1., there are no codas in Saramaccan, and the vast majority of instances of *m* that may appear to be coda consonants in practical orthographies for the language instead mark vowel nasalization before a labial onset.

The consonant *mb*

Saramaccan has a series of prenasalized stops, represented orthographically here as nasal-stop sequences. They are reported as appearing both word-initially and word-medially. However, at least for our main consultant, expected word-initial prenasalized stops were typically reduced to a simple nasal. It is not known if this represents an idiolectal feature or is representative of more systematic dialectal variation. Given such variation, the prenasalized stop *mb* is perhaps best represented phonologically as /m^b/ – that is, as a nasal consonant with a secondary oral stop release, though other representations are also imaginable (within previous descriptions, this representation is more consistent with Voorhoeve's [1959: 440] treatment of them as "fortis nasals" rather than their more usual characterization as prenasalized stops).

Since non-final nasalized vowels are expressed in common orthographies as a sequence of *VNCV* representing *ṼCV*, in principle in these orthographies a sequence like *VNDV* (where *D* represents a voiced stop) would be ambiguous between a parsing *V.NDV*, with a prenasalized stop, or *Ṽ.DV*, with a nasalized vowel. This issue was discussed by Voorhoeve (1959: 439) in the first proposed orthography of the language, who was evidently not particularly concerned about the lack of means to represent the distinction because of its relatively low (if even existent) functional load. In fact, Voorhoeve (1959: 439) even seems to imply the distinction is not employed to make phonemic contrasts. In principle, the transcription system used here is not ambiguous in this regard since it marks nasalization diacritically rather than via nasal consonants. However, if there is a distinction, it is possible that it may have gone unnoticed and words exhibiting the contrast could be mistranscribed. While we believe this to be unlikely, there are a number of cases in Saramaccan segmental phonology where there is evidence for a contrast with low functional load (see, for example, the sections on *b*, *d*, *kp~kw*, and *gb~gw*), meaning that, barring targeted investigation into the issue, it would be premature to rule out the possibility entirely. See also section 1.1.3.2. on nasalized vowels for relevant discussion.

As discussed below in section 1.2.2., prenasalized stops are known to be subject to co-occurrence restrictions wherein they do not appear word-initially before the lax mid vowels *ɛ* and *ɔ*. They also are not well attested before or after nasalized vowels.

Some examples of words containing *mb* include: *mbéi* 'make,' *mbíi* 'mill,' *sɛmbɛ* 'person,' and *kámba* 'room.' Some minimal pairs/sets for *mb* with similar consonants include: *mbíi* 'mill' vs. *bíi* 'beer' vs. *míi* 'child'; and the near minimal pair *tómbi* 'spill' vs. *tógbo* 'great grandparent.' As can be seen from a comparison of the word *míti* 'meet,' cognate with English *meet*, and *mbéti* 'animal,' cognate with English *meat*, the distinction between *m* vs. *mb* is not simply the result of direct transfer of *mb* in lexical items from African languages into Saramaccan.

The consonant *n*

The Saramaccan consonant *n* has a comparable realization to English *n*, but with a more dental articulation, and no known significant distributional restrictions, except for a possible gap involving its presence before the mid tense vowels *e* and *o* and a poor attestation after nasalized vowels, both to be discussed below in section 1.2.2. As discussed in the section on *nd*, for certain speakers, some of the words given as containing an *nd* in some sources may be realized with *n* instead, in particular when *nd* would be expected word-initially. Some examples of words containing *n* include: *néti* 'net,' *náki* 'hit,' *maaní* 'screen,' and *kínɔ* 'film.' Some minimal pairs for *n* with similar consonants include: *tené* 'tear' vs. *tendé* 'stretch'; *né* 'name' vs. *dé* 'there'; and the near minimal pairs *namá* 'touch' vs. *njúma* 'term of address' and *náki* 'hit' vs. *ndjaká* 'crisscross' (though our consultants have produced a variant pronunciation of this latter word with an initial *dj* rather than *ndj*). (The lack of clear minimal pairs involving palatal nasals appears to be largely due to the fact that they are not particularly common in the Saramaccan lexicon.)

Except for a few possible exceptions involving *m* discussed in section 1.2.1., there are no codas in Saramaccan, and instances of *n* that may appear to be coda consonants in practical orthographies for the language, in fact, mark vowel nasalization (though see section 1.1.3.2. for discussion of an alternation between vowel nasalization and a final velar nasal).

The consonant *nd*

As discussed above in the section on *mb*, Saramaccan is generally described as having a series of prenasalized stops which can appear both word-initially and word-medially. However, for our main consultant, expected word-initial prenasalized stops were typically reduced to a nasal, thus suggesting a phonological representation of /n^d/ for this consonant – that is, as a nasal with a secondary oral stop release. See the section on *mb* for relevant discussion on the intepretation of orthographic and transcribed nasal-stop sequences intervocalically.

As discussed above in reference to *mb* and below in section 1.2.2., prenasalized stops do not appear word-initially before the lax mid vowels *ɛ* and *ɔ* and are also not well attested before or after nasalized vowels.

Some examples of words containing *nd* include: *ndéti* 'night,' *míndi* 'middle,' *kɛndé* 'heat,' and *déndu* 'inside.' As indicated by the first two of these words, the presence of *nd* in Saramaccan cannot be solely attributed to transfer of words with an *nd* sequence, since both derive from English words which do not contain *nd*. Some minimal pairs for *nd* with similar consonants include: *tendé* 'stretch' vs. *tené* 'tear'; *béndi* 'bend' vs. *bédi* 'bed'; and the near minimal pair *sendé* 'shine' vs. *sembɛ* 'person.'

The consonant *nj*

The consonant *nj* is a palatal nasal, though in Saramaccan orthographies it may be ambiguous between a palatal nasal and a nasalized vowel followed by a *j*. Its distribution is somewhat restricted, appearing primarily word-initially, as observed by Rountree and Glock (1977: 40). In the few exceptional cases where it is known to appear word-medially, some of the relevant words are transparently formally reduplicated with the medial instance of *nj* simply being the initial sound of the second instance of the reduplicated stem as in, for example, *njãnjã́* 'food,' *njũ̌njũ* 'new,' and, for our consultants, *njũ̌ẽnjũẽ* 'lizard type' (which has an alternate pronunciation with *ndj* rather than *nj*) (the exceptional status of the first two words was pointed out by Rountree and Glock [1977: 40]). One other exception that we have found is the word *sipanjólu* 'Spanish,' and Rountree (1972b: 26) also reports the word *mũnjã́* 'wet' as showing a medial *nj*. (This latter word is also atypical insofar as it shows a nasal consonant after a nasalized vowel, a pattern that otherwise is uncommon – see section 1.2.2.) Even in initial position, the sound is not particularly common.

Additional examples of words containing *nj* include: *njã́* 'eat,' *njengí* 'wasp type,' and *njawí* 'lizard type.' Due to the relative infrequency of *nj*, true minimal pairs involving this consonant are difficult to find. Some minimal pairs and near minimal pairs for *nj* with similar consonants include: *njúma* 'term of address' vs. *namá* 'touch'; *njũ̌njũ* 'new' vs. *ndjú* 'peanut type' (though this second word was not known by our consultants); *njũ̌su* 'news' vs. *djũ̌su* 'soon'; and *njóku* 'young' vs. *ngáku* 'stutter.'

Since the transcription system here encodes nasalization diacritically rather than via nasal consonants, it allows for unambiguous marking of the distinction between nasalized vowel followed by *j* and a post-vocalic palatal nasal. However, due to the presence of a minor nasal harmony rule involving the palatal glide and the palatal nasal, it is possible that some instances of $\tilde{V}nj\tilde{V}$ could have been misapprehended as $\tilde{V}j\tilde{V}$ due to the phonetic overlap between the sequences (see section 1.1.3.2. for further discussion).

The consonant *ndj*

The consonant *ndj*, a palatal prenasalized stop, is not particularly frequent in Saramaccan, though it has been long recognized as distinctive, phonologically pairing with *nj*. As with the other prenasalized stops, our main consultant did not articulate the stop portion of *ndj* when in word-initial position. In word-medial position, the stop release was not as strongly affricated as what was found for the *dj* consonant, suggesting a transcription closer to [nʲ] than [nᵈʒ] (see the sections on *mb* and *nd* for justification for treating the stop articulations as secondary for this class of consonants in Saramaccan), though phonologically there is no reason not to group *dj*, *nj*, and *ndj* into a single palatal stop series. Voorhoeve (1959: fn. 9) suggests that *ndj* could be analyzed as *ndi* preceding a vowel, specifically applying this analytical possibility to the word *ndjú* 'peanut type' and suggesting something along the lines of *ndiú* as a possible transcription. He opts for an analysis along the lines of *ndj* by appealing to a preference for an overall symmetry in Saramaccan's phonemic system. An additional reason for choosing an analysis employing an *ndj* consonant is the presence of sets of words like *gándji* 'sour' and *faádji* 'menstruation' vs. *gandí* 'crocodile' and *gadíi* 'porch' and *díi* 'three,' which seem to clearly indicate a contrast between *dji* sequences and *di* sequences making it difficult to treat *ndj* as simply the surface reflex of *ndiV*. A word *didía* 'daylight' is particularly revealing in this regard. However, no comparable word with an *ndiV* sequence was found in Rountree, Asodanoe, and Glock (2000), making it impossible to unequivocally rule out Voorhoeve's proposed alternative analysis for this sound.

Further examples of words containing *ndj* include: *(a)djíndja* 'ginger,' *bandja* 'side,' *bóndji* 'cluster,' and *ndjaká* 'crisscross' (though this last word was preferably pronounced *djaká* by consultants when checked). Some minimal and near minimal pairs/sets for *ndj* with similar consonants include: *mandjá* 'stain' vs. *mandá* 'send'; *gándji* 'sour' vs. *adjí* 'game type'; *ndjú* 'peanut type' vs. *njũnjũ* 'new' vs. *djú* 'Jew' (though the word *ndjú* was not known by our consultants); and *miindjá* 'urine' vs. *miingá* 'aluminum band.'

The consonant *ng*

Unlike nasal consonants at other places of articulation, there is no distinction made between a plain velar nasal and a prensasalized velar stop in Saramaccan. Rather, one finds only one velar nasal, generally written as *ng* and grouped phonologically with the prenasalized stops, with typical phonological realization representable as /ŋᵍ/ (see the sections on *mb* and *nd* for justification of this representation). Unlike the other prenasalized stops, our main consultant did pronounce the stop release of the velar nasal even when it was in initial position (though such words are uncommon in the language). However, in some cases, for example in the word *íngísi* 'English,' a reduction of *ng* to [ŋ] was observed. See the section on *mb* for relevant discussion on the intepretation of orthographic and transcribed nasal-stop sequences intervocalically.

Examples of words containing *ng* include: *ngáku* 'stutter,' *ngɔ́tɔ* 'ditch,' *taánga* 'strong,' *píngo* 'pig type,' *dúngu* 'dark,' and *zεngéni* 'sway.' Some minimal pairs and near minimal pairs for *ng* with similar consonants include: *hánga* 'hang' vs. *hága* 'pellets'; and *miingá* 'aluminum band' vs. *miindjá* 'urine.'

1.1.2.3. Fricatives

The consonant *f*

The Saramaccan consonant *f* has a comparable realization to English *f* and no known significant distributional restrictions. Some examples of words containing *f* are: *fási* 'manner,' *féífi* 'five,' and *fufúu* 'steal.' Some minimal pairs for *f* with similar consonants include: *fulá* 'spray' vs. *vulá* 'rain' (in a secret language); and the near minimal pairs *háfu* 'half' vs. *avó* 'grandparent'; *fitjá* 'overgrown' vs. *vítje* 'monkey type'; and *fáa* 'fell' vs. *sáa* 'pity.' (Due to a relative lack of words containing *v*, it is difficult to find clear minimal pairs between *v* and other consonants. In addition to the ones listed above, Voorhoeve [1959: 440] suggests *a fiti hẽ́* 'it fits him' vs. *aviti* 'drill.')

The consonant *v*

The Saramaccan consonant *v* has a comparable realization to English *v*. It is not particularly frequently found in the language, and a fairly high proportion of words where it is found are ideophones. Some examples of words containing *v* are: *vẽtu* 'wind,' *vínde* 'throw,' *vítje* 'monkey type,' *vũvṹ* 'hummingbird,' *avó* 'grandparent,' and *aviɔ́* 'airplane.' As mentioned in the discussion of *f*, there does not appear to be a good exact minimal pair between *v* and *f*. However, there are some relevant pairs including *vulá* 'rain' (in a secret language) vs. *fulá* 'spray,' which is a minimal pair, but not an ideal one due to the fact that *vulá* is not a word in the regular language, and there are also the near minimal pairs *háfu* 'half' vs. *avó* 'grandparent' and *fitjá* 'overgrown' vs. *vítje* 'monkey type.' There are similar problems for *v* and *w*. However, one does find the near minimal pairs *vodú* 'snake type' vs. *wɔ́du* 'proverb' and *avó* 'grandparent' vs. *awoo* 'old.' Finally, a near minimal pair between *v* and *z* is *vẽtu* 'wind' vs. *zũtu* 'near.' Overall, the phonemic status of *v* seems clear, and the lack of minimal pairs is presumably attributable to accidental gaps arising from the general infrequency of *v* in the first place.

The consonant *s*

The Saramaccan consonant *s* has comparable realization to English *s* and no known significant distributional restrictions. Examples of words containing *s* are: *Saamáka* 'Saramaccan,' *sę́* 'shame,' *básu* 'bottom,' and *bósi* 'kiss.' Some minimal pairs and near minimal pairs for *s* with similar consonants include: *basiá* 'undercaptain' vs. *baziá* 'descend'; and *síkísi* 'six' vs. *sikífi* 'write.'

Unlike Sranan, but like Ndjuka, Saramaccan does not have an alveopalatal fricative [ʃ] (often written as *sj* or *sy* for Sranan) in its consonant inventory. The inclusion of *sj* in the Saramaccan consonant inventory in Bakker, Smith, and Veenstra (1995: 170) appears to be a mistake, as no other source reports such a consonant for any variant of the language.

The consonant *z*

The Saramaccan consonant *z* has a comparable realization to English *z* and no known significant distributional restrictions. Examples of words containing *z* are: *zé* 'sea,' *zõká* 'coals,' *azã* 'frond,' and *piizíi* 'celebration.' Some minimal pairs and near minimal pairs for *z* with similar consonants include: *baziá* 'descend' vs. *basiá* 'undercaptain'; and *zų́tu* 'near' vs. *vę́tu* 'wind' (see the discussion on *v* for comments regarding the lack of a clear minimal pair between *z* and *v*).

The consonant *h*

The Saramaccan consonant *h* is a voiceless glottal fricative with comparable realization to English *h*. While *h* appears before all Saramaccan vowels word-initially, intervocalically its distribution is quite restricted. Excluding compounds, based on an examination of Rountree, Asodanoe, and Glock (2000), one finds it only preceded by *a* and *o* and followed by *a*, *o*, *ɔ*, and *u* (i.e. non-front vowels). Furthermore, one does not find *h* after nasalized vowels of any quality (as is also the case with *w*).

As is discussed in the section on *w*, there is some indication that there may be a marginally phonemic voiceless labialized velar approximant *hw* in Saramaccan, and all of the words in Rountree, Asodanoe, and Glock (2000) indicated as containing *hw* are also associated with variants where an *h* replaces *hw* (sometimes with vocalic changes as well).

Examples of words containing *h* are: *ahala* 'forked stick,' *ahɔ́* 'hoe,' *híti* 'throw,' *húku* 'hook,' *hę́* '3ST,' and *hų́jã* 'nail.' Some minimal pairs for *h* with similar consonants are: *hái* 'haul' vs. *wái* 'happy'; and *hípi* 'pile' vs. *sípi* 'ship.'

As with *j* and *w*, there is a class of words which alternate with respect to the presence or absence of an initial *h* (see also section 17.2.). Examples include: *hákísi/ákísi* 'ask,' *hédi/édi* 'head,' and *hópo/ópo* 'stand up.' (In Rountree, Asodanoe, and Glock 2000, the *h*-initial variants are all treated as the main entries.) Unlike the case of the *j*/Ø and *w*/Ø alternations, there does not appear to be any specific phonological conditioning to this alternation. While it appears to affect the majority of *h*-initial words, there are also words which do not permit the alternation, for example *hą́so* 'attractive' and *heépi* 'help' (which consultants reported as having an alternate form of *jeépi* instead). Therefore, this alternation appears to be best characterized as primarily lexical in nature. Finally, as also found with the alternations involving *j* and *w*, there are numerous vowel-initial words which never appear with a preceding *h* (or other consonant). So, while *h*-initial words often have a vowel-initial variant, the generalization does not go in the other direction.

1.1.2.4. Approximants

The consonant *l*

The Saramaccan consonant *l* has a comparable realization to English *l* and no known significant distributional restrictions. There is a relatively small set of words showing an alternation (whose conditioning factors are not known, but are presumably sociolinguistic in nature) where an intervocalic *l* may alternate with nothing. Some examples of such words (with variants ordered following which form is given the main entry in Rountree, Asodanoe, and Glock 2000) are: *baí/balí* 'sweep,' *baláta/baáta* 'rubber,' and *hía/híla* 'much.' The presence of these pairs is related to a sound change, with fairly complex conditioning factors (see Smith [1987b: 210–224] for relevant discussion), deleting word-medial *l*'s (which, in some cases, go back historically to other alveolar consonants like *d* or *r*). This sound change partly explains, for example, the form of the words *béi* 'bury' (from English *bury,* passing through a stage with a form like *béri*) and *fúu* 'full' (from English *full*, passing through a stage with a form like *fúlu*). (Earlier forms of each of these words with the intervocalic alveolars are, in fact, documented by Schumann 1778.) Instances of words where *l* alternates with nothing intervocalically simply represent cases where, for some reason, the sound change is not consistently applied synchronically (perhaps due to dialect borrowing or influence from other Surinamese creoles which did not undergo the sound change but show otherwise similar forms in some cases).

Examples of words containing *l* are: *lalá* 'grate,' *líba* 'month,' *akulí* 'Hindustani,' and *alulú* 'rice type.' Some minimal pairs for *l* with similar consonants include: *ló* 'clan' vs. *jó* 'melt'; *lái* 'load' vs. *wái* 'happy'; and *lúsu* 'loosen' vs. *dúsu* 'thousand.'

The consonant *j*

The consonant *j*, a palatal glide, has a realization comparable to English *y*, and no known significant distributional restrictions except for an apparent prohibition on the sequence *ji,* parallel to the prohibition on *wu* to be discussed below in the section on *w* and in section 1.2.2. Comparable to *w*, while *j* clearly has phonemic status in many words, for example, *jáa* 'year' and *wójo* 'eye,' there are some cases where a *j* is transcribed both here and in other sources on the language but where its phonemic status is somewhat ambiguous due to the fact that the sound could simply represent an automatic transition between two vowels that would otherwise be adjacent. Thus, for example, it does not appear to be the case that the word written as *alijá* 'animal type' could contrast with a sequence like *aliá.* Furthermore, there are cases like this where authors explicitly indicate that a transcription either with or without a *j* is possible. Thus, Smith (2003: 100) offers both *teéa* and *teéja* as possible transcriptions of 'star' (and one finds the former transcription in, for example, Donicie and Voorhoeve 1963 and the latter in Rountree, Asodanoe, and Glock 2000). Similarly Rountree, Asodanoe, and Glock (2000) list *fijáá* as a variant form of the ideophone *fiáá* 'completely gone.' As with similar variation found in the transcription of intervocalic *w*, it is possible that the presence/absence of *j* in a word like *teéja/teéa* 'star' represents dialectal or idiolectal differences, but it seems equally possible (and, in our view, more likely) that it simply represents different conventions on the part of various authors for transcribing vowel sequences where a phonetic *j* would appear automatically.

It is important to point out that, as will be discussed below in section 1.1.3.3., a factor that makes arriving at a resolution of this issue difficult is that, while one might expect that it would be possible to appeal to general principles of syllabification in Saramaccan to argue for one transcription over another, the language, in fact, independently allows for a very wide range of vowel combinations without any requirement that some kind of consonant must intervene between the vowels. Thus, while in another language, one might opt to rule out a transcription like *teéa* for 'star' because of general constraints against extra long vowels or long vowel plus short vowel hiatus, words like *buúu* 'blood' or *beéi* 'braid' show that such combinations do not appear to be intrinsically problematic in Saramaccan.

Here, we have attempted to standardize the transcriptions in favor of indicating the presence of a *j* between the vowels when it is salient phonetically based on impressionistic evidence, though in doing this, we are not making any phonological claims.

Further examples of words containing unambiguous instances of phonemic *j* in Saramaccan are: *jejé* 'shadow,' *jekɛjekɛ* 'fringe,' *agúja* 'needle,' and *ajṍ* 'onion.' Some minimal and near minimal pairs for *j* with similar consonants include: *jaakú* 'ant type' vs. *waakú* 'fish type'; *jɔ́* 'melt' vs. *lɔ́* 'clan'; and *jabí* 'open' vs. *njawí* 'lizard type.' (The lack of a true minimal pair for *j* vs. *nj* is at least partially due to the restriction on *nj* where it is found primarily only in word-initial position.)

Similar to alternations between initial *wo* and *o* to be discussed in the section on *w* below, there are a number of words in Saramaccan that alternate between an initial *je* and *e*. Examples of such words include *éti/jéti* 'yet' and *jéside/éside* 'yesterday' (the order within each pair lists the form of the main entry for the word in Rountree, Asodanoe, and Glock 2000 first). As with the *wo/o* alternation, this alternation cannot be considered purely phonological, since there are some words beginning with *je* that do not show variant forms without *j*, for example *jési* 'ears' and *jéi* 'hear.'

Nevertheless, despite such exceptions, the general pattern does appear to be that words beginning with the sequence *je* can also be realized without the initial *j*, thus making it possible to treat this as a kind of phonological rule – one that can, in fact, be generalized to initial combinations of glides followed by tense mid vowels with a similar articulation. However, it is important to point out that the generalization only appears to go one way since there are a handful of words beginning with *e* which are not associated with variants beginning with *je*. (This class of words, however, is much smaller than a parallel class of words beginning with *o*, but not also associated with variants beginning with *wo*; see discussion in the section on *w* below.) Examples of such words include: *édi* 'head' (variant form of *hédi*), *ekísee* 'sneeze' (variant form of *hekísee*) (see the section on *h* for further discussion of *h~Ø* variation), and *ée/éfi* 'if.'

Finally, in the transcription used here, as well as in commonly employed orthographic systems for Saramaccan, *j* is not only used to represent a glide but also is part of the digraphs *dj*, *nj*, and *tj*, as well as the trigraph *ndj*, each representing a palatal consonant of a different manner of articulation. Due to the lack of consonant clusters in Saramaccan, of these, only *nj*, when present intervocalically, presents any possible ambiguities as to whether the *j* represents a glide or is part of a multigraph representation of a consonant. Specifically, *VnjV* sequences can, in principle, be analyzed as $\tilde{V}jV$ or *VjnV*. However, the consonant *nj* is quite infrequent in intervocalic position in Saramaccan, as is discussed in the section devoted to that sound. Therefore, in orthographies marking nasalization by means of symbols normally associated with nasal consonants, *VnjV* will usually represent $\tilde{V}jV$.

The consonant *w (hw)*

The Saramaccan consonant *w* has a comparable realization to English *w* and no known significant distributional restrictions, except that it does not appear to be allowed after nasalized vowels (except in reduplications) and there is an apparent prohibition on the sequence *wu*, parallel to the prohibition against *ji* discussed above and to be discussed in section 1.2.2. Because it is not present after nasalized vowels, it does not participate in the nasal harmony pattern associated with *j*, discussed in section 1.2.2.

Comparable to what is described above with respect to *j*, while *w* has clear phonemic status in many words, for example, *wéi* 'weather' and *awaá* 'palm type,' there are some cases where it is transcribed but its phonemic status is more ambiguous due to the fact that it could also represent an automatic transition between two vowels that would otherwise be adjacent. This is the case, for example, in words like *uwíi* 'leaf' or *túwɛ* 'throw,' and there does not appear to be any phonemic distinction between, say, a sequence like *uwíi* or a hypothetical sequence like *uíi* (though one does find comparable sequences transcribed in some sources, for example, in the word *duídui* 'insect type' in Rountree, Asodanoe, and Glock 2000). And, not surprisingly, the sources are inconsistent in their transcription of such sequences. Rountree, Asodanoe, and Glock (2000) give variant forms with and without intervocalic *w* for the words *kúákúa/kúwákúwa* 'raw' and *sukuáti/sukuwáti* 'chocolate,' for example. Similarly, the word *túwɛ* 'throw,' mentioned above, is written here with an intervocalic *w*, but is found as *túɛ* in other sources (e.g., in Donicie and Voorhoeve 1963). (See section 1.1.3.3. for further discussion of this word.)

Here, we have attempted to standardize the transcriptions in favor of indicating the presence of a *w* between the vowels when it is salient phonetically based on impressionistic evidence, though in doing this, we are not making any phonological claims.

The fact that *w* is not clearly attested after nasalized vowels gives us a potential criterion for treating some possible cases of transcribed intervocalic *w* as not present phonemically, for instance, *tũẽti* 'twenty' (written as *túwénti* in Rountree, Asodanoe, and Glock 2000). When elicited from one consultant this word showed nasalization as indicated in the transcription which, if an intervocalic glide were present phonemically, would be phonologically exceptional.

Examples of words containing *w* where it is clearly phonemic, in addition to those mentioned above, are *wáta* 'water,' *wíni* 'win,' and *mawí* 'bird type.' Near minimal pairs with *v* are *wṍdu* 'proverb' vs. *vodú* 'snake type' and *awoo* 'old' vs. *avó* 'grandparent' (see the section on *v* for discussion on why finding true minimal pairs involving *v* is difficult). Minimal pairs/sets with other similar consonants include: *waakú* 'fish type' vs. *jaakú* 'ant type'; and *wái* 'happy' vs. *kpái/kwái* 'tree type' vs. *lái* 'load' vs. *hái* 'haul' (see the section on the voiceless labial-velar stop for discussion of the *kp~kw* alternation).

There are a handful of words recorded in other sources that indicate the possibility of a marginal voiceless labialized velar approximant consonant [ʍ] in at least some Saramaccan varieties, though we have not found it with consultants who have been specifically questioned regarding this. This sound is written as *hw* both here and in other sources. Words where it has been reported as being found include *ahwámã̃ũ* 'shoulder' (which also has a variant form *ahõ̃mã̃ũ*) and *hwɛ́nɔ* 'bird type' (which also has a variant form *hénɔ*). No minimal pairs for *hw* and *w* have been found in sources reporting it. However, the element *ahwá* in the word *ahwámã̃ũ*, which does not stand on its own but is partially analyzable by virtue of the fact that *mã̃ũ* means 'hand,' could form a very near minimal pair with *awáa* 'at last' in a speaker whose variety makes the distinction. It appears to be the case that all words attested with *hw* also have variants not making use of *hw*, though what conditions the variation is not known.

Finally, parallel to the class of words which alternate between initial *je* and *e*, discussed in the section on *j* above, there is a large class of words which alternate between initial *wo* and *o* (see also section 17.2. for additional discussion), with some examples being *ómi/wómi* 'man' and *wójo/ójo* 'eye' (the order within each pair lists the form of the main entry for this word in Rountree, Asodanoe, and Glock 2000 first). As with the *je/e* alternation, this alternation cannot be considered purely phonological since there are a few words invariably beginning with *wo* that do not have a variant beginning with *o*. One of these is *woóko* 'work,' and another is *wówa* 'yawn' which has a variant form *hóha* but no variant **ówa*. Nevertheless, despite such exceptions, the general pattern does appear to be that words beginning with the sequence *wo* can also be realized without the initial *w*, thus making it possible to treat this as a kind of phonological rule which can be generalized to initial combinations of glides followed by tense mid vowels with a similar articulation. However, it is important to point out that, more robustly with *wo/o* than with *je/e*, the generalization only appears to go one way: words beginning with *wo* have variants without initial *w*, but, at the same time, there are many words beginning invariantly with *o*. Words in this category that have been checked with consultants include: *óbia* 'obeah,' *okási* 'opportunity,' *olóisi* 'clock,' and *opaláni* 'airplane.'

1.1.3. Vowels

1.1.3.1. Basic vowel qualities

As was seen in Table 2, Saramaccan has a symmetrical seven vowel system with two distinct sets of mid vowels, which we characterize here as an upper mid and a lower mid set, though the precise articulatory distinction has not been investigated, and we cannot rule out that it may involve factors other than height, as will be discussed below in the sections on the relevant vowels. This characterization should, therefore, be understood as a descriptive expediency rather than a specific phonetic claim. Only two noteworthy distributional restrictions on the appearance of the vowels have been noted. First, as mentioned above, word-initially, there are restrictions on the appearance of nasals before mid vowels, at least for those speakers maintaining a distinction between prenasalized stops and plain nasals word-initially. Second, though there are exceptions, there appears to be a general restriction on the appearance of mid vowels of different heights in adjacent syllables of a morpheme. Both of these restrictions will be discussed in section 1.2.2.

At least for a native English speaker, the most difficult vowel contrasts to reliably perceive are probably those between the members of the front pair and back pair of mid vowels. This is perhaps because the upper mid vowels are not accompanied by the diphthongization that characterizes English vowels commonly associated with [e] and [o], but it could also be a consequence of their articulation involving a phonetic distinction that is fundamentally difficult for an English speaker to perceive, along the lines of an ATR feature of the sort associated with West African languages.

The vowel *i*

The Saramaccan vowel *i* has a realization that can be reasonably characterized as IPA [i]. Some minimal pairs and near minimal pairs for *i* with similar vowels include: *físi* 'fish' vs. *fési* 'face' and *bési* 'bus' vs. *bése* 'frog type'; *díí* 'three' vs. *deé* 'dry' and *méti* 'meter' vs. *mɛté* 'meddle'; and *fiká* 'remain' vs. *fuká* 'distress' and *bási* 'boss' vs. *básu* 'bottom.'

The vowel *e*

For our main consultants, the Saramaccan vowel *e* would appear to be broadly transcribable as IPA [e], that is, as a higher mid front vowel. Such a transcription is in agreement with Rountree's (1972b) transcription of this vowel in a description of the Upper River dialect of the language. (Our consultants, however, speak the Lower River dialect.) Voorhoeve's (1959: 438) description of the Lower River dialect transcribed this vowel as [ɪ], suggesting a higher phonetic realization than what is implied by [e], and the vowel chart he gives further implies that *e* is not only lower than *i* but also further back in articulation than either *i* or *ɛ*. We are not able to verify the articulation of the vowel as compared to the other front vowels to such a high degree of accuracy.

It is important to point out here that Voorhoeve's transcription of *e* as [ɪ] should not be taken to mean that *e* is treated in Saramaccan phonology as a lax vowel (as might be an English vowel transcribed this way). First, it is not clear that the notions "tense" and "lax" are, in fact, relevant to the phonological structure of the Saramaccan vowel system. Furthermore, when phonological descriptions of Saramaccan do adopt the terms "tense" and "lax," *e* is uniformly treated as tense, while *ɛ* is treated as lax, this convention being adopted presumably under the influence of standard descriptions of the English vowel system. None of this is to say that a distinction between tense and lax vowels – or related concepts like [±ATR] – does not play an important role in the phonological system of Saramaccan. Rather, use of such concepts does not straightforwardly yield a more insightful description of the language's vowel system than simply specifying two distinct mid vowel heights, except perhaps in understanding the nature of some vowel co-occurrence restrictions to be discussed in section 1.2.2. (Smith and Haabo [2004: 528] do suggest that the lower mid vowels "would appear to be [-ATR]" while the rest are [+ATR], but it is not clear what their evidence is for this.) For further points on this matter, see the discussion of the vowel ε.

Some minimal pairs and near minimal pairs for *e* with similar vowels include: *bégi* 'request' vs. *bígi* 'big' and *bése* 'frog type' vs. *bési* 'bus'; *wéti* 'white' vs. *wéti* 'law' and *bé* 'let' vs. *bɛ* 'red'; and *kési* 'coffin' vs. *kósi* 'scold' and *kulé* 'run' vs. *kiló* 'kilogram.'

The vowel ε

The vowel written here as ε is broadly transcribable as [ε], that is, as a lower mid front vowel. This transcription is found in most sources, including Voorhoeve's early (1959) work and subsequently. In orthographic systems of Saramaccan, this vowel has been represented as è (or as ě when also marked for high tone) and as ë. As noted above in the discussion of *e*, Saramaccan does not obviously show a tense/lax distinction in its vowel system and, therefore, at least given the present state of our knowledge of Saramaccan phonetics, we characterize the opposition between ε and *e* in terms of height, as a matter of convenience but not as a specific phonetic claim. Rountree (1972b) suggests that the distinction can instead be understood as involving an opposition between bright and muffled vowels, with *i, u,* ε, and ɔ being bright, while *e* and *o* are muffled, giving the transcription [ẹ] for ε. (Such a classification, incidentally, would appear to run counter to one in which ε and ɔ are treated as lax and/or [-ATR] with *i, u, e, o* as [+ATR].) Based on our own impressions, this description does not seem implausible. However, we cannot verify it since the bright/muffled distinction, at least as understood by Rountree (1972b: fn. 2), is expected to correlate articulatorily with a more open/closed pharyngeal cavity, an aspect of phonetic description we have not explored. (Also, it is worth repeating the fact that, as mentioned above, Rountree 1972b was a description of the Upper River dialect, while we worked primarily with Lower River speakers, and the vowel systems of the two dialects, while of the same basic structure, may very well involve distinct phonetic realizations.)

Some minimal pairs and near minimal pairs for ε with similar vowels include: *deέ* 'dry' vs. *dií* 'three' and *mɛté* 'meddle' vs. *méti* 'meter'; *wéti* 'law' vs. *wéti* 'white' and *bɛ* 'red' vs. *bé* 'let'; *mɛté* 'meddle' vs. *mɔté* 'motor' and *sέ* 'side' vs. *sɔ́* 'so'; *héngi* 'hang' vs. *hángi* 'hunger' and *fiέ* 'burn' vs. *fiá* 'argue.'

The vowel *a*

Saramaccan *a* has a realization that can be reasonably characterized as IPA [a]. Some minimal pairs and near minimal pairs for *a* with similar vowels include: *hángi* 'hunger' vs. *héngi* 'hang' and *fiá* 'argue' vs. *fiέ* 'burn'; and *kálu* 'corn' vs. *kɔ́lu* 'guilder' and *ba* 'carry (water)' vs. *bɔ́* 'bow.'

The vowel *u*

Saramaccan *u* has a realization that can be reasonably characterized as IPA [u], though sometimes at the end of words it was observed to be perceptually close to [o], at least to the ears of a native English speaker, suggesting a possible lowering rule. Some minimal pairs and near minimal pairs for *u* with similar vowels include: *búnu* 'good' vs. *bónu* 'bone' and *mángu* 'thin' vs. *mángo* 'mangrove'; *húngɔ* 'gizzard' vs. *hɔ́ndɔ* 'hundred' and *djɔ́kú* 'hip' vs. *djɔ́kɔ́* 'nod'; and *fuká* 'distress' vs. *fiká* 'remain' and *básu* 'bottom' vs. *bási* 'boss.'

The vowel *o*

The Saramaccan vowel *o* presents comparable descriptive complications to those found for the vowel *e*. It can be reasonably given a broad transcription of [o]. Parallel to his transcription of *e* as [ɪ], Voorhoeve (1959: 438) transcribes *o* as [ʊ], and, comparable to the way his vowel chart implies *e* is further back than *i* or *ɛ*, it implies that *o* is further front than *u* or *ɔ*. We are not able to verify the articulation of the vowel as compared to the other back vowels to such a high degree of accuracy. Rountree's (1972b) description of the sound also transcribes it as [o], though, as noted, she was working primarily with Upper River speakers. As with the opposition between *e* and *ɛ*, there is not a clear indication that a distinction between tense and lax is relevant to understanding the difference between *o* and *ɔ*, and we descriptively characterize the distinction as one of height here, though without intending to make a specific articulatory claim (but see discussion of *ɛ* and *ɔ* on the possibility of a bright/muffled distinction and section 1.2.2. for some evidence of a possible ATR distinction).

Some minimal pairs and near minimal pairs for *o* with similar vowels include: *bónu* 'bone' vs. *búnu* 'good' and *mángo* 'mangrove' vs. *mángu* 'thin'; *kóto* 'skirt' vs. *kɔ́tɔ* 'cold' and *agó* 'knot' vs. *ahɔ́* 'hoe'; and *kósi* 'scold' vs. *kési* 'coffin' and *kiló* 'kilogram' vs. *kulé* 'run.'

The vowel *ɔ*

The Saramaccan vowel *ɔ* presents comparable descriptive complications to the vowel *ɛ*. It can be broadly transcribed as [ɔ], as found in Voorhoeve's early (1959) work and subsequently. In orthographic systems of Saramaccan, this vowel has been represented as *ò* (or as *ǒ* when also marked for high tone) and as *ö*. As noted above in the discussion of *e*, Saramaccan does not obviously show a tense/lax distinction in its vowel system and, therefore, at least given the present state of our knowledge of Saramaccan phonetics, we describe the opposition between *ɔ* and *o* in terms of height without making a specific phonetic claim. As noted in the discussion of *ɛ*, however, Rountree (1972b) suggests that the distinction can instead be understood as involving an opposition between bright and muffled vowels, with *ɔ* being bright and *o* muffled, and she suggests the transcription [o̞] for *ɔ*. As with the transcription of [e̞] for *ɛ*, based on our own impressions, this description does not seem implausible. However, we cannot verify this for the reasons discussed in the section on *ɛ*.

Some minimal pairs and near minimal pairs for *ɔ* with similar vowels include: *hɔ́ndɔ* 'hundred' vs. *húngɔ* 'gizzard' and *djɔ̃kɔ́* 'nod' vs. *djɔ̃kú* 'hip'; *kɔ́tɔ* 'cold' vs. *kóto* 'skirt' and *ahɔ́* 'hoe' vs. *agó* 'knot'; and *kɔ́lu* 'guilder' vs. *kálu* 'corn' and *bɔ́* 'bow' vs. *ba* 'carry (water).'

1.1.3.2. Nasal vowels

Saramaccan has distinctive vowel nasalization. All vowel qualities have nasalized variants, with no reduction of the vowel inventory under nasalization (though see section 1.2.2. for brief discussion of a small set of phonological environments where certain nasal vowels have been observed to significantly change their articulation). The distinctions among the front and back series of vowels are often more difficult to perceive under nasalization, in particular for each pair of mid vowels. Here, all phonemic nasal vowels are transcribed directly with a tilde. However, as mentioned above, most sources transcribe nasalization by means of silent "coda" nasal consonants (with an *m* before labial stops and an *n* elsewhere), analogous to the way nasalization is marked in French orthography. Thus, for example, *tõpi* 'stump' would be rendered as *tómpi*, *lõká* 'snore' would be rendered as *lonká*, and *sɛ̃* 'shame' would be rendered as *sén*.

For the most part, this latter convention works reasonably well since Saramaccan's fairly simple syllable structure generally results in apparent coda consonants serving as unambiguous markers of vowel nasalization. As noted in the discussion of *mb* and *nj*, this convention theoretically results in ambiguities in the case of digraphs whose first character is a nasal. In practice, however, this is not as problematic as it would first appear. On the one hand, the language does not seem to contrast sequences along the lines of *VNDV* with *ṼDV* – that is, the distinction between nasalized and non-nasalized vowels is apparently neutralized before prenasalized stops (in a pattern extending to nasal consonants more generally – see section 1.2.2.). On the other hand, while some cases of a true intervocalic *nj* have been found (see the discussion of *nj*), these are quite infrequent and, for the most part, one can assume that an orthographic *Vnj* sequence represents *Ṽj*.

Impressionistically, at least to the ears of a native English speaker, Saramaccan nasalization can be fairly "weak," especially when word-final. However, this may be due, at least partially, to the fact that vowel quality, in general, remains fairly constant in both nasalized and non-nasalized variants of the vowel. Therefore, there are not major secondary cues for nasalization. The specific perception of weak nasalization word-finally may also be due to the frequent presence of a degree of devoicing in this position in elicitation contexts, which reduces perceptual cues to vowel distinctions more generally. When appearing preconsonantally, nasalized vowels (again, to the ear of a native English speaker) are somewhat easier to perceive since they typically sound like *NC* sequences. In fact, Rountree (1972b: 26) even reports that intervocalic orthographic *NT* sequences (where *T* is a voiceless consonant) can actually be realized along the lines of [nt], [mp], [ŋk], etc., and we have found this as well, at least to a limited extent, when words are carefully articulated.

Word-finally, Rountree (1972b: 26) further implies that vowel nasalization (i.e. *Ṽ#*) can alternate with a sequence containing a final velar nasal (i.e. *Ṽŋ#*). While we have not examined this phenomenon extensively, we did encounter this as a possibility for a word Rountree cites, *sḗ* 'shame,' for example, as well as with the word *agbá̃* 'pot type,' when informally examined with one consultant. Thus, a nasalized vowel followed by a velar nasal appears to be a possible allophonic variant of vowel nasalization, at least word-finally in careful speech.

Examples of words containing each of the seven vowel qualities nasalized are given in Table 3. Where found, minimal or near minimal pairs across the different vowels are given across the word sets, especially for vowels with comparable articulation. It is generally harder to find true minimal pairs among the nasal vowels than the oral vowels, largely because nasal vowels are overall less frequent than oral vowels.

Minimal and near minimal pairs for nasal vowels with their oral counterparts include those given in Table 4. (As above, a relative infrequency of nasalized vowels makes finding true minimal pairs in some cases difficult.)

1.1.3.3. Long vowels and vowel combinations

All Saramaccan vowels appear in short and long forms, and the language also shows a fairly large range of vowel combinations. Both long vowels and vowel combinations are transcribed here simply by means of two adjacent vowels, with both vowels being the same in the case of a long vowel. Just like short vowels, long vowels and vowel combinations have nasalized variants. In some cases, the nasalized variants may only be poorly attested, or not at all, but due to the general prevalence of nasalized long vowels and vowel combinations, there is no reason to believe that such gaps are not simply accidental.

Examples of long vowels for each of the vowel qualities are given in Table 5.

Table 3. Examples of nasal vowels in Saramaccan

VOWELS	EXAMPLES
ĩ	así 'vinegar,' kwĩtí 'banana type,' síkíi 'body,' síta 'snake type,' wĩ 'wine'
ẽ	keléki 'chamber pot,' pẽ 'pin,' lẽtí 'edge,' tẽ 'time,' sẽsi 'since,' vẽtu 'wind'
ɛ̃	dẽkú 'energetic,' fɛ̃ 'break off,' hɛ̃pi 'shirt,' sɛ̃si 'cent,' wɛ̃wɛ̃ 'fly'
ã	báku 'bank,' dã 'rapids,' fã 'talk,' lãti 'government,' lãza 'spear,' pãpía 'paper'
ũ	ahũ 'grass,' gũsá 'pig type,' hũjã 'nail,' kũsu 'pillow,' sũ 'swim,' tũtá 'spit'
õ	ajõ 'onion,' kõtu 'legend,' opiõ 'poison,' põpa 'tip of boat,' tõõ 'time'
ɔ̃	hɔ̃ 'uproot,' hɔ̃jɔ̃hɔ̃jɔ̃ 'insect type,' kɔ̃ku 'betray,' sipɔ̃su 'sponge,' tɔ̃ɔ̃ 'rodent type'

Table 4. Minimal pairs for vowel nasalization

VOWELS	EXAMPLES
i/ĩ	sí 'see' vs. así 'vinegar'; síki 'sick' vs. síkíi 'body'
e/ẽ	bé 'let' vs. bẽ 'beam'; péti 'puddle' vs. pẽti 'comb'
ɛ/ɛ̃	dɛ́ 'there' vs. dɛ̃ 'rooster's comb'; pɛ́pɛ 'pepper' vs. hɛ̃pi 'shirt'
a/ã	dá 'give' vs. dã 'rapids'; hási 'horse' vs. hãsi 'ant'
u/ũ	háfu 'half' vs. ahũ 'grass'; núsu 'nose' vs. njũsu 'news'
o/õ	jajó 'loose living' vs. ajõ 'onion'; kóto 'skirt' vs. kõtu 'legend'
ɔ/ɔ̃	násɔ 'or' vs. nasĩɔ̃ 'nation'; mɔ́sɔ 'mix' vs. mɔ̃ɔ̃sɔ 'never'

Examples of minimal or near minimal pairs/sets across short and long vowels for each of the vowel qualities are given in Table 6.

At least on a surface level, in addition to regular long vowels, one also finds extra long vowels in words like: *giíi* 'stingy,' *beɛ́ɛ* 'bread,' *baáa* 'brother,' and *buúu* 'blood.' (Long vowel sequences like these are also found in ideophones – see 1.2.3. However, this is less striking since ideophones possess a number of distinct phonological properties.) Generally (and perhaps exclusively), these extra long sequences are the result of a relatively recent sound change wherein intervocalic alveolars were deleted (see the section on *l* for further discussion). Thus, for example, a word like *baáa* 'brother,' derived from the English word with the same meaning, is given as *brára* in Schumann's word list, with the present Saramaccan form resulting from deletion of the intervocalic liquids in a form along the lines of *barára* (with initial epenthesis between the *b* and *r* of the etymological *br* sequence).

Table 5. Examples of long vowels in Saramaccan

VOWELS	EXAMPLES
ii	afìikǎ 'African,' bíi 'beer,' bíibi 'belief,' gĩĩtá 'roar,' síkii 'body'
ee	bēēki 'tin can,' djeési 'imitate,' fééda 'Friday,' kúndjée 'wood type,' peetá 'crowd'
ɛɛ	bɛ́ɛ 'belly,' bɛɛ 'very red,' fɛ̃ɛ̃ 'for.3SO,' fɛɛbé 'boil,' pɛɛ́ 'play'
aa	akáa 'soul,' baasá 'embrace,' gã̌ã 'big,' sitááfu 'punishment,' taánga 'strong'
uu	buúku 'pants,' duumí 'sleep,' gũũjǎ 'complain,' púu 'produce,' sugúu 'darkness'
oo	boóko 'break,' boongó 'alligator type,' gõ̌õ 'ground,' kókóo 'shell,' kóóko 'yellow'
ɔɔ	bɔɔ́ 'blow,' kɔɔdéi 'rope type,' mɔ̃̌ɔ̃ 'more,' nɔ́ɔ 'NI,' sikɔ́ɔ 'school'

Table 6. Minimal pairs for vowel length

VOWELS	EXAMPLES
i/ii	kíki 'move' vs. kiíki 'creek'; nínga 'suppose mistakenly' vs. niingá 'refuse'
e/ee	hébi 'heavy' vs. heépi 'help'; péni 'enclosure' vs. peéni 'plane (wood)'
ɛ/ɛɛ	bɛ 'red' vs. bɛɛ 'very red'; kɛ́ 'want' vs. kɛɛ́ 'cry'
a/aa	paká 'pay' vs. pakáa 'dowry' vs. paaká 'bird type'
u/uu	búku 'book' vs. buúku 'pants'; pú 'pool' vs. púu 'pull'
o/oo	kókóo 'shell' vs. kóóko 'yellow'; sópu 'soap' vs. soópu 'swell'
ɔ/ɔɔ	hɔ́ni 'bee' vs. hɔɔní 'bird type'; tɔ́tɔ 'push' vs. tɔɔ́tɔ 'crooked'

A general analytical issue involving long vowels in Saramaccan is whether they should be treated phonologically as adjacent single vowels which happen to be of the same quality, or as true long vowels. As was first pointed out by Voorhoeve (1959: 437), each half of a long vowel is a separate tone bearing unit, and historically, it is clearly the case that many long vowels – not just extra long vowels – are the result of the recent sound change deleting intervocalic liquids just discussed. Voorhoeve (1959: 437), in fact, seems to favor an analysis of long vowels as simple concatenations of two short vowels, and Rountree (1972b: 25) reports that in words with extra long vowels speakers themselves treat each transcribed vowel as a separate syllable. We are not aware of unambiguous evidence that would resolve this issue generally, and it does not even seem to be possible to exclude – at least without delving into analysis going well beyond traditional description – the idea that some "long" vowels may be true long vowels, while other "long" vowels may be the surface manifestation of two adjacent short vowels. Below in this section, the possibility that patterns of vowel nasalization may be relevant to this issue will be briefly discussed.

In addition to long vowels, Saramaccan allows for a fairly extensive set of vowel combinations as well. At least some of these vowel combinations are frequent enough that it would be reasonable to refer to them as diphthongs, though we refrain from applying that label generally here since, as with the complications of the long vowels just discussed above, we are unaware of unambiguous evidence that would suggest these vowel sequences are treated as a single phonological unit in a way that is analogous to, for example, English diphthongs. As with long vowels, each transcribed vowel in a vowel combination serves as a separate tone bearing unit, suggesting that they exhibit at least some phonological independence from each other.

Table 7 summarizes the possibility/impossibility of the various logically possible vowel combinations (ignoring long vowels) in Saramaccan. A blank indicates that a given vowel combination is well attested, a "—" that it does not appear to be at all attested, and a "*" that it is attested, but only infrequently. The distinction between "well attested" and "infrequent," however, has been made on impressionistic grounds. There is much variation in the attestation of even the combinations classified as well attested here, and at least a few of the vowel combinations (especially *ea, iɛ, iɔ, oa,* and *ɔi*) are borderline cases.

As can be seen in Table 7, vowel combinations are more common when involving the high vowels *i* and *u*, though the third apex vowel *a* is also found fairly often in them. Furthermore, vowel combinations are more common the greater the difference in height between the vowels, with no possible combinations among the mid vowels. Perhaps the most surprising feature of the vowel combinations is the contrast (exemplified below) between *ei* and *ɛi* sequences and *ou* and *ɔu* sequences.

Table 7. Vowel combinations

V1↓ V2→	i	e	ɛ	a	o	ɔ	u
i		*	✓	✓	✓	✓	—
e	✓		—	✓	—	—	*
ɛ	✓	—		—	—	—	*
a	✓	—	—		*	—	✓
o	✓	—	—	✓		—	✓
ɔ	✓	—	—	*	—		✓
u	✓	✓	*	✓	—	—	

Examples of the well-attested vowel combinations (i.e. the ones indicated with a checkmark in Table 7) are given below in Table 8 (if an instance of the combination in nasalized form is not given, it is because no clear example could be found). All of the examples of the sequence *oa* are given as *owa* in Rountree, Asodanoe, and Glock (2000). Three of those words are also found in de Groot (1977), and two, *mboa* 'plant type' and *sóa* 'spoil,' are written without *w*, while the third, *koóa* 'sawdust,' is written with an *owa* sequence. See the section on *w* for further discussion. The forms for the sequence *ue* are written as *uwe* in both Rountree, Asodanoe, and Glock (2000) and de Groot (1977) (when found in the latter). Many of the forms for the sequence *ua* are written as *uwa* in Rountree, Asodanoe, and Glock (2000) but are found as *ua* elsewhere (for example in de Groot 1977). Some of the words with the *ui* sequence are written with an intervening *w* in Rountree, Asodanoe, and Glock (2000) while others are not. One, *uíi* 'leaf,' is written with a *uwi* sequence in both Rountree, Asodanoe, and Glock (2000) and de Groot (1977). See the section on *w* as to why it may be reasonable to treat the *w* as non-phonemic in these sequences. (See also related discussion in the section on *j*, though none of the examples given here which might contain a phonetic intervocalic *j* were transcribed as such in Rountree, Asodanoe, and Glock 2000.) As discussed above, in this grammar we have generally attempted to standardize the transcriptions in favor of indicating the presence of a glide between vowels when it is salient phonetically based on impressionistic evidence, although in doing this, we are not making any phonological claims. However, our transcriptions in this section are exceptional: for the purposes of describing the possible vowel combinations, we have assumed that glides that can be reasonably analyzed as being the automatic result of a transition between two vowels are not phonologically present and, in contrast to our more general practice, we do not transcribe them here. Obviously, the precise analysis one adopts for these glides could have significant consequences for the catalog of attested vowel combinations in Saramaccan, and the assumptions made here result in a description that gives the largest reasonable inventory.

Examples of the poorly attested vowel combinations are given in Table 9. The examples attempt to be exhaustive for monomorphemic words in Rountree, Asodanoe, and Glock (2000) (excluding ideophones). At least one of these words, *túwɛ* 'throw,' plays an important grammatical role in Saramaccan (see sections 8.2. and 13.3.2.2.), and is, therefore, used quite frequently. The fact that *uɛ* is otherwise unattested suggests that, at least for this word, an analysis of the intervocalic *w* found in some orthographic representations (including ours) as phonemic might be warranted. (We should also note that the glide transition seems impressionistically more prominent in *túɛ* than in the phonetically similar word *túɛ́ti* 'twenty,' showing an otherwise more common combination, which may provide further evidence for such an analysis.) We were not able to verify all the transcriptions of Rountree, Asodanoe, and Glock (2000), and this is noted when the relevant examples are presented.

Across morpheme boundaries there do not appear to be any restrictions on vowel combinations. Thus, reduplicated forms and compounds involving vowel-initial morphemes will sometimes also result in further examples of poorly attested vowel combinations or combinations that are otherwise unattested. For example, a further example of the sequence *ie* is found in *ediédi* 'dirt grains' (which is a formal reduplication of a bound stem – see section 3.1.1.4. – and is also associated with a variant form *ɛniéni*). Similarly, one finds the sequence *iu* in a word like *bíúdu* 'tree type' which is a compound consisting of an apparently bound morph *bí* followed by the morpheme *údu* 'wood.'

Impressionistically, in elicitation contexts, nasalization is stronger towards the end of long nasalized vowels and vowel combinations, at least when they are not preceded by a nasal consonant (as in a word like *mɔ̃ɔ̃* 'more' – which is a phonologically unusual word as will be discussed in section 1.2.2.). This was observed, for example, in the words *gõṍ* 'ground,' *pẽẽ́jã* 'fish type,' and *tũẽ́ti* 'twenty.' In work with one consultant, there seemed to be an almost complete lack of nasalization in the first vowel of *fẽáti* 'animosity' (and an *n* also appeared to be phonetically present in the recorded tokens after the *a*). This word has a variant form *felã́ti*, and the pattern of nasalization suggests perhaps the two vowels are not interpreted as being part of the same syllable even when the *l* is not found and indicates more generally that differential patterns of nasalization in long vowels or vowel combinations may be probative in determining the phonological structure of these patterns in some cases. However, while we would not rule out the possible discovery of a few marginal cases suggesting a contrast between $V\tilde{V}$ and $\tilde{V}\tilde{V}$ sequences, it does not appear to be a significant area of contrast even if, phonetically, nasalization is not necessarily spread out evenly within long vowels or vowel combinations.

Table 8. Examples of vowel combinations

VOWELS	EXAMPLES
ia	*aviaté* 'pilot,' *bía* 'beard,' *biá* 'turn,' *gani̋ã* 'chicken'
iɛ	*fié* 'burn,' *ni̋ɛ̃* 'strand,' *temíɛmaipa* 'tree type,' *piɛpiɛ páu* 'tree type'
io	*fíófio* 'spirit revenge,' *lío* 'river,' *milĩő* 'million,' *tapióka* 'tapioca'
iɔ	*biɔ́ngɔ* 'obeah medicine,' *losĩɔ̃* 'lotion,' *nasĩɔ̃* 'nation,' *tapiɔ́kɔ* 'insect type'
ei	*féífi* 'five,' *mbéi* 'make,' *léi* 'learn,' *seí* 'ant type,' *wéi* 'tired'
ɛi	*éísi* 'ice,' *léi* 'drive,' *sikéíki* 'fright,' *wɛi* 'dedicate'
ea	*fɛ̃áti* 'animosity,' *kandéa* 'resin,' *matééa* 'spray'
ai	*agãĩ* 'fish type,' *djakaí* 'monkey type,' *maipá* 'tree type,' *páíti* 'priest'
au	*laú* 'crazy,' *matjáu* 'axe,' *mãṹ* 'hand,' *sauké* 'fish type'
oa	*mboa* 'plant type,' *sóa* 'spoil,' *kooá* 'skim,' *koóa* 'sawdust'
oi	*asõítábaku* 'tobacco type,' *bói* 'cook,' *bóíti* 'except,' *hói* 'hold,' *olóísi* 'clock'
ɔi	*kɔ́i* 'walk around,' *mɔ́i* 'soft,' *mɔ́íti* 'effort,' *nɔ́íti* 'never'
ou	*dóu* 'arrive,' *fitoóu* 'trust,' *fóu* 'bird,' *góútu* 'gold'
ɔu	*fɔ́útu* 'mistake,' *kɔúsu* 'socks,' *tɔ́ɔu* 'marriage,' *wɔ́útu* 'words'
ue	*akúsue* 'rodent type,' *duéngi* 'force,' *ndjuéndjue* 'lizard type,' *tűéti* 'twenty'
ua	*kambalúa* 'reed type,' *kúákúa* 'raw,' *suálufu* 'matches,' *sũãpu* 'swamp'
ui	*búi* 'chain,' *duídui* 'insect type,' *matúítui* 'bird type,' *suí* 'bird type,' *uíi* 'leaf'

Table 9. Marginal vowel combinations

VOWELS	EXAMPLES	NOTES
ie	bobíēte 'undeveloped maripa fruit'	bóbíɛte when checked with one of our consultants
ao	kakáo 'cacao,' laláo 'whale'	difference between *ao* and *au* could not be detected in elicitation
eu	léu 'lion'	variant form of léũ; when checked with one consultant, found *léu*
ɛu	lɛ́ũ 'lion'	variant form *léu*; when checked with one consultant, found *léu*
ɔa	amɔatawé 'vine type'	when checked with a consultant, the word was not recalled
uɛ	túɛ 'throw'	

1.2. Phonotactics

1.2.1. Syllable structure and epenthetic vowels

Contemporary Saramaccan only clearly allows syllables of shapes *V* and *CV* (though earlier varieties may have allowed for a wider range of syllable structures [Aceto 1996]), assuming that sounds like *mb*, *nd*, *ndj*, *ng*, *kp/kw*, and *gb/gw* are treated as single segments (and, as far as we are aware, there is no reason not to, given that, otherwise, there is no evidence for consonant clusters in the language). Rountree (1972b: 23) further analyzes the language as showing *CVN* syllables, as a kind of allophonic variant of vowel nasalization. For example, the word represented here as *lãza* 'spear' is transcribed by her as [lánza]. However, there is no evidence for a contrast between $\tilde{V}$ and *VN* sequences in Saramaccan, and it is not clear to us that there is often a true phonetic nasal consonant in words like *lãza* as opposed to a perceived nasal, though we have occasionally found tokens where true nasals in comparable positions seem to be found. As discussed in section 1.1.3.2., in word-final position, there is also the possibility of a final velar nasal appearing as an allophonic (free) variant of vowel nasalization, which is obviously less susceptible to being the result of misperception than a word-medial nasal. Therefore, it seems that, on a phonetic level, at least $C\tilde{V}\eta\#$ syllables are found. Phonologically, however, since apparent coda nasals, when reported, are almost always allophonically related to vowel nasalization, it would seem more accurate to describe the Saramaccan syllable canon as *(C)V* with the suprasegmental feature of vowel nasalization sometimes resulting in more complex phonetic realizations.

Beyond the above possible exceptional cases, there are also a handful of words showing apparent coda *m*. Several examples of these found in Rountree, Asodanoe, and Glock (2000) are ideophones (cf. section 1.2.3.): *gbalam* 'thunder,' *gbemm* 'hit and falling,' *kám* 'full,' *tjam* 'piercing,' and *tóm* 'sitting straight.' (The last of these has a variant form *tó̃*.) The remaining examples in that source are: *adamkilo* 'measuring worm,' *adjámtóo* 'rice type,' and *komsáka* 'athlete's foot.' A presumably recent borrowing (drawn from Glock and Rountree [2003]) showing such a syllable is *pomté* 'potato' (ultimately from French *pomme de terre*). Thus, the syllable shape *CVm* also appears to be marginally possible in the language. However, we have not checked these words with consultants, and it may be the case that some of these apparent instances of coda *m* are syllabic, resulting from the loss of a vowel that was earlier present after them (see the discussion on *m* above). In addition, one ideophone was recorded from a consultant with the form *kpáp* for the sound of an arrow being let loose, the only instance known to us of a word with a *p* coda.

There are numerous vowel-initial words in Saramaccan, especially for the vowel *a* (see section 3.2.3.). Some examples include: *agó* 'knot,' *ée* 'if,' *éísi* 'ice,' *íngi* 'Amerindian,' *óbia* 'obeah,' *ɔ́fu* 'oven,' and *údu* 'wood.' Such words clearly attest the possibility for syllables of shape *V* in the language. In addition, as discussed in section 1.1.3.3., it may be possible to analyze some vowel sequences as consisting of separate syllables, in which case a non-initial syllable could also have shape *V*. Thus, for example, Rountree (1972b: 25) states that her consultants syllabified a word like *baáa* 'brother' as *ba-á-a*. We leave open the question of how best to analyze such sequences phonologically, but clearly it has consequences regarding the prevalence of syllables of shape *V* in the language.

Saramaccan's simple syllable structure has resulted in extensive vowel epenthesis, both to break up consonant clusters and to prevent the appearance of word-final codas, in transferred and borrowed words. In the contemporary language, the most frequent epenthetic vowels are the high vowels *i* and *u*, though older vocabulary indicates that at an earlier stage of the language other strategies may have been employed. Whether *i* or *u* is chosen is dependent on the adjacent consonants as well as on nearby vowels. (The relevant epenthetic vowels in the examples below are all bolded.)

Round vowels in a borrowed word are often associated with the appearance of an epenthetic *u*, and other vowels with the appearance of an *i*. Thus, for example, on the one hand, one finds an epenthetic *u* in words like *suwálufu* 'matches' adapted from Sranan *swarfu* 'match,' *sukúfu* 'screw' adapted from Sranan *skrufu* 'screw,' and *fɔlúku* 'fork' from Sranan *forku* 'fork.' On the other hand, one finds an epenthetic *i* in words like *póbíki* 'doll' from Sranan *popki* 'doll,' *báíki* 'beam' from Sranan *barki* 'beam,' and *féífi* 'paint' from Sranan *ferfi* 'paint' – in the case of the last two words the vowels no longer appear as epenthetic because of the loss of intervocalic *l* (see the section on that consonant above), either because of a historical sound change affecting these words directly or as the result of an established Sranan transfer rule. In addition to the quality of adjacent vowels, the quality of the consonants being broken up by the epenthetic vowel can also be relevant. For example, the epenthetic vowel in *Cw* clusters is generally *u* as in *suwáki* 'sick' from Sranan *swaki* 'weak' and *tuwálúfu* 'twelve' from Sranan *twarfu* 'twelve,' while the epenthetic vowel in *sk* clusters is generally *i*, as in *sikɔ́ɔ* 'school' from Sranan *skoro* 'school' and *sikópu* 'kick' from Sranan *skopu* 'kick,' except when the following vowel is *u* as in *sukúfu* just given above. However, it should be noted that exceptions to these patterns are not, in general, hard to find.

1.2.2. Co-occurrence restrictions and related kinds of patterns

Various co-occurrence restrictions among segments have been detected in Saramaccan roots. Due to the relative lack of morphology in the language, none of these restrictions result in allomorphy, and they therefore only take the form of morpheme structure constraints.

Plain nasals and prenasalized stops and mid vowels: As mentioned in the discussion of *mb* and *nd* above, there is a restriction on word-initial nasal-vowel sequences where, for those speakers distinguishing between prenasalized stops and plain nasals word-initially, before the high mid vowels *e* and *o* one finds only prenasalized stops, while before the low mid vowels *ɛ* and *ɔ* one finds only plain nasals. Thus, for example, for at least some speakers/dialects, one finds word pairs like *mbéti* 'animal' vs. *méti* 'meter,' but no forms like *méti or *mbéti. (Recall, however, that for our main consultant, a word like *mbéti* was, in fact, rendered as *méti*.) Other examples of words illustrating this restriction are *ndéti* 'night' vs. *néti* 'net,' *mbookó* 'fish type' vs. *mɔtjɔ́* 'prostitute,' and *ndófu* 'a lot' vs. *nɔ́bu* 'identifier,' though it should be said that for some of these combinations there are not many words containing them to start with. This restriction on prenasalized stops before lower mid vowels does not hold word-internally as seen in words like *mémbɛ* 'remember,' *pendé* 'colored,'and *hɔ́ndɔ* 'hundred.' However, examples of plain nasals before upper mid vowels word-internally appear to be close to non-existent, with no clear examples found in Rountree, Asodanoe, and Glock (2000). With respect to *ng*, the one prenasalized stop not paired with a plain nasal, there is no apparent restriction on what vowels it can precede. While very few words begin with *ng* in Saramaccan, the only one whose first vowel is mid in Rountree, Asodanoe, and Glock (2000), *ngɔ́tɔ* 'ditch,' contains a low mid vowel, contrary to the pattern found for the other prenasalized stops. Furthermore, word-internally, one finds examples of *ng* followed by both upper mid and lower mid vowels, for example, in *gengé* 'bell,' *malɛ́ngɛ* 'lazy,' *píngo* 'pig type,' and *dɔɔ́ngɔ* 'drunk.'

Before non-mid vowels, *mb* and *nd* can clearly contrast with *m* and *n*, respectively, as seen in minimal pairs and near minimal pairs like: *mbíi* 'mill' vs. *míi* 'child,' *mbata* 'deer type' vs. *máta* 'mortar,' *mbulu* 'receding hairline' vs. *múlu* 'uterus,' and *namá* 'touch' vs. *nambá* 'strap'; and *hɔ́ndi* 'hunt' vs. *hɔ́ni* 'bee,' *pína* 'pin' vs. *pindá* 'peanut,' and *kándúu* 'amulet type' vs. *kaánu* 'tree type.' However, there are still some potentially noteworthy gaps in attested contrasts – for example, the lack of an *n/nd* distinction before *a* word-initially given that there are many words beginning with *na* in the language (in contrast to *nu*, for example, which is much less common to begin with, rendering the lack of *n/nd* distinction word-initially before *u* less striking).

Nasal consonants and nasalized vowels: The occurrence of plain nasal consonants and prenasalized stops immediately before or after nasalized vowels is relatively uncommon, though some exceptions have been noted including a variant form of an ideophone *gíngí/gíngĩ́* 'stuck fast' found in Rountree, Asodanoe, and Glock (2000), the word *mũnjã̌* 'wet' (also unusual for allowing a word-medial palatal nasal), and several words containing long vowels or vowel combinations, such as *mɔ́̃ɔ̃* 'more,' *mã́ũ* 'hand,' and *ganĩ́ã* 'chicken.'

Prenasalized stops in a single morpheme: Multiple prenasalized stops in direct succession in a single morpheme are quite rare, with the only clear case we are aware of being *bingúngu* 'stink bug.' The occurrence of multiple prenasalized stops even anywhere within a single morpheme is rare, in fact, and we are aware of only one further case, *mbáfumbá* 'animal type.' Otherwise, excepting compounds, multiple prenasalized stops in a single word are generally only found in words containing reduplicated elements, some of which, like *malɛmbélɛmbɛ* 'medicinal plants' and *jengéjenge* 'rice type,' contain instances of reduplicated stems not found in isolation.

Upper mid and lower mid vowels: Generally, upper mid and lower mid vowels do not appear together within a single morpheme (see also Smith [1975]). Thus, one readily finds forms like *kóto* 'skirt,' *kɔ́tɔ* 'cold,' *bése* 'frog type,' *bétɛ* 'better,' *kɔ́ndɛ* 'village,' and *éndolé* 'stork type' containing multiple mid vowels of the same height, while forms like *kɔɔdéi* 'rope type,' *pikoléti* 'bird type,' and *tóṍjɔ̃* 'spirit type' are much less frequent, with around ten or so cases found in Rountree, Asodanoe, and Glock (2000). This co-occurrence restriction is reminiscent of what is found in West African languages exhibiting ATR harmony (see Casali [2008]), suggesting a possible basis for analyzing the mid vowels in Saramaccan as contrasting across ATR rather than height.

Contextualized nasalized vowel allophony: As noted by Rountree (1972b: 24–25), in environments involving nasalized vowels and following voiceless stops, the distinctions between nasalized vowels and their plain counterparts can involve relatively salient quality changes in the nasalized vowels.

For instance, in a word like *lótu* 'go around,' the first vowel sounds like something in between [o] and [ɔ], and in a word like *vĕtu* 'wind' the first vowel sounds perceptually closer to English [ɪ] than the expected vowel [e]. By contrast, the long vowel in a word like *pēẽjã* 'fish type' appears to match [e] fairly well (and certainly much more so than in *vĕtu*), clearly indicating this effect is not merely connected to vowel nasalization but, rather, involves nasalization in specific contexts.

Nasal harmony: As first pointed out by Rountree (1972b: 26), there is a minor nasal harmony pattern in Saramaccan wherein vowels on either side of a *j* or a *nj* within a morpheme must both be either nasalized or non-nasalized. Thus, one finds numerous instances of words containing sequences like *VjV*, such as *fája* 'fire,' *wójo* 'eye,' *adója* 'plant type,' and *mujéɛ* 'woman,' and words containing sequences like *ṼjṼ*, such as *hɔ̃jɔ̃hɔ̃jɔ̃* 'insect type,' *hũjã* 'nail,' *kũjã* 'bird type,' *pēẽjã* 'fish type,' and *pãjã̌* 'hold,' but words containing *VjṼ* or *ṼjV* are quite uncommon. The only two clear cases of the first pattern we have found within a morpheme are *ajṍ* 'onion' and *mapijɔ̃́* 'louse type,' as reported in Rountree, Asodanoe, and Glock (2000). An additional word showing this pattern, *kɛijɔ̃́* 'pencil,' is associated with a variant *kɛ̃jɔ̃́* that does show nasalization harmony. This disharmonic pattern is also reported in *azɔ̃kíjẽjɛ̃* 'firefly' whose form, from the perspective of both tone and vowel co-occurrences, suggests that it is etymologically complex (though it does not appear to be analyzable synchronically). This word is disharmonic in both directions exhibiting *VjṼ* and *ṼjV* patterns. The pattern *ṼjV* appears to be more marginal, with the clearest possible case in Rountree, Asodanoe, and Glock (2000) being *sãājá* 'give away,' which is also associated with a harmonic variant form *saajá* (and this latter was the form produced when checked with a consultant).

Due to the fact that intervocalic *nj* is relatively uncommon in Saramaccan (see the discussion in the section on that consonant), words exemplifying nasal harmony involving this consonant are also relatively uncommon but the pattern can be seen, for example, in *njũ̌njũ* 'new,' *njãnjã̌* 'food,' and *sipanjólu* 'Spanish.'

Homorganic glide-vowel sequences: As discussed above in the sections on *j* and *w*, there appears to be a ban on the sequences *ji* and *wu* in the language, which are unattested in Rountree, Asodanoe, and Glock (2000). This can be understood as a general ban on a glide followed by a vowel with the same place of articulation. See the sections on *j* and *w* respectively for additional discussion of patterns of alternation observed for *je* and *wo* sequences.

1.2.3. Ideophones

Saramaccan has an extensive array of ideophones with distinct phonological characteristics from the rest of the vocabulary. Section 2.2.3.5. discusses their tonal features and section 14.7. discusses their syntax. Here, we touch briefly upon their segmental features.

Perhaps the most striking segmental feature of ideophones is that a handful of them allow a nasal coda of form *m* – otherwise the language only very rarely allows coda consonants. As mentioned above in section 1.2.1., five ideophones with this property are given in Rountree, Asodanoe, and Glock (2000) (some of which are associated with variants without nasal codas): *gbalam* 'thunder,' *gbemm* 'hit and falling,' *kám* 'full,' *tjam* 'piercing,' and *tóm* 'sitting straight.'

Another noteworthy feature of ideophones, not surprising given their sound symbolic status, is that transcribed long vowels in ideophones are often extra long – of roughly comparable length to sequences of three or more transcribed vowels. Thus, "long" vowel transcriptions in ideophones are typically used to indicate a stylistically lengthened vowel rather than a "regular" long vowel. For example, the ideophone transcribed as *fã́ã́* 'very white' in Rountree, Asodanoe, and Glock (2000) would appear, in some instances at least, to be uttered closer to IPA [fã́::] (if not longer) than [fá:]. Similarly, transcriptions containing sequences of three or four vowels in an ideophone should also be taken as indications of stylistic lengthening rather than, say, an analysis of those sequences as consisting of three or four moras.

With respect to consonant distribution, although ideophones draw on the same segmental inventory as non-ideophones, certain sounds are much more common in ideophones than in the rest of the vocabulary. For example, *gb* (but not *kp*) is quite characteristic of ideophones but otherwise not especially common. Though the distribution is less skewed, the same can be said for *f* and *v*, as well.

Finally, the overall patterning of segments in ideophones of more than one syllable can be described as generally "repetitive" both because they often contain apparent cases of full or partial reduplication and because they also often show total vowel harmony. Examples of apparent full reduplication in ideophones include: *bugubugu* 'shaking out,' *fiafia* 'energetically,' and *gbéîgbéî* 'iron hitting iron.' Examples of apparent partial reduplication in ideophones include: *dalala* 'straight,' *dílílíí* 'unwrinkled,' and *tjúlúlúú* 'without a thing.' Additional examples of ideophones wherein there is full vowel harmony include: *fãjãã* 'messy,' *fèlelɛ* 'shallow,' and *gbɔlɔ* 'lukewarm.' However, these patterns are only tendencies, and there are many ideophones not adhering to them, for example, *dimbaa* 'heavy object on water,' *fɔkííí* 'pale,' and *kpatii* 'many.'

See section 1.4. for discussion of sporadic phonological alternations, in which some ideophones participate.

1.3. Lexical strata

A noteworthy feature of the Saramaccan lexicon which we will not explore in detail here, but which is worth pointing out at least briefly, is the apparent "layering" of different strata of vocabulary. Historically speaking, some of these strata are no doubt the result of Saramaccan's origins as a contact language and its acquisition of vocabulary from a range of source languages: English, Portuguese, Gbe languages, western Bantu languages, Dutch, Sranan, Amerindian languages, etc. (see Good [2011] for a discussion of "loanwords" in Saramaccan where the sources of the Saramaccan lexicon are discussed in more detail).

The most prominent synchronic aspects of the stratification of the Saramaccan lexicon are prosodic in nature and will be discussed in more detail in section 2.2. However, there are segmental features that appear to define different layers of vocabulary as well. For example, there is an unexpectedly large set of nouns beginning with an *a* that is reminiscent of a Niger-Congo noun class prefix (and in some cases, at least, is presumably a transfer of such a prefix) (see section 3.2.3.). While normally one would not necessarily view a category of words defined by their initial segment as a "stratum," in the Saramaccan case, there is a noted imbalance holding among words beginning with vowels where, overall, they are not particularly common when one excludes those beginning with *a*. For example, in Rountree, Asodanoe, and Glock (2000), there are nearly 300 *a*-initial words against less than 100 for all other vowels combined. Furthermore, there are a number of words which alternate between *a*-initial and *a*-less variants, for example *(a)kulí* 'Hindustani' (where the *a*-initial variant is clearly a Saramaccan innovation with the word ultimately deriving from the same source as English *coolie*), *(a)tengútengú* 'limping,' and *(a)dikpókpo* 'mushroom,' suggesting there is more to the presence of *a*- than mere accident. Perhaps the *a*- can be interpreted as a prefix, but, if so, it would seem impossible to devise any conditioning environment for its presence since the class of words showing *a*- is not obviously semantically coherent.

Another apparent stratum was discussed in the section on *h* (see also the sections on *j* and *w*). As mentioned, there is a class of words characterized by showing an alternation between beginning with *h* or simply a vowel. Membership in this class is not directly predictable from a word's form since some *h*-initial words are not associated with a vowel-initial variant and there are a vast number of vowel-initial words not associated with an *h*-initial variant. It, therefore, seems reasonable to consider this class of words to be a special lexical stratum.

Synchronically, the status of other, apparent strata is unclear for the same reason that the status of many possible morphophonological patterns (see section 1.2.2.) is unclear: namely, without extensive morphology, evidence for the strata primarily takes the shape of static word form distributions rather than productive alternations.

1.4. Sporadic alternations

There are a handful of classes of sporadic alternations not discussed above found in the Saramaccan lexicon which seem worthy of mention but which are not systematic enough for one to arrive at a general characterization of their conditioning factors, though they may be dialectal in nature in some cases. The alternations described here are purely lexical – see Chapter 3 for discussion of irregular morphophonemic alternations and see Chapter 17 for further discussion of lexical variation. This discussion is not exhaustive, and other sporadic alternations can be found by an examination of variant forms in Rountree, Asodanoe, and Glock (2000).

Vowel shortening: A few words show alternations between long and short vowels including *heelú/helú* 'curse,' *kúúkútu/kúkútu* 'insect type,' and *hekísee/hekíse* 'sneeze.'

Long vowels and vowel combinations: A few words show variant forms with a simplification of *Vi* vowel combinations to *VV* including *adjãĩsi/adjã̃ã̃si* 'spider,' *beipé/beepé* 'graveyard,' and *péikáa/péékáa* 'horsepower.'

***wi~u*:** At least two words show variant forms where the sequence *wi* alternates with *u*. These words are *wiwíi/uwíi* 'leaf' and *kwíndji/kúndji* 'squeeze.' While an alternation involving just two words might not seem obviously noteworthy, it bears mentioning here because it follows the pattern mentioned in the section on *w* wherein the sequence *wu* is unattested in Saramaccan. This presumably partly explains why the alternation is between *wi* and *u* instead of the perhaps more expected *wi* and *wu*. This alternation is, thus, additional evidence for this co-occurrence restriction.

Palatalization of *k*: A few words show an alternation involving palatalization of a velar before *i*. Examples include *kína/tjína* 'taboo' and *lémíki/lémítji* 'lime tree.' However, there is no indication that this is the result of a productive phonological process in the language and, as discussed in the section on *k*, these pairs may be the result of borrowing variant Sranan forms, where allophonic palatalization of velars before high front vowels is found.

Chapter 2
Prosodic phonology

2.1. Introduction

A particularly striking feature of Saramaccan prosodic phonology is the apparent maintenance of two distinct word-level prosodic systems, one accentual and the other tonal. The phrasal phonology is most saliently characterized by a process of tonal plateauing as well as a number of intonational sentence-level processes and has already been relatively well-described in the literature, making Saramaccan one of the best-studied creole languages in terms of its suprasegmental phonology. (This chapter focuses only on tonal and accentual aspects of phonology in Saramaccan. Other suprasegmental aspects of the language's phonology, e.g. syllable structure, are discussed in section 1.2.) The discussion of word-level prosody here will, in some ways, deviate from traditional description insofar as it will include not only illustrative examples of phenomena but also significant analytical argumentation. This is necessary to establish the existence of an apparent accentual/tonal split in the Saramaccan lexicon. Furthermore, since such a pattern is typologically unusual, it requires a greater level of detail in its description than a typologically "normal" system would.

It should be noted that tonal patterns in Saramaccan are often not transcribed at all in other sources on the language and, even when they are, one not infrequently finds inconsistent transcriptions. Some of this is likely due to genuine dialectal or idiolectal variation. At the same time, more than in other features of the language's grammar, a good deal of this variation is probably due to inconsistencies or misapprehensions on the part of the analyst – no doubt some of which will be found in this chapter as well, though hopefully to a much less significant degree than elsewhere. Section 2.5. discusses some analytical problems associated with tonal transcription in Saramaccan relating to its split prosodic system and should be examined by any reader interested in making use of the data here to advance specific claims regarding Saramaccan's prosody.

Tonal transcriptions (for examples not given a source in the literature) are based on impressionistic evidence, often augmented with instrumental data. Most of the phrasal data in this chapter, when drawn from other sources, has been double-checked with our consultants, though this has not always been possible, and a significant number of the words cited as exemplifying specific prosodic patterns have not been double-checked, primarily in cases where they merely offer further examples of patterns already determined to be fairly robust.

2.2. Word-level prosody

2.2.1. Introduction

As discussed in detail in Good (2004), Saramaccan shows an apparent split wherein the majority of its words are marked for pitch accent but a noteworthy minority are marked for tone. At a very general level, the source of the split seems straightforward: tonal "African" words and accentual "European" words have both contributed to the Saramaccan lexicon without leveling of the language's prosodic structure in favor of one type of system over another. In this respect, the Saramaccan split appears to be different in degree, but not in kind, from what is found in languages like English or Japanese where distinct prosodic strata are found associated historically with massive borrowing of Latinate and Sinitic vocabulary respectively.

Obviously, the presence of such a split complicates the description of the language's prosodic system considerably, especially given that a high pitch – apparently phonetically indistinguishable from a lexical high tone (see Good 2006) – is part of the surface manifestation of accent in the language. As a descriptive preliminary, we define our senses of the terms *accent*, *pitch accent*, *stress*, and *tone* in (1) below. While the particular wording of the definitions is our own, it is our impression that the way we use these terms is as close to "standard" as possible given the extensive variation found in their use in the literature.

(1) a. **Accent**: An abstract indication of linguistic prominence distinguishing one syllable from the other syllables within a word – hence, a marking of syntagmatic contrast within the word.
   b. **Pitch accent**: The realization of accent as a specific tone (or tone contour) which is placed with reference to an accented unit.
   c. **Stress**: The realization of accent by making primary use of acoustic parameters other than pitch – typically amplitude, duration, and segment quality.
   d. **Tone**: The linguistic use of pitch to mark paradigmatic contrasts – that is, one toneme must contrast with other tonemes that can appear within the same domain.

The importance of surface pitch fluctuations to Saramaccan grammar has been well-recognized as least as far back as Voorhoeve (1961). Until recently, these pitch fluctuations have generally been considered to be manifestations of "tone." However, the nature of Saramaccan surface tonal patterns in fact suggests that, while one can characterize Saramaccan surface phonology in terms of high and low "tonal" targets (as can also be done for the intonational systems of uncontroversially non-tonal languages like English), it is not quite accurate to describe Saramaccan as tonal in the technical sense intended by (1d). This is because, for the majority of the vocabulary, there is no evidence for a paradigmatic contrast of tonemes in the relevant domain, which for Saramaccan is the single vowel of a short syllable or either half of a long vowel or vowel combination (or, more rarely, *m*; see the discussion of *m* in section 1.1.2.2.). Accordingly, we divide the rest of our discussion of Saramaccan word-level prosody into three sections: the first (section 2.2.2.) treats those elements of the vocabulary which are most easily interpreted as being marked for accent, the second (section 2.2.3.) discusses those elements of the vocabulary which are most easily interpreted as being marked for true tone, and the third (section 2.2.4.) discusses some exceptional cases. Compounds and reduplications are not treated in this section but, rather, in section 2.3.1.1.

In the transcription system used here, any orthographic vowel is a tone bearing unit (TBU). Analytically speaking, it may, in fact, make sense to treat the TBU as a single mora, though we will not generally adopt such terminology in the following description, only raising the issue where particularly relevant. As discussed in section 1.1.3.3., the precise status of surface long vowels is not completely clear insofar as we are unaware of clear-cut evidence that crucially bears on whether they should be treated as true long vowels or as sequences of two vowels which happen to have the same quality. Resolution of this issue is a prerequisite for making a clear determination regarding whether the TBU is better treated as a vowel or a mora.

The transcription of tone in this chapter will differ from what is found generally in the grammar (though some of its conventions are found elsewhere, as in section 14.7. on ideophones). In particular, rather than only marking the high tones that are found in the citation forms of lexical items, the full tonal patterns of surface forms will often be indicated as well, and a transcription system will be used which distinguishes between TBU's bearing true low tones, which will be explicitly marked with a grave accent in both underlying and surface forms, and TBU's treated as underlyingly unspecified for tone (which surface as low in citation contexts), which will only be marked with a grave accent (where appropriate) in surface forms. Where relevant, stress will be indicated using the IPA stress marks. See section 2.5. for brief discussion of how to phonetically interpret the tonal transcriptions used here.

2.2.2. Accentual words

2.2.2.1. Words with high tones and TBU's unspecified for tone

As first explicitly recognized by Rountree (1972b), building on Voorhoeve's (1961) seminal work, lexical items in Saramaccan can be subdivided into a number of "tonal" classes, the largest of which is composed of words with either one high tone or two adjacent high tones in their citation form and whose other TBU's surface predictably with either high or low tones depending on their phonosyntactic environment. Here, TBU's of this latter type will be referred to as TBU's unspecified for tone. Because sources on the Saramaccan lexicon do not generally clearly distinguish between TBU's unspecified for tone and TBU's which are consistently low tone (see section 2.2.3.) – assuming, that is, that they mark tone at all – it is difficult to determine precisely what percentage of words in Saramaccan fall into the class of words that is the focus of this section, but we estimate that it comprises, perhaps, ninety-percent or so of the language's vocabulary.

An illustrative example is given in (2), which shows the underlying and surface tones in the word *taánga* 'strong' in both its citation form and within a noun phrase. In particular, what should be noted is the contrasting tonal realization of the final TBU in this word in (2a) versus (2b).

(2) a. *taánga* → *tàángà* 'strong'
    b. *dí   taánga wómi* → *dí tàángá wómì*
       DEF strong man
       'the strong man'

In section 2.3. the phrasal environments conditioning tonal alternations like the one seen in (2) will be discussed in detail. Roughly speaking, we can understand the alternations as resulting from the fact that (i) some TBU's in Saramaccan are not lexically specified for tone in any way and (ii) these TBU's acquire their tones either through a kind of "default" rule assigning them a low tone or as a result of a process of high-tone plateauing wherein a TBU unspecified for tone, but flanked by high-tone TBU's, is realized with a high tone in a well-defined set of syntactic environments, one of which is an adjective and a following noun, as in (2b). In this section, we will be concerned with the patterns of tonal specification for words containing TBU's unspecified for tone, not the details of the plateauing process, though it is primarily through observations related to plateauing that a word's lexical tonal specifications can be reliably determined. Specifically, this plateauing process clearly distinguishes between TBU's unspecified for tone, which will be realized as high in plateauing environments, and TBU's specified for true low tones, which never appear as high.

As discussed in detail in Good (2004), the restrictions on the surface tone patterns of Saramaccan words indicate that the language seems most reasonably characterized as one where high tones appearing on citation forms of most words are a realization of accent (thus, making Saramaccan a language exhibiting pitch accent) but, in some cases, are instead manifestations of true lexical tone. The situation can be most succinctly characterized by saying that Saramaccan is primarily a pitch accent language which nevertheless contains a stratum of vocabulary which is truly tonal. Setting more theoretical aspects of this issue aside, the basic descriptive generalizations underlying this characterization are as follows: (i) a number of logically possible but unattested (or only very poorly attested) citation tone patterns; (ii) apparent manifestations of stress correlated with the presence of high tones in one class of words, but not another; and (iii) phonological evidence for a distinction between low tones and unspecified tones.

The rest of this section focuses on the description of the prosodic behavior of the class of words which we characterize as showing marking for accent, which is more or less the same as the class of words containing TBU's unspecified for tone.

2.2.2.2. Accented words with short syllables

Table 10 shows all the common tone patterns for words of two, three, or four syllables that contain TBU's unspecified for tone. Words containing only one TBU are excluded because, as will be discussed in section 2.2.3.2., their minimal size makes it difficult (and, in some cases, perhaps impossible) to determine whether they belong to the accentual class or the tonal one. Clear examples of monomorphemic words of five syllables are difficult to find in Saramaccan, and, even when they are found, appear to be semi-opaque compounds like *kelebétête* 'painted parakeet' (which, despite attestation of neither element as a separate word, seems decomposable as *kelebé* and *tête*, with the latter form perhaps derived from Portuguese *tinta* 'paint' in some way), partial reduplications as in *malembélembe* 'medicinal plant,' or words showing an apparent initial *a*-formative, as in *asubusúba* 'plantain type' (see section 2.2.4.). Therefore, the discussion here only covers words of up to four syllables, which are relatively well-attested. For ease of exposition, only words with syllables containing one TBU will be discussed at this point. Longer syllables will be covered in section 2.2.2.3.

Three generalizations emanating from Table 10 are of particular relevance here: (i) the lack of any low-tone TBU's in these words; (ii) the fact that, even in cases where there are multiple high-tone TBU's, they are adjacent; and (iii) the number of attested tone patterns is never greater than the number of syllables in a word. (The symbol "Ø" in the table is used as a placeholder for a TBU not specified for tone.) Despite these restrictions, we should make clear at the outset that the placement of high tones in words like those in Table 10 is not phonologically predictable, and numerous minimal pairs exist which differ in their citation forms solely on the basis of placement of high-tone TBU's (see section 2.2.2.5.).

Table 10. Tone patterns on accented words

WORD	TONES	GLOSS
foló	ØH	'flower'
náki	HØ	'hit'
makisá	ØØH	'step on'
kamísa	ØHØ	'loincloth'
hákísi	HHØ	'ask'
alukutú	ØØØH	'soursop (fruit)'
afokáti	ØØHØ	'lawyer'
minísíti	ØHHØ	'minister'

The restricted range of patterns for tones in words of the type seen in Table 10 suggests a descriptive analysis treating them as marked for accent rather than tone since there is nothing to suggest a paradigmatic contrast among different tonemes. Rather, we see a syntagmatic contrast where part of a word is signaled for a kind of prominence, most saliently realized via a high tone. There are some complications to this analysis, in particular involving words with high tones on two TBU's. However, these can be clarified by proposing a specific accentual analysis for these words. The schematizations in (3) illustrate the common patterns for words of two, three, and four syllables. The schematizations in (4) illustrate how these patterns can be analyzed in terms of treating one TBU as being marked for syntagmatic prominence (with boldface and underlining being used as a prominence marker).

(3) a. 2-σ words: CVCV́ CV́CV
    b. 3-σ words: CVCVCV́ CVCV́CV CV́CVCV
    c. 4-σ words: CVCVCVCV́ CVCVCV́CV CVCV́CVCV

(4) a. 2-σ words: CVC**V** C**V**CV
    b. 3-σ words: CVCVC**V** CVC**V**CV C**V**CVCV
    c. 4-σ words: CVCVCVC**V** CVCVC**V**CV CVC**V**CVCV

As illustrated in (4), the tone patterns of words like those in Table 10 can be described in terms of a prosodic system which makes use of final, penultimate, and antepenultimate accent. A high tone on the accented TBU then becomes one of the manifestations of accent. There is an additional complication insofar as, in words showing antepenultimate accent, a high tone appears not only on the accented TBU but also on the penultimate TBU. This pattern would be problematic for an accentual analysis of these words if tone patterns like (CV)CV́CVCV were robustly attested, but, in fact, they are not. Rountree, Asodanoe, and Glock (2000) actually do transcribe many words with such a pattern. However, while we have not systematically verified the tones on all of these, many of those we have checked turn out to have been mistranscribed or semi-analyzable complex morphological structures, though there do appear to be some genuine exceptions (see section 2.2.4.). (The dictionary, however, should not be strongly faulted in cases where it fails to transcribe penultimate high tones in words with antepenultimate accent since the fact that they have little role in marking contrast makes their distribution largely irrelevant outside of academic studies.) As will be discussed in section 2.2.2.4., one way to analyze the appearance of two high tones in words with apparent antepenultimate accent is to appeal to aspects of the metrical structure of these words.

In Table 11, we give more examples of the words exhibiting the tonal patterns for two- and three-syllable words schematized in (3). Four-syllable words are not included because there are relatively few examples. However, as we will see in 2.2.2.3., this is due to a relative lack of words with four short syllables. When we look at words with four TBU's, the patterns of final, penultimate, and antepenultimate accent (counting by TBU, not syllable) seen in (3) are fairly well-attested.

Table 11. Examples of accented words

ACCENT	EXAMPLES
CVCV́	*ajṍ* 'onion,' *botó* 'mushroom type,' *bulí* 'move,' *kiní* 'knee,' *lakwá* 'cross,' *mɛkú* 'crab type,' *pikí* 'little,' *sipó* 'vine type,' *soní* 'thing,' *zŏká* 'coals'
CV́CV	*ábi* 'have,' *bási* 'boss,' *bítju* 'worm,' *dágu* 'dog,' *féni* 'find,' *gúdu* 'riches,' *hǎse* 'handsome,' *jési* 'ears,' *tófu* 'miraculous,' *wíni* 'win'
CVCVCV́	*alibí* 'kidney,' *dimbolí* 'wrap up,' *gbaniní* 'eagle,' *jamasú* 'vulture,' *kaluwá* 'lizard,' *kujaké* 'toucan,' *matapí* 'reed press,' *potigé* 'Portuguese,' *pangulá* 'plant type,' *sakatá* 'toss and turn'
CVCV́CV	*azéma* 'vampire,' *bakúba* 'banana,' *fìlígi* 'kite,' *gangása* 'shelter,' *gulǔtu* 'vegetables,' *kabéti* 'false teeth,' *makpénu* 'container type,' *pakúsi* 'fish type,' *sabána* 'grasslands,' *tabáku* 'tobacco'
CV́CV́CV	*djákíti* 'jacket,' *élúfu* 'eleven,' *fékísi* 'salve type,' *kwálíki* 'quarter (coin),' *lémíki* 'lime tree,' *sákása* 'living room,' *póbíki* 'statue,' *túlíngi* 'twins,' *sékéti* 'dance type,' *wákíti* 'guard'

2.2.2.3. *Accented words with "heavy" syllables*

We use the term *heavy syllable* here informally to refer to cases where two orthographic vowels appear directly adjacent to each other. As discussed in section 1.1.3.3., it is not clear when these should be interpreted as true heavy syllables as opposed to two distinct syllable nuclei where the second syllable has no onset consonant. However, understanding the way that the accentual system of Saramaccan operates with respect to heavy syllables does not require resolution of this issue. Rather, the generalizations involving accentual placement in final, penultimate, or antepenultimate position extend straightforwardly to words with heavy syllables if we count from the end of the word by TBU rather than syllable. Relevant examples are given in Table 12.

The patterns seen in Table 12, in fact, suggest that the Saramaccan accentual system may be better understood in terms of units of syllable weight, i.e. moras, rather than syllables.

While there are relatively few examples, the basic patterns seen in Table 12 for four-TBU words extend to five-TBU words – that is, one finds cases of final, penultimate, or antepenultimate accent but not preantepenultimate or initial accent. Some relevant examples include: *anakitapú* 'burlap sack,' *apeesína* 'orange,' and *kookóódẽ* 'plant type.' Some other possible cases of these patterns found in, for example, Rountree, Asodanoe, and Glock (2000) are actually compounds, and it may be the case that at least some apparent monomorphemic five-TBU words fitting these patterns are diachronically derived from now opaque compounds as well.

In Table 13, we give further examples of words containing heavy syllables exhibiting the patterns seen in Table 12.

Looking at words both with only light syllables and with heavy syllables, it appears that penultimate TBU accent is most frequent, followed by final TBU accent, with antepenultimate TBU accent the least common (even when two-TBU words are not included in the count).

Table 12. Tone patterns on words with heavy syllables

WORD	TONES	GLOSS
tuú	ØH	'true'
máũ	HØ	'hand'
sumέε	ØHØ	'smell'
toóbi	ØHØ	'trouble'
bεέε	ØHØ	'bread'
sipaí	ØØH	'stingray'
paandí	ØØH	'plant'
síkii	HHØ	'body'
góútu	HHØ	'gold'
asokeé	ØØØH	'lizard type'
afiiká	ØØØH	'African'
paasóo	ØØHØ	'umbrella'
pakiséi	ØØHØ	'think'
piimísi	ØØHØ	'pardon'
mbutíkáa	ØHHØ	'wasps'
kotóígi	ØHHØ	'witness'
kεέkíti	ØHHØ	'funnel'

2.2.2.4. Manifestations of stress and possible foot structures

While pitch is impressionistically the most prominent cue for accent in Saramaccan, there is also evidence for the presence of stress in the language, whose appearance can be predicted from the position of the pitch accent. (See Good [2004: 586–588] for additional discussion of stress in Saramaccan including a critique of aspects of Rountree's 1972a description of stress, which apparently adopts a different sense of stress than the one used here.) Specifically, the syllable containing the TBU marked for pitch accent will also receive a primary stress. The stress is realized both as perceptual prominence and through lengthening and reduction rules, where stressed syllables can be lengthened under emphasis (e.g. when a word is repeated carefully in elicitation) and unstressed syllables can be shortened (especially during normal speech).

The most important difference between the placement of pitch accent and stress is that pitch accent is manifested on TBU's whereas stress is manifested on syllables. Therefore, there can be pitch accent/stress "mismatches" in words of certain shapes. The schematizations in (5) give the placement of stress with respect to tone in words containing only short syllables.

Table 13. Accented words containing heavy syllables

ACCENT	EXAMPLES
ØH	*dãã́* 'rum,' *dií* 'three,' *kaí* 'fall,' *peé* 'play,' *seí* 'ant type'
HØ	*bái* 'warn,' *díi* 'dear,' *fóu* 'bird,' *hói* 'hold,' *sáa* 'pity'
ØØH	*baasá* 'embrace,' *djaaí* 'bathing area,' *kaabã́* 'charcoal type,' *mandoó* 'bird type,' *pootí* 'poor'
ØHØ	*akáa* 'soul,' *baái* 'broad,' *bẽ́ẽki* 'tin cup,' *joóka* 'spirit type,' *sugúu* 'darkness'
HHØ	*féífi* 'five,' *kándúu* 'amulet type,' *kókóo* 'shell,' *kóóko* 'yellow,' *sáápi* 'slow'
ØØØH	*aviaté* 'pilot,' *fãteisí* 'lace,' *kakaakú* 'fish type,' *kapiiwá* 'capybara,' *sangaafú* 'plant type'
ØØHØ	*adãã́ũ* 'sandwasp,' *baasía* 'watermelon,' *bɔɔtjási* 'broadcast,' *fuuféi* 'bore,' *mataási* 'mattress'
ØHHØ	*adáái* 'pot type,' *folóísi* 'move,' *kãtóóli* 'circle in canoes,' *matééa* 'spray,' *sitááti* 'street'

(5) a. 2-σ words: CV'CV́   'CV́CV
     b. 3-σ words: CVCV'CV́   CV'CV́CV   'CV́CV́CV
     c. 4-σ words: CVCVCV'CV́ CVCV'CV́CV CV'CV́CV́CV

One of the easiest places to see the mismatch between pitch accent and stress is in words with antepenultimate accent when the antepenultimate and penultimate vowels are spread across two syllables. Such words show high tones on both the antepenultimate and penultimate TBU's, but stress is only found on the antepenultimate syllable. The data in (6) gives examples of specific words instantiating the patterns given in (5). (These words are glossed in Table 10.)

(6) a. 2-σ words: *fo'ló*   *'náki*
    b. 3-σ words: *maki'sá*   *ka'mísa*   *'hákísi*
    c. 4-σ words: *aluku'tú*   *afo'káti*   *mi'nísíti*

One additionally sees the mismatch between pitch accent and stress in words containing V́V or VV́ sequences, where the high tone associated with the pitch accent is associated with only one half of a long vowel. Based on impressionistic evidence, VV́ syllables are always stressed and V́V are stressed in cases where the high is derived from penultimate accent, as opposed to being the second high-tone TBU in a word with antepenultimate accent. Thus, one has words like *'toóbi* 'trouble' and *sum'éɛ* 'smell' where the contoured heavy syllable is also stressed as opposed to a word like *'síkii* 'body,' where the high tone of the contoured heavy syllable is the second high tone associated with antepenultimate accent and, therefore, the heavy syllable is not stressed. Again, based on impressionistic evidence, sequences of "extra-long" vowels (orthographically represented as three-vowel sequences) like *beéɛ* 'bread' appear to be stressed if they contain an accented TBU.

In words of sufficient length, there are additional impressionistically stressed syllables on alternating syllables preceding or following the syllable whose stress coincides with pitch accent. Relevant examples, drawing on the words given in (6), are given in (7). An IPA secondary stress mark (",") is used to mark these additional stressed syllables.

(7) a. 3-σ words: ˌ*maki'sá*   *'hákíˌsi*
    b. 4-σ words: *aˌluku'tú*   ˌ*afo'káti*   *mi'nísíˌti*

The patterns in (7) suggest a characterization of Saramaccan wherein words are parsed into (moraic) trochaic feet based on the position of the accented TBU. Thus, for example, the words in (6) would have foot structures as in (8) where parentheses are used to mark off feet and "<" and ">" to mark off syllables not parsed into feet. As seen in (8), such an analysis implies the possibility of defective feet at the right edge, but not the left edge, of a word. An analysis along these lines allows us to describe the environment for the appearance of high tones in two TBU's in terms of foot structure: high tones appear in both TBU's of any non-final foot containing accent. (In fact, given the independent presence of a rule lowering a final high-tone TBU in utterance-final contexts – see section 2.4.2. – this rule could even be taken as applying to all feet but being overridden by this intonational process in final feet.)

(8) a. 2-σ words: <*fo*>('*ló*)   ('*náki*)
    b. 3-σ words: (ˌ*maki*)('*sá*)   <*ka*>('*mísa*)   ('*hákí*)(ˌ*si*)
    c. 4-σ words: <*a*>(ˌ*luku*)('*tú*)   (ˌ*afo*)('*káti*)   <*mi*>('*nísí*)(ˌ*ti*)

While most of our transcriptions of stress here are based on impressionistic evidence, as mentioned above there is also evidence for stress in Saramaccan involving vowel lengthening and shortening which is less susceptible to misinterpretation. The conditions under which such lengthening and shortening occurs do not allow us to verify all aspects of the impressionistic analysis, but they are helpful in some cases. In particular, non-final stressed vowels can be lengthened under emphasis and non-final unstressed vowels can be shortened. In the case of high vowels in *sIT* or *TIs* sequences (where *T* represents a voiceless stop), this shortening has even been observed to render the high vowel as little more than a release.

To take some examples, under emphasis in elicitation contexts, a word like *sákása* 'living room' can be pronounced along the lines of *sá:kása*. Furthermore, the *a* in the second syllable of such a word is notably shorter in articulation than the other two *a*'s. This reduction is particularly salient in words like *síkísi* 'six,' *bókúsu* 'box,' or *minísíti* 'minister' where the reduction of the penultimate high vowels (here taken not to be accented – see (4)) can render them almost inaudible. (This reduction may be indicative of the influence of Sranan on some Saramaccan speakers insofar as clusters like *ks* or *st* are permissible in that language.) If we take such lengthening to be associated with stress and shortening with lack of stress, then these phenomena can be used as relatively concrete evidence for stressed/unstressed syllables in Saramaccan. They are perfectly consistent with the analysis based on impressionistic evidence but are not easily applicable to all environments, for example, word-final high vowels in unstressed syllables can never be shortened to the same degree as medial high vowels.

2.2.2.5. Minimal pairs

There is no question that accent in Saramaccan (however it may be analyzed) must involve lexical specification on some level. This is because of the presence of numerous minimal pairs involving the placement of accent. Furthermore, to the extent that the placement of accent is predictable, this can only be done using diachronic, not synchronic, criteria (for example, by knowing what language was the ultimate source of a given word). For instance, the word for 'begin' in Saramaccan is *bigí* with final accent, reflecting that it entered Saramaccan as a result of transfer of the English word *begin* which is stressed on the final syllable. The word for 'big,' by contrast, is *bígi* with initial accent on the vowel associated with the single vowel of the English word *big*, while the historically epenthetic vowel is unaccented. The opposition between *nási* 'dirty' (from English *nasty*) and *nasí* 'grow' (from Portuguese *nascer* 'be born') also illustrates this pattern. Good (2009a, b) provides etymologies for a large number of Saramaccan words which provide many further examples and others can be found in the short wordlist included with the grammar which, where possible, includes etymologies.

In addition to those just given above, we give a number of other accentual minimal pairs here for reference. These are primarily drawn from Rountree, Asodanoe, and Glock (2000): *adjindjá* 'porcupine' vs. *adjíndja* 'ginger,' *bajá* 'dance' vs. *bája* 'friend,' *biá* 'turn' vs. *bía* 'beard,' *bisí* 'wear' vs. *bísi* 'polish,' *botó* 'mushroom type' vs. *bóto* 'boat,' *dií* 'three' vs. *díi* 'dear,' *fií* 'liberty' vs. *fíi* 'feel,' *fingá* 'tuck in' vs. *fínga* 'finger,' *kaí* 'fall' vs. *kái* 'call,' *kandá* 'song' vs. *kánda* 'candle,' *kondá* 'count' vs. *kónda* 'necklace,' *koowá* 'skim' vs. *koówa* 'chaff,' *lalú* 'okra' vs. *lálu* 'clap,' *laú* 'crazy' vs. *láu* 'smell,' *maaká* 'mark' vs. *maáka* 'sign,' *mandá* 'send' vs. *mánda* 'basket,' *mindí* 'bind' vs. *míndi* 'middle,' *otó* 'automobile' vs. *óto* 'story,' *paí* 'give birth' vs. *pái* 'father-in-law,' *papá* 'dirge' vs. *pápa* 'porridge,' *pasá* 'pass' vs. *pása* 'compass,' *pikí* 'little' vs. *píki* 'answer,' *poobá* 'try' vs. *poóba* 'gun powder,' *puumá* 'shed' vs. *puúma* 'fur,' *saí* 'be' vs. *sái* 'tree type,' *seí* 'ant type' vs. *séi* 'sell,' *tuú* 'true' vs. *túu* 'all,' *watjí* 'tree type' vs. *wátji* 'wait.'

We are not aware of any minimal pairs involving words containing the lower mid vowels, but we believe this is purely accidental, arising from the fact that they are less common, in general, than the other vowels. Furthermore, as will be seen in section 2.2.3.3., there are minimal pairs between accentual words with these vowels and tonal words.

2.2.3. Tonal words

2.2.3.1. High tones and low tones

Section 2.2.2. focused on words containing TBU's unspecified for tone along with one high-tone TBU or two adjacent high-tone TBU's. The high tones in these words were seen to be readily viewed as manifestations of pitch accent. However, the Saramaccan prosodic system presents significant descriptive complications because of the presence of a class of words which do not appear to be marked for accent at all but, rather, are truly tonal. The first important characteristic of this class of words is that, rather than exhibiting a distinction between high-tone TBU's and TBU's unspecified for tone, there is, instead, an apparent opposition between high-tone TBU's and low-tone TBU's.

In citation contexts, TBU's unspecified for tone and low-tone TBU's are indistinguishable. However, in other contexts, most notably in environments where tonal plateauing is found (illustrated in (2b) and discussed in detail in 2.3.1.), these two classes of TBU's are readily distinguished. This can be seen in the contrast between (9a) and (9b).

(9) a. Dí   wómi   kulé   alá.   → Dí wómí kúlé àlá.
       DEF man   run   yonder
       'The man runs there.'   (Rountree 1972a: 316)

   b. Dí   kàìmà   kulé   alá.   → Dí kàìmà kùlé àlá.
       DEF crocodile run yonder
       'The crocodile runs there.'   (Rountree 1972a: 316)

The last word of a subject and a following verb form a syntactic environment in which high-tone plateauing can take place if the right phonological conditions are met. These conditions are that two high tones (regardless of whether their source is pitch accent or true tone) flank one or more TBU's unspecified for tone. These conditions are met in (9a) and, thus, the last TBU of the subject wómi 'man' and the first TBU of the verb kulé 'run' are both realized with high tone. By contrast, in (9b) plateauing is not found. This is because the last two TBU's of the word kàìmà 'crocodile' are marked for low tone and not merely unspecified for tone. Their tones are always realized as low, and they block high-tone plateauing. Thus, not only are the final tones of kàìmà not realized as high in (9b), they also prevent the first TBU of kulé from being realized with a high tone.

As will be shown, the distinction between words like wómi and kàìmà goes beyond details of tonal specification. Rather, it is indicative of a more fundamental "cut" in Saramaccan grammar between words marked for accent and those which are apparently purely tonal and give no evidence for entering into an accentual system. Table 14 gives examples of words containing no TBU's unspecified for tone, showing a range of tone patterns involving high tones and low tones. Clear examples of some logically possible tone combinations have yet to be found. In some cases, such as the lack of an unambiguous instance of a word with a single high-tone TBU, the issue is not a matter of surface tonal patterns but, rather, analytical indeterminacy, as discussed in section 2.2.3.2. In other cases, a word with the pattern is recorded in other sources, but we have not been able to verify its tones with our consultants. This is the case, for instance, with éndòlé 'stork type,' a word which was simply not known when checked with two consultants. Similarly, while one consultant gave the tones indicated in Table 14 for the word for 'woodpecker' (also found in Rountree, Asodanoe, and Glock 2000), others showed a pattern that appeared best characterized as totómboti, showing an exceptional ØHØØ pattern (see section 2.2.4.) with stress on the high-toned TBU.

Words like those in Table 14 demonstrate that a fairly wide range of high and low tone combinations are attested on Saramaccan lexical items. The existence of words with only low tones is important in this context insofar as their lack of any high tone means that none of their TBU's are candidates for being marked for pitch accent of the sort described for words with TBU's unspecified for tone in section 2.2.2.

Our impression is that words fully marked for tone comprise perhaps around ten percent or less of the Saramaccan vocabulary.

Table 14. Words fully specified for tone

WORD	TONES	GLOSS
bà	L	'carry (water)'
jàà	LL	'sow'
kédé	HH	'box'
bɔ̀sɔ̀	LL	'loosen'
káìmà	HLL	'crocodile'
lògòsò	LLL	'turtle'
tótómbòtí	HHLH	'woodpecker'
séségùùsé	HHLLH	'fish type'

2.2.3.2. Indeterminacy in determining if a word is marked for tone or accent

A split prosodic system raises descriptive difficulties not found in languages with more consistent prosody, and we should briefly comment here on the conventions we have adopted regarding the possibility of analytical indeterminacy of a word's prosodic type.

Words containing just one high-tone TBU, like the tonic third-person singular pronoun hḯ (see sections 2.2.3.3. and 5.1.), for instance, appear to be equally well-treated as being specifically marked with a high tone on their one TBU or as marked for accent on that TBU, which is consistently realized as a high tone. A similar issue arises for some words that only ever surface with a single low-tone TBU. A word like kù 'with,' for example, could presumably be analyzed as simply being unaccented or as not ever being subject to plateauing for syntactic reasons (see section 2.3.1.3.), making it impossible to distinguish its surface low tone as resulting from a lack of accent or from a true low tone. At the same time, there are other words with single low-tone TBU's which could not be analyzed this way, such as bà 'carry (water).' Being a verb, this word would not be expected to be unaccented, and it can also appear in environments otherwise associated with plateauing, making an analysis of it as being specified with a low tone the more straightforward one. For consistency, we treat all words with a single TBU that always appears with a low tone as being specified for that tone in the transcriptions in this chapter.

There are also cases of words with more than one TBU which, for syntactic reasons, do not allow for straightforward determination regarding whether they should be analyzed tonally or accentually. For instance, there is only one preposition containing more than one TBU, bóíti 'except.' It never undergoes plateauing, but this could be reasonably seen as deriving from general phonosyntactic principles or as a result of it actually having an underlying form bóítì (see section 2.3.1.3.). We treat it as being specified for accent here since its surface shape is consistent with a word with accent on the antepenultimate TBU, an otherwise well-attested class in Saramaccan, though this is clearly weak evidence. Similar issues also arise with respect to two elements that appear at the end of the noun phrase, akí 'here' and alá 'yonder,' which will be discussed in section 2.3.1.2., and the word ée 'if.' At least in cases where words like these have multiple syllables, detailed investigation into the phonetic properties of stress in Saramaccan may reveal criteria allowing less equivocal assignment of such words to either the accentual or tonal class (see sections 2.2.2.4. and 2.2.3.4.).

2.2.3.3. Minimal pairs and tonal features of morphological processes

One of the clearer areas of Saramaccan grammar where words surfacing with low tones can be opposed to words surfacing with high tones in a way that suggests a paradigmatic opposition between two tonemes involves the distinction between the subject series and the tonic series of pronouns (see Chapter 5). These are given in Table 15.

As seen in Table 15, for four of the six pronouns, the sole formal distinction between the subject and tonic series involves tone. Thus, the pronominal system offers one possible set of minimal pairs evincing a paradigmatic distinction between high tone and low tone. There are comparable minimal pairs outside of the pronominal system, for example *kù* 'with' vs. *kú* 'vagina' and *tù* 'also' vs. *tú* 'two.' However, because one-TBU high-tone words are open to an analysis as being accented, it would be possible to offer an alternative analysis of the pronominal patterns as well as these other minimal pairs in terms of an accented/unaccented distinction (see section 2.2.3.2.). And, in fact, that is presumably the analysis one would adopt without question were there not additional evidence for a true tonal opposition in Saramaccan.

Table 15. Tone in pronouns

	SUBJECT		TONIC	
	SG	PL	SG	PL
1	*mì*	*ù*	*mí*	*ú*
2	*ì*	*ũ̀*	*í*	*únu*
3	*à*	*dè*	*hɛ̃́*	*dé*

Less ambiguous evidence for the presence of an opposition between words marked for pitch accent and those marked for true tone comes from the phonological behavior of the agentive suffix *-ma* (see sections 3.1.2. and 3.4. for further discussion). This suffix appears with a low tone when appearing immediately after a high-tone TBU or a TBU unspecified for tone but with a high tone when following a true low-tone TBU, as illustrated by the data in Table 16. (The forms in Table 16 are independently attested except for *káìmàmá*, which was specifically elicited and thus lacks a translation, though it would be expected to mean something like 'alligator man.') This suffix thus offers further evidence for a distinction between low-tone TBU's and TBU's unspecified for tone by suggesting a clear contrast in their phonological influence on a following element.

Table 16. Agentive nouns

WORD	TONES	GLOSS	TRANSLATION
lúku-mà	HØL	'look-AG'	'spectator'
koósu-mà	ØHØL	'skirt-AG'	'woman'
paí-mà	ØHL	'give.birth-AG'	'child-bearer'
lègèdè-má	LLLH	'lie-AG'	'liar'
káìmà-má	HLLH	'crocodile-AG'	—

As reported by Voorhoeve (1961: 155), there is comparable evidence involving the formative *wã́* (clearly related to the word *wã́* 'one'), which can form nouns from other parts of speech. One finds, for example, words like *ótowã̀* 'other one,' *búnuwã̀* 'good one,' and *kuléwã̀* 'flowing one' against *tàkùwã́* 'evil one' and *bɔ̀sɔ̀wã́* 'loose one.'

While we are not aware of any clear-cut (i.e. non-monomoraic) cases of minimal pairs of true tone words with each other, there are a number of minimal pairs for such words with words marked for accent. Examples drawn from Rountree, Asodanoe, and Glock (2000) include: *àkàtà* 'headpad' vs. *akáta* 'crossed legs,' *bààkà* 'menstruation' vs. *baáka* 'black,' *bàndjà* 'side' vs. *bandjá* 'dance type,' *bùbù* 'roughest part of rapids' vs. *bubú* 'jaguar,' and *jàà* 'broadcast' vs. *jáa* 'year.' There is also the minimal quadruplet *tjàkà* 'rash type' vs. *tjaká* 'rattle' vs. *tjáka* 'too short' vs. *tjáká* 'sudden and quick (ideophone).' While the opposition between *tjàkà* and *tjáká* may appear to be a minimal pair for two unambiguously fully-toned words – since neither word shows patterns associated with pitch accent – this is not an ideal example because the special prosodic characteristics of ideophones (see section 2.2.3.5.) make their status as appropriate comparanda with non-ideophones in cases like this unclear.

2.2.3.4. Lack of evidence for stress

Words fully marked for tone have a final feature which distinguishes them from words marked for accent: the lack of any evidence that their syllables participate in a stressed/unstressed opposition. This is true both in impressionistic terms and, to the extent that this can be tested, using phonological criteria as well.

For example, no syllable in words like *lògòsò* 'turtle' or *lègèdè* 'lie' is impressionistically stressed. To the ears of a native English speaker, in a word like *séségùùsé* 'fish type' the final syllable sounds possibly stressed, but this is presumably due to English's general association of high pitch with stressed syllables and the fact that this syllable is preceded by low-toned TBU's. (Furthermore, instrumental evidence from one speaker uttering the word *séségùùsé* did not indicate any significant increase in amplitude on that syllable.) Less ambiguously, one has a word like *pùkùsù* 'bat' which does not allow any kind of medial vowel reduction like that seen for a word like *bókúsu* 'box,' despite a similar segmental shape. In general, in fact, the lengthening and reduction rules described for accented words in section 2.2.2.4. have not been observed in truly tonal words. Such observations are significant to the extent that they indicate that tonal words do not just differ from accented words in their deployment of pitch. Rather, they do not show any evidence of the opposition between prominent and non-prominent positions associated with accent.

2.2.3.5. Ideophones

Ideophones have a number of exceptional prosodic features (much as they have exceptional segmental features – see section 1.2.3.). The first is a strong tendency to consist solely of high-tone TBU's or low-tone TBU's. Thus, the prosodic patterns exemplified in ideophones like *fáá* 'very white,' *kúlúlúú* 'straight,' *gbìtìì* 'many,' and *sììì* 'close quietly' are typical. Attested, but much less common, are ideophones like *bàngùlá* 'walking drunkenly' and *vùngúvùngù* 'floating in space' (drawn from Rountree, Asodanoe, and Glock 2000). The syntactic properties of ideophones (see section 14.7.), wherein they are somewhat "detached" from clausal phrase structure, mean that they do not participate in the process of tonal plateauing exemplified in (2b) nor are they subject to the same intonational processes as non-ideophones. Because this means that their surface tones are never observed to change, we describe them together with other words classified as being specified for tone here.

The results of Good (2006) suggest that the low tones in ideophones are phonetically the same as low tones found elsewhere in Saramaccan, but that high tones in ideophones are phonetically distinct and, perhaps, better classified as "super-high."

2.2.4. Word-level prosody: Exceptions

While the description given above covers most of the prosodic patterns in the Saramaccan lexicon, there are a number of words that are exceptional in various ways. On the one hand, there are words with unspecified TBU's which do not conform to the patterns described in section 2.2.2. Examples include: *fóótóo* 'photograph,' which exceptionally has three high-tone TBU's and preantepenultimate high tone; *hékísee* 'sneeze,' which exceptionally has a preantepenultimate high-tone TBU as well as an antepenultimate high tone without a penultimate one; *bobíete* 'undeveloped maripa fruit,' which exceptionally has an antepenultimate high tone without a penultimate one; and *adjáási* 'spider,' which shows the same irregularity as *bobíete*. (These examples have been verified with consultants. So, their exceptional status seems clear.)

On the other hand, there are also a handful of words identified as containing both TBU's unspecified for tone and true low-tone TBU's. The known words of this type all begin with a vowel and involve an initial TBU (or set of TBU's) unspecified for tone followed by TBU's fully specified for tone. Examples include: *anákìtá* 'biting ant,' *asoóbònú* 'taboo name for cow,' and *obílògbḗ* 'snake type.' (The first of these has been verified with consultants.) Voorhoeve (1961: 154) lists some others, and all known examples begin with *a* except for the last word in the list just given (see section 3.2.3. for further discussion of these *a*-initial words). The initial vowels of these words along with their relatively long form (always four or more syllables) as well as the fact that they all lack obvious European etymologies suggests that they may derive from West African compounds. This could provide a historical explanation for their exceptional tonality.

A number of other apparent exceptions result from words being morphologically complex, or at least semi-analyzable. For instance, one finds words like *bákatẽ* 'later,' *fésitẽ* 'antiquity,' *líbitẽ* 'lifetime,' and *písitẽ* 'a while,' which all exceptionally show antepenultimate, but not penultimate, high tone. However, they also all appear with a final element *tẽ*, clearly relatable to *tḗ* 'time.' Many other apparent exceptions in Rountree, Asodanoe, and Glock (2000) are easily analyzed as compounds (see section 2.3.1.1.).

While the tone patterns on reduplicated forms generally follow what is observed in compounds (see section 2.3.1.1.) – a fact first described by Voorhoeve (1961: fn. 15) (see also Rountree [1972a: 317–318]) – there are some reduplicated forms whose tone patterns diverge from what might otherwise be expected, though these unusual patterns appear to be limited to frozen or semantically irregular reduplications. For example, the frozen reduplication *kpḗjḗkpẽjẽ* 'newborn' shows two low tones on its last syllables when elicited, but appears with all high tones in the expression kpéjékpéjé míi 'newborn baby.' This is most consistent with positing an underlying tonal representation of the word as HHØØ, but there is no way to derive this if one assumes that both parts of the reduplicated structure have the same tonal representation. Other examples of this pattern include: fíófío 'spirit revenge,' jángájanga 'fish type,' and wátéwáte 'immediately' (which is related in some way to wáté 'right away'). While this pattern appears restricted to frozen or opaque reduplicated forms, it is not the case that all irregular reduplications follow it. For instance, it is not seen in words like mɔsimɔ́si 'mouse' or wasiwási 'wasp' (both of which only appear reduplicated in Saramaccan; cf. 3.1.1.4.). Unlike a word like kpéjékpéjé (whose HHØØ tone pattern has been verified with consultants), while these words are irregular in the sense of being frozen reduplications, their ØØHØ tonal form otherwise conforms to broader patterns of Saramaccan prosody. See section 3.1.1.6. for additional relevant discussion.

2.3. Phrasal prosody

Saramaccan phrasal prosody is dominated by a process of high-tone plateauing (illustrated above in (2)) wherein TBU's unspecified for tone are realized as high tones when flanked by high tones in certain syntactic contexts. Example (10) repeats example (2) for purposes of illustration. As indicated, a number of the examples in this section are drawn from other authors.

(10) a. taánga → tàángà 'strong'
      b. dí   taánga wómi → dí tàángá wómì
          DEF   strong man
          'the strong man'

Example (10a) shows the citation form of the word taánga 'strong,' which is a word associated with penultimate accent. In (10b), the first TBU unspecified for tone surfaces as low, and the second as high. The latter is affected by high-tone plateauing, but the former is not. This is because, while both are flanked by high tones and, therefore, in the right phonological environment, only the latter TBU is also in the right syntactic environment, which, in this case, can be characterized informally as a noun and the word immediately preceding it within the noun phrase.

Example (11) repeats example (9) to show how words with TBU's specified for low tone interact with high-tone plateauing. As can be seen in the contrast between the surfacing form of the first TBU of kulé 'run' in (11a) vs. (11b), even though a verb and the word preceding it in the subject noun phrase form the right syntactic environment for plateauing, the low-tone TBU's in a word like káìmà 'crocodile' block the process by virtue of not providing the right phonological environment. In the sections to follow, further examples of the non-application of plateauing when the requisite phonological environment is lacking will be given when available.

(11) a. Dí   wómi kulé   alá.   → Dí wómí kúlé àlá.
          DEF   man   run   yonder
          'The man runs there.'   (Rountree 1972a: 316)

      b. Dí   káìmà   kulé   alá.   → Dí káìmà kùlé àlá.
          DEF   crocodile run   yonder
          'The crocodile runs there.'   (Rountree 1972a: 316)

Section 2.3.1. discusses tonal plateauing phenomena, listing all environments where it is known to occur and suggesting some descriptive generalizations. Section 2.3.2. then discusses the more difficult case of tone raising in serial verb constructions, which are affected both by high-tone plateauing as well as other less straightforwardly phonological effects. In the data given in these sections, processes classified as intonational (see section 2.4.) are not transcribed. Accordingly, surface tonal realizations may differ from those indicated. The most prominent intonational process in this regard is lowering of a final high tone which, in some cases, can cause tonal plateauing not to occur when it might otherwise be expected.

2.3.1. Tonal plateauing

We begin by discussing a range of syntactic environments, providing data relevant to establishing whether high-tone plateauing does or does not occur within them. See section 2.5. for discussion of some difficulties involved in testing for the presence of plateauing in certain environments.

2.3.1.1. Compounds and regular reduplication

Compounds form a syntactic plateauing environment as shown by the examples in (12). As seen in (12d), this environment can span multiple words. The same prosodic pattern is also found in reduplicated adjectives (cf. section 6.2.), as in (12g).

(12) a. *beéi*   *gaási*   → *bèéí gáásì*
          eyeglasses   glass
          'eyeglass lens'

      b. *hédi*   *uwíi*   → *hédí úwíi*
          head   hair
          'hair (of head)'

      c. *boóko*   *jési*   → *bòókó jésì*
          break   ear
          'deaf'   (Rountree, Asodanoe, and Glock 2000)

      d. *báka   míndi   bónu*   → *báká míndí bónù*
          back   middle   bone
          'spine'   (Rountree, Asodanoe, and Glock 2000)

      e. *síkísi   téni*   → *síkísí ténì*
          six   ten
          'sixty'   (Rountree 1972a: 319)

      f. *wósu   paimá*   → *wósú páímá*
          house   payment
          'rent'

      g. *lánga-lánga*   → *lángá-lángà*
          tall-tall
          'tall'

As was discussed in section 2.2.4., there are also prosodically irregular reduplicated forms which do not follow the pattern seen in (12g).

2.3.1.2. Noun phrases

Within a noun phrase, a noun and its preceding word form a plateauing environment, as in (13). The elements appearing in this position can be articles, adjectives, and other kinds of modifiers that can immediately precede a noun. Example (13e) shows the lack of plateauing when the relevant phonological environment is not found. The prosodically irregular noun in (13d) seems like a good candidate for having derived from a West African compound form (see section 2.2.4.).

(13) a. dí   mujéɛ   → dí mújéɛ̀
         DEF   woman
         'the woman'   (Rountree 1972a: 318)

    b. dí   há̌so   wómi   → dí há̌só wómì
         DEF   handsome man
         'the handsome man'   (Rountree 1972a: 321)

    c. dí   sósó   mujéɛ   → dí sósó mújéɛ̀
         DEF   only   woman
         'the only woman'

    d. déé   azɔbítɔtɔ   → déé ázɔ́bítɔ̀tɔ̀
         DEF.PL   butterfly
         'the butterflies'

    e. dí   taánga   lògòsò   → dí tàángà lògòsò
         DEF   strong   turtle
         'the strong turtle'

Elements before the noun generally do not plateau with each other. For example, an article and a following adjective do not trigger plateauing, nor two adjectives, as in (14).

(14) a. dí   taánga   wómi   → dí tàángá wómì
         DEF   strong   man
         'the strong man'

    b. dí   gã̌ã   wósu   → dí gã̀ã̌ wósù
         DEF   big   house
         'the big house'

    c. dí   lánga   há̌so   wómi   → dí lángà há̌só wómì
         DEF   tall   handsome man
         'the tall, handsome man'   (Rountree 1972a: 321)

Modifiers denoting nationality, however, do form a plateauing environment with a preceding prenominal element, as in (15). This suggests they should either be treated as a special class of adjectives or as forming compounds with the nouns they modify and, therefore, not having a syntactic adjectival function.

(15) a. síkísí olánsi wómi → síkísí ólánsí wómì
six Dutch man
'six Dutch men' (Rountree 1972a: 319)

b. dí taánga amɛɛká̌ wómi → dí tàángá ámɛ́ɛ́ká̌ wómì
DEF strong American man
'the strong American man'

While most prenominal modifiers behave the same as an article with respect to plateauing insofar as they only form part of a plateauing environment when immediately preceding a noun, at least one modifier óto 'other' has apparently exceptional behavior (see also Kramer 2007). Relevant examples are given in (16).

(16) a. óto lánga hǎso wómi → ótó lángà hǎsó wómì
other tall handsome man
'other tall, handsome man' (Rountree 1972a: 319)

b. dí óto síkísi sèmbè → dí ótò síkísì sèmbè
DEF other six person
'the other six people' (Kramer 2007: 47)

c. dí óto sèmbè → dí ótó sèmbè
DEF other person
'the other person' (Kramer 2007: 47)

In (16a), if we assume the basic tonal pattern of óto is HØ, as given in previous descriptions, then the word plateaus with a following adjective, which is different behavior from clear adjectives as exemplified in (14c). However, in (16b) óto does not plateau with a following numeral. More surprisingly, the word has been described as appearing with a final high tone when followed by a word specified with low tones, in a process that cannot be plateauing as described here since the relevant phonological conditions are not found. This pattern is comparable to effects found in serial verb constructions where such "spurious" high tones are also found (cf. 2.3.2.). It is difficult to make sense of data like that in (16) in the context of the rest of the Saramaccan prosodic system, and we offer no specific analysis. It could be the case that the basic tonal pattern of óto has been misanalyzed, or, perhaps, we are dealing with an area of the grammar where the clash between Saramaccan's tonal and accentual prosodic patterns makes a tonal transcription with the level of precision indicated in (16) inadvisable – an issue that will be discussed in more detail in section 2.5.

In addition to prenominal elements, plateauing is also observed between a noun and certain postnominal elements including the demonstrative dé 'there' and the relative pronoun dí (see (17)). The two other demonstrative markers akí 'here' and alá 'yonder' (see section 4.2.) do not plateau with a preceding noun (see (18)), suggesting either morpheme-specific rules are involved with plateauing in this environment (as implied by the transcription here) or that the first TBU's of akí and alá are lexically low rather than unspecified (see section 2.2.3.2.).

(17) a. dí mujéé dé akí seépi → dí mújéé dé àkí séépì
DEF woman there here self
'this woman here herself' (Rountree 1972a: 319)

	b.	dí	bóto	dí	mì	músu	téi	→	dí bótó dí mì músú téì
		DEF	boat	REL	1S	must	take		
		'the boat which I must take'							(Rountree 1972a: 321)

(18)	a.	dí	mujée	akí	ù	mí	→	dí mújéè àkí ù mí
		DEF	woman	here	POSS	1S		
		'this woman of mine'						(Rountree 1972a: 320)

	b.	dí	búku	alá	ù	mí	→	dí búkù àlá ù mí
		DEF	book	yonder	POSS	1S		
		'that book (over there) of mine'						

2.3.1.3. Adpositional phrases

True prepositional phrases do not generally show plateauing effects with preceding or following elements. The most common prepositions, locative *à*, possessive *fù*, and comitative *kù*, are all monosyllabic, showing invariant low tones, meaning that plateauing effects would probably not be expected on purely phonological grounds (though see section 2.2.3.2. for discussion of ambiguities regarding the analysis of their prosody). There is at least one longer preposition, *bóíti* 'except,' which contains a high tone and, therefore, in principle could form one side of a plateauing environment. As seen in (19), it does not exhibit plateauing with a following noun.

(19) bóíti koósu   →   bóítì kòósù
      except clothes
      'except clothes'   (Rountree 1972a: 321)

The data in (19) suggests that prepositions do not form a plateauing environment with a following noun. However, since there is only one known preposition that allows for testing this environment, the generalization cannot be considered very strong. Indeed, we are not aware of any synchronic evidence that *bóíti* could not be analyzed as *bóítì* – that is, as a word ending with a specified low tone.

Exceptions to this pattern are found with at least one of the special forms associated with the possessive *fù*, as in (20).

(20)	dí	mujée	u	mí	akí	→	dí mújéé ú mí àkí
	DEF	woman	POSS	1S	here		
	'my woman here'						(Rountree 1972a: 320)

If the *u* of *u mí* in (20) were to be strictly associated with *fù*, which is certainly the case historically, one would not expect it to show a high tone. The fact that it does has been taken as an indication that it has been reanalyzed as something like a prefix to the word *mí* (Voorhoeve 1961: 159). Given the generally unpredictable forms associated with the combination of *fù* plus pronoun (see section 3.3.1.), such an interpretation (or something like it) seems reasonable.

While Saramaccan does not have elements which are unambiguous postpositions, there are a number of locative nouns like *líba* 'above, top,' *básu* 'under, bottom,' or *bàndjà* 'side,' which can follow noun phrases to create larger noun phrases with locative meanings, as in (21). In such phrases, the locative noun plateaus with the immediately preceding word if the phonological conditions for plateauing are met, which is the case in (21a) and (21b), but not (21c).

(21) a. dí táfa ù dí kónu líba → dí táfà ù dí kónú líbà
       DEF table POSS DEF king top
       'the top of the king's table'   (Rountree 1972a: 320)

   b. dí sitónu básu   → dí sítónú básù
      DEF stone   under
      'under the stone'

   c. dí wósu   bàndjà   → dí wósù bàndjà
      DEF house side
      'the side of the house'

As can be seen in (21a) the two elements in the plateauing relation in this construction need not have a particularly close syntactic connection. Because of the fact that the locative noun in such a construction can be understood to be the head of the noun phrase, the plateauing seen in an example like (21) can be straightforwardly viewed as a special case of a noun plateauing with a preceding element in its noun phrase in the way exemplified in (13).

2.3.1.4. Tones in the verbal complex

The future tense marker *ó*, the imperfective marker *tá*, and the negative marker *á* form a plateauing environment with the following verb (see Chapter 7 for discussion of the syntax of these markers). The low-tone past marker *bì* does not, as would be expected on the basis of patterns of plateauing seen elsewhere.

(22) a. Mì   tá   kulé tidé.   → Mì tá kúlé tìdé.
       1S   IMF run   today
       'I am running today.'

   b. Mì   ó   bebé kofi.   → Mì ó bébé kòfi.
      1S   FUT drink coffee
      'I am going to drink coffee.'   (Rountree 1972a: 322)

   c. Mɛ́   á   makisá   dí   sɔ́fu kã́   kó   paáta. →
      Mɛ́   á   mákisá   dí   sɔ́fú kã́   kó   páátà.
      1S.NEG NEG step.on DEF   soda can come flat
      'I did not squash the soda can flat.'

   d. Mì   bì   kulé éside.   → Mì bì kùlé ésìdè.
      1S   PAST run   yesterday
      'I ran yesterday.'

2.3.1.5. Simple clauses

In monoverbal monoclausal structures, the basic pattern regarding plateauing is that the last word of a subject noun phrase and the first element of a verb complex (i.e. a verb preceded by any TMA markers) form a syntactic plateauing environment, while a verb and a following nominal object do not. Relevant examples are given in (23) for the subject-verb environment and in (24) for the verb-object environment. Examples (23d) and (23e) show the non-application of plateauing when the requisite phonological environment is not found.

(23) a. Dí   mujéɛ   tá   wáka.   → Dí mújéé tá wákà.
        DEF   woman   IMF   walk
        'The woman walks.'   (Rountree 1972a: 324)

   b. Dí   wómi,   hɛ̃́   kulé   dé.   → Dí wómì, hɛ̃́ kúlé dé.
        DEF   man   3ST   run   there
        'The man, he runs there.'   (Rountree 1972a: 324)

   c. Dí   gṍṍ   à   Saamáka   héi.   → Dí gṍṍ à Sààmáká héì.
        DEF   ground   LOC   Saramaka high
        'The ground in Saramaka is high.'

   d. Dí   lògòsò kulé   alá.   → Dí lògòsò kùlé àlá.
        DEF   turtle   run   yonder
        'The turtle runs there.'   (Rountree 1972a: 315)

   e. Páulu   lègèdè   → Páúlù lègèdè
        Paul   lie
        'Paul lies.'

(24) a. Mì   lápu   koósu.   → Mì lápù kòósù.
        1S   mend   clothes
        'I mend clothes.'

   b. À   náki   dí   tatái.   → À nákì dí tátáì.
        3S   hit   DEF   rope
        'He hits the rope.'

   c. Kofí   féni   Ámba.   → Kòfí fénì Ámbà.
        Kofi   find   Amba
        'Kofi found Amba.'

High-tone pronominal objects, however, do form a plateauing environment with a preceding verb, suggesting that they have some sort of clitic status. This dovetails with some of the facts regarding their segmental patterns discussed in section 5.2.

(25) Dí   sitónu   tá   náki   mí   à   mí   fútu.   →
     Dí   sitónú   tá   nákí   mí   à   mí   fútù.
     DEF stone   IMF   hit   1S   LOC   1S.POSS   foot
     'The stone hits me on my foot.'   (Rountree 1972a: 323)

2.3.1.6. Adverbial expressions

Modifiers with adverbial function generally do not participate in plateauing, as seen in (26), though exceptions to this pattern have been noticed for the temporal elements nɔ́u 'now' and (j)éti 'yet.' (The use of nɔ́u 'now' in unreduplicated form in (27b) is unusual in Saramaccan – see section 3.1.1.2. – and its appearance here may be due to the influence of Sranan where the element can normally stand on its own. See also section 5.3.)

(26) a. Mì   wáka   lóngi.   → Mì wákà   lóngì.
         1S   walk   far
         'I walk far.'

    b. Dí   wómi   tá   wooko   taánga   lóngi.   →
        Dí   wómí   tá   wóókò   tàángà   lóngì.
        DEF   man   IMF   work   strong   long
        'The man works hard and long.'   (Rountree 1972a: 322)

(27) a. Mì   wáka   éti.   → Mì wáká étì.
         1S   walk   yet
         'I am still walking.'

    b. Mì   wáka   nɔ́u.   → Mì wáká nɔ́ù.
        1S   walk   now
        'I am walking now.'

The word *mɔ̃ɔ̃* 'more' also participates in plateauing and is a somewhat special case. It plateaus with the word it most directly modifies whether it precedes or follows it.

(28) a. Mì   hã́so   mɔ̃ɔ̃   i.   → Mì hã́só mɔ̃ɔ̃́ í.
         1S   handsome more   2S
         'I am more handsome than you.'   (Rountree 1972a: 323)

    b. Mì   wáka   hési   mɔ̃ɔ̃   i.   → Mì wákà hésí mɔ̃ɔ̃́ í.
        1S   walk   fast   more   2S
        'I walk faster than you.'   (Rountree 1972a: 322)

    c. Mì   wáka   mɔ̃ɔ̃   hési.   → Mì wákà mɔ̃ɔ̃́ hésì.
        1S   walk   more   fast
        'I walk faster.'

2.3.1.7. Interaction between intonational processes and plateauing

In one area, a significant interaction between plateauing and an intonational process has been found. This is illustrated in the data in (29), where the final low tones in the examples depart from the transcription conventions of the rest of this section by indicating this intonational process (though see section 2.4.2. for a refinement of the transcriptions of the tones on the final TBU's).

(29) a. Dí   bóto   kó.   → Dí bótò kò.
         DEF   boat   come
         'The boat comes.'   (Rountree 1972a: 325)

    b. Dí   bóto   kó   éside.   → Dí bótó kó ésìdè.
        DEF   boat   come   yesterday
        'The boat came yesterday.'

c. *Dí   wómi   kulé.*   → *Dí wómì kùlè.*
   DEF   man   run
   'The man runs.'

d. *Dí   wómi   kulé   alá.*   → *Dí wómí kúlé àlà.*
   DEF   man   run   yonder
   'The man runs over there.'

e. *Mi   tá   kulé.*   → *Mì tá kùlè.*
   1S   IMF   run
   'I am running.'

f. *Mi   tá   kulé   tidé.*   → *Mì tá kúlé tìdè.*
   1S   IMF   run   today
   'I am running today.'

As discussed in section 2.3.1.5., a noun phrase and a following verb form a syntactic plateauing environment. Example (29b) accordingly shows the last TBU of the subject with a high tone. By contrast, in (29a), this TBU appears with a low tone due to the fact that an utterance-level intonation process (see section 2.4.2.) has lowered the final high tone of the sentence, suggesting that intonational lowering, in some sense, has "precedence" over plateauing. The same basic pattern holds for the pairs (29c) and (29d) and (29e) and (29f). In (29d) and (29f), the lowering affects the last word of each sentence, but the presence of these additional words, as compared to (29c) and (29e), allows plateauing to take place between the verb and a preceding element.

2.3.2. Tones in serial verb constructions

Serial verb constructions (see Chapter 8) represent a particularly complex area in terms of their tonal properties, and their tonal patterns have been the subject of relatively extensive investigation (Good 2003, 2004; Kramer 2004). In part, their plateauing patterns can be seen to derive from a number of the more general patterns described above. In particular, adjacent serial verbs plateau with each other, in a manner comparable to what is found in compounds (see section 2.3.1.1.), as seen in (30). (The word *pói* 'too much' seen in (30b) is verbal in Saramaccan despite its adverbial gloss and translation, and in (30c) the relevant interaction involves the last two verbs.) In addition, serial verbs and following noun phrases do not form a plateauing environment, just as is the case in VO structures, while noun phrases appearing between two serial verbs do plateau with the following verb comparable to the plateauing found between subjects and verbs (see section 2.3.1.5.), as seen in (31). (Example (31b) illustrates the lack of plateauing when the requisite phonological environment is not found.) While their precise syntactic analysis is another matter, at least some auxiliary-like elements, for example *músu* 'must' in (17b), also behave like serial verbs with respect to plateauing.

(30) a. Mì   hópo   kumútu   à   dí   wósu.   →
         Mì   hópó   kúmútù   à   dí   wósù.
         1S   stand.up exit   LOC DEF   house
         'I get up and go out of the house.'   (Rountree 1972a: 324)

   b. Mì   wáka   pói.   →
       Mì   wáká   pòi.
       1S   walk   too.much
       'I walk too much.'

   c. Mì   makisá   dí   sófu   kã̂   kó   paáta.   →
       Mì   màkìsá   dí   sófú   kã̂   kó   páátà.
       1S   step.on DEF   soda   can   come flat
       'I squashed the soda can flat.'

(31) a. Mì   tá   tjá   deési   gó à   dí   wómi.   →
         Mì   tá   tjá   dèésí   gó à   dí   wòmì.
         1S   IMF   carry medicine go LOC DEF   man
         'I am taking medicine for the man.'   (Voorhoeve 1961: 151)

   b. Dè   féni   lògòsò   butá   à   téla.   →
       Dè   fénì   lògòsò   bùtá   à   télà.
       3P   find   turtle   put   LOC shore
       'They found the turtle and put it at the shore.'

However, there are aspects of tone in these constructions which are somewhat unexpected and are difficult to describe in any consistent way. Various work (Rountree 1972a; Good 2003, 2004; Kramer 2004) has discussed the relevant issues, in some cases in a fair degree of detail, and here we summarize the relevant problems without offering a specific new analysis. Rountree (1972a: 325) was the first to discuss a key kind of data, given in (32), using her tonal transcription. (We have had trouble re-eliciting (32b) due to the lack of coherence of the coded events. Therefore, it has been difficult to verify the relevant tones.)

(32) a. Mì   wási   koósu   butá   à   dí   sónu.   →
         Mì   wásí   kòósú   bútá   à   dí   sónù.
         1S   wash   clothes put   LOC DEF   sun
         'I wash clothes and put them in the sun.'

   b. Mì   ó   náki   dí   lògòsò kulé   gó à   mí   wósu.   →
       Mì   ó   nákí   dí   lògòsò kúlé   gó à   mí   wósù.
       1S   FUT hit   DEF   turtle run   go LOC 1S.POSS   house
       'I am going to hit the turtle and run to my house.'

Setting aside complications of tonal transcription in sentences containing serial verb constructions, which we will come back to shortly below, what Rountree (1972a) takes as notable about these sentences are the apparent high tones at the right edges of non-final verbs in the serial verb construction and the left edges of non-initial verbs (e.g. the final high tone on *wási* 'wash' in (32a) and the initial high tone on *kulé* 'run' in (32b)). An important aspect of (32b) is the interposition of a word with TBU's specified for low tone between the two verbs in order to determine whether or not a plateauing analysis could account for the appearance of certain high tones, which in the case of *kulé* in (32b) does not seem possible due to its being immediately preceded by the word *lògòsò* 'turtle,' which only contains low tones.

Rountree (1972a) treats the appearance of high tones like these in serial verb phrases as resulting from a kind of non-local plateauing, where two verbs are interacting with each other as though the intervening object were phonologically "invisible." Good (2003) provided apparent counterevidence to these examples using minimal pair sentences like those in (33) (see Good [2003: 107]), making use of verbs specified with low tones to test Rountree's analysis.

(33) a. *À   náki   dí   tatái.* →
       À   nákì   dí   tátâi.
       3S hit   DEF rope
       'He hit the rope.'

   b. *À   náki   dí   tatái   bɔ̀sɔ̀.* →
      À   nákí   dí   tátâi   bɔ̀sɔ̀.
      3S   hit   DEF rope   loosen
      'He hit the rope loose.'

The transcriptions in (33) indicate a difference in the final tone of *náki* 'hit' in the two sentences, with sentence (33a) showing an expected low tone on the word (consistent with the pattern more generally exemplified in (24) where verbs and following objects do not form a plateauing environment). In (33b), however, there is an unexpected high tone when the verb is found within a serial verb construction. Notably, the second verb in the construction, *bɔ̀sɔ̀* 'loosen,' contains only low tones, and thus should not be associated with plateauing (whether local or non-local) on phonological grounds. Comparable instances of apparent "spurious" high tones are found in (34) – these high tones are found both at the right edge of non-final verbs in serial verb constructions and the left edge of non-initial verbs. All of these examples contain the low-tone verb *bà* to rule out the possibility that the high tones result from non-local plateauing between the relevant serial verbs.

(34) a. *À   wáka   bà   wáta   gó   à   wósu.* →
       À   wáká   bà   wátà   gó   à   wósù.
       3S walk   carry water go   LOC   house
       'He walked the water into the house.'   (Good 2003: 109)

   b. *Kofi   féni   wáta   bà   à   wósu   bebé   éside.* →
      Kòfi   féní   wátà   bà   à   wósú   bébé   èsìdè.
      Kofi   find   water carry LOC house drink yesterday
      'Kofi found water, carried it home, and drank it, yesterday.'   (Good 2003: 110)

   c. *À   féni   wáta   bà   butá   à   wósu.* →
      À   féní   wátà   bà   bùtá   à   wósù.
      3S find   water carry put   LOC   house
      'He found water and carried it home.'   (Good 2003: 110)

In (34a), there is an unexpected high tone on the last TBU of *wáka* 'walk.' In (34b), there is an unexpected high tone on the last TBU of *féni* 'find' and the first TBU of *bebé* 'drink.' In (34c), there is an unexpected high tone on the last TBU (again) of *féni*. Notably, in (34c), the first TBU of *butá* is low, as would normally be expected. Good (2003) takes examples like these to be indicative of the presence of tonal morphology on Saramaccan serial verbs which marks the right edge of a non-final verb and the left edge of a non-initial verb not immediately preceded by another verb.

Good (2004) and Kramer (2004) add to the dataset and show that the reality appears to be more complex than this, however, as indicated by the examples in (35). (Example (35a) repeats (31b).)

(35) a. Dè   féni   lògòsò   butá   à   téla.   →
       Dè   fénì   lògòsò   bùtá   à   télà.
       3P   find   turtle   put   LOC   shore
       'They found a turtle and put it at the shore.'   (Good 2004: 612)

   b. Dè   féni   dí   lògòsò   butá   à   téla.   →
      Dè   féni   dí   lògòsò   bùtá   à   télà.
      3P   find   DEF   turtle   put   LOC   shore
      'They found the turtle and put it at the shore.'   (Good 2004: 612)

   c. Dè   súti   dí   lánga   sèmbè.   →
      Dè   sùtì   dí   lángà   sèmbè.
      3P   shoot   DEF   tall   person
      'They shot the tall person.'   (Good 2004: 614)

   d. Dè   súti   dí   lánga   sèmbè kíi.   →
      Dè   súti   dí   lángá   sèmbè kîi.
      3P   shoot   DEF   tall   person kill
      'They shot the tall person dead.'   (Good 2004: 614)

The sentence pair in (35a) and (35b) indicates that the presence/absence of a right-edge high tone on a non-final serial verb can be sensitive to the presence of a (high-tone) definite article on the intervening noun phrase. The sentence pair in (35c) and (35d) suggests that serial verb high tones may appear on an adjective in an intervening noun phrase, not just a verb. Good (2004) takes these facts as indicative of tension between the intonational and the tonal aspects of Saramaccan prosody, specifically resulting from an attempt to impose a general LHL intonational contour across an entire sentence as a kind of "overlay" on top of the more local plateauing processes. Under such a view, while lexical low tone specifications cannot be overridden, unspecified TBU's may become "raised" unexpectedly as a result of the imposition of the LHL pattern.

The discussion to this point has glossed over a key issue that will be returned to in section 2.5.: what does it mean to transcribe TBU's as "high" or "low" in a language where lexical items can be drawn from an intonational or tonal lexical stratum? Indeed, informal instrumental investigation of the pitch of Saramaccan utterances has not revealed a system where TBU's can be neatly segregated into high and low tones, most notably because the high "tones" in stressed syllables are often noticeably higher in pitch than high tones which result from plateauing. Furthermore, in many of the sentences just discussed, the spurious high tones are not particularly high. For example, while the transcription of the phrase 'the tall person' in (35d) as *dí lángá sèmbè* does not seem unreasonable if one assumes only the possibility of a strict high/low contrast, instrumental data would actually suggest an alternative transcription along the lines of *dī lángā sèmbè*, with mid tones on *dí* and the second (unstressed) TBU of *lánga*. Furthermore, within the context of the serial verb construction, this phrase is notably shorter than in (35c), making tonal perception more difficult as well as compressing the pitch range by virtue of reducing the time between tonal transitions. Therefore, apparent spurious high tones in serial verb constructions, at least partly, may, in fact, be an artifact of an imposition of a binary high/low transcription model on a system where pitch can align somewhat more "elastically" with segmental material in the way usually associated with intonational languages. In the scope of the present description, it, therefore, seems best to simply say that serial verb constructions are a part of Saramaccan grammar where the "clash" between its intonational and tonal aspects is particularly pronounced, rendering their precise tonal analysis difficult – at least using conventional means of the analysis of pitch changes.

2.4. Intonational processes

2.4.1. Overview

In addition to the phrasal phonological processes discussed in section 2.3., there are also a number of significant utterance-level processes in Saramaccan. One of these, final lowering, was already introduced in section 2.3.1.7. and will be further discussed here. Another is a special falling pattern found at the end of negative clauses. In addition, there are the issues of the overall pitch contour of utterances, including the role of pitch in signaling emphasis, and the formation of yes/no questions using intonational cues. Each of these will be discussed in turn below.

Our general impression of Saramaccan clausal intonation is that it is more reminiscent of what is found in English, for example, than of West and Central African languages. In particular, there is a flexibility in the deployment of pitch across utterances, for instance to mark emphasis (see section 2.4.4.), that is typical of an accentual language like English, but not as readily exploitable in truly tonal languages, where the manipulation of pitch to express different degrees of pragmatic emphasis is typically more restricted. Also, while we have not examined the phenomenon in detail, it appears that clauses in the language are subject to a tendency towards downdrift.

Rountree (1972a: 309–314) discusses a number of intonational phenomena that are not specifically treated here, in large part either because we encountered difficulties in uncovering the same generalizations with our consultants or because the nature of her descriptions left us unsure as to how precisely to interpret her analysis, in particular regarding her sense of the word "stress." So, while, overall, her descriptions can be said to be fairly accurate within the descriptive framework she adopted, we cannot verify all the details she discusses. Some of the examples below are borrowed from her work, though specific citations are not always given because our tonal transcriptions differ from hers.

The surface transcriptions given in this section differ from most of those given in the previous sections of this chapter by virtue of transcribing intonational processes via tone marks rather than restricting the transcription to "pure" phrasal tonal patterns.

2.4.2. Utterance-final lowering

A general process in Saramaccan positive declaratives is utterance-final lowering in which the final TBU of a clause is realized as low, even if this would not be expected given its lexical form. (Final TBU's which would be expected to surface as low simply remain low.) As noted by Rountree (1972a: 317), the final-lowering process does not affect all high-tone TBU's uniformly. Specifically, high-tone TBU's which would normally be expected to enter into a plateauing relationship with the word appearing before them appear as low, while high-tone TBU's which would not be expected to plateau with the word before them appear to be somewhat lower than might otherwise be expected, but are still clearly higher than a low-tone TBU preceding them. Rountree treats this as a "mid" tone, though this must be understood as a transcription indicating a relative pitch level rather than as an indication of a third distinctive toneme. Relevant examples are given in (36). Examples (36a) and (36b) give cases where a final high tone is realized at a level that seems most readily interpreted as low, and examples (36c), (36d), and (36e) give cases where the level is best described as between low and high (and hence, transcribed as mid).

(36) a. Mí   bì   paká   mí   wósu   paimá.   →
       Mí   bì   pàká   mí   wósù   pàìmà.
       1S   PAST pay   1S.POSS house payment
       'I paid my rent.'

   b. Mí   tá   kulé.   →
      Mí   tá   kùlè.
      1S   IMF   run
      'I am running.'

   c. Mí   tá   kulé   tidé.   →
      Mí   tá   kúlé   tìdē.
      1S   IMF   run   today
      'I am running today.'

   d. Dí   lògòsò   kulé   alá.   →
      Dí   lògòsò   kùlé   àlā.
      DEF   turtle   run   yonder
      'The turtle runs over there.'

   e. Mí   ó   bebé   kofí.   →
      Mí   ó   bébé   kòfī.
      1S   FUT   drink   coffee
      'I am going to drink coffee.'   (Rountree 1972a: 322)

It is difficult to understand the exact source of this differential lowering pattern. The most straightforward way to look at it is presumably to see it as resulting from a phrasal phonological effect specifying one primary accent per phonological phrase, where the phonological phrase is understood as a plateauing domain and the primary accent is found on the first high-toned TBU. Cases like (36a) and (36b) would then surface in the way seen due to the fact that the final high tones would not be primarily accented and, thus, would shift to being completely unaccented, in pitch terms, when phrase-final. By contrast, in (36c), (36d), and (36e), the final words of these sentences stand in their own plateauing group and, therefore, have only one high-tone TBU available for primary accent. In final position, this high tone may be lowered but not completely effaced due to its status as bearing primary phrasal accent. This is a somewhat speculative interpretation, but it may, nevertheless, help at least make the overall descriptive facts surrounding this pattern clearer.

In addition to final tone lowering, utterance-final position is also frequently associated with partial devoicing of final vowels.

2.4.3. Negative lowering

Rountree (1972a: 310) reports that in negative sentences the final two TBU's of the last word appear with low tones, in a pattern reminiscent of what is found in Central African languages showing VONeg structures (see Dryer 2009). This intonational coding does not appear to have been seriously explored since Rountree (1972a) and, at least based on the speech of one consultant, we can refine the earlier description somewhat. The lowering of tones in negation is not realized as simple low tones but, rather, as a falling pattern across the last two TBU's of the final word of a sentence, whether or not these TBU's are found in the same syllable. If the final word only contains one TBU, then the pattern is realized within the span of that one TBU. In principle, utterance-final lowering (see section 2.4.2.) could produce a similar pattern in certain phonological contexts. However, the lowering involved in negative sentences is clearly distinguishable phonetically from utterance-final lowering by virtue of being associated with lower pitch targets, at least in those cases where the two processes might otherwise be expected to result in phonetically identical intonational patterns.

Examples are given in (37) where positive and negative sentences are paired. A downstep marker is used to transcribe those cases where negative sentences are associated with a final falling pattern that starts from a lower initial pitch than comparable falls in positive sentences. The single TBU of the word *njǎ* 'eat' in examples (37e) and (37f) is transcribed with a circumflex to indicate that it is realized with a phonetic fall (which would more usually be transcribed as low in the positive sentence) across its one TBU in both positive and negative sentences (though starting from a lower initial pitch and with a more compressed fall in the negative variant). In example (37l), the final falling pattern in the negative does not involve downstep, but, due to the way utterance-final lowering applies to the affirmative variant in (37k), there is still a difference in the intonational realization of the final word in each of the two sentences, with a final falling pattern only in (37l).

(37) a. *Mì   tá   wáka.* →
      Mì   tá   wákà.
      1S   IMF   walk
      'I am walking.'

   b. *Mέ   á   tá   wáka.* →
      Mέ   á   tá   ꜜwákà.
      1S.NEG NEG IMF walk
      'I am not walking.'

   c. *Mì   tá   hákísi.* →
      Mì   tá   hákísì.
      1S   IMF   ask
      'I am asking.'

   d. *Mέ   á   tá   hákísi.* →
      Mέ   á   tá   háꜜkísì.
      1S.NEG NEG IMF ask
      'I am not asking.'

   e. *Mì   tá   njǎ̂.* →
      Mì   tá   njâ̂.
      1S   IMF   eat
      'I am eating.'

   f. *Mέ   á   tá   njǎ̂.* →
      Mέ   á   tá   ꜜnjâ̂.
      1S.NEG NEG IMF eat
      'I am not eating.'

g. Mì   súti   dí   dágu   kíi. →
   Mì   sútí   dí   dágú   kîi.
   1S   shoot   DEF   dog   kill
   'I shot the dog dead.'

h. Mé   á   súti   dí   dágu   kíi. →
   Mé   á   sútí   dí   dágú   ˈkîi.
   1S.NEG NEG   shoot DEF   dog   kill
   'I did not shoot the dog dead.'

i. Mì ké bái dí sutúu dí à bì sindó nɛ̃ɛ̃́ déndu. →
   Mì ké bái dí sútúú dí à bì sìndó nɛ̃ɛ̃́ déndù.
   1S want buy DEF chair REL 3S PAST sit LOC.3S.POSS inside
   'I want to buy the chair that he sat in.'

j. Mé á ké bái dí sutúu dí à bì sindó nɛ̃ɛ̃́ déndu. →
   Mé á ké bái dí sútúú dí à bì sìndó nɛ̃ɛ̃́ ˈdéndù.
   1S.NEG NEG want buy DEF chair REL 3S PAST sit LOC.3S.POSS inside
   'I don't want to buy the chair that he sat in.'

k. Mì   tá   kulé. →
   Mì   tá   kùlè.
   1S   IMF   run
   'I am running.'

l. Mé   á   tá   kulé. →
   Mé   á   tá   kúlè.
   1S.NEG NEG   IMF   run
   'I am not running.'

This final negative contour does seem to be best described as affecting the final word of a sentence, rather than some other constituent, since it has been found to affect words with a variety of syntactic roles and which are unified only by their position in the utterance. This is most clearly seen by looking at sentence (37i) where the final word is within a distinct clause from the negation.

The transcriptions used above to indicate the nature of this contour do not encode some important nuances regarding its realization (see also section 2.5.). For instance, in the pair in (37e) and (37f), while there is a phonetic fall on the final syllable of the utterance in both cases, perceptually, the fall in (37f) was somewhat longer and more salient and, therefore, appeared more like a "true" fall than the one found in (37e) which, more likely, simply represented the necessary transition between the penultimate high tone and the final low tone due to utterance-final lowering.

2.4.4. Emphasis within a clause

As mentioned above, our impression overall is that Saramaccan clausal intonation is closer to that of, say, English than languages of West and Central Africa. Where this seems particularly clear is in the language's use of pitch fluctuations where a higher pitch can be found on words that are "emphasized" in one way or another. For instance, in the pair in (38), two different words can be in focus (depending on the associated pragmatic context), and this focus results in two significantly different pitch realizations. In (38a), where the first word *alá* 'yonder' is in focus, its pitch is noticeably raised to the point where its initial low tone is around the same level as the high tone of the following word *njãnjá* 'food.' (This is indicated with a downstep marker in the surface transcription.) In (38b), by contrast, the tone patterns are more consistently realized across the utterance.

(38) a. **Alá**   njãnjá   dé.   → Àlá ˈnjãnjá̂ dè.
          yonder   food   be
          'Food is *over there*.'

     b. Alá   **njãnjá**   dé.   → Àlá **njãnjá̂** dè.
          yonder   food   be
          '*Food* is over there.'

Comparable patterns are found in information questions (see section 11.2.). Specifically, the question word (and, in some cases, an associated element modified by the word) can receive a higher pitch than is found for other high tones in the utterance.

(39) Ǔ   wómi   tá   wáka?   → Ǔ wómí ˈtá wákà?
     which   man   IMF   walk
     'Which man is walking?'

An additional way of indicating emphasis (over a whole clause) involves the use of a clause-final particle *é* (see section 15.4.5.). (This element is transcribed as *ɛ́* in Rountree [1972a: 312], perhaps because the contrast between *e* and *ɛ* can be hard to discern sentence-finally where some reduction in voicing is often found.) Like yes/no question markers (see section 2.4.5.), this particle is not subject to the utterance-final lowering rule and forms a plateauing environment with a preceding element.

(40) Mí   tá   wáka   é!   → Mí tá wáká é!
     1S   IMF   walk   INJ
     'I am walking!'

2.4.5. Yes/no questions

The intonation patterns of yes/no questions (see section 11.1.) involve a higher pitch at the end of an utterance by virtue of a final high-tone question marker, which the utterance-final lowering rule (see section 2.4.2.) also fails to apply to. Less commonly, a yes/no question can be marked purely intonationally, in which case it, again, ends in a high tone either by virtue of utterance-final lowering not applying to a final high-tone TBU or by the raising of a final tonally-unspecified TBU. In affirmative questions, a final question marker plateaus with the word preceding it. In negative questions, the negative falling contour (see section 2.4.3.) targets the word before the question particle, plateauing is not found, and the particle surfaces with the same kind of "mid" pitch discussed in section 2.4.2. as appearing in certain final-lowering contexts.

(41) a. Mì   tá   wáka   nɔ́?   → Mì tá wáká nɔ́?
        1S   IMF   walk   INT
        'Am I walking?'

b. À   sindó?   → À sìndó?
    3S   sit
    'Is he sitting down?'

c. Mì   tá   wáka?   → Mì tá wáká?
    1S   IMF   walk
    'Am I walking?'

d. Á   tá   wáka   nó?   → Á tá ʼwákà nɔ́?
    3S.NEG   IMF   walk   INT
    'Isn't he walking?'

2.5. Notes on tonal and intonational phonetics and problems of analysis

As already indicated above, the split nature of the Saramaccan lexicon, into accentual and tonal strata, raises analytical difficulties, in particular in the realm of phrasal phonology. Beginning with Voorhoeve (1961), there has been a descriptive tradition in the language, continued here, of describing phrasal patterns in terms of sequences of high and low tones, as one might expect in a regular tone language. At the same time, there are cases in the grammar when it is not clear if the pitch patterns should be described via individual pitches on TBU's as opposed to larger intonational "arcs." This tension comes through most clearly in serial verb phrases (see section 2.3.2.), but is also an issue in understanding patterns of marking emphasis which exploit pitch (see section 2.4.4.). It should further be noted that, while the transcriptions above with high and low tones are, we believe, a reasonable expression of the nature of the phonological opposition in the Saramaccan sound system, it can not always be assumed that they offer a clear transcription of how a given utterance is actually rendered by speakers. In particular, there appears to be a system of phrase-level accentuation which results in an accented high tone appearing with a higher pitch than other adjacent high tones.

For instance, in the citation form of a basic affirmative clause, like *Mì tá wáka* 'I am walking,' instrumental evidence indicates that the "high" tone in *tá* can actually appear at more or less the same level as the "low" tone in *mì*. Nevertheless, the indication of a high tone on *tá* seems justified on the basis of plateauing effects and the fact that, in other contexts (e.g. interrogative sentences), it can surface with an unambiguous high tone. Ultimately, issues like this are directly connected to the fact that the descriptive devices for prosody tend to be geared towards systems which are either primarily tonal or accentual in their deployment of pitch. To the extent that Saramaccan mixes the two, these descriptive devices are not fully adequate for understanding the system as a whole.

Chapter 3
Morphology and morphophonemics

3.1. Derivational morphology

3.1.1. Reduplication

Saramaccan's principal overt derivation mechanism is reduplication.

Productive reduplication is total. There is a small closed set of partially reduplicated items (e.g. *tái* 'to tie,' *tatái* 'rope'; *búnu* 'good,' *bumbúu* 'fine'; *kɔkɔ́ni* 'rabbit'), which are likely the result of phonetic erosion over time of original forms with total reduplication.

Reduplication has several productive functions in the grammar, which will be discussed in turn.

3.1.1.1. Deverbal resultatives

With dynamic transitive verbs, reduplication renders a resultative meaning:

(1) dí   láilái   bóto
    DEF   load.RD   boat
    'the loaded boat'

(2) Dí   bóto   dé   láilái.
    DEF   boat   be   load.RD
    'The boat is loaded.'

(3) Dí   né   dé   sikífisikífi   nɛ̃ɛ̃.
    DEF   name   be   write.RD   LOC.3SO
    'The name is written down on it.'

(4) Dí   mbéti   dé   a   dí   táfa   líba   kótikóti.
    DEF   meat   be   LOC   DEF   table   top   cut.RD
    'The meat is on the table cut up.'

For details on syntactic and other aspects of this usage, see 6.4.

For property items expressed with stative verbs, these deverbal resultatives convey counterexpectational semantics. For example, one reading of *boóko* is as the property item 'broken.' A semantically neutral sentence would be:

(5) Dí   sutúu   boóko.
    DEF   chair   break
    'The chair is broken.'

But if one is pointing out that a chair is broken, as a warning to someone about to sit in it as opposed to other chairs surrounding it, then the reduplicated resultative can be used:

(6) Dí sutúu dé boókóbóóko.
    DEF chair be break.RD
    'The chair is broken.'

See 6.2. for details.

3.1.1.2. Intensification

Reduplication can also be used to intensify meaning: *bandja* 'side, beside,' *bandjabandja* 'right alongside'; *hésíhési* 'very fast'; *sáápísáápi* 'very slow.' In some cases, the meaning of the reduplicated form has specialized somewhat from a strictly compositional meaning of intensification. *Lánga* 'long,' for example, when reduplicated means 'all the way' (or also 'along'):

(7) Mi ó   gó lángálánga   té   a   Miami.
    1S FUT   go long.RD   until LOC Miami
    'I am going to go all the way to Miami.'

Similarly, *fósu* 'first' but *fósúfósu* 'formerly'; *mɔ́õ* 'more,' *mɔ́õmɔ́õ* 'again.' Also relevant is when the intensification conveys generations' remove: *avó* 'grandparent,' *avóávó* 'ancestors.'

Nɔ́unɔ́u 'now' is a case where this intensification has fossilized (*nɔ́u*).

3.1.1.3. X-like

Reduplication can also derive a word that describes a quality of the root. Examples include *wáta* 'water,' *wátáwáta* 'watery'; *síndja* 'ashes,' *síndjásíndja* 'gray'; and the partial reduplication example *wawã́* 'alone' from *wã́* 'one.'

3.1.1.4. Aggregate plural

Nouns can be reduplicated to convey that the referent exists in high number. This reduplication occurs mainly in descriptive parts of vivid narratives; it is not an entrenched plural-marking strategy.

(8) wáka   a   déé   kamíãkámíã
    walk   LOC   DEF.PL   place.RD
    'walk to various places'

(9) U   bi   sí písípísi   fẽẽ   akí   kaa.
    1P PAST   see home.RD   POSS.3SO   here CPLT
    'We saw those houses he had all over the place here.'

In a closed set of nouns referring to entities usually encountered in groups or masses, only the reduplicated form is used. These can be seen as frozen forms of the aggregate plural construction, e.g. *mɔsimɔ́si* 'mouse,' *wasiwási* 'wasp' (cf. *wási* 'to wash'), *kɔkɔ́ni* 'rabbit,' *gbɛnɛgbénɛ* 'moss,' *ɛniɛ́ni* 'dirt grains.' *Gɔɔgɔ́ɔ* 'Adam's apple,' 'chicken craw' is an exception in not referring to an aggregate entity; this item can be treated as onomatopoeic.

3.1.1.5. Nominalization

The Saramaccan lexicon includes a set of frozen reduplicated items that indicate that at an earlier stage of the grammar, reduplication also created deverbal nouns. Instruments thus created include *wawái* 'fan' (< *wái* 'to wave') and *tatái* 'rope' (< *tái* 'to tie'). Other cases include *buábua* 'gnat' (< *buwá* 'to fly') and *njănjã́* 'food' (< *njã́* 'to eat'). A semantically distorted case is *bebɛ* 'yolk' (< *bɛ* 'red').

The partial reduplication in some of these forms is itself a suggestion that these words are especially antique within the lexicon, to the point that usage has eroded the first syllable somewhat.

3.1.1.6. Tone plateauing in reduplicated words

When a root with the tonal pattern HØ is reduplicated, there is high tone plateauing in the reduplicated item: /nákináki/ > [nákínáki] 'beaten.' Otherwise:

1. Plateauing does not occur when the unreduplicated form is bisyllabic and both syllables have high tone (Rountree 1972a: 318): *wãté* 'right away,' *wãtéwãte* 'immediately' (see 2.2.4. for further discussion). This applies also with ideophones formed from the reduplication of a sequence of two syllables with high tone, such as *kélékele* 'Indeed!' or *lébélebe* 'long and thin' from *lébéé* 'thin,' which with its high tones on each syllable classifies as an ideophone. When only the final syllable of the unreduplicated form is high, as in *kopíkopi* 'termite' or *buábua* 'gnat,' then plateauing occurs at the phrasal level: *kopíkópí*. However, in citation form, an utterance-final lowering rule (cf. 2.4.2.) lowers the final syllable of the reduplicated form, which then allows the penultimate syllable to go low as well.

2. The basic rule that there is plateauing in reduplicated forms composed of a bisyllabic HØ root is contravened in a particular semantic class: natural entities commonly encountered in the plural. Examples include *mɔsimɔ́si* 'mouse,' *patupátu* 'duck,' *kesikési* 'squirrel monkey,' *hɔnjɔhɔ́njɔ́* 'type of large fly,' *gbɛnɛgbéne* 'moss,' *gobogóbo* 'large peanut,' and *ɛniéni* 'dirt grains.' Thus there is an ØØHØ template specified for this class when the root is HØ – but only then (cf. above *kopíkopi* 'termite,' *buábua* 'gnat'). It would appear that in all of these cases, the unreduplicated form is not attested.

3. Plateauing does not occur when the form is onomatopoeic: *tekúteku* 'hiccup,' *kúsikúsi* 'whisper,' *kɔɔkɔ́ɔ* 'cough,' *kasikaási* 'wound.' This last item is a partial reduplication from *kaási* 'to scratch' (cf. the form in Saramaccan's ancestor Sranan *krasi*, which is less phonetically evolved beyond English *scratch*) and thus derived from the mimetic 'scratch-scratch.'

4. We are aware of one idiosyncratic exception to the above generalizations about plateauing, namely *pusipúsi* 'cat' (given that domesticized cats are not typically encountered in groups), as well as an exception that is only apparent: *bíi* 'beer,' *biibíi* 'flood, swamp.' *Biibíi* is a borrowing from a local Amerindian language, likely Carib, and thus not a reduplication of *bíi*. *Pusipúsi*'s immunity to plateauing could be an analogy with other animal names with the same tone pattern.

Voorhoeve (1961: 156) argues that words in which plateauing does not apply are borrowings from Sranan and that their tones preserve a Sranan stress pattern, but this seems unlikely. All of the cases that Voorhoeve gives fall under the exceptional classes above except for the word for 'cat.' Why would that single ordinary word and possibly a few more be borrowed from Sranan after Saramaccan was already formed, and thus preserved in a form against the phonological grain of the language, as opposed to concepts more clearly associated with the world outside of Saramaka culture?

See 2.2.4. for other cases of lexically specified exceptions to plateauing.

3.1.2. The nominalizers -*ma* and -*wã́*

Beyond reduplication, Saramaccan makes very little use of bound morphemes for derivational processes. The agentive marker -*ma* (< *man*) derives agentives from verbs, as in *hóndima* 'hunter' and *tákima* 'leader' (< *táki* 'to talk'), and from nouns, as in *hédima* 'leader' ('headman') and *néma* 'famous person' ('name man').

Despite its etymology, this marker is gender-neutral: *paíma* 'woman who gives (or just gave) birth' (< *paí* 'to give birth').

The marker -*ma* can also mark roots composed of two constituents, such as verb + object:

tjá-bóto-ma	< carry-boat-AG	'boat carrier'
subí-kúnunu-ma	< climb-mountain-AG	'mountain climber'

or those composed of a constituent modified by a prepositional phrase adjunct:

síki-a-édi-ma < sick-LOC-head-AG 'retarded person'

Our informants do not accept, *pace* Bakker, Smith, and Veenstra (1995: 173–174), roots with more than two constituents such as serial verb constructions:

**subí-kúnunu-gó-a-líba-ma*
climb-mountain-go-LOC-top-AG
'mountain climber'

or those with two clauses, such as:

*bigí-u-woóko-ma
start-NF-work-AG
'first worker'

When the preceding syllable in the root has an unchangeable low tone, -*ma* takes a high tone: *lεgεdεmá* 'liar' (cf. 2.2.3.3. for more examples).

The item *wã́* 'one' occurs as a nominalizer, not to the extent of -*ma*, but with a similar tonal alternation at least in some words: *búnu-wã* 'good one' versus *taku-wã́* 'bad one' (cf. 2.2.3.3.).

3.1.3. An incipient derivational affix?

Tế 'time' when used as part of compound words often loses its high tone: *físitẽ* 'antiquity,' *hiniwã́tẽ* 'all the time,' *líbitẽ* 'lifetime,' *písitẽ* 'a while,' *bákatẽ* 'later.' This could be analyzed as the beginning of the grammaticalization of *tế* into an affix denoting time. However, the process remains incipient at this point, as in other cases *tế* retains the high tone, e.g. *naṹtế* 'when,' *bitế* 'before daylight.'

3.2. Inflectional morphology

Saramaccan is essentially an inflectionless language. However, there are three features that can be treated as inflectional.

3.2.1. Imperfective *tá* with *gó* 'to go'

Imperfective marker *tá* has fused with *gó* 'to go': *mi nángó* 'I am going' (**mi tá gó*). This fusion of *tá* occurs with only this verb, clearly because of the especially frequent usage of the collocation. The *nán-* form here has all of the hallmarks of inflectionhood:

1. It is significantly phonetically removed from its source independently of phonological rules.

2. It is indisputably a bound form: the occurrence of the second [n] in *nán-* before a consonant (the [g] in *nángó*) is an example of a nasal-stop sequence that is only allowed in Saramaccan phonology within a word (i.e. *nángó* cannot be analyzed as a hypothetical *nán gó*). *Tá* is derived from *stand*, with the second [n] in *nán-* the descendant of *stand*'s [n]; in Saramaccan's phonology, etymological word-final nasal consonants are rendered as nasality on the preceding vowel, e.g. *kã* 'can (be),' or leave no remnant, e.g. past marker *bi* from *been*.

3. Finally, *nán-* is highly selective, occurring only with *gó*, rather than occurring more generally as clitics tend to (Zwicky and Pullum 1983: 503).

Nevertheless, the fact remains that this would appear to be the sole segmental inflectional morpheme in the entire language (but cf. 3.2.3. below). As such, it is also coherent to treat *nángó* as a portmanteau morpheme within an inflectionless language. Clearly, here, *chacun à son goût*.

3.2.2. Tonal marking of verb serialization

Good (2003) also proposes that Saramaccan has an inflectional tonal morpheme which marks the syntactic status of a verb as serial within a serial verb construction. As discussed in 2.3.2., there is normally high tone plateauing between serial verbs which "skips" the intervening object. This can be seen in the sentence below, in which the bolded segments are ones that are low tones in isolation but are raised to high by plateauing:

(10) Mi ó nákí dí logoso kúlé gó a mí wósu.
 1S FUT hit DEF turtle run go LOC 1S.POSS house
 'I will hit the turtle and run to my house.' (Rountree 1972a: 325)

But there is a subclass of Saramaccan words marked with unchangeable low tones that are insensitive to plateauing, and in serial verb constructions with verbs of this subclass, stipulating mere plateauing between the verbs is insufficient. A first serial verb without unchangeable low tones plateaus "phantom style" even when the second one has unchangeable low tones and thus cannot, such as *bɔsɔ* 'loosen':

(11) A nákí dí tatái bɔsɔ.
 3S hit DEF rope loosen
 'He hit the rope and loosened it.'

Also, the first syllable of a second verb without unchangeable low tones is marked high even when the first verb is one with such unchangeable low tones, such as *ba* 'carry':

(12) *A   ba   wátá   bébé   éside.*
      3S   carry   water   drink   yesterday
      'He carried water and drank it yesterday.'

3.2.3. Nominal marker *a-*?

A few hundred nouns in Saramaccan begin with *a*, contrasting with the fact that only about 20 begin with *o* (and most of these occur optionally with an initial *w*: *óto* / *wóto* 'story' [cf. 17.2]) and very few at all begin with *e*, *i*, or *u*.

The nouns with initial *a-* are almost all African borrowings, and one might suppose that the frequency of initial *a-* in the Saramaccan lexicon is due to the fact that *a-* is a common nominal class marker in Niger-Congo languages (albeit often occurring only in fossilized fashion, as in Fongbe). However, two facts could suggest that *a-* is a morpheme.

The *a-* is optional with a few words, which exhibit no common phonetic trait that could be treated as conditioning the optionality; e.g. *amakudjá* / *makudjá* 'passion fruit,' *amusói* / *musói* 'amsoi (a green leafy vegetable).' This could be analyzed as suggesting that *a-* has status as a separate morpheme.

Also, in many cases, the source etymon lacks an initial *a-*, suggesting that Saramaccan's creators appended the *a-* via analogy with the wealth of *a-*initial nouns, again suggesting a possible morphemic analysis. Examples include *adikpókpo* / *dikpókpo* 'mushroom,' from Fongbe *džikpo*; *agó* 'knot,' from Fongbe *gó*; *akata* 'head pad,' from Kikongo *nkata*; *ambóló* 'large lizard,' from Kikongo *ki-mboolo*; and *akulí* / *kulí* 'Hindustani,' from Hindi *kulī*.

Further research is necessary to determine whether the optionality of *a-* applies to more than a compact set of words (i.e. is a general matter of elision in rapid speech). In any case, if *a-* is a nominal marker, it is not productive.

3.3. Morphophonemics

In Saramaccan, morphophonemic processes occur most often with pronominals.

3.3.1. Possessive *(f)u*

Possession can be indicated with prepositional phrases postposed to the possessum (statistically more often with alienables; cf. 4.3.), in which case various distortive processes are conventionalized: either the phonetic shortening of the possessive marker *fu* or the subsumption of the pronoun into a portmanteau morpheme in which *fu*'s vowel assimilates to the pronoun's vowel (assuming the latter is not [u]):

Table 17. Fu + pronominal portmanteau morphemes

1S	u mi, u m	1P	fuu
2S	fii	2P	fuunu
3S	fɛɛ̃	3P	u de

3.3.2. Other morphophonemic processes with *fu*

A similar morphophonemic process occurs when *fu* is followed by third-person subject pronominal *a*, so that /fu a/ > [faa]:

(13) A   kandá   ká   **faa**   bajá.
      3S   sing   where for.3S   dance
      'He sings instead of dancing.'

Fu also assimilates to the initial vowel of *alá* 'yonder':

(14) Mi   ná   **fa**   alá.
      1S   NEG   of   yonder
      'I'm not from there.'

3.3.3. Negation and pronouns

When occurring after subject pronouns, negator *á* is subsumed into portmanteau morphemes that result from assimilation processes or, in the third-person singular, erosion (only with the third-person plural pronoun does no change occur). Note that first-person singular *má* is the Upper River dialect form:

Table 18. Subject pronoun + negator portmanteau morphemes

1S	mé / má	1P	wá
2S	já	2P	wá
3S	á	3P	de á

Cf. 7.1.2. for details.

3.3.4. Third-person singular ẽ

Third-person singular oblique pronoun ẽ is subject to a morphophonemic rule stipulating that it causes assimilation in a preceding [a] or [ɛ] and yields a long (or bisyllabic) lax mid vowel in a particular set of contexts:

3.3.4.1. After a verb

/paká ẽ/ > [pakɛ́ɛ̃] 'pay him'
/túwɛ ẽ/ > [túwɛ̃ɛ̃] 'throw him'

(15) A   **biɛ́ɛ̃**   (< biá ẽ)   gó   a   básu.
      3S   turn.3SO   go   LOC   under
      'He turned it upside-down.'

(16) Hɛ̃́   a   **butɛ́ɛ̃**   (< butá ẽ)   a   dí   táfa   líba.
      then 3S   put.3SO   LOC   DEF   table   top
      'Then he put it on the table.'

Note from the above examples that the morphophonemic rule is not sensitive to tone, occurring with both high-tone and low-tone final syllables (e.g. *túwɛ*).

With other vowels, the rule does not apply:

bebé ɛ̃ 'drink it'
subí ɛ̃ 'climb it'
sindó ɛ̃ 'sit on it'
sɔ́ɔ́tɔ ɛ̃ 'lock it'
tjɔkɔ́ ɛ̃ 'prick it'
lúku ɛ̃ 'look at it'

However, even within its phonological domain, the cliticization of *ɛ̃* is variable. In some cases it is grammatical for the morphophonemic rule not to apply, as seen in examples such as:

(17) Ma té John fã, nɔ́ɔ híi sɛmbɛ tá **háika ɛ̃**. (cf. *háikɛ̃ɛ̃*)
but when John talk NI all person IMF listen 3SO
'But when John talks, everybody listens to him.'

(18) A téi u kúma díi dáka sɔ́ fu **kabá ɛ̃**. (cf. *kabɛ́ɛ̃*)
3S take 1P like three day such NF finish 3SO
'It took us about three days to finish it.'

In our data, these forms are not restricted to elicited sentences – they also occur in our corpus of spontaneous speech. They thus cannot be analyzed as symptoms of especially explicit speech.

Frequency of usage affects the occurrence of the cliticization. For example, it is obligatory with core verb *dá* 'give':

(19) De ábi u mbéi wǎ lánga bédi **dɛ́ɛ̃**.
3P have NF make INDF long bed give.3SO
'They had to make a longer bed for him.'

Frequency also allows this cliticization in phonetic contexts beyond those in which it regularly applies. Our data include its occurrence with a verb whose final vowel would normally bar its application: *ábi* 'to have,' with a final [i]. The object pronoun does not always cliticize with *ábi*:

(20) Mi músu **ábi** ɛ̃.
1S must have 3SO
'I must (i.e. have to) have it.'

But in some cases it does, likely because it is such a high-usage item:

(21) Wá sábi ambé **ábɛ́ɛ̃**.
1P.NEG know who have.3SO
'We don't know who owns it.'

3.3.4.2. With locative marker *a*

When the locative marker *a* (in the form of the allomorph *na*) is followed by *ɛ̃*, the two obligatorily fuse into a portmanteau morpheme: /(n)a ɛ̃/ > [nɛ̃ɛ̃] 'LOC.3SO' (cf. 3.3.5. below):

(22)　Dí　né　dé　sikífisikífi　**nɛ̃́ɛ̃**.　　(*... a ɛ̃.)
　　　 DEF　name　be　write.RD　LOC.3SO
　　　 'The name is written down on it.'

3.3.4.3. With negator ná

(23)　Mi　**nɛ̃́ɛ̃**　　　tatá.
　　　 1S　NEG.POSS.3SO　father
　　　 'I am not his father.'

3.3.4.4. With copula da

/da ɛ̃/ > [dɛ̃ɛ̃] 'be his/hers'

(24)　Mi　**dɛ̃̂ɛ̃**　　tatá.
　　　 1S　be.POSS.3SO　father
　　　 'I am his father.'

3.3.4.5. With njã́ 'eat' and fõ̌ 'beat'

With these particular two monosyllabic verbs, both of which end with nasal vowels, this clitic does not cause assimilation of the verb's vowel. It instead occurs with a preceding epenthetic [m] due to the surfacing of an underlying syllable-final nasal consonant:

/njã́ ɛ̃/　>　[njã́mɛ̃] 'eat it'
/fõ̌ ɛ̃/　>　[fõ̌mɛ̃] 'beat it'

In contrast to what is presented in Kouwenberg (1987), our data do not indicate that the clitic in these forms is long or bisyllabic.

3.3.5. Locative (n)a

Usually, Saramaccan's locative morpheme is *a*:

(25)　A　wáka　gó　**a**　wósu.
　　　 3S　walk　go　LOC　house
　　　 'He walked home.'

However, it occurs in certain contexts as allomorph *na*. First, *na* occurs fossilized in wh-words. It is preserved in *naũté* 'when' (< *na* 'LOC' *ǔ* 'which' *tě* 'time') and *naásé* 'where' (as well as with its variant *naŭsé*). More broadly, it occurs with *ǔ* 'which' when the latter is used independently and with its derivant *úndi* 'which one':

(26)　**Na**　ǔ　kɔ́ndɛ　Jeff　kumútu?
　　　 LOC　which　village　Jeff　exit
　　　 'Which village did Jeff come from?'

(27) Á   toóbi, i   sá   njã̌   **na** ű   júu   i   ké   é.
     3S.NEG trouble 2S can eat   LOC   which hour 2S want INJ
     'It's no big deal – you can eat at whatever time you want.'

(28) **Na**   úndi   u   déé   táfa   básu   i   tá   tjubí?
     LOC   which of   DEF.PL table   under 2S IMF   hide
     'Which of the tables did you hide under?'

Second, it is preserved with deictic adverbials *na akí* 'at this place,' *na alá* 'at yonder place,' and *naandé* 'at that place.'

Finally, it surfaces in morphophonemic conjunction with third-person singular oblique *ɛ̃* (or its possessive form *ɛ̃́*), as in:

(29) Dí   wósu   dé   **nɛ̃ɛ̃́**   (*a ɛ̃́)   báka   de   bi   tá   bósi.
     DEF   house there LOC.3S.POSS   back   3P   PAST IMF   kiss
     'That's the house they kissed in back of.'

3.3.6. Hortative verb *bé*

In the first-person plural, *bé* has combined with pronoun *u* 'we' yielding the portmanteau *bóo*:

(30) Dísi   ó   taánga –   **bóo**   poobá.
     this   FUT   strong   HORT.1P   try
     'This is going to be hard – let's try.'

(31) **Bóo**   u   síngi   ká   fuu   bajá.
     HORT.1P   1P   sing   where for.1P dance
     'Let's sing instead of dancing.'

3.4. Compounding

Compounding has been a fertile source of the Saramaccan lexicon, given its development from an abbreviation of the lexicons of its source languages. Thus 'blind' is *boóko-wójo* 'broken eye,' 'leprosy' is *tjína-síki* 'taboo sickness,' and so on. Compounding would appear to be more common in Saramaccan than in European languages (albeit less so than in many East and Southeast Asian languages).

Compounds in Saramaccan are generally right-headed. Most compounds are formed from nominal heads, although the resultant compounds include adjectives and sometimes verbs as well as nouns:

AN: *bɛ-wójo* < red-eye 'to threaten,' *kúa-uwíi* < raw-leaf 'spring' (describing the color green)
VN: *kulé-wáta* < run-water 'running water,' *síngi-fóu* 'singing bird'
NN: *mamá-fóu* < mother-bird 'bush hen,' *gangáa-wáta* < neck-water 'phlegm'

For information on what could be termed verbal compounding, cf. Chapter 8 on serial verb constructions.

There are a few left-headed compounds, such as *agó-mã̌ũ* 'elbow' (lit. 'knot-hand'), *agó-fútu* 'heel' (lit. 'knot-foot'), and *ahwá-mã̌ũ* 'shoulder' (lit. 'shoulder-hand'). These are certainly the result of the elision of *u* in what were initially associative constructions, e.g. *agó u mã̌ũ* 'knot of hand.' Support for this analysis includes current terms such as *keké u máũ* 'wrist' (*keké* 'small tool for spinning thread'), in which assimilation of *u* is apparently blocked by the frontness of the preceding vowel.

Compounding is not distinguished by any specific phonological or tonal alterations. Tone sandhi rules, for example, apply in compounds as they do elsewhere (cf. 2.3.1.1).

Nor is it distinguished by contravening of phrasal word order along the lines of English's *birdcatcher* (**I birdcatch*):

tjá-bóto-ma   (*bóto-tjá-ma)
carry-boat-AG
'boat carrier'

bebé-buúu-máku   (*buúu-bebé-máku)
drink-blood-mosquito
'blood-sucking mosquito'

Rather, compounding is distinguished mostly semantically, in that compounds' meanings have often lexicalized somewhat away from strict compositionality:

síngi-fóu   'singing bird'
kandá-fóu   'birds whose song is not pretty, such as chickens'

kulé-wáta-físi < run-water-fish 'freshwater fish'
wáta-físi   'ocean fish'

píki-táki-ma
answer-talk-AG
'interlocutor' (lit. 'answer leader' [cf. *tákima* 'leader'])

There are some idiosyncratic cases, however, where compounding has occasioned phonetic distortion. The vowels in *deé* 'dry' assimilate from lax to tense due to the following element's vowel in *píki-deé-wéi-líba* 'April' (lit. 'little-dry-weather-month'). A type of fish is referred to alternately as *alogohédi*, in which *hédi* 'head' is phonetically intact, or *alogoídi*. The purpleheart tree is *pópúáti*, in which the initial segment of *háti* 'heart' has been elided.

Also, the eclipse of lexical items when used independently has left cranberry morphemes in occasional cases such as *kokóába* 'maipa palm tree,' in which *ába* (today meaning 'to cross') is derived from a now-defunct early Saramaccan item *abra* 'tree,' itself derived from Portuguese's *arvore*.

Exocentric compounds are not common, but include *góni-gógo* 'wasp' (lit. 'gun-butt'), *alátu-lábu* 'type of plant' (lit. 'rodent-tail'), and *kúkútú-lábu* 'scorpion' (lit. 'small.biting.insect-tail').

Compounding in Saramaccan also includes a derivational strategy: the inversive is rendered with negator morpheme *ná*. Examples include:

ná-buwá-fóu   <   NEG-fly-bird   'flightless bird'
ná-tɔɔ́u-ma   <   NEG-marry-AG   'unmarried man'
ná-jasájásá-pindá < NEG-fry.RD-peanut   'uncooked peanuts'

There are no formal grounds for treating this usage of *ná* as an affix (e.g. along the lines of English *un-*), as it undergoes no segmental or tonal alteration. Unlike agentive *-ma*, for example, it retains its high tone. (*-Ma*, derived from *man*, presumably entered the Saramaccan lexicon with high tone, as evident in its current derivant *mánu* 'husband,' but then lost it in becoming an affix.)

3.5. Rapid speech phenomena

Some of the elisions that occur in rapid Saramaccan speech are so common as to qualify as regularized contractions, occasionally even given by informants in elicited isolated sentences.

For instance, certain heavily used verbs occur quite often in shortened form: *ábi / á* 'to have,' *músu / mú* 'must,' *lóbi / ló* 'to like, to love,' *sábi / sá* 'to know,' and *táki / táa* 'to talk.' In the latter three cases, the shortened forms can be used in grammaticalized functions as well (cf. 7.3.3., 7.4.2.2., and 8.3.4.).

The definite determiner/relativizer *dí* (cf. 4.1., 4.4.) undergoes alterations in rapid speech. For example, after a word ending in [i], *dí* is reduced to a high tone on the preceding word's final syllable:

(32) De nákí̵   (< náki dí) lábu   u   mi.
      3P hit.DEF   tail   POSS 1S
      'They hit my tail.'

Also, after a word ending in [a] or a preceding occurrence of *dí*, *dí* loses its consonant and cliticizes on to the preceding syllable:

(33) A séi   mi dá-í̵   (< dá dí) dágu.
      3S sell 1S give-DEF   dog
      'He sold me to the dog.'

(34) Mi sí   kúma a   ó   gó dí   líba-í̵   (< líba dí) tá   kó.
      1S see how   3S FUT go DEF month-REL   IMF   come
      'It looks like he will leave next month.'

(35) I   lúku   í   seéi   a-í̵   (< a dí) sipéi   ó?
      2S look   2S   self   LOC-DEF   mirror INT
      'Are you looking at yourself in the mirror?'

(36) Dí-í̵   (< Dí dí) mésite   tá   lési, hɛ̃   déé   míi   tá
      when-DEF   teacher IMF   read   then DEF.PL child IMF

      woóko gó dóu.
      work   go arrive
      'While the teacher was reading, the kids kept on working.'

Andí 'what' often loses its second syllable in rapid speech:

(37) Ũ   tá   jéi   **an**   tá   pasá   a   múndu.
      2P IMF   hear   what   IMF   happen LOC world
      'You were hearing what was happening in the world.'

(38) **An**   da   dí   búnu   soní   d-u   (< dí u) mú   dú?
      what   be   DEF   good   thing REL-1P   must do
      'What is the best thing we can do?'

Note also in example (38) above that *dí*, here serving as a relative marker, fuses with the following pronoun.

In the case of *andí pasá* 'why,' there is an alternate single-word form in which the final consonant of the truncated *an* form assimilates to the initial consonant of the succeeding *pasá*:

(39) Má   sábi   **ampasá**   a   dú   ẽ.
      1S.NEG know   what.happen   3S   do   3SO
      'I don't know why he did it.'

Before future marker *ó*, first-person plural pronoun *u* tends in rapid speech to reduce to [w] and become the onset of a portmanteau morpheme [wó]:

(40) Wɛ   nɔ́ɔ, wɛ   i   sí,   fá   **wó**   bigí   alá ...
      FOC   NI   FOC   2S   see   how   1P.FUT   start yonder
      'So now, you'll see how we're going to start there...'

and second-person singular pronoun *i* often becomes a palatal glide onset yielding [jó]:

(41) Mé   sábi   ée   **jó**   sá   kái   mi   amã́jã́.
      1S.NEG know   if   2S.FUT   can   call   1S   tomorrow
      'I don't know if you can call me tomorrow.'

Deictic adverb *alá* 'yonder' is often pronounced [aá]:

(42) Mé   gó   **aá**.
      1S.NEG go   yonder
      'I'm not going there.'

(43) U   músu   gó   dóu   **aá**?
      1P   must   go   arrive yonder
      'Do we have to keep going (now that we have gone on to *that* point)?'

Given the wealth of literature on variation in creole languages charting the relationship between variation and social class or variation and access to European standard varieties, it must be noted that these contractions in Saramaccan are not conditioned by sociological factors of this kind. They are, in the present stage of the grammar, rapid speech phenomena controlled by all speakers of the language.

Chapter 4
The noun phrase

The basic constituent order of the Saramaccan noun phrase is that of English: determiner/ /quantifier – adjective – noun, with relative clauses occurring postnominally. However, demonstratives are circumnominal elements. Adjectives will be discussed in Chapter 6.

4.1. Determiners

For marking singular nouns, Saramaccan has a definite article *dí* (< *dísi* 'this,' still current) and an indefinite article *wã́* ('one').

(1) *Já   músu wási **dí** wági.*
    2S.NEG must wash DEF car
    'You don't have to wash the car.'

(2) *Ná gó sɔ́ndɔ tapá **dí** dɔ́ɔ.*
    NEG go without close DEF door
    'Don't go without closing the door.'

(3) *Mi ábi **wã́** pusipúsi.*
    1S have INDF cat
    'I have a cat.'

(4) *Méni **wã́** pusipúsi dé akí.*
    be.careful INDF cat be here
    'Careful, there's a cat here.'

As shown in the above sentences, the occurrence of the determiners is affected by referentiality; when the noun is non-referential (refers to no real-world entity), it can occur without a determiner:

(5) *Mi ná ábi dágu!*
    1S NEG have dog
    '(But) I don't *have* a dog!'

(6) *I bi bisí hẽ́pi.*
    2S PAST wear shirt
    'You put on a shirt.' (as advice or description of a generic event)

(7) *Mi á ké gó lúku film, mi wéi.*
    1S NEG want go look movie 1S tired
    'I don't want to go to a movie, I'm tired.'

However, as stated above, referentiality only affects, rather than determines, the occurrence of determiners. For one, the definite article *dí* can occur even when the referent is non-referential:

(8) Ó, andí da **dí** búnu soní dí u mú dú?
     oh what be DEF good thing REL 1P must do
     'Oh, what is the best thing that we can do?'

And then, the indefinite article *wã́* is not ungrammatical with non-referential referents, and occurs with them as often as it does not:

(9) Súku **wã́** mánu dám nɔ́?
     look.for INDF husband give.1S INT
     'Look for a husband for me?'

(10) Já fu gó bái **wã́** njũ̀njũ wági.
     2S.have NF go buy INDF new car
     'You need to buy a new car.'

Relevant here is that the informant who was the source for the sentence about the dog in (5) actually said in full *Mi ná ábi wã́ dágu ... mi ná ábi dágu!* giving the sentence with an indefinite article first, and then without it.

The plural definite determiner is *déé*, which occurs only with specific referents:

(11) Dí dí mésíte tá lési, hɛ̃́ **déé** míi tá
     when DEF teacher IMF reading, then DEF.PL child IMF

     woóko gó dóu.
     work go arrive
     'While the teacher was reading, the children continued working.'

(12) Híbi wã́ u **déé** tú sɛmbɛ ábi wã́ dágu.
     all one of DEF.PL two person have one dog
     'Each one of the two people has one dog.'

Déé is used with inanimate as well as animate references; our data do not indicate animate reference as the more likely context for *déé*:

(13) Bɛ wĩ́ ó dé wã́ u **déé** bebé amã̀jã́.
     red wine FUT be one of DEF.PL drink tomorrow
     'Red wine will be one of the drinks tomorrow.'

(14) A léi mi **déé** fóótóo.
     3S show 1S DEF.PL photo
     'He showed me the photographs.'

(15) Bóo gó nɔ́ɔ wã́ u **déé** dáka akí?
     HORT.1P go NI one of DEF.PL day here
     'Why don't we go one of these days?'

There is no plural indefinite determiner. In that English's is *some* (as in *Some cats were living under the house*), Saramaccan does have an etymological reflex, but it is used only in the partitive (cf. also section 16.4. and examples (119–121) in this chapter):

(16) Abíti mɔ́ɔ̃ mi ó jasá **só** óbo.
 a.little more 1S FUT fry some egg
 'I'll be frying some eggs in a minute.'

Só cannot be used as a plural indefinite determiner:

(17) ***Só** pusipúsi bi tá líbi a wósu básu.
 some cat PAST IMF live LOC house under
 'Some cats were living under the house.'

Other than *déé* there is one other overt grammatical marker of plurality in Saramaccan, reduplication, used with or without *déé*. Reduplication is used only when a speaker desires to highlight that a referent exists in the aggregate, usually in narratives:

(18) wáka a déé **kamíãkámíã**
 walk LOC DEF.PL place.RD
 'walk to various places'

(19) U bi sí **písípísi** fẽẽ akí kaa.
 1P PAST see home.RD POSS.3SO here CPLT
 'We saw those houses he had all over the place here.'

(A closed set of nouns referring to entities most commonly encountered in groups occur only in lexicalized reduplicated form, such as *wasiwási* 'wasp' and *mɔsimɔ́si* 'mouse' [cf. 3.1.1.4.].)

This is not an entrenched plural-marking strategy, however. Generally in the grammar, with non-specific referents (generics), plurality is left to context:

(20) Lúku búnu é! Dágu dé a mátu dé!
 look good INT dog be LOC forest there
 'Be careful! There are dogs in the woods.'

(21) Andí mbéi fóu tá síngi?
 what make bird IMF sing
 'Why do birds sing?'

(22) U bi ábi féti a dí kɔ́ndɛ; tɔkúsééi, a ábi u
 1P PAST have fight LOC DEF country nevertheless 3S have NF

 gó dóu.
 go arrive
 'We have had fights in the country; however, we have to move on.'

Plurality is unmarked, for example, with inherently plural quantifiers:

(23) Dí tjúba kaí u **téni** dáka.
 DEF rain fall for ten day
 'It rained for ten days.'

(24) **Hía** sɛmbɛ á lóbi ɛ̃.
 many person NEG like 3SO
 'Many people don't like her.'

4.2. Demonstratives

Saramaccan demonstrative adjectives occur according to three degrees of proximity, indicated with determiner *dí* before the noun and adverbials *akí* 'here,' *dɛ́* 'there,' and *alá* 'over there, yonder' after:

(25) **Dí** soní **akí** á kã́; ná tuú.
DEF thing here NEG can NEG true
'This thing can't be so; it's not true.'

(26) Mi ó tjumá **dí** wósu **akí**.
1S FUT burn DEF house here
'I am going to burn down this house.'

(27) A **dí** wósu **dɛ́** mi nángó.
LOC DEF house there 1S IMF.go
'To that house is where I am going.'

(28) **Dí** búku **alá** u mi.
DEF book yonder POSS 1S
'Yonder book is mine.'

The demonstrative adjectives are pluralized via the plural determiner:

(29) **Déé** óbo **akí** á jasá tjiká.
DEF.PL egg here NEG fry suffice
'These eggs aren't fried enough.'

(30) **Déé** wómi **alá** de bi kó a dí fésa.
DEF.PL man yonder 3P PAST come LOC DEF party
'Those are the men who came to the party.'

When the referent is both possessed and modified by a demonstrative, the possessive marker (if preposed, as opposed to postposed [cf. 4.3.]) carries the definiteness in place of the determiner:

(31) Mé sí kúma i lóbi **i** kijɔ́ɔ **dɛ́** wã́ dáka.
1S.NEG see how 2S like 2S.POSS fellow there one day
'I don't think you've ever liked that friend of yours.' (i.e. 'that your friend')

The postposed adverbials modify noun phrases as well as nominals:

(32) **Dí** sé u dí táfa **akí** sṹdju.
DEF side POSS DEF table here dirty
'This part of the table is dirty.'

(33) **Dí** óto boóko **dɛ́** da u mi.
DEF car break there be POSS 1S
'That broken car is mine.'

(34) **Dí** wómi dí mi sábi **dé** sindó.
      DEF   man   REL 1S know there sit
      'That man whom I know sat down.'

This usage of the demonstratives can also serve a discourse function, when the distal *dé* is used in an abstract sense to set one part of an utterance as removed spatially or temporally, in a pragmatic fashion untranslatable as deictically locating its noun phrase in a literal fashion (e.g. in the following sentence, the translation cannot be 'That last week'):

(35) Dí   wíki dí   bi   pasá **dé**, mé   bi   sá   peé,
      DEF week REL PAST pass there   1S.NEG   PAST can   play

      ma   nɔ́ɔ mi kó   tá   peé   báka.
      but NI   1S come IMF play again
      'Last week I couldn't play, but now I'm playing again.'

The demonstrative pronouns are *dísi* 'this one' (less often *dí akí*), *dídé* (from determiner *dí* and *dé* 'there') 'that one' (less often *dínaandé* [*naandé* 'there']), and *dialá* 'that one over there' (cf. 13.2.):

(36) Dí   páu   akí   héi   mɔ́ɔ̃   **dísi**.
      DEF tree here high more   this
      'This tree is taller than this one.'

(37) **Dídé** da dí   fíí.
      that   be DEF POSS.2S
      'That one is yours.'

4.3. Possession

The possessive pronouns are the following:

Table 19. Saramaccan possessive pronouns

1S	mí	1P	ú
2S	í	2P	ú / únu
3S	ɛ́ / hɛ́	3P	dé

Most of these forms are tonic pronouns, meaning they are segmentally identical to their corresponding subject pronouns, but are marked with high tone. However, the third-person singular possessive pronouns are exceptional: *hɛ́* is tonic but differs segmentally from the corresponding subject pronoun, and *ɛ́* is oblique (cf. 5.1.).

There is a moderately conventionalized distinction between inalienable and alienable possession. (Much of the data on this point was elicited by Suzanne Wilhite, to whom sincere thanks are appropriate.) The possessive pronouns are usually used for inalienably possessed referents:

(38) **Mí**   fútu boóko.
      1S.POSS   foot break
      'My foot is broken.'

(39) **ú**   míi
      1P.POSS   child
      'our children'

(40) **dé**   asákpáa
      3P.POSS   thigh
      'their thighs'

In the third-person singular, both the oblique and tonic pronominal forms are used in the possessive interchangeably (the former with a high tone it does not have otherwise), with no difference in meaning:

(41) A   tuúsi   **é́**   finga   gó   a   dí   baáku   déndu.
      3S   push   3S.POSS   finger   go   LOC   DEF   hole   inside
      'He pushed his finger into the hole.'

(42) Djǔsu   Djéfi   gó   mbéi   de   seeká   **hé́**   hǔjã   dě̃ẽ.
      just   Jeff   go   make   3P   care.for   3S.POSS   nail   give.3SO
      'Jeff just got his nails done.'

In the second-person plural, both tonic forms (with high tone) are used interchangeably:

(43) **ǔ**   máti
      2P.POSS   friend
      'your friend'

(44) Méni   bé   wǎ   náki   **únu**   fútu.
      be.careful   HORT   2P.NEG   hit   2P.POSS   foot
      'Be careful not to hit your (own) feet (on something).'

With an alienable possessum, a postposed prepositional phrase, consisting of (*f*)*u* 'for' as the possessive marker and a pronominal (the oblique form in the third-person singular), is usually used, with morphophonemic transformations affecting all six instances (cf. 3.3.1.):

Table 20. Fu + pronominal portmanteau morphemes

1S	u mi, u m	1P	fuu
2S	fii	2P	fuũnu
3S	fɛ̃ɛ̃	3P	u de

(45) Dí   wági   **u**   **mi**   boóko.
      DEF   car   POSS   1S   break
      'My car is broken.'

(46) Dí   táfa   **fii**   boóko.
      DEF   table   POSS.2S   break
      'Your table is broken.'

(47) Dí   móni   **u**   **de**   gũǔũ.
      DEF   money   POSS   3P   green
      'Their money is green.'

The alienability contrast is marked not only with pronouns, but also with full nouns:

(48) Djéfi   m'má
      Jeff   Mom
      'Jeff's Mom'

(49) dágu   mamá
      dog   mother
      'dog's mother'

(50) dí   kɔkɔ́ni fútu
      DEF   rabbit   foot
      'the rabbit's foot'

(51) Dí   táfa   u   Rohít   boóko.
      DEF   table   POSS   Rohit   break
      'Rohit's table is broken.'

The distinction is maintained in noun phrases that include both kinds of possession:

(52) Djéfi   mã́ũ   lánga   dí   píngo   fuu   fútu.
      Jeff   leg   long   DEF   pig   POSS.1P   foot
      'Jeff's legs are longer than our pig's legs.'

With nominal possessors, possessive marker *u* can be expressed in its source form *fu*. The variation is free, not conditioned by sound quality of the initial segment of the noun:

(53) Dísi   da   dí   búku   (f)u   Ámba / Rohít.
      this   be   DEF   book   POSS   Amba / Rohit
      'This is Amba's / Rohit's book.'

However, the alienability differentiation is a tendency rather than a rule. Informants often give examples going against the tendency, including ones semantically identical to examples conforming to it. They also readily accept such examples when presented with them, even though they may be less likely to produce them spontaneously. For example, for 'pig's mother,' informants spontaneously give:

(54) píngo   mamá
      pig   mother
      'pig's mother'

but when presented with:

(55) dí   mamá   u   dí   píngo
      DEF   mother POSS   DEF   pig

they accept it preliminarily, but if asked to compare the two, judge the latter "not as good" upon reflection, rather than rejecting it as ungrammatical. Similarly:

(56) Dí   fútu   **u**   **mi**   boóko.
      DEF   foot   POSS   1S   break
      'My foot is broken.'

(57) **Mí**   wági   boóko.
    1S.POSS   car   break
    'My car is broken.'

(58) Dí   wómi-míi   u   **mi** kabá   dí   héi   sikɔ́ɔ   a   dí
    DEF   man-child   POSS   1S   finish DEF   high   school   LOC   DEF

    jáa   akí.
    year   here
    'My son is finishing high school this year.'

(59) Mi   ké   gó   a   **mí**   njũ̌njũ   wósu.
    1S   want go   LOC   1S.POSS   new   house
    'I want to go to my new house.'

The presence of an adjectival modifier does not condition the "flouting" in the above sentence, as equivalent cases are grammatical with the postposed possessive marking:

(60) De   náki   mi   a   dí   hãso   uwíi   u   **mi**!
    3P   hit   1S   LOC   DEF   pretty   hair   POSS   1S
    'They hit my nice coiffure!' (someone being hit in the head with a ball after having their hair done)

While our data give no indication of a semantic conditioning of the "flouting," one informant stated that the use of the postposed marker in the following sentence is more narratively vivid:

(61) A   náki   dí   tatá   u   **mi**.
    3S   hit   DEF   father POSS   1S
    'He hit my father.'

A similar example may well be the following, from an emotional narrative about homesickness, in which both kinds of possessive markings are applied to the same possessum:

(62) Mi   ó   gó   dé   a   **mí**   síki   m'má   u   **mi**.
    1S   FUT   go   there LOC   1S.POSS   sick   Mom   POSS   1S
    'I'll go there to my ailing Mom.'

Since the determiners do not occur in juxtaposition with the possessive pronouns (*dí mí fútu 'the my foot,' cf. Italian *il mio piede*), the use of the plural specifier *déé* forces the use of the postposed construction regardless of alienability:

(63) Mi   ké   u   déé   míi   u   **mi** musu   dé   límbólímbo.
    1S   want NF   DEF.PL   child   POSS   1S   should be   clean.RD
    'I want my children to be clean.'

External possessor marking, in which the possessor is expressed with a separate constituent from an inalienable possessum (such as a body part) (e.g. English's *He hit me in the eye*), is largely absent, except as in English, in which it is used to a minor extent to lend narrative immediacy:

(64) I   náki   mí   fútu.
    2S   hit   1S.POSS   foot
    'You hit my foot.'

(65) A   náki   mi a   mí   fútu.
      3S hit   1S LOC   1S.POSS   foot
      'He hit me in my foot.'

To express emphasis upon the possessive pronoun, the *fu* + pronominal construction, with high tone on the pronominal, is preposed to the referent. This also cancels the alienability distinction:

(66) Méni   bé   i   á   náki   mi a   dí   *u*   *mí* fútu.
      be.careful HORT 2S NEG hit 1S LOC DEF POSS 1S foot
      'Be careful that you don't hit *my* foot.' (contrastive reading)

When the possessum is referred to pronominally as a noun phrase, it is rendered with the *fu* + pronominal expression, here used as a discrete constituent rather than as a modifier:

(67) *U*   *mí* dé   a   dí   táfa   líba.
      POSS 1S be   LOC DEF table   top
      'Mine is on the table.'

(68) *Fií*   a   dí   búku   akí   ó?
      POSS.2S   be   DEF book   here INT
      'Is this book yours?' (lit. 'Yours is this book?')

The pronominal occurs variably with the definite determiner:

(69) Í   fési   háso   mɔ́ɔ   *dí*   *u*   *mí*.
      2S.POSS face   pretty more   DEF   POSS 1S
      'Your face is prettier than mine.'

(70) Dídé   da   *dí*   *fií*.
      that   be   DEF   POSS.2S
      'That one is yours.'

(71) Mí   fútu   hɛ́   a   náki,   ná   *dí*   *fɛ̃ɛ̃*.
      1S.POSS foot 3ST   3S hit   NEG   DEF   POSS.3SO
      'He hit my foot, not his.'

These expressions are pluralized via the plural determiner:

(72) Hɛ́   da   *déé*   *u*   *mí*.
      3S   be   DEF.PL   POSS   1S
      'Those are mine.'

However, when the possessor is a nominal rather than a pronoun, the determiner does not occur:

(73) Dí   pindá   (da)   *u*   *mí*   mamá.
      DEF   peanut be   POSS   1S.POSS mother
      'The (bowl of mashed) peanut is my mother's.'

(Cf. 12.1.4. for demonstration of irregularities in nonverbal predicative expressions conditioned by possessive pronominals when in the form of separate arguments.)

4.4. Relative clauses

Relative clauses are postnominal, and marked by the relativizers *dí* for singular heads and *déé* for plural ones (*dí* has a wide range of functions in the grammar; cf. 4.1., 4.2.):

(74) dí   mujéε   **dí**   tá   bebé   buúu
      DEF   woman   REL   IMF   drink   blood
      'the woman who sucks blood'

(75) Dí   wómi   **dí**   mi   sábi   sindó.
      DEF   man   REL   1S   know   sit
      'The man I know sat down.'

(76) Déé   wómi   **déé**   mi   sábi   sindó.
      DEF.PL   man   REL.PL   1S   know   sit
      'The men I know sat down.'

The relativizers are obligatorily expressed except with obliques (see below): *dí wómi mi sábi 'the man that I know.'

4.4.1. The accessibility hierarchy

The examples above show relativization of subject and object. In terms of the accessibility hierarchy of relativization – subject / object / indirect object / oblique / possessor – indirect objects relativize easily. Indirect objects can be relativized from dative-alternation constructions with ditransitives (cf. 10.2.1.):

(77) Dí   wómi   **dí**   mi dá   dí   jási   kó   kéndi.
      DEF   man   REL   1S give DEF   jacket   come   warm
      'The man I gave the jacket got warm.'

while with verbs that mark arguments for the dative overtly, this is not with an adposition, but with serial use of the verb *dá* 'give,' which stays in place:

(78) Dí   wómi   **dí**   mi mandá dí   bíífi   dá   ø   kεέ   dí   a
      DEF   man   REL   1S send   DEF   letter   give   cry   when   3S
      lési   ε̃.
      read   3SO
      'The man I sent the letter to cried when he read it.'

However, at the next step on the hierarchy, obliques, relativization requires a resumptive pronoun:

(79) Dí   wósu   dí   mi   tá   líbi   **nε̃ε̃**   hãso   téé.
      DEF   house   REL   1S   IMF   live   LOC.3SO pretty   very
      'The house I live in is really pretty.'

(80) Mi ké u bái dí sutúu dí a bi sindó **nɛ̃ɛ̃**
1S want NF buy DEF chair REL 3S PAST sit LOC.3S.POSS

déndu.
inside
'I want to buy the chair that he sat in.'

(81) Dí wómi dí mi ku ɛ̃ gó fɛ́ɛɛ.
DEF man REL 1S with 3SO go afraid
'The man I went with is afraid.'

(82) Dí matjáu dí mi tá kóti údu ku ɛ̃ boóko.
DEF axe REL 1S IMF cut wood with 3SO break
'The axe I chop wood with is broken.'

It is possible to elicit relativized obliques without pronoun retention, but only with great effort, and with informants gifted with a natural "sense of language" and especially comfortable with Dutch and/or English. It is questionable that such sentences qualify as genuine constructions of the language (they also do not occur in any of our recordings of running speech):

(83) Dídé da dí táfa básu dí mi tjubí té mí háti
that be DEF table under REL 1S hide when 1S.POSS heart

tá boónu.
IMF burn
'That's the table I hide under when I'm angry.'

The relativizer *dí* is optionally omissible with obliques:

(84) Mi á wã̌ baási mí né sikífi nɛ̃ɛ̃.
1S have INDF balloon 1S.POSS name write LOC.3SO
'I have a balloon with my name written on it.'

(85) Dí wómi mi ku ɛ̃ gó fɛ́ɛɛ.
DEF man 1S with 3SO go afraid
'The man I went with is afraid.'

At the tail end of the relativization hierarchy, possessors relativize with the possessor rendered in a paratactic relationship with the possessum and its relative clause:

(86) Hɛ̃́ da dí wómi dé né **dí** mé sá méni.
3S be DEF man there name REL 1S.NEG can remember
'That's the man whose name I can't remember.'

This, too, is a sentence type only given upon elicitation, and even then, with a certain unmistakeable air of indulgence on the part of the informant. Most readily, for relativized possessors, informants render the possessum argument of the relative clause as a topic:

(87) Dí   mujéɛ-míi   u   dí   wómi   dɛ́,   hɛ̃́   mi   bósi   a
    DEF   woman-child   POSS   DEF   man   there   3ST   1S   kiss   LOC

   dí   ndéti   pasá   akí.
   DEF   night   past   here
   'That's the man whose daughter I kissed last night.' (lit. 'The man there's daughter, it was her I kissed last night.')

Similarly, sentences in which in English a nonverbal predicate head is relativized (e.g. *That is the man that I sit on*) are usually rendered otherwise in Saramaccan. Saramaccan often renders the head of what would be the relative clause in English as a topic, followed by a comment with a resumptive pronoun:

(88) Déé   wómi   alá,   de   bi   kó   a   dí   fésa.
    DEF.PL   man   yonder   3P   PAST   come   LOC   DEF   party
    'Those are the men who came to the party.'

In such cases with obliques, what in English is the subordinate clause verb is, as in the core argument cases, a matrix verb, and its verb-phrase—internal argument is fronted along with its oblique markers:

(89) Dí   wómi   dɛ́   líba   mi   tá   sindó.
    DEF   man   there   top   1S   IMF   sit
    'That's the man I sit on.'

(90) A   dí   wósu   dɛ́   mi   nángó.
    LOC   DEF   house   there   1S   IMF.go
    'That's the house I go to.'

(91) Dí   wósu   dɛ́   nɛ̃ɛ̃́   báka   de   bi   tá   bósi.
    DEF   house there   LOC.3S.POSS   back   3P   PAST   IMF   kiss
    'That's the house that they kissed in back of.'

4.4.2. Headless relatives

In headless relatives, the referent is usually expressed with the corresponding wh-word.
   When the referent is 'what,' then the item is *andí* 'what,' alternately rendered as the head of a relative clause as *andí dí*:

(92) Lúku   **andí**   i   dú!
    look   what   2S   do
    'Look at what you did!'

(93) Ũ   tá   jéi   **andí**   tá   pasá   a   múndu.
    2P   IMF   hear   what   IMF   happen   LOC   world
    'You were hearing what was going on in the world.'

(94) Dí   a   tooná   kó,   hɛ̃́   a   léi   **andí**   **dí**   a   bái.
    when   3S   return come   then   3S   show   what   REL   3S   buy
    'When he came back, he showed all the things he bought.'

Andí ku andí is a variant:

(95) Dí   a   tooná   kó,   hɛ̃́   a   léi   **andí**   **ku**   **andí**   (**dí**)   a   bái.
     when   3S   return   come then 3S   show   what   with   what   REL   3S   buy
     'When he came back, he showed all the things he bought.'

Other headless relatives similarly use the corresponding wh-word:

(96) Wá   sábi   **ambé**   ábɛ̃ɛ̃.
     1P.NEG   know   who   have.3SO
     'We don't know who owns it.'

(97) Mi   á   lóbi   **ambé**   mi   sí.
     1S   NEG   like   who   1S   see
     'I don't like who I see.'

(98) Má   sábi   **andí**   mbéi   a   dú   ɛ̃.
     1S.NEG   know   what   make   3S   do   3SO
     'I don't understand why he did that.'
     (also *andí pasá* [*pasá* 'happen'] *a dú ɛ̃*)

Only with locative headless relatives is an item other than the wh-word used, *ká* (rather than interrogative *naásé*):

(99) Nɔ́ɔ   **ká**   a   dé   alá,   ée   a   náki   máku,   nɔ́ɔ   né   fɛ̃ɛ̃
     NI   where   3S   be   yonder   if   3S   hit   mosquito   NI   name   POSS.3SO

     ó   pói.
     FUT   spoil
     'Where she was, if she smacked the mosquito it would ruin her reputation.'

(*Ká* is also used with locational adverbial complements; cf. 9.2.3.3.)

4.5. Quantifiers

'Many' or 'a lot of' is *híla*, or its alternate form *hía*:

(100) **Híla**   pusipúsi   dé   akí.
      many   cat   be   here
      'There are a lot of cats here.'

(101) **Híla**   wági   dé   akí.
      many   car   be   here
      'There are a lot of cars here.'

(102) **Hía**   sɛmbɛ   á   lóbi   ɛ̃.
      many   person   NEG   like   3SO
      'Many people don't like her.'

(103) De á **hía** dágu a dí mátu.
 3P NEG.have many dog LOC DEF forest
 'There aren't too many dogs in the woods.'

The item can also occur as a verb, in which case it occurs after the noun:

(104) Méni, pɛndémbéti **híla** akí.
 be.careful jaguar many here
 'Careful, there are a lot of jaguars here.'

The mass/count distinction does not affect the grammaticality of the item's occurrence (cf. English *many peas*, *many water):

(105) Dí bási ábi **hía** mɔ́ni.
 DEF boss have many money
 'The boss has a lot of money.'

As in many languages, 'little' in the sense of 'a few of' in Saramaccan is not expressed with a lexical item or discrete expression, but via negation, i.e. 'not' + [verb] or 'not much of' (cf. a similar trait in comparative constructions; 6.5.4.):

(106) Mɛ́ mbéi **híla** mɔ́ni tidé.
 1S.NEG make many money today
 'I didn't make a lot of money today.'

'All (of)' is *híi* when preposed to the referent:

(107) De bujá ku dé seéi **híi** ndéti.
 3P argue with 3P self all night
 'They argue with each other all night.'

(108) **Híi** mí síkii mũnjã́.
 all 1S.POSS body wet
 'I'm all wet.'

(109) Mi bi ké u **híi** ũ tú kó akí.
 1S PAST want NF all 2P two come here
 'I wanted both of you to come here too.'

However, 'all (of)' is also rendered with postposed *túu*:

(110) a déé kamíã **túu**
 LOC DEF.PL place all
 'in all the places'

This occurs obligatorily when it would be impossible for the quantifier to be preposed to its referent because the referent is encliticized to its host, as in the case of the third-person singular object pronoun after a verb:

(111) I njã́mɛ̃ **túu**.
 2S eat.3SO all
 'You ate it all.'

or in conventionalized constructions such as:

(112) Mi ábi de fɔ́ **túu**.
       1S have 3P four all
       'I have all four of them.'

The concepts of 'everything' and 'everybody' are expressed with *híi* + *soní* 'thing' and *sɛmbɛ* 'person':

(113) Nɔ́ɔ **híi soní** nángó búnu.
       NI all thing IMF.go good
       'So everything was going well.'

(Cf. alternate form *híi soní túu* demonstrating word order conditioning of 'all [of].')

(114) Té a fã nɔ́ɔ **híi sɛmbɛ** tá háika ɛ̃.
       when 3S talk NI all person IMF listen 3SO
       'When he talks, everybody listens to him.'

'Each' or 'every':

(115) **Híbi** wã́ / **híi** wã́ / **híni** wã́ sɛmbɛ ábi u sólúgu
       all one / all one / all one person have NF care.for

       dá dé seéi.
       give 3P self
       'Everyone has to care for themselves.'

(116) Dí wági akí músu wási **híbi** wã́ wíki.
       DEF car here must wash all one week
       'This car has to be washed every week.'

(*Híbi* and *híni* apparently occur only with *wã́*; *híi* is of more general occurrence.)
    'So many':

(117) Akí **sɔ́méni** mbéti píi.
       here so.many animal quiet
       'So many animals are laying quiet (i.e. killed).'

Here and *ṹ méni* 'how many' (cf. 11.2.) notwithstanding, *méni* alone cannot connote 'many'; rather, it is a verb meaning 'think' or 'be careful (mind).'

    'Both of' is rendered as 'they two' + [noun]:

(118) De tú sɛmbɛ, kandé de ábi dí fɔ́útu.
       3P two person may.be 3P have DEF mistake
       'It could be that both of them have the mistake.'

'Some (of)' (the partitive) is rendered with *só*, invariant according to the mass/count distinction:

(119) Abíti mɔ́ɔ̃ mi ó jasá **só** óbo.
a.little more 1S FUT fry some egg
'I'll be frying some eggs in a minute.'

(120) Lénim **só** mɔ́ni.
lend.1S some money
'Lend me some money.'

(121) **só** u dí njãnjã́
some of DEF food
'some of the food'

'Some' is also expressed, in the meaning of 'a few,' with *wã́lɔ*:

(122) **Wã́lɔ** sɛmbɛ kumútu téé a Saaná gó lúku dí bási.
some person exit all.the.way LOC Surinam go look DEF boss
'Some people came all the way from Surinam to see the boss.'

Also, *(h)áfu* (< *half*) is used to refer not only to a half, but to an unspecified subset:

(123) I sá tjái **háfu** wáta kó dá mi nɔ́?
2S can carry half water come give 1S INT
'Could you please bring me some water?'

'A little bit of' is *pikí sɔ́* ('little so'), or alternately *abíti*, *wã́ pikí sɔ́* (cf. 6.5.2.), or *sɔ́ wã́ pikí*:

(124) Mi njã́ wã́ háfu fóu ku **pikí sɔ́** batáta.
1S eat INDF half bird with little so sweet.potato
'I ate half of a bird with some sweet potatoes.'

'Enough' is expressed not with a nominal quantifier as in English, but with a verb used as the second in a serial verb construction, translating as 'suffice' (cf. 8.5.2.):

(125) I ábi njãnjã́ **tjiká** ɔ́?
2S have food suffice INT
'Do you have enough food?'

(126) Mɛ́ ábi mɔ́ni **tjiká**.
1S.NEG have money suffice
'I didn't have enough money.'

4.6. Coordination

The coordination marker for nouns is *ku* 'with':

(127) I   sá   bebé   té, sukuáti, **ku**   wĩ,   ma   ná   dãã́.
       2S   can   drink tea chocolate with   wine but NEG rum
       'You can drink tea, chocolate, and wine, but not rum.'

(128) Mi tá   sindó a   Susanne **ku**   Marvin míndi.
       1S IMF sit   LOC Susanne with   Marvin between
       'I am sitting between Susanne and Marvin.'

'Or' is (*ée*) *náá* (*só*) 'if not so':

(129) Ée i   ké,   i   sá   njã́   mbéti **náá** (**só**) físi.
       if 2S want 2S can eat   meat   or   fish
       'If you want, you can eat meat or fish.'

(130) Mamá   **ée náá só**   tatá?
       mother or   father
       'Mother or father?'

'Either ... or' is *náá ... náá*:

(131) I   sá   njã́   **náá** mbéti **náá** físi.
       2S can eat   or   meat   or   fish
       'You can eat either meat or fish.'

but, as in English, can also be conveyed with the 'or' word alone:

(132) Mi sí   kúma a   bái   búku **ée náá só** pɔtɔlɔ́tɔ.
       1S see how   3S   buy   book or   pencil
       'I think he bought either books or pencils.'

4.7. Gerunds

Deverbal nominals can be marked by definite article *dí*:

(133) A   léi   (**dí**) **sṹ**   tjiká   a   kó   sábi andí a   tá   dú.
       3S learn DEF   swim   suffice   3S come know what 3S IMF do
       'He learned how to swim (he learned swimming) enough to end up knowing what he was doing (i.e. get the hang of it).'

The definite article is required when the action denoted by the nominal has an overt subject:

(134) Gã́ã́tã́ngi   fu   **dí** i   **lúku** dí   míi   dá   mi.
       thank.you for DEF   2S look   DEF child give 1S
       'Thank you for looking after my children.'

4.8. Adjective + *wá* 'one'

When a noun phrase identifies the bearer of a property, then as in English, 'one' (*wá*) is used as a nominal head:

(135) Hḗ   da dí   mɔ́ɔ̃   **lánga** **wá** a   u   déndu.
      3S   be DEF more tall   one   LOC   1P   inside
      'He is the tallest one among us.'

This nominalization marking does not occur, however, with demonstrative pronouns:

(136) Dí   búku akí   u   mí,   dídé   (***wá***) fíi.
      DEF   book here POSS   1S   that   POSS.2S
      'This book is mine, that one is yours.'

Chapter 5
Personal pronouns

5.1. Pronominal inventory

Saramaccan pronouns are distributed according to a basic six-way split between person and number.

Table 21. Saramaccan pronouns

	TONIC	SUBJECT	OBLIQUE
1S	mí	mi, m	
2S	í	i	
3S	hɛ́̃	a	ɛ̃
1P	ú	u	
2P	ṹ, únu	ũ, únu	únu
3P	dé	de	

There is one exclusively oblique pronoun, third-person singular ɛ̃:

(1)   *A   náki   ɛ̃.*
      3S   hit   3SO
      'He hit him.'

In the second-person plural, in our data (both elicited and spontaneous) either *ũ* or *únu* are possible in subject position although the former is more common; however, in the oblique, only *únu* occurs:

(2)   *Ũ   kóni.*
      2P   smart
      'You are smart.'

(3)   ***Únu***   *lúku   ṹ   seéi   a   dí   sipéi.*
      2P   look   2P   self   LOC   DEF   mirror
      'You look at yourselves in the mirror.'

(4)   *Mi   sá   kó   lúku   **únu**   tidé   ó?*
      1S   can   come   look   2PO   today   INT
      'Can I come visit you today?'

These forms are classified as oblique in that they can be used not only as direct objects but also as indirect objects and objects of prepositions:

(5)   *Léni   ɛ̃   só   móni.*
      lend   3SO   some   money
      'Lend him some money.'

(6) Mi   bi   tá   poobá u   dá   kái   **únu**.
     1S   PAST IMF   try   NF give   call   2PO
     'I was trying to call you.'

(7) Mí   fútu hḗ   a   náki, ná   dí   **fɛ̰́ɛ̰́**.   (< fu ɛ̰́)
     1S.POSS   foot 3ST 3S hit   NEG DEF   POSS.3SO
     'He hit my foot, not his.'

In Saramaccan, oblique forms are also required under coordination; subject forms are ungrammatical:

(8) mi ku   ɛ̃   / *a
     1S with 3SO   /   3S
     'me and him / her'

(9) Mi ku   **únu** músu gó a   Saaná.
     1S with 2PO   must go LOC Surinam
     'Me and you have to go to Surinam.'

The second-person plural pronoun can be used with a single addressee to convey respect, although this is in no way as socially conventionalized as in many European languages.

Most of the pronouns have tonic forms identical to the subject ones but distinguished by high tone; in the third-person singular, however, there is a distinct tonic form hḗ.

(10) Mí, dísi.
     1S   this
     'It's me.' (i.e. 'This is me talking to you.')

(11) A   táa   '**Hḗ**!' / *a.
     3S   talk 3ST   /   3S
     'He said 'Him!'.'

(12) Móni,   **hḗ**   / *a   mi ké.
     money   3ST   /   3S   1S want
     'It's money I want.' (i.e. 'Money, it, I want.')

On first- and second-person pronouns and the third-person plural pronoun, various distinctions are marked by high tone: possessive (cf. 4.3.), tonicity (cf. discussion above), and reflexive (along with the reflexive pronoun seéi 'self') (cf. 5.5.). For purposes of clarity in interpretation, glossing of pronouns in examples sometimes explicitly codes functional distinctions (such as possessive) that are not associated with distinct forms.

5.2. Clitic status

5.2.1. Third-person singular oblique ɛ̃

Third-person singular oblique pronoun ɛ̃ is rendered as a clitic under the morphophonemic rule stipulating that it causes assimilation with a preceding [a] or [ɛ] and yields a long (or bisyllabic) lax mid vowel (cf. 3.3.4. for further coverage of the morphophonemics of ɛ̃):

/paká ẽ/ > [pakẽ́ẽ] 'pay him'
/túwɛ ẽ/ > [túwẽ̃ẽ] 'throw him'

(13) A biẽ́ẽ   gó   a   básu.   (< biá ẽ)
     3S turn.3SO go   LOC bottom
     'He turned it upside-down.'

(14) Hẽ́   a   butẽ́ẽ   a   dí   táfa   líba.   (< butá ẽ)
     then 3S put.3SO   LOC DEF table   top
     'Then he put it on the table.'

Note from the above examples that the morphophonemic rule is not sensitive to tone, occurring with both high-tone and low-tone final syllables. With other vowels, the rule does not apply:

bebé ẽ 'drink it'
subí ẽ 'climb it'
sindó ẽ 'sit on it'
sɔ́tɔ ẽ 'lock it'
tjɔkó ẽ 'prick it'
lúku ẽ 'look at it'

5.2.2. First-person singular *m*

First-person singular *mi* can occur as *m*:

(15) Mi bi   ó   wái   ée **m** bi   sá   féni   wã́   kámba.
     1S PAST FUT happy   if 1S   PAST can   find   INDF   room
     'I'd be happy if I found a room.'

(16) **M** sá   hái!
     1S   UFUT haul
     'I'll pull!'

Its cliticized status is apparent in that when occurring as an internal argument it sandhis with the preceding verb:

(17) Lénim   só   mɔ́ni.   >   Léní   **ṁ** só   mɔ́ni
     lend.1S   some money
     'Lend me some money.'

M is primarily a rapid speech phenomenon, in that even in rapid speech it occurs only variably, and would never be spontaneously offered by an informant as a translation of 'I.' When used as an object, it usually occurs with verbs of transfer, a high-frequency context in which phonetic elision is especially likely. The above sentence is an example. Pointedly, it is with core transfer verb *dá* 'give' that object *m* occurs the most – i.e. virtually regularly in unmonitored speech:

(18) Súku   wã́   mánu   dám   nɔ́?
     look.for INDF husband give.1S   INT
     '(Could you) look for a husband for me?'

5.3. Second-person singular *ju*

Sources such as Voorhoeve (1961) and others have posed *ju* as an alternate tonic second-person singular pronoun. However, this is not confirmed by our data. Rather, *ju* occurs as a variant of *i*, in not only tonic but atonic, non-emphatic contexts (and neither is it indexed to formality):

(19) A mɔ́ɔ̃ bétɛ dá ju, ée i wási dí wági.
      3S more advisable give 2S if 2S wash DEF car
      'It would be better for you, if you wash the car.'

(20) Mí wɛ tá fã ku i / ju.
      1S FOC IMF talk with 2S / 2S
      'It's *me* talking to you.'

Our data suggest that *ju* is an interference from Sranan. Saramaccan is a sister language to Sranan, its grammar as similar to Sranan's as Portuguese is to Spanish. Since Sranan is the vernacular lingua franca of Surinam, many Saramaccan speakers (including all of our informants) also speak it. Inevitably, then, Sranan influence from such speakers has percolated into Saramaccan itself, such that a "pure" Saramaccan is an abstract idealization rather than a reality. In elicitation sessions, Saramaccan speakers often discuss with one another whether a given item is Saramaccan or Sranan, and regardless of the verdicts in each individual case, it is clear that "bleeding" from Sranan is a regular aspect of real-life usage of Saramaccan.

In our data, *ju* qualifies as an example of this. It is a borrowing from Sranan, used in occasional free variation with Saramaccan's *i*.

Crucially, one sentence in our data in which *ju* is used tonically is one in which Sranan influence is unequivocal. The first word in the sentence below, *na*, would be incoherent in Saramaccan in which it would mean 'not.' However, in Sranan, *na* is the affirmative copula, cognate to Saramaccan's *da* (cf. 12.1.; Sranan's negated equative copula is not *na*, but *ano*):

(21) Na jú ó lúku dí wɛ́kɛ.
      be 2S FUT look DEF store
      'It's *you* who is going to look after the store.'

5.4. Pleonastic pronoun

The pleonastic pronoun is third-person singular *a*, whose omission in such cases is ungrammatical:

(22) *(A) kéndi / kɔ́tɔ.
       3S   warm / cold
       'It's hot / cold.'

5.5. Reflexives

The reflexive is formed with *seéi* 'self,' or its alternate form *seépi*. The pronominal element is tonic in the reflexive, except that in the third-person singular, the exclusively oblique form is optionally used as well (*ɛ̃ seéi* 'him/her/itself'):

(23) *Mi lúku mí seéi a dí sipéi.*
 1S look 1S self LOC DEF mirror
 'I look at myself in the mirror.'

(24) *Mi kóti dí mbéti mí seépi.*
 1S cut DEF meat 1S self
 'I cut the meat myself.'

(25) *I lúku i seéi a dí sipéi ó?*
 2S look 2S self LOC DEF mirror INT
 'Are you looking at yourself in the mirror?'

(26) *Ú lúku ű seéi a dí sipéi.*
 2P look 2P self LOC DEF mirror
 'You looked at yourselves in the mirror.'

(27) *A ndéti u nángó wási ú seéi a lío.*
 LOC night 1P IMF.go wash 1P self LOC river
 'At night we go wash ourselves in the river.'

As in English, the reflexive is also used as an equivalent to focusing the subject to highlight their agency:

(28) *Mí seéi ó bói ẽ.*
 1S self FUT cook 3SO
 'I will cook it myself.'

Bare object pronouns cannot have reflexive reading in reference to the subject of the clause they occur in:

(29) *John$_i$ wasi ẽ$_{*i,j}$.*
 John wash 3SO
 'John washed him(*self).'

Reflexive reading within the clause requires reflexive marking:

(30) *A téi wã fóótóo fẽẽ seéi.*
 3S take INDF photo for.3SO self
 'He took a picture of himself.'

Only across a clause boundary can a bare object pronoun be interpreted, optionally, as reflexive (as in English):

(31) *John$_i$ bi ké u Mary náki ẽ$_{i,j}$.*
 John PAST want NF Mary hit 3SO
 'John wanted Mary to hit him.' ('him' = either John or another man)

Unlike many creoles, Saramaccan does not use the word for 'body' as a reflexive marker. *Síkíi* is not used reflexively. For example, *náki mí síkíi* cannot mean 'hit myself,' but only conveys an idiomatic phrase translating literally as 'hit my body':

(32) Mi wási mí síkíi ku sópu.
    1S wash 1S.POSS body with soap
    'I wash my body.'

(33) Mi náki mí síkíi (taánga).
    1S hit 1S.POSS body strong
    'I worked hard.'

5.6. Reciprocals

Reciprocals are expressed with *seéi* as well:

(34) Awáa de kó lóbi dé seéi.
    at.last 3P come like 3P self
    'They came to like one another.'

(35) De bujá ku dé seéi híi ndéti.
    3P argue with 3P self all night
    'They argue with each other all night.'

(36) De féífi dé seéi hǔjã.
    3P paint 3P self nail
    'They paint each other's nails.'

Chapter 6
Adjectives

6.1. Definition of adjectival class

When used attributively, property items in Saramaccan occur before the noun:

(1) U   ó   bebé   **bɛ**   wí   amã́jã́.
     1P   FUT drink red   wine tomorrow
     'We will drink red wine tomorrow.'

(2) A   dé wã́   **súti** soní.
     3S be INDF   sweet   thing
     'It is a good thing.'

However, when used as predicates, property items behave as verbs, specifically intransitive stative verbs. For example, rather than occurring after a *be*-verb that carries the sentence's tense and aspect, they take tense and aspect markers themselves, like verbs (cf. 7.2., 7.3.).

(3) Ée   i   njã́ dí   soní   akí, i   **ó**   (*dé) síki.
     if   2S   eat DEF thing here 2S FUT   be   sick
     'If you eat this thing, you will get sick.'

(4) Ée   ná   mi **bi** síki, mi bi   ó   gó a   wowójo.
     if   NEG 1S PAST   sick   1S PAST FUT go LOC market
     'If I weren't sick, I would go to the market.' (recall that *bi* is a past marker and not a form of 'be')

Just as imperfective marker *tá* encodes the inchoative with stative verbs (cf. 7.3.1.):

(5) Mi   **tá** lóbi de.
     1S   IMF   love 3P
     'I am coming to love them.'

it also encodes this meaning with property item predicates:

(6) Mi   **tá** síki.
     1S   IMF   sick
     'I'm getting sick.'

Predicate property items also demonstrate their verbal status in occurring in a focusing construction involving predicate cleft with copy, which occurs only with verbs (other constituents when focused do not leave a copy; cf. 15.1.):

(7) Nɔ́nɔ, **jéi**   mi **jéi**   dí   a   tá   kó.
     no   hear   1S hear   REL   3S IMF   come
     'No, I *hear* him coming.'

(8) Wɛ   nɔɔ   dí   tɛ̋   dé,   de   bi   sábi   kaa   táa   **dédɛ**
     FOC   NI   DEF   time   there 3P   PAST   know   CPLT   COMP   dead

   a   **dédɛ**.
   3S dead
   'At that time, they knew that he was dead.' (Aboikoni and Glock 1997: 1)

Predicate property items also occur in serial verb constructions, serving as main verbs modified by grammaticalized ones, such as *dá* 'give' which in serial constructions is Saramaccan's benefactive marker (cf. 8.3.1.):

(9) Andí   súti   dá   i   sɔ́?
     what   sweet   give   2S   so
     'What's so funny?' (lit. 'What is so sweet to you?')

It would appear that we could say that property items occur as adjectives when used attributively and as stative verbs when used as predicates. However, certain constructions allow a more precise definition.

For one, when a predicate property item is fronted, it leaves behind *dé* 'to be' in its place, whose occurrence would be ungrammatical if the verb were not fronted:

(10) Ű   bígi   dí   wósu   **dɛ́**?
     how   big   DEF   house   be
     'How big is the house?' (Kramer 2001: 36)

(11) *Dí   wósu   **dɛ́**   bígi.
      DEF   house   be   big
      'The house is big.'

This means that when fronted, property items depart from the verbal class, becoming nonverbal predicates like adjectives in European (and other) languages.

Then, when property items occur as complements to predicates, such as perception verbs, they do not exhibit verbal behavior, and again behave as adjectives:

(12) I   ó   gó   a   wooko amãjá̋   ée   i   fíi   síki   ɔ́?
     2S   FUT   go   LOC   work tomorrow if   2S   feel   sick   INT
     'Will you go to work tomorrow if you feel sick?'

(13) I   lúku   hã́so.
     2S   look   pretty
     'You look pretty.'

This shows that property items do not occur as verbs when they are arguments within the predicate.

A descriptive statement, then, is that property items in Saramaccan behave as intransitive stative verbs when they are predicate *heads that are not fronted*, and as adjectives elsewhere. The predicate can also be a secondary one:

(14) A   kumútu   a   dí   wósu   dɔɔ́ngɔ.
     3S   exit   LOC   DEF   house   drunk
     'He came out of the house drunk.'

(15) Mi féífi dí wósu bɛ.
1S paint DEF house red
'I painted the house red.'

One item varies suppletively according to attributive and predicative occurrence: 'big' is *gã́ã́* when attributive and *bígi* when predicative:

(16) Úndi (andí) da dí **gã́ã́** fóto a Kirghizstan?
which what be DEF big capital LOC Kirghizstan
'What is the capital of Kirghizstan?'

(17) Ée a **bígi** seéi, ma á taánga.
if 3S big self but 3S.NEG strong
'Even though he is big, he is not strong.'

6.2. Adjectives and reduplication

The semantics of property item reduplication in Saramaccan are almost impossible to identify via sentential elicitations alone. The function of reduplication in this domain is conditioned by an interaction between verbal *Aktionsart* and pragmatics, of a sort that speakers are no more consciously aware than English speakers are of what determines whether one says *I will go tomorrow*, *I'm going tomorrow*, or *I go tomorrow*. As such, fieldwork in Surinam by Marvin Kramer was crucial to this section and section 6.4. (cf. Kramer 2001: 22–80). Sentences from Kramer (2001) are cited with "K" followed by the page number.

When reduplicated, property items' connotation is not intensified, but rendered counterexpectational. In contrast to the neutral usage of *boóko* 'broken' in the following sentence:

(18) Bigá dí wági u mi **boóko**, hɛ̃ mi téi dí bus.
because DEF car POSS 1S break then 1S take DEF bus
'Because my car is broken, I am taking the bus.'

in the sentence below, the reduplication of *boóko* conveys that the broken bottle shards are an unusual phenomenon requiring special attention:

(19) Kɔ́ni dí **boókobóóko** báta dé.
be.careful DEF break.RD bottle there
'Be careful of that broken bottle.' (K44)

When reduplicated property items occur as predicates, they occur after *dé* 'be' and thus are adjectives rather than stative verbs:

(20) Dí sutúu dé **boókobóóko**.
DEF chair be break.RD
'The chair is broken.'

An informant gave this sentence in warning one of the authors that the dining room table chair that he was about to sit on was rickety for the time being; i.e. in counterexpectational fashion.

Kramer (2001), on the basis of his experiences in a Saramaccan village, gives the example of:

(21) dɛɛ́dɛ́ɛ́   físi
      dry.RD   fish
      'dry fish' (K41)

which referred to fish that had been dried contrary to usual custom, in contrast to other fish varieties normally dried.

The counterexpectational aspect of the semantics can also be quite moderate, rooted in fine-grained pragmatic aspects of experience. For example, in:

(22) Mi ké   u   déé   míi   u   mi musu dé **límbólímbo**.
      1S want NF   DEF.PL   child POSS   1S should be clean.RD
      'I want my children to be clean.'

the reduplication is motivated by the implication that there is an alternate contrasting possibility, undesired, that the children would not be clean. Similarly, in:

(23) I, dɔɔ́ngɔ́dɔ́ɔ́ngɔ nɔ́ɔmɔ   i   tá   dé.
      2S drunk.RD   always 2S   IMF   be
      'You're just a total drunk.'

the reduplication indicates that the person in question is constantly drunk, counterexpectationally to the normal case in which drunkenness is an occasional state.

6.3. Irregularities in reduplication of property items

The counterexpectational denotation of reduplication of property items has led to irregularities in a few cases.

Búnu 'good' denotes goodness in a general sense, while the reduplicated form *bumbúu* is a separate lexical item denoting 'good' in the sense of 'all right' or 'proper.'

(24) Kobí   da   wã̂   (mɔ́ɔ̃) **búnu** dáta   mɔ́ɔ̃   Ámba.
      Kobi   be   INDF   more   good   doctor more   Amba
      'Kobi is a better doctor than Amba.'

(25) Dídé   **búnu**.
      that   good
      'That one is good.' (i.e. verdict that a proposed Saramaccan sentence is grammatical in contrast to some previous renditions that were not)

(26) Dí   wómi   dé   **bumbúu**   sɛmbɛ,   dídé.
      DEF   man   there good.RD   person   that
      'That man is a good person.' (i.e. 'good guy')

Informants allow *búnu sɛmbɛ* only with hesitation, and never produce it. The reduplicated form is not conditioned by pragmatics, but is a lexicalized item (indicated in part by its phonetic distortion from its presumed source *búnubúnu*). Its meaning is used in various expressions in which unreduplicated *búnu* would be ungrammatical, such as:

(27) Mi bi a dí **bumbúu** nɔ́bu.
    1S PAST LOC DEF good.RD number
    'I got the right number (on the phone).'

The semantics of *bumbúu* can be assumed to be rooted in an initial sense of goodness in a counterexpectational sense; i.e. remarking that someone is a good person in implicational acknowledgment that not all people are good. However, goodness and its degrees and shades is central enough to human experience that the item has evolved into a separate lexical entry from *búnu*, connoting 'right' or 'okay.'

Some property items occur only in reduplicated form, such as *njũnjũ* 'new' (there exists no word *njũ). This is likely due to the fact that newness is inherently salient – that is, counterexpectational – such that it was subject to reduplication so consistently that the reduplicated form became conventionalized as the sole one:

(28) Dí ósu u mi bi dé **njũnjũ**, nɔ́unɔ́u a kó gaándi.
    DEF house POSS 1S PAST be new   now   3S come old
    'My house used to be new, but now it's getting old.'

(29) Já fu gó bái wã̌ **njũnjũ** wági.
    2S.have NF go buy INDF new car
    'You need to buy a new car.'

Similar is *kúakúa* 'raw,' again an inherently counterexpectational trait. Informants reject *kúa* (one immediately said it was "too short"). Yet an item on the margins of the language, *kúa uwíi gũũũ* 'aqua' (lit. 'raw leaf green') (Aboikoni and Glock 1997: 68, cited in K48), indicates that this is a conventionalization of an item that once occurred unreduplicated.

With a few other items, the reduplicated form no longer encodes counterexpectational semantics, such as *tuú* 'true':

(30) Dí wóto akí **tuú**.
    DEF story here true
    'This story is true.'

The attributive form occurs only reduplicated, but has a neutral connotation:

(31) Mi ó kondá wã̌ **tuútuu** wóto dá i.
    1S FUT tell INDF true.RD story give 2S
    'I am going to tell you a true story.'

such that the reduplicated form used after *dé* 'be' is semantically identical to the unreduplicated predicate:

(32) Dí óto dé **tuútuu**, dídé ɔ́?
    DEF story be true.RD that INT
    'Is that story true?'

This has likely happened because the semantics of 'true' are inherently counterexpectational; to designate something as true is to contrast it with a tacit awareness that mendacity is sadly common. *Wái* 'to be happy' is a like case:

(33) Mi **wái** táa i kó.
    1S happy COMP 2S come
    'I'm glad you came.'

(34) A bi dé súti, **wáíwái** soní.
    3S PAST be sweet happy.RD thing
    'It was a fine, happy thing.'

Here, the reduplicated form is pragmatically neutral, again because happiness is a condition that it is natural to the human condition to consider an evanescent gift.

Tuú is also irregular in occurring variably with the identificational copula *da*, which typically occurs with nonverbal nominal predicates (e.g. *Mi da í tatá* 'I am your father'; cf. Chapter 12):

(35) Ma da **tuú**?
    but be true
    'But is it true?'

Correspondingly, *tuú* can also occur with the suppletive negative form of *da*, *ná*:

(36) Ná **tuú**!
    NEG true
    'It isn't true!'

This appears to be due to the fact that *tuú* also occurs as a noun, meaning 'truth,' as in:

(37) Ée i bi fã dí **tuú** dá mi, mí háti á
    if 2S PAST talk DEF truth give 1S 1S.POSS heart NEG

    bi ó boónu.
    PAST FUT burn
    'If you'd told me the truth, I wouldn't be angry.'

Thus the occurrence of *tuú* with copular forms used with nonverbal nominal predicates is nominal itself. This compatibility with *da* also explains the otherwise curious occurrence of *tuú* unreduplicated after the other *be*-verb *dé*, which obligatorily occurs in place of *da* in the context of modification by tense, aspect, or mood (cf. 12.1.2.). Thus:

(38) Á sá dé **tuú**!
    3S.NEG can be truth
    'It couldn't be!'

is like a typical tensed nonverbal predicate such as:

(39) A bi dé dí kabiténi. (*A bi da dí kabiténi.)
    3S PAST be DEF captain
    'He was the captain.'

6.4. Resultative adjectives

When dynamic rather than (intransitive) stative verbs are reduplicated, the outcome is Saramaccan's resultative adjectives, which do not have the counterexpectational semantics that reduplicated intransitive statives connote:

(40) dí **láilái** bóto
 DEF load.RD boat
 'the loaded boat'

(41) Dí bóto dé **láilái**.
 DEF boat be load.RD
 'The boat is loaded.'

These forms can also be used as resultative secondary predicates:

(42) Dí mbéti dé a dí táfa líba **kótíkóti**.
 DEF meat be LOC DEF table top cut.RD
 'The meat is on the table cut up.'

Verbs yielding deverbal resultatives must be ones entailing a high degree of effect upon the object, and thus the construction is impossible with unergative, transitive stative and perception verbs:

(43) *wákáwáka hási
 walk.RD horse
 'the having walked horse'

(44) *sábísábi kɔ́tu
 know.RD tale
 'the known tale'

(45) *sísí fufúuma
 see.RD thief
 'the seen thief' (K54)

When occurring unreduplicated in the attributive position, dynamic verbs are present participles:

(46) **síngi** fóu
 sing bird
 'singing bird'

(47) **kɛɛ́** míi
 cry child
 'crying child'

When occurring unreduplicated in the predicate position, dynamic verbs encode the passive:

(48) Déé físi **kóti**.
 DEF.PL fish cut
 'The fish were / have been cut.' (K60)

This allows a subtle semantic distinction between the resultative and the passive meaning:

(49) Déé   paabí   dé **wásíwási** kaa.
     DEF.PL   plate   be wash.RD   CPLT
     'The plates are washed (up).'

(50) Déé   paabí   **wási** kaa.
     DEF.PL   plate   wash   CPLT
     'The plates were / have been washed.' (K60)

The following table illustrates how verbal *Aktionsart* interacts with reduplication to create various types of adjectival items:

Table 22. Reduplication and property items

	PROPERTY ITEMS	DYNAMIC VERBS
ATTRIBUTIVE UNREDUPLICATED	neutral modifier *dí deé físi* 'the dry fish'	present participle *dí bái dágu* 'the barking dog'
ATTRIBUTIVE REDUPLICATED	counterexpectational *dí deédéé físi* 'the dried fish' (that aren't usually)	resultative *dí láilái bóto* 'the loaded boat'
PREDICATE REDUPLICATED	counterexpectational *dí físi dé deédéé* 'the fish are dried' (rather than not)	resultative *dí bóto dé láilái* 'the boat is loaded (up)'
PREDICATE UNREDUPLICATED	neutral stative *dí físi deé* 'the fish is dry'	passive *dí bóto lái* 'the boat has been loaded'

There is, however, a certain bleeding between the property item and dynamic categories depending on real-world realities. Example: the real-world nature of chopping means that in concatenation with a noun, *latjá* 'to chop' will refer most often to a result rather than a property. Objects are much more often being or having been chopped than themselves engaged in chopping. As such, in unreduplicated form, when modifying a noun such as *údu* 'wood,' *latjá* means not 'chopping' (i.e. 'chopping wood,' or 'wood that chops') but 'chopped.' Thus, the contrast between its unreduplicated and reduplicated form parallels the one described for property items:

(51) **latjá**   údu
     chop   wood
     'chopped wood'

(52) **latjálátjá**   údu
     chop.RD   wood
     'chopped wood' (K45–46)

in which the second phrase was used to refer to wood chopped by Kramer, who was not as experienced in the activity as the Saramaka who taught it to him and thus had results different from those with a lifetime's experience.

6.5. Comparative constructions

6.5.1. Positive comparison

The comparative is expressed with *mɔ́ɔ̃* 'more,' used both to express degree and as the comparative marker:

(53) Déé   míi   fuu   **mɔ́ɔ̃** hǎse   **mɔ́ɔ̃** déé   fii.
     DEF.PL   child POSS.1P more   pretty more   DEF.PL   POSS.2S
     'Our children are better-looking than yours.'

The first *mɔ́ɔ̃* in such constructions is optional:

(54) A (**mɔ́ɔ̃**) lánga **mɔ́ɔ̃** ju.
     3S more   tall   more   2S
     'He is taller than you.'

(55) A   tá   kulé   (**mɔ́ɔ̃**) hési   **mɔ́ɔ̃** mi.
     3S IMF run   more   fast   more   1S
     'He runs faster than me.'

(56) Tidé   mi mbéi   (**mɔ́ɔ̃**) móni   **mɔ́ɔ̃** éside.
     today   1S make   more   money   more   yesterday
     'Today I made more money than yesterday.'

(57) Kobí   bái   (**mɔ́ɔ̃**) wági   **mɔ́ɔ̃** baisígi.
     Kobi   buy   more   car   more   bicycle
     'Kobi bought more cars than bicycles.'

When the object of comparison is verbal, then the *mɔ́ɔ̃* comparative marker is followed by *fá* or *kumafá* 'how, as, like':

(58) Dí   dɔ́ɔ   héi   **mɔ́ɔ̃** **fá**   a   baái.
     DEF   door   high   more   how   3S   wide
     'The door is taller than it is wide.'

The verb *pasá* 'pass' can be used in a serial verb construction to express the comparative (cf. 8.3.2.), but *pasá* is not especially grammaticalized in this usage, and is only used thus for circumstances in which its lexical connotation is applicable. For example,

(59) I   lánga   **pasá**   dí   dɔ́ɔ.
     2S   tall   pass   DEF   door
     'You are too tall (to pass through the) door.'

denotes less 'You are taller than the door' than that your height surpasses its height such that your getting through it will be difficult. Or, an alternate way of expressing:

(60) Dí   páu   akí   héi   **mɔ́ɔ̃**   dísi.
     DEF   tree   here   high   more   this
     'This tree is taller than this one.'

is:

(61) Dí   páu   akí   gɔɔ́   **pasá**   dísi.
     DEF   tree   here   grow   pass   this
     'This tree is taller than this one.'

but this is only possible because the nature of the growth of trees is such that one tree can grow "past" another one. However:

(62) *Mi   wái   **pasá**   de.
     1S   happy   pass   3P
     'I am happier than them.'

because happiness cannot physically pass anything.

Saramaccan has incorporated one of English's suppletive comparative adjectives, *better*, as *bétɛ* 'better.' However, *bétɛ* is not the comparative form of *búnu*, but a separate lexical entry. Saramaccan renders *búnu* comparative in regular fashion with *mɔ́ɔ̃*:

(63) Kobí   da   wã̌   (**mɔ́ɔ̃**)   **búnu**   dáta   **mɔ́ɔ̃**   Ámba.
     Kobi   be   INDF   more   good   doctor   more   Amba
     'Kobi is a better doctor than Amba.'

(64) Ée já   peé   mɔ́ɔ̃,   já   ó   peé   **mɔ́ɔ̃**   **búnu**.
     if 2S.NEG   play   more   2S.NEG   FUT   play   more   good
     'If you don't play more, you won't get better.'

Bétɛ has two meanings. One occurs in deontic propositions and translates as 'advisable.' In this usage it is itself modified by *mɔ́ɔ̃*, showing that it is not simply a comparative form of *búnu*, but rather a semantically narrower concept within 'good':

(65) A   **mɔ́ɔ̃**   **bétɛ**   já   dú   dí   soní   dé.
     3S   more   advisable   2S.NEG   do   DEF   thing   there
     'You'd better not do that.'

(66) A   bi   ó   **mɔ́ɔ̃**   **bétɛ**   ée   i   wási   dí   wági.
     3S   PAST   FUT   more   advisable   if   2S   wash   DEF   car
     'It would be better to wash the car.'

Bétɛ can also mean 'to improve,' 'to get better,' in which case it is not modified by *mɔ́ɔ̃*:

(67) U   mɔ́ɔ̃   i   peé,   u   mɔ́ɔ̃   i   kó   **bétɛ**.
     for   more   2S   play   for   more   2S   come   get.better
     'The more you play, the better you get.'

This would explain DeGroot's (1977: 34) designation of *bétɛ* as referring to healing from sickness, as in:

(68) A   bi   kó   **bétɛ**   kaa.
     3S   PAST   come   get.better   CPLT
     'He is already better (i.e. healed).'

6.5.2. Degree of comparison

Comparison is reinforced by *híla / hía* 'many' and tempered by *wã̂ pikí sɔ́* 'a little' (lit. 'a little so') (cf. 4.5.):

(69) Kobí bái (mɔ́ɔ̃) **híla** wági mɔ́ɔ̃ Ámba.
Kobi buy more many car more Amba
'Kobi bought lots more cars than Amba.'

(70) Kobí (mɔ́ɔ̃) lánga **wã̂ pikí sɔ́** mɔ́ɔ̃ Ámba.
Kobi more tall INDF little so more Amba
'Kobi is a little taller than Amba.'

The construction for 'the more X ... the more Y' is expressed as in English with *mɔ́ɔ̃*, and optionally with *u* (< *fu*) 'for' before both clauses:

(71) (U) **mɔ́ɔ̃** i pɛɛ́, (u) **mɔ́ɔ̃** i kó béte.
for more 2S play for more 2S come get.better
'The more you play, the better you get.'

6.5.3. Equal comparison

Equal comparison is expressed with *kumafá* with verbal and sentential complements (cf. 6.5.1.) and *kúma* elsewhere:

(72) Kobí taánga tidé **kumafá** a bi dé féífi jáa pasá.
Kobi strong today as 3S PAST be five year pass
'Kobi is as strong today as he was five years ago.'

(73) Mi mbéi mɔ́ni tidé **kúma** éside.
1S make money today as yesterday
'I made as much money today as yesterday.'

'As many' is expressed with *híla / hía* 'many':

(74) Kobí bái **híla** wági kúma Ámba.
Kobi buy many car as Amba
'Kobi bought as many cars as Amba.'

6.5.4. Negative comparison

There is no word in Saramaccan for 'less.' As in many languages, negative comparison is expressed via negation of an expression of equal comparison (this is, for example, what informants spontaneously give as translations):

(75) Á bái wági híla kúma Ámba.
3S.NEG buy car many as Amba
'He bought fewer cars than Amba.' (lit. 'He didn't buy as many cars as Amba.')

(76) Á   móni   kumafá   mi ábi.
    3S.NEG.have money as   1S have
    'He has less money than me.' (lit. 'He doesn't have as much money as I do.')

(77) Mé   mbéi   móni   tidé   kúma   éside.
    1S.NEG   make   money today as   yesterday
    'I made less money today than yesterday.' (lit. 'I didn't make as much money today as yesterday.')

Negative comparison can also be expressed in ways beyond comparative constructions:

(78) Á   bái   dóu   téni   wági.
    3S.NEG   buy   arrive ten   car
    'He bought fewer than ten cars.' (lit. 'The number of cars he bought did not reach ten.')

6.5.5. Superlatives

For a language to have a strategy exclusively devoted to distinguishing a referent as the one out of many that displays a property to the highest degree is, in the strict sense, unnecessary, despite the familiarity of European languages' words for 'most' and suffixes like English's *-est*. The referent that is comparatively, for example, 'bigger' is, by definition, the biggest: 'the bigger one' is, logically, 'the biggest one.'

Saramaccan is one of many languages that lacks, therefore, any markers of the superlative alone. Rather, a noun is rendered superlative via marking with the definite article and modification with *mɔ́ɔ*:

(79) **dí**   **mɔ́ɔ**   gãá   wã́
    DEF   more   big   one
    'the biggest one'

(80) Hɛ́   da   **dí**   **mɔ́ɔ**   lánga   wómi   u   dí   kóndɛ.
    3S   be   DEF   more   tall   man   POSS   DEF   village
    'He is the tallest man in the village.'

(81) Hɛ́   da   **dí**   **mɔ́ɔ**   lánga   wã́   a   u   déndu.
    3S   be   DEF   more   tall   one   LOC   1P   inside
    'He is the tallest one among us.'

6.5.6. Excessives

There are two main strategies for the excessive. One is the adverb *túmísi* (alternate form *túmúsi*) 'too much':

(82) I   lánga   **túmísi**,   báa.
    2S   tall   too.much   brother
    'You're too tall, brother.'

(83) A háti mi **túmísi**.
    3S hurt 1S too.much
    'It hurt me too much.'

The other is the use of the verb *pói* 'spoil' as the modifying second verb in a serial verb construction (cf. 8.3.2.), as in:

(84) De tá   peé dí   póku taánga **pói**.
    3P IMF play DEF poku strong too.much
    'They played poku music too loud.'

(85) U   hángi   u sí   únu **pói**.
    1P hungry NF see 2PO too.much
    'We were *really* longing to see you.' (i.e. to the point that it was getting to be too much to bear)

6.6. Color terms

Saramaccan color terms conform neatly to Berlin and Kay's (1969) prediction as to the implicational hierarchy that constrains which focal colors a language will have words for.
    Berlin and Kay specified that this hierarchy is:

white			green						purple
	>	red >		>	blue	>	brown	>	pink
black			yellow						orange
									gray

In Saramaccan, the focal colors are:

wéti			gũũũ						paars
	>	bɛ >		>	baáu	>	bruin	>	ros
baáka			kóóko						oranje
									síndjásíndja

The colors through *baáu* 'blue' are Saramaccan words, conforming to the language's phonotactics. After this, however, most of the colors are rendered in Dutch. *Bruin, paars,* and *oranje* are unchanged from Dutch. 'Pink' in Dutch is *rose* rather than *ros*, but the Saramaccan *ros* remains foreign to Saramaccan's phonology, since [r] does not occur in Saramaccan itself and *ros* also contravenes Saramaccan's CV(N) phonotactics. Meanwhile, *síndjásíndja* 'gray' is derived from the reduplication of Saramaccan's *síndja* 'ash, ashes,' but in this, is disqualified from Berlin and Kay's hierarchy in being a transparently descriptive term rather than a discrete, unanalyzable item referring to color exclusively.

Chapter 7
Core predicate phrase modifiers:
Negators, tense, aspect, and modals

Saramaccan has various preverbal particles (phonological clitics and auxiliaries) which interact to encode negation, tense, aspect, and modality.

7.1. Negation

7.1.1. Predicate negation

The negator of verbal predicates is usually *á* (in the Upper River dialect, in which many sources on Saramaccan are couched, this morpheme is *ã́*):

(1) Kobí   *á*   tɔ́tɔ   dí   wómi   túwɛ.
     Kobi   NEG   push   DEF   man   throw
     'Kobi didn't push the man down.'

It is invariant for tense or aspect; it precedes the markers of these categories:

(2) De *á*   tá   kó   akí   mɔ̃́ɔ̃.
     3P NEG   IMF   come   here   more
     'They don't come anymore.'

Despite its frequency of occurrence, however, the conditioning of *á* is highly specific, with *ná* serving as the negator in a greater range of contexts. *Ná* is the negator in presentational constructions:

(3) *Ná*   Rohít,   ku   Henry   i   tá   fã.
     NEG   Rohit   with   Henry   2S   IMF   talk
     'It's not Rohit – you're talking to Henry.'

(4) *Ná*   mí   dú   ɛ̃.
     NEG   1S   do   3SO
     'It's not me who did it.'

(5) Nɔ́nɔ,   *ná*   tapá   dí   sípi   tá   tapá,   síngi   a   tá   síngi.
     no   NEG   stop   DEF   ship   IMF   stop   sink   3S   IMF   sink
     'No, the ship isn't *stopping*, it's *sinking*.'

(6) Nɔ́ɔ   *ná*   u   kabá   ɔ́?
     NI   NEG   1P   finish   INT
     'So we're done, aren't we?' ('So isn't it that we're done?')

Ná is the negator in cases of verbal ellipsis:

(7) I sá bebé té, sukuáti, ku wí̧, ma **ná** dã́ã́.
    2S can drink tea chocolate with wine but NEG rum
    'You can drink tea, chocolate, and wine, but not rum.'

as well as with verbless predicates, such as equative ones with *da*, which does not exhibit verbal behavior (cf. 12.1.2.); *ná* is, then, the negative copula:

(8) Mi da í máti.
    1S be 2S.POSS friend
    'I'm your friend.'

(9) Mi **ná** í máti. (*Mi á da í máti.)
    1S NEG 2S.POSS friend
    'I'm not your friend.'

Similarly *ná* occurs with another verbless predicate type composed of possessive pronouns (cf. 4.3.), which occur either with *da* or alone:

(10) Dí pindá (da) u mi.
     DEF peanut be POSS 1S
     'The peanut is mine.'

(11) Nda dí wági **ná** u mi, nɔ́ɔ i ó paká fẽ́ẽ.
     since DEF car NEG POSS 1S NI 2S FUT pay for.3SO
     'Since the car is not mine, you're going to pay for it.'

Ná is also used when emphasis is intended:

(12) Mi **ná** ábi dágu.
     1S NEG have dog
     'I don't *have* a dog!'

and to negate the imperative:

(13) **Ná** dú ná wã́ soní.
     NEG do NEG one thing
     'Don't do anything.'

(14) **Ná** gó alá!
     NEG go yonder
     'Don't go there!'

Thus it can be stated that *á* is the negator in the particular case of verbal (but not nonverbal) predicates marked with an overt subject in neutral assertions; *ná* can be seen as the "elsewhere" negator.

Yet the domain of *á* is narrowed even more by one more factor: when the subject is a theme (i.e. in passive sentences), *ná* is optionally used, in which case it is assertionally neutral. Thus:

(15) Déé   óbo   akí   **á**   jasá   tjiká.
     DEF.PL   egg   here   NEG   fry   suffice
     'These eggs aren't fried enough.'

but:

(16) Dí   góni   **ná**   lái.
     DEF   gun   NEG   load
     'The gun isn't loaded!' (Kramer 2001: 61)

(17) Dí   físi   **á**   /   **ná**   kóti.
     DEF   fish   NEG   /   NEG   cut
     'The fish isn't cut (up).' (as I asked for)

(18) Dí   wómi   **á**   /   **ná**   fṍ.
     DEF   man   NEG   /   NEG   beat
     'The man isn't beaten.'

(See 2.4.3. on tonal patterns connected with negation.)

7.1.2. Irregularity in surface manifestation of negative marking

When occurring after subject pronouns, *á* is subsumed into portmanteau morphemes that result from assimilation processes (only with the third-person plural pronoun does this not occur). The Upper River dialect paradigm differs from that of the Lower River dialect in that the first-person singular form is *má*:

Table 23. Subject pronoun + negator portmanteau morphemes

1S	mé / má	1P	wá
2S	já	2P	wã́
3S	á	3P	de á

(19) **Mé**   kumútu   a   dí   wósu.
     1S.NEG   exit   LOC   DEF   house
     'I did not leave the house.'

(20) Dí   i   sí   Djéfi   dé   akí,   hẽ́   da   **á**   síki.
     because   2S   see   Jeff   be   here   3S   be   3S.NEG   sick
     'Since you see Jeff is here, he must not be sick.'

The uncontracted forms are not ungrammatical, but occur only when the negation is highlighted in the discourse (recall that if the negation of a predicate is outright emphasized, then *ná* is used; cf. 7.1.1.):

(21) Té   i   dá   mi piimísi,   bifɔ́   **mi á**   ó   fã   ku   i.
     until   2S   give   1S pardon   for.now   1S NEG   FUT   talk   with   2S
     'Until you apologize to me, I will not talk to you.'

(22) **I á** bi njã́.
2S NEG PAST eat
'You didn't eat.' (i.e. if the expectation was that you should have eaten)

There is an optional contracted form when *á* modifies *ábi* 'to have.' Thus while the full verb can be negated in regular fashion:

(23) Mé féni dí pãpía, bigá mi **á ábi** móni tjiká.
1S.NEG find DEF paper because 1S NEG have money suffice
'I didn't get the paper because I didn't have enough money.'

just as common is a contracted form *áá* in which only the first syllable of *ábi* (which occurs quite often as a shortened form *á*) remains:

(24) Mi **áá** máti.
1S NEG.have friend
'I don't have friends.'

(25) Dí dágu u mi **áá** móni.
DEF dog POSS 1S NEG.have money
'My dog doesn't have money.'

7.1.3. Negative quantifiers

Negative quantifiers can occur in conjunction with a marker of predicate negation (double negation).

(26) Mé ló ná wã́ (kódo) sɛmbɛ.
1S.NEG like NEG one single person
'I don't like anybody.'

(27) Mé mbéi ná wã́ (kódo) soní.
1S.NEG make NEG one single thing
'I don't make anything.'

(28) Ná wã́ soní mbéi mi kɛɛ́.
NEG one thing make 1S cry
'Nothing makes me cry.'

This double negation is obligatory except when the negative quantifier is the subject, in which case double negation is ungrammatical:

(29) Ná wã́ (kódo) sɛmbɛ (*á) lóbi ɛ̃.
NEG one single person NEG like 3SO
'Nobody likes him.'

(*Kódo* is 'single,' and is included in the quantifiers for person and entity more by some speakers than others; some speakers also variably use *hójɔ*.)

(30) Ná   wã́   hójɔ   soní   mbéi   mi kɛɛ́.
      NEG   one single thing make   1S cry
      'Nothing makes me cry.'

(31) Já   mú   gó ná   wã́   kamiã tidé.
      2S.NEG   must go NEG one place today
      'Don't go anywhere today.'

(32) Á   tá   kó   mɔ́ɔ̃sɔ.
      3S.NEG IMF come   never
      'He never comes.'

To express 'never,' there is also a form restricted to negative polarity in negated clauses, along the lines of Standard English's paradigm of required *any-* forms with negative quantification (e.g. *I don't have anything*). *Wã́ dáka*, lexicalized from 'one day,' is used with the predicate to connote English's *ever*:

(33) Mé   míti   ẽ   **wã́** **dáka**.
      1S.NEG meet   3SO one   day
      'I've never seen him.' (lit. 'I haven't met him ever.')

Like English's *any-* forms, *wã́ dáka* is used elsewhere as an indefinite adverb:

(34) I   gó alá   **wã́** **dáka** ɔ́?
      2S go yonder one   day   INT
      'Have you ever (i.e. anytime) been there?'

'(Not) ... either' is expressed with predicate negation and *tu* 'also':

(35) Ma   í   seéi **já**   tá   peé   báli **tu**.
      but 2S self 2S.NEG   IMF play ball also
      'But you don't play soccer either.'

7.1.4. Expletive negation

Expletive negation occurs in subordinate clauses with the mood verb *kandé* (cf. 7.4.2.3.):

(36) Nɔ́nɔ, á   **kandé** de á   ó   wíni.   (*Nɔ́nɔ, á kandé de ó wíni.)
      no   3S.NEG may.be   3P NEG FUT win
      'No, it couldn't be that they will win.'

7.2. Tense markers

7.2.1. Past marker *bi*

The past marker *bi* occurs before the verb. While etymologically derived from a form of English's 'be' verb (*been*), it has no relation to Saramaccan's 'be' verbs (*da* and *dé*) and is exclusively a marker of tense.

(37) Dí   baisígi   u   mi,   hɛ̃́   **bi**   boóko.
      DEF   bicycle   POSS   1S   3ST   PAST   break
      'It was my bicycle that broke down.'

The default reading of bare dynamic verbs is past, such that they are often zero-marked for past, whether transitive or intransitive. This is true not only in running speech, but is also evident in that in elicitations, informants almost always render past dynamics as bare.

(38) De   táki   táa   bé   i   tapá   dí   dɔ́ɔ.
      3P   talk   COMP   HORT   2S   close   DEF   door
      'They said for you to close the door.'

(39) A   féni   wã́   wósu   dá   mi.
      3S   find   INDF   house   give   1S
      'He found a house for me.'

(40) I   njã́mẽ   túu.
      2S   eat.3SO   all
      'You ate it all.'

(41) A   sindó   a   dí   líba   fẽ́ẽ.
      3S   sit   LOC   DEF   top   POSS.3SO
      'He sat on top of it.'

(42) Kobí   wáka   sɔ́ndɔ   kaí.
      Kobi   walk   without   fall
      'Kobi walked without falling.'

As such, *bi* with dynamic verbs can convey a pluperfect (past-before-past) meaning:

(43) Nɔ́ɔ   fá   a   kó   já   sábi;   u   **bi**   sí   písípísi
      NI   how   3S   come   2S.NEG   know   1P   PAST   see   piece.RD

      fẽ́ẽ   akí   kaa.
      POSS.3SO   here   CPLT
      'So, how it came about you don't know; we had seen pieces scattered around here.'

Stative verbs, on the other hand, are generally interpreted as present tense when bare:

(44) Mi   lóbi   ɛ̃   tuútuu.
      1S   love   3SO   true.RD
      'I love him so much.'

(45) Mɔ́ni   hɛ̃́   mi   ké.
      money   3ST   1S   want
      'It's money I want.'

such that past marking requires *bi*:

(46) *Mi á* **bi** *ké.*
 1S NEG PAST want
 'I didn't want it (to be so).'

In this utterance from spontaneous running speech, we see a bare dynamic verb connoting past reference and a stative one within the same time frame marked with *bi*:

(47) *A háti mi só taánga táa kúma ... fá mi* **bi** *sábi Ameeká.*
 3S hurt 1S so strong COMP as how 1S PAST know America
 'It hurt me so much that ... the way I knew America.' (i.e. what it was like)

Thus there is a tendency according to which *bi* is conditioned by the following schema:

Table 24. Past marking according to *Aktionsart*

	BARE	MARKED WITH *bi*
STATIVE	present *mi lóbi* 'I love'	past *mi bi lóbi* 'I loved'
DYNAMIC	past *mi wáka* 'I walked'	pluperfect *mi bi wáka* 'I had walked'

However, alone, this schema is an oversimplification. The dynamic/stative difference in marking with *bi* is not an absolute rule, as exceptions are hardly uncommon. For example, with *lési* 'to read,' a technically dynamic action that has an inherent nature leaning towards the stative pole, the bare form is easily interpreted as non-past:

(48) *Mi lési híla.*
 1S read much
 'I read ([ri:d]) a lot.' (intended in the habitual, not past)

The past reading of dynamics is also overridden in adverbial temporal complements of non-past tense, in which dynamic verbs occur bare and yet do not have past reference:

(49) *Té mujée* **sí** *Kobí, nɔ́ɔ de tá kulé.*
 when woman see Kobi NI 3P IMF run
 'When women see Kobi, they run.'

(50) *Mi sábi táa té mi* **gó** *a déndu naandé, nɔ́ɔ de ó*
 1S know COMP when 1S go LOC inside there NI 3P FUT

 disá u woóko.
 leave NF work
 'I know that when I go in there, they will stop working.'

(51) *U lóbi té Jeff hɛ̃* **jasɛ́ɛ̃**.
 1P love when Jeff 3ST fry.3SO
 'We love it when *Jeff* fries them.'

A more precise analysis is that *bi* is a relative past marker, situating the action at a time before the locus of time that the utterance refers to, rather than necessarily the time that the utterance is expressed. Thus *bi* often marks dynamic verbs that would not be rendered in the pluperfect in English, but where the narrative frame of the utterance includes indication that the marked verb's action preceded another one:

(52) Dí   mi   **bi**   jabí   dí   dóɔ,   hɛ̃́   mi   sí   dí   gõó̌   mũnjǎ.
     when 1S   PAST   open   DEF   door   then   1S   see   DEF   ground wet
     'When I opened the door, I saw the ground wet.'

(53) Mi ké   u   bái   dí   sutúu   dí   a   **bi**   sindó   nɛ̃ɛ̃́
     1S want   NF   buy   DEF   chair   REL   3S   PAST   sit   LOC.3S.POSS

     déndu.
     inside
     'I want to buy the chair that he sat in.'

Note that it is relatively easy to conceive of an "alternate universe" variety of English in which these verbs would be rendered as pluperfect. *When I had opened the door, I saw the ground wet* would be grammatical to most English speakers, if slightly infelicitous. Saramaccan has conventionalized pluperfect marking somewhat more than English, therefore.

But this *bi*-marking of dynamics also occurs in monoclausal utterances, in which it is pragmatically significant that the action occurred before the time of the utterance. In such cases, there is no overlap with European languages' pluperfect:

(54) Andí   a   **bi**   dá   i?
     what   3S   PAST   give   2S
     'What did he give you?'

Here, 'What had he given you?' is a hopeless translation; *bi* serves here only as a "lookback" strategy. This question is most likely asked between people well acquainted, in a context set off temporally and emotionally from the one in which the giving occurred. Thus the giving's occurrence in a context distinctly separated from the asking, and specifically, separated in time, is pragmatically salient, making the use of *bi* natural.

Bi marks a verb only at the point when a new situation in time is required; afterwards, the tendency is for following verbs to be bare. A nice example is the answer to the sentence above; the exchange was:

(55) a. Andí   a   **bi**   dá   i?
         what   3S   PAST   give   2S
         'What did he give you?'

     b. A   dám   wã̌   pen.
         3S   give.1S   INDF   pen
         'He gave me a pen.'

7.2.2. Future marker ó

Future tense is marked by ó (< gó 'to go'). Its meaning does not vary according to the dynamic/stative distinction.

(56) Mí seéi **ó** bói ɛ̃.
 1S self FUT cook 3SO
 'I will cook it myself.'

(57) Té dí mamá fɛ̃ɛ̃ dédɛ, a **ó** tjɛ̃ɛ̃ gó béi.
 when DEF mother POSS.3SO die 3S FUT carry.3SO go bury
 'When his mother dies, he will bury her.'

(58) Dísi **ó** taánga – bóo poobá.
 this FUT strong HORT.1P try
 'This is going to be hard – let's try.'

(Cf. 7.4.2.3. for a second future marker with an irrealis connotation.)

7.3. Aspect markers

7.3.1. Imperfective marker tá

The marker tá expresses both the progressive and the habitual, and thus is an imperfective marker. Examples of its progressive usage:

(59) Mi **tá** sindó a Susanne ku Marvin míndi.
 1S IMF sit LOC Susanne with Marvin between
 'I am sitting between Susanne and Marvin.'

(60) Tjúba seéi **tá** kaí!
 rain really IMF fall
 'Boy, it's really raining, isn't it?'

(61) Máku **tá** njã́ mi éti é!
 mosquito IMF eat 1S yet INJ
 'But mosquitos are still biting me!'

With stative verbs, tá marks an unbounded inceptive meaning:

(62) Mi **tá** lóbi de.
 1S IMF love 3P
 'I am coming to love them.'

However, the inceptive is also marked lexically, with kó 'to come,' in its reflex as 'become':

(63) Awáa de **kó** lóbi dé seéi.
 at.last 3P come like 3P self
 'They came to like one another.'

(64) Mi wási ẽ té a **kó** límbo.
1S wash 3SO until 3S come clean
'I washed it until it was clean.'

In this usage, *kó* can co-occur with *tá* with no change in meaning:

(65) U (**tá**) **kó** wéi.
1P IMF come tired
'We're getting tired.'

When a verb marked with *tá* occurs as the second verb of a serial construction (cf. Chapter 8), it translates as a present participle modifying the first verb:

(66) Mi sindó dé **tá** mbéi hóha.
1S sit there IMF make yawn
'I sat there yawning.'

(67) Dí wíki dí bi pasá dé, mé bi sá peé,
DEF week REL PAST pass there 1S.NEG PAST can play

ma nɔ́ɔ mi kó **tá** peé báka.
but NI 1S come IMF play again
'Last week I couldn't play, but now I'm back playing again.' (lit. 'have come and am playing again')

With *gó* 'to go,' *tá* has fused with the verb: *nángó* (*tá gó). Thus *nán-* is perhaps Saramaccan's sole segmental inflectional affix (cf. 3.2.1.).

(68) A nángó bái soní.
3S IMF.go buy thing
'He is going to buy something.'

(69) Naásé i nángó?
where 2S IMF.go
'Where are you going?'

Tá is also used to encode the habitual (cf. 7.3.3. and 7.3.4. for other habitual markers):

(70) Á **tá** woóko taánga sɔ́ mɔ́ɔ.
3S.NEG IMF work strong so more
'He's not working as hard as before.'

(71) Dí ganíã á **tá** kandá kumafá a bi kandá mɔ́ɔ.
DEF chicken NEG IMF sing like 3S PAST sing more
'The chicken isn't singing like it used to.'

(72) Té mi kabá u njá a dí sónúáti njãnjã́, nɔ́ɔ hángi
when 1S finish NF eat LOC DEF noon food NI hunger

tá kísi mi éti.
IMF catch 1S yet
'After I finish eating lunch, I am (always) still hungry.'

(73) Té   mi fã   ná   wã̌   kódo sɛmbɛ tá   háika mi.
     when   1S talk NEG   one single person IMF listen 1S
     'When I talk nobody listens to me.'

(74) Andí mbéi fóu   tá   síngi?
     what make bird IMF sing
     'Why do birds sing?'

7.3.2. Grammatical status of *bi*, *ó*, and *tá*

These three "particles" are the most frequently occurring predicate phrase modifiers in Saramaccan other than the negators. Taxonomically, they are auxiliary verbs. Unlike clitics, they can occur without a host:

(75) I   á   bi   njã̌.   –   Aái, mi **bi**.
     2S   NEG PAST eat   yes   1S PAST
     'You didn't eat. – Yes, I did.'

(76) Kobí kulé mɔ́ɔ̃ taánga tidé   mɔ́ɔ̃   Ámba **bi**   éside.
     Kobi run   more strong today more Amba PAST   yesterday
     'Kobi ran faster today than Amba did yesterday.'

(77) Aái, mi **ó**.
     yes   1S FUT
     'Yes, I will.'

(78) Mɛ́   sábi   ũfá dí   pási **ó**   tidé.
     1S.NEG know   how DEF road FUT   today
     'I don't know how the roads will be today.'

(79) De tá   peé   ɔ́?   –   Aái, de **tá**.
     3P IMF   play INT   yes   3P IMF
     'Are they playing? – Yes, they are.'

7.3.3. Habitual marker *ló*

To encode more literal shades of habituality, the marker is *ló*, a contracted form of *lóbi* 'like, love,' which occurs with or without nonfinite marker *u*. In contrast to the more abstract and grammaticalized habitual connotation that *tá* lends when used in the habitual (cf. 7.3.1.), *ló* translates more as '(is) in the habit of' or 'is always':

(80) Mɛ́   **ló** sí   ɛ̃   sónde.
     1S.NEG HAB   see 3SO   Sunday
     'I never see him on Sundays.'

(81) A   bi   **ló**   u   baláki té   a   kabá   u   njã̂,   ma   nɔ́unɔ́u
     3S   PAST HAB   NF   vomit when   3S finish NF eat   but now

     á   tá   baláki mɔ́ɔ̃,   a   tá   hói   ɛ̃   nɛ̃ɛ̃́   bɛ́ɛ.
     3S.NEG   IMF   vomit more 3S IMF   hold 3SO   LOC.3S.POSS belly
     'He used to throw up after eating, but now he doesn't throw up anymore; he holds it in
     his belly.'

Ló, as a marker of salient habituality, can correspond to the English *keeps* [verb]-*ing*, *is always*
[verb]-*ing* construction:

(82) A   **ló**   u   kó   náki a   dɔ́ɔ   u   mi té   mi tá   duumí.
     3S   HAB   NF   come   hit   LOC   door   POSS 1S when   1S IMF sleep
     'He keeps knocking on my door when I'm asleep.'

Ló is grammaticalized enough that it is not restricted to human or animate subjects:

(83) Akí   **ló**   u   tapá   a   bundji.
     here HAB   NF   cover   LOC   fog
     'It's always foggy in here.'

There remain instances in which its semantics remain equidistant between 'to like' and a habitual
marker:

(84) Aluási   fá   mé   **ló**   u   gafá   sɛmbɛ   seéi,   ma   ũ   kɔ́ni.
     even.though how   1S.NEG   HAB   NF   praise person even   but 2P   smart
     'Though I don't like to praise people, you are smart.'

Ló qualifies as a contraction rather than a new morpheme in its own right (cf. 3.5.), partly because
of usages such as the above, and partly because *lóbi* also occurs in contracted form in its original
meaning:

(85) Mé   **ló**   ná   wã̂   kódo   sɛmbɛ.
     1S.NEG like   NEG   one   single   person
     'I don't like anybody.'

7.3.4. Past habitual marker *náa*

Although *ló* is used in the past as well as the present, there is also a past habitual marker, *náa*:

(86) Mi   bi   **náa**   gó a   San Francisco.
     1S   PAST HAB   go LOC   San Francisco
     'I used to go to San Francisco.'

(87) Sɔ́   u   bi   **náa**   dú.
     thus 1P   PAST   HAB   do
     'That's how we used to do it.'

Our informants only accept *náa* in past contexts, finding it uninterpretable in present-tense sentences.

Náa appears, from our data, to be a rather marginal item in the language in terms of frequency of use. Our informants have never produced it spontaneously in sessions: instead they give sentences with *ló*. When presented with *náa*, they respond to it as rather exotic (one informant: "I haven't heard that word for so long!").

The etymology of *náa* is as an allomorph of imperfective marker *tá* used with the locative marker (*n*)*a* as *tá a*. This would have been modelled on the usage of *a*- as a marker of the progressive or habitual in regional British dialects, such as that of Cornwall: *I've a keept 'n* 'I've kept it' (Hancock 1994: 104). Three things support this. 1) The initial consonant of *tá* has also nasalized amidst its bounding to *gó* 'to go' in the irregular form *nángó* (< *tá gó*) (cf. 3.2.1., 7.3.1.). 2) This source would explain the habitual semantics of *náa*. 3) This source would also explain why *náa* cannot occur before past marker *bi*, given that neither can *tá* (cf. 7.5.):

(88) *Só   de   **náa**   bi   béi   sɛmbɛ.
     thus   3P   HAB   PAST   bury   person
     'That's how they buried people.' (Veenstra 1996: 27)

7.3.5. Durativity

Repetition of stative verbs can convey a durative meaning:

(89) Mí   wági   boóko   boóko.
     1S.POSS   car   break   break
     'My car is breaking.' (i.e. slowly falling apart) (Kramer 2001: 62)

(90) Híi   fá   de   dé   duumí   duumí,   nɔ́ɔ   hɛ̃́   sɛmbɛ   kó   a
     all   how   3P   be   sleep   sleep   NI   then   person   come   LOC

     dí   wósu.
     DEF   house
     'While they were sleeping, people came into the house.'

This construction does not entail, as it may appear, reduplication, given that true verb reduplication in Saramaccan includes tone sandhi between the verbs (cf. 3.1.1.), while there is no sandhi between verbs used in this durative meaning:

Dí sutúu dé /boókoboóko/ > [boókóbóóko] 'The chair is broken.'
Mí wági /boókoboóko/   > [boókoboóko] 'My car is falling apart.'

7.3.6. Completive marker *kaa*

Kaa, which is postposed to the verb, marks the end of an action (it is derived from *kabá* 'to finish'). It can translate as 'already':

(91) Dí   mi   bi   kó   lúku   de,   nɔ́ɔ   de   bi   duumí   **kaa**.
     when   1S   PAST   come   look   3P   NI   3P   PAST   sleep   CPLT
     'When I came to see them, they were (already) asleep.'

But more generally, its function is to connote the completive, when the observation that a given event ended is relevant to the discourse:

(92) Mi dú ẽ   dí   de gó **kaa**.
     1S do 3SO   when 3P go CPLT
     'I did it after they left.'

(93) A gó a   dɔ́ɔ   **kaa** ɔ́?
     3S go LOC door   CPLT   INT
     'Did he go (and stay) outside?'

(94) Hɛ̃́   da John gó **kaa**.
     3S   be John go CPLT
     'John must have left.'

(95) A láti **kaa**, gó a   wósu.
     3S late CPLT   go LOC house
     'It's late, go home.'

Kaa is often used with passive predicates, which distinguishes them as actions, as opposed to reduplicated verbal items which refer to states (cf. 6.4.):

(96) Dí   físi kóti **kaa**.
     DEF fish cut   CPLT
     'The fish has been cut.' (cf. *Dí físi dé kótíkóti* 'The fish is cut up')

Note that in the above sentences after the first one with *kaa*, an 'already' translation is impossible, despite other sources on Saramaccan's treatment of *kaa* as an adverbial. The following sentence shows the 'already' translation to be even more unsuitable: the pronoun has been fronted, leaving a zero-copula (one of the few contexts in which zero-copula is grammatical in Saramaccan; cf. 12.1.3.):

(97) Nɔ́ɔ u nɔ́ɔ ø   dísi **kaa**.
     NI 1P NI   this CPLT
     'This is the way we are.'

Other sources on Saramaccan also treat *kaa*'s source verb *kabá* 'to finish' as a co-existing completive marker:

(98) Dí   wósu wɛ   a   mbéi   **kabá**.
     DEF house FOC 3S make   finish
     'He finished building the *house*.'

However, *kabá* is much less grammaticalized as a completive marker than *kaa*. Byrne (1987: 224) and Veenstra (1996: 96–98), for example, note its narrower semantic application than *kaa*, occurring with achievements and accomplishments but not states and activities, such that for example:

(99) Mi fɔ̃́mɛ̃   **kabá**.
     1S beat.3SO finish
     'I finished beating him.'

(100) Mi fɔ̃mɛ̃ **kaa**.
1S beat.3SO CPLT
'I beat him up.' (e.g. such that he is/was lying there defeated and the event was over)

This semantic restriction is due to *kabá*'s lesser grammaticalization: post-verbal *kabá* can be treated as simply a lexical item meaning 'finish.' This explains its incompatibility with states and activities, which do not constitute processes with ending points at which finishing would be describable. In addition, the post-verbal use of *kabá* is an alternate construction to its use before the modified verb, in which case this latter is an ordinary verb-phrase complement to *kabá*:

(101) Té a **kabá** u mbéi dí ósu, nɔ́ɔ u sá gó déndu.
when 3S finish NF make DEF house then 1P can go inside
'When he is finished building the house, we will be able to go into it.'

Many verbs take verb-phrase complements in the same construction:

(102) Amã́jã́ mi ó **bigí** u séti dí ósu.
tomorrow 1S FUT begin NF set DEF house
'Tomorrow I will start to build the house.'

(103) A **biingá** u náki ɛ̃.
3S rush NF hit 3SO
'He rushed to / was itching to hit him.'

Yet we would not classify *bigí* as a grammaticalized "inceptive marker": rather, we would say that Saramaccan, like all languages, has ways of expressing the inceptive, and its verb meaning 'begin' is one of them. Similarly, *biingá* is not a grammaticalized "haste marker." Given that post-verbal *kabá* has the same meaning and semantic application as the *kabá* + complement usage, there is little motivation for treating it as a "completive marker."

Thus in cases where one English translation is compatible with a "completive" analysis such as this one:

(104) Mi njã́mɛ̃ **kabá**.
1S eat.3SO finish
'I ate it up.'

we can also note that 'I finished eating it' is an equally good translation, and that the truly grammaticalized completive marker, occurring with all verbal types and often untranslatable as 'finish' or 'already,' is *kaa*.

Yet "completive" *kabá* is indeed somewhat more grammaticalized than *bigí* 'begin' or *biingá* 'rush' in that it occurs in a serial (paratactic) construction at all; for example:

(105) *Mi mbéi dí wósu **bigí**.
1S make DEF house begin
'I started building the house.'

Occurrence in serial constructions distinguishes a verb as having conventionalized in its concatenation with main ones, such that its semantics often drift away from the original lexical meaning, down the pole of grammaticalization (cf. *dá* 'to give' in 8.3.1. and *túwɛ* 'to throw' in 13.3.2.2.). *Kabá* has indeed undergone this process, leading to the separate item *kaa*. Serial *kabá* itself, however, is a persisting early layer in the process.

7.3.7. *Kó* as completive marker

Kó 'come' is used in a fashion that could be analyzed as completive when context focuses on the process leading to the completion rather than on the completion having already been accomplished:

(106) A   téi   lóngi u   mi **kó**   féni   léti   andí   mi tá   súku.
      3S take   long NF 1S come   find   exactly what 1S IMF look.for
      'It took a while for me to find (succeed in finding) exactly what I was looking for.'

(107) Nɔ́ɔ hɛ̃́   wɛ   a   **kó**   dú   ɛ̃.
      NI   then   FOC   3S come   do   3SO
      'And so then she managed to do it.'

This could also, however, be seen as a lexicalized usage of *kó* to mean 'manage to (do)'; preferences will differ as to whether this is considered a grammaticalized enough concept to qualify as a completive marker.

7.3.8. Continuative marker *gó dóu*

The core meaning of *dóu* is 'to arrive':

(108) Akí   mi **dóu**!
      here   1S arrive
      'Here I am!'

(109) Dí   u   mí   té̌   **dóu**.
      DEF   POSS   1S   time   arrive
      'It's my turn.' (i.e. 'My turn has arrived.')

However, *dóu* occurs in paratactic serial usage with *gó* 'to go' in conventionalized expression of 'to keep on / continue [verb]-ing.'

(110) Déé   míi   tá   woóko **gó dóu**.
      DEF.PL   child   IMF   work   go   arrive
      'The kids kept on working.'

This qualifies as a grammaticalized continuative marker in that its connotation is so far evolved from the compositional meaning of the two verbs. That is, compositionally *gó dóu* would indicate 'to go up to' and thus 'to reach,' 'to get to,' given that when used in other serial verb constructions (cf. 8.2.) elsewhere *dóu* in its 'arrive' meaning connotes the 'up to' meaning expressed prepositionally in English:

(111) A   héi   **dóu**   a   mí   hédi.
      3S   high   arrive   LOC   1S.POSS head
      'It came all the way up to my head.'

(112) Á   bái   **dóu**   téni   wági.
      3S.NEG   buy   arrive   ten   car
      'He bought fewer than ten cars.' (lit. 'The number of cars he bought did not arrive at ten.')

It would appear that the *gó dóu* semantics are rooted in a framing which originally included the end point, i.e. 'keep/kept going until the end' rather than English's leaving the telicity unspecified. This is indicated, for example, in the expression:

(113) **Gó dóu** té i kabá.
go arrive until 2S finish
'Carry on.'

However, in the current stage of the grammar, the *gó dóu* expression can apply to contexts in which an end point plays no logical part in the semantics, such as this sentence from an informant who had been conversing with another speaker for our recordings and after a while jokingly asked whether they had to keep going. This context was one where there was obviously no set end point, and yet:

(114) U músu **gó dóu** alá?
1P must go arrive yonder
'(Come on,) do we have to keep going (now that we have gone on so long)?'

7.4. Modal markers

Most of the elicitations of modal markers were done by Heiko Narrog; cf. Narrog (2005) for a separate treatment of this aspect of Saramaccan grammar.

7.4.1. Deontic

The verb *músu* expresses the deontic, as in:

(115) Já **músu** wási dí wági.
2S.NEG must wash DEF car
'You don't have to wash the car.'

(116) Mi táa i **músu** heépi mi.
1S talk 2S must help 1S
'I insist that you help me.'

Músu can be tensed:

(117) Mi bi **músu** háika andí de bi táki dá mi.
1S PAST must listen what 3P PAST talk give 1S
'I had to listen to what they said to me.'

but not marked for aspect:

(118) *Mi tá **músu** wási dí wági.
1S IMF must wash DEF car
'I have to wash the car (right now).'

It frequently occurs in a contracted form:

(119) Já **mú** fã ku ná wã́ sεmbε a dɔ́ɔ sé.
2S.NEG must talk with NEG one person LOC door side
'Don't talk to anyone (outside) today.'

but can also occur in "expanded form" mediating its main verb with nonfinite marker (f)u; this appears to be a feature of especially explicit speech – informants give it only occasionally, and only in direct translations of sentences presented to them:

(120) I **músu** u dú ɛ̃.
2S must NF do 3SO
'You must do it.'

Músu also occurs as a main verb, meaning 'to force':

(121) Ná wã́ kódo sεmbε **músu** mi u wási dí wági.
NEG one single person force 1S NF wash DEF car
'Nobody is forcing me to wash the car.'

Without its high tone, *musu* connotes the less forceful 'should' instead:

(122) I **musu** háika andí dí máti fíi táki dá i.
2S should listen what DEF friend POSS.2S talk give 2S
'You have to listen to what your friend says to you.'

(123) Já **musu** tã́ akí mɔ̃́ɔ̃, i **músu** gó a wósu.
2S.NEG should stand here more 2S must go LOC house
'You shouldn't stand here anymore, you have to go home.'

(124) I bi **musu** táki dɛ̃́ɛ̃.
2S PAST should talk give.3SO
'You should have told him.'

The deontic can be expressed in the subordinate clause as well as the matrix:

(125) Mi ké u déé míi u mi **músu** dé límbólímbo.
1S want NF DEF.PL child POSS 1S must be clean.RD
'I want my children to be clean.' (cf. English **I want that my children must be clean*.)

An alternate deontic expression, synonymous with *músu*, is *ábi f(u)* 'have to':

(126) Mi **ábi** (f)u wási dí wági.
1S have NF wash DEF car
'I have to wash the car.'

There is also the *a dé fu* + pronominal expression, 'It is for you (to).'

(127) **A dé fíiúnu** wási dí wági.
      3S be for.2P wash DEF car
      'It's time for you to wash the car.'

A variation on this is *fu* + pronominal followed by *músu*. Such sentences are anomalous structurally; a challenge, for example, would be to identify their subject:

(128) **Fií músu** dú ẽ.
      for.2S must do 3SO
      'You must do it.'

In many Atlantic English-based creoles, the *for*-derived item alone can convey the deontic, as in Jamaican *Unu fi dwiit* 'You have to do it' (Hancock 1987: 295). This construction does not exist in Saramaccan: informants readily and conclusively correct *Mi fu gó to *Mi á(bi) fu gó* ('I have to go') and we have encountered no sentences of the *Mi fu gó* sort in our informants' spontaneous speech or any transcriptions of Saramaccan speech by others. *Fu* conveys the deontic only within the *a dé fu* and *fu*-pronoun + *músu* constructions. There have been analyses that take the proposed *Mi fu gó* sentence type as indicating that *fu* is even a full verb, with various implications for the question as to whether Saramaccan has nonfinite clauses. It would appear that this analysis of *fu* as a verb is mistaken.
  (Cf. 8.3.5. on hortative marking.)

7.4.2. Epistemic

7.4.2.1. Probability

Probability can be expressed with the 'must' verb, as in English:

(129) A **músu** tá peé dí báli.
      3S must IMF play DEF ball
      'He must be playing ball.'

(130) A **músu** kó amãjã́.
      3S must come tomorrow
      'He must be coming tomorrow.'

It is also expressed with the expression *hẽ́ da* 'It is':

(131) **Hẽ́ da** mi bi duumí.
      3S be 1S PAST sleep
      'I must have fallen asleep.'

(132) **Hẽ́ da** mi dɔ́ngɔ.
      3S be 1S drunk
      'I must have gotten drunk.'

(133) Nɔ́ɔ   ée   i   náki   máku,   nɔ́ɔ   **hɛ̃́ da** já   ábi
      now   if   2S   hit   mosquito NI   3S be 2S.NEG   have

      dégi   áti.
      thick   heart
      'If you smash the mosquito, then it is that you have no (you must not have) courage.'

7.4.2.2. Ability

Ability is conveyed with *sá* 'can':

(134) A   **sá**   dé   sɔ́,   ma   áá   fu   dé   sɔ́.
      3S   can   be   thus   but   3S.NEG.have   NF   be   thus
      'It can be that way, but it doesn't have to be.'

(135) Mé   bi   **sá**   sí   déé   teéja.
      1S.NEG   PAST   can   see   DEF.PL   star
      'I couldn't see the stars.'

Sá is also used to convey politeness:

(136) Mi   **sá**   tɔ́ɔu   ku   dí   mujéɛ-míi   fíi   ɔ́?
      1S   can   marry   with   DEF   woman-child   POSS.2S   INT
      'Can I marry your daughter?'
(137) I   **sá**   tapá   dí   dɔ́ɔ   ɔ́?
      2S   can   close   DEF   door   INT
      'Could you close the door?'

Sá is derived from *sábi* 'to know,' which itself often occurs in contracted form as *sá*:

(138) Mé   **sá**   fá   u   táki   ɛ̃   nɔ́ɔ.
      1S.NEG   know   how   1P   talk   3SO   just
      'I just don't know how we say it ...!'

(139) Wá   **sá**   fá   u   dú.
      1P.NEG   know   how   1P   do
      'We didn't know how to go about things.'

Sá is used with a meaning intermediate between the full verb *sábi* 'to know' and the modal in reference to remarking on someone's high ability. In this construction, our informants reject the use of *sábi* itself, however:

(140) A   **sá**   /   *sábi   (u)   pɛɛ́   dí   báli.
      3S   know   /   know   NF   play   DEF   ball
      'He can really play soccer!'

(141) Pele   bi   **sá**   /   *sábi   (u)   pɛɛ́   dí   báli.
      Pele   PAST   know   /   know   NF   play   DEF   ball
      'Pele could really play soccer!'

Our informants do accept *sábi*, however, in reference to language competence:

(142) Aái,   a   **sábi**   u   fã   Saamáka   tóngɔ.
      yes   3S   know   NF   talk   Saramaka   language
      'Yes, he can speak Saramaccan.'

This can be treated as an idiom specific to *fã*.

The relatively recent development of *sá* from a full verb is also indicated in that like *bi*, *ó*, and *tá*, it is an auxiliary rather than a clitic, occurring independently as in:

(143) Aái,   mi   **sá**.
      yes   1S   can
      'Yes, I can.'

7.4.2.3. Possibility

Given the intimate relationship between futurity and possibility, the semantic range of *sá* extends into indicating the uncertain future, contrasting with the asserted future marked by *ó* (cf. 7.2.2.). In this function, it translates essentially as 'may':

(144) Mé   sábi   tu,   ma   dí   pási   **sá**   ógi.
      1S.NEG   know   also   but   DEF   road   UFUT   bad
      'I'm not sure, but the road may be bad.'

(145) Kandé   déé   sɛmbɛ   **sá**   háika.
      may.be   DEF.PL   person   UFUT   listen
      'Maybe the people will listen.'

(146) Fá   i   ó   sá   fá   i   **sá**   dú   sɛmbɛ?
      how   2S   FUT   know   how   2S   UFUT   do   person
      'How will you know how you will treat people?'

This spontaneous utterance nicely demonstrates the difference between *sá* and *ó*; the passage is in narrative present:

(147) Mé   sí,   dí   soní   dé   naandé,   a   **sá**   kó   nɔ́ɔ,
      1S.NEG   see   DEF   thing   there   there   3S   UFUT   come   just

      fá   a   **ó**   kó   já   sábi.
      how   3S   FUT   come   2S.NEG   know
      'I didn't see – the situation there, it could just come out ... how it's actually going to come out you didn't know.'

Here, *sá* is used to refer to uncertainty as to how things would go, and then *ó* is used only in a complement clause to *já sábi* 'you didn't know.' *Ó* is used in a hypothetical sense: one could not have the certainty of *ó*, and as such it is used "in quotation marks," as a concept unavailable to the speaker in his mental state as described in the utterance.

Possibility of a more overtly asserted degree is expressed with *kandé* (< *kã́ dé* 'can be'), which is a matrix verb after which the proposition it refers to is a subordinate clause.

(148) **Kandé**   a   sábi.
may.be   3S know
'Probably he knows.' / 'He might know.'

(149) **Kandé**   a dé u mi wási dí   wági.
may.be   3S be for 1S wash DEF car
'I might have to wash the car.'

Kandé also occurs with pleonastic *a*:

(150) A **kandé**   John ó   gó.
3S may.be   John FUT go
'It's possible that John will go.'

(151) A **kandé** a ó   kó   amãjã, ma mé   sábi (tu).
3S may.be 3S FUT come tomorrow but 1S.NEG know also
'He might come tomorrow, but I don't know.'

It can also stand alone as an independent clause: *Kandé* 'Could be.'

Kandé is not compatible with tense or aspect marking:

(152) *A ó   **kandé**   de wíni.
3S FUT may.be   3P win
'They might win the game.'

Kandé conditions expletive negation in the subordinate clause:

(153) Nɔ́nɔ, á   **kandé**   de á   ó   wíni. (*Nɔ́nɔ, á kandé de ó wíni.)
no   3S.NEG may.be   3P NEG FUT win
'No, it couldn't be that they will win.'

Ká̰ can occur independently:

(154) **Ká̰**   John gó kaa.
may.be John go CPLT
'John must have left.'

(155) A **ká̰**   fu u   kumútu akí.
3S may.be NF 1P exit   here
'It may be that we get out of here.'

(156) Á   **ká̰**!
NEG may.be
'It couldn't be!'

However, its meaning is identical to that of *kandé*; it is not a separate item meaning 'to be able,' a function fulfilled by *sá*. This is clear, for example, in that *ká̰* occurs only in third-person impersonal constructions, and not with first- or second-person pronouns:

(157) *Mi / *i / *u **ká̰**.
1S / 2S / 1P may.be
'I / you / we can.'

7.5. Order of occurrence

Negator and tense, aspect, and mode morphemes occur in an inviolable order:

NEG *bi* *ó* *sá* *tá* *músu* VERB *kaa*

The ordering of *sá* and *tá* is not often evidenced in the language in use, but is indicated by sentences such as:

(158) Mi **sá** **tá** pɛɛ́.
 1S can IMF play
 'I can be playing.'

Tá occurs with tense markers to express the past and future progressive:

(159) Dí a **bi** **tá** duumí, hɛ̃́ mi gó kumútu dɛ́.
 when 3S PAST IMF sleep then 1S go exit there
 'When he was sleeping, I left.'

(160) U **bi** **tá** fã, hɛ̃́ a gó djééé.
 1P PAST IMF talk then 3S go up.and.go
 'We were talking, and then she just up and left.'

(161) A **ó** **tá** kandá déé kandá.
 3S FUT IMF sing DEF.PL song
 'He will be singing the songs.'

(162) De **ó** **tá** kó háika.
 3P FUT IMF come listen
 'They will be coming to listen.'

When dynamic verbs are marked by *tá*, they no longer rely as much on context to indicate the past: *bi* then usually co-occurs with *tá* just as it does with statives, as shown above in section 7.2.1. This is, however, a strong tendency rather than a rule, given sentences such as this one where *tá* occurs without *bi* in the embedded clause:

(163) A téi lóngi u mi kó féni léti andí mi **tá** súku.
 3S take long NF 1S come find exactly what 1S IMF look.for
 'It took a while for me to find exactly what I was looking for.'

The combination of *bi* and *ó* creates the conditional:

(164) Mi méni táa a **bi** **ó** kó.
 1S think COMP 3S PAST FUT come
 'I thought she would come.'

(165) Ée ná mi bi síki, mi **bi** **ó** gó a wojowójo.
 if NEG 1S PAST sick 1S PAST FUT go LOC market
 'If I weren't sick, I would go to the market.'

In narratives, even in the conditional dynamic verbs continue to tend towards a default past interpretation that allows the omission of past marker *bi*, such that *ó* alone can mark the conditional:

(166) *A   bi   dé   súti,   wáíwái   soní,   fá   déé   zangers*
       3S   PAST   be   sweet   happy.RD   thing   how   DEF.PL   singers

       Frank Sinatra,   a   ó   kó   a   TV,   a   ó   tá   kandá
       Frank Sinatra   3S   FUT   come   LOC   TV   3S   FUT   IMF   sing

       déé   kandá,   tá   kandá   "It's My Way."
       DEF.PL   song   IMF   sing   "It's My Way."
       'It was a great, super-happy thing, how those singers, Frank Sinatra, would come on TV, he'd be singing those songs, singing "It's My Way".'

Combinations of more than two markers are possible:

(167) *Mé   sí   kúma   mi   bi   ó   sá   dé   só   lóngi,   ma   mi   sindó*
       1S.NEG   see   how   1S   PAST   FUT   can   be   so   long   but 1S   sit

       te   a   kabá.
       until   3S   finish
       'I didn't think I could sit there for so long, but I sat till it was over (i.e. sat through it).'

(168) *Ée   tjúba   á   bi   tá   kaí,   nɔ́ɔ   u   bi   ó   tá*
       if   rain   NEG   PAST   IMF   fall   NI   1P   PAST   FUT   IMF

       peé   nɔ́unɔ́u.
       play   now
       'If it wasn't raining, we would be playing now.'

Chapter 8
Verb serialization

8.1. Diagnostic issues

8.1.1. Taxonomy

Verbs in Saramaccan can occur in the same clause without markers of coordination or subordination, depicting single events that entail both actions. In this relationship, usually one of the verbs has grammaticalized or semantically drifted to some degree and modifies the other verb. However, other cases simply reveal Saramaccan as a grammar in which parataxis plays a greater role than in European languages.

One traditional diagnostic of serial verbs is that the second verb is not marked for tense or aspect. Saramaccan partially flouts this, in that imperfective *tá* (cf. 7.3.1.) can mark both verbs in a serial construction. In the following sentence *tá* marks only the first verb:

(1) Mi **tá** tjá wáta gó butá a dí bóto déndu.
    1S IMF carry water go put LOC DEF boat inside
    'I am carrying water into the boat.'

But in the following sentences, it marks both:

(2) A **tá** kulé **tá** lǒtu.
    3S IMF run IMF go.round
    'He is running in circles.'

(3) A **tá** wáka **nán**gó a lío, tééé gó dendá a
    3S IMF walk IMF.go LOC river all.the.way go enter LOC

    wáta déndu.
    water inside
    'She was walking going all the way down to the river and entering it.'
    (the *nán-* on *nángó* is an allomorph of *tá* occurring only with *gó* [cf. 3.2.1., 7.3.1.])

(4) Nɔ́ɔ hɛ̃́ wɛ a **tá** kondá dá de **tá** táki táa wɛ,
    NI then FOC 3S IMF tell give 3P IMF talk COMP FOC

    sɔ́ dí soní dí mbéti pɛndé.
    such DEF thing DEF animal colored
    'So then he was telling them that, it's like this, the animals were colored.'

Such cases could be analyzed as matrix verbs modified by present participles, as *tá* occurs in subordinate clauses to convey the same:

(5) Mi sindó dé **tá** mbéi hóha.
    1S sit there IMF make yawn
    'I sat there yawning.'

Thus, the verb phrases in examples (2) and (3) above could be read as 'running (while) going in circles' and 'walking heading towards the river.'

In any case, tense markers (for which there is no construction akin to that above in which they occur in a subordinate clause while the matrix verb is bare) cannot mark both verbs:

(6) *Mi **bi** bái dí wósu **bi** dá dí mujée.
    1S PAST buy DEF house PAST give DEF woman
    'I bought the house for the woman.'

8.1.2. Constraints on argument sharing

Saramaccan serial verb constructions can be described as occurring in three main configurations. In one, the verbs occur in juxtaposition and share a subject:

(7) A **wáka gó** a dí wósu déndu.
    3S walk go LOC DEF house inside
    'He walked into the house.'

In a second, they share an object, as here, where *dágu* is the object both of *súti* and *kíi*:

(8) A **súti** dí dágu **kíi**.
    3S shoot DEF dog kill
    'He shot the dog dead.'

In the third, when the second verb is a motion verb, the shared argument serves as the object of the first verb and the subject of the second. In this, Saramaccan can flout another commonly cited diagnostic of verb serialization, that both verbs have the same subject.

(9) A **sikópu** dí báli **gó** a wósu.
    3S kick DEF ball go LOC house
    'He kicked the ball into the house.' (*'He kicked the ball and went into the house.')

(10) A **sikópu** dí báli **kó** a John.
     3S kick DEF ball come LOC John
     'He kicked the ball to John.' (from John's perspective) (*'He kicked the ball and came to John.')

(11) A **sikópu** dí báli **kumútu** a wósu.
     3S kick DEF ball exit LOC house
     'He kicked the ball out of the house.' (*'He kicked the ball and came out of the house.')

(12) **Vínde** ɛ̃ **pasá** a dí wall.
     throw 3SO pass LOC DEF wall
     'Throw him through the wall.'

(13) Mi **túwɛ** dí páu **kaí** a wáta.
     1S throw DEF tree fall LOC water
     'I threw the tree down into the water.'

Kó 'come' can also occur as the second argument-sharing verb in its reflex meaning 'become,' in a verb phrase translating as a small clause in English:

(14) Mi **makisá** dí sɔ́fu kã̂ **kó** paáta.
1S step.on DEF soda can become flat
'I stomped the soda can flat.'

(15) Mi **féífi** dí wósu **kó** bɛ.
1S paint DEF house become red
'I painted the house red.'

8.2. Directional serials

Serial verbs carry much of the load in conveying direction (cf. 13.3. for a more detailed address of direction). Despite its phonetic resemblance to Romance languages' [a] 'to, at,' Saramaccan's *a* expresses only location. Direction is conveyed by second verbs in serial constructions:

(16) Sáka dí dágu disá bé a kulé **gó** a dɔ́ɔ. (*...kulé a dɔ́ɔ.)
descend DEF dog leave let 3S run go LOC door
'Put the dog down and let him go out.'

When *gó* has no internal argument, it conveys 'onward, away':

(17) Dí tape tá kulé **gó** éti.
DEF tape IMF run go yet
'The tape is still running.'

(18) De tá tjá soní **gó**.
3P IMF carry thing go
'They are carrying things away.'

(19) Kumútu a mi líba **gó**!
exit LOC 1S top go
'Get off of me!'

Kó 'come' conveys movement towards the speaker or referent:

(20) A dí dɔ́ɔ akí, a wáka **kó** a déndu.
LOC DEF door here 3S walk come LOC inside
'He walked in through this door.'

Gó and *kó* can also be used before the main verb serially, analogous to their use in many languages that otherwise lack serial verbs (e.g. English's *go get, come see*):

(21) Mi **nángó** **súku** dí pusipúsi.
1S IMF.go look.for DEF cat
'I'm going to look for the cat.'

(22) A ló   u   **kó**   **náki**   a   dɔ́ɔ   u   mi té   mi tá   duumí.
    3S HAB NF come   hit   LOC door POSS 1S when 1S IMF sleep
    'He keeps knocking on my door when I'm asleep.'

Kumútu 'exit' and *púu* 'pull' encode that an argument shared with a first serial verb moves out of or away from a location. *Kumútu* is used when the first serial verb is intransitive and *púu* when the first verb is transitive:

(23) A   fusí   **kumútu**   a   sitááfu   wósu.
    3S sneak   exit   LOC   punishment   house
    'He escaped from jail.'

(24) A   gó   féki   dí   keéti   **púu**   a   dí   bóutu.
    3S go   dust.off   DEF   chalk   pull   LOC   DEF   blackboard
    'He's going to wash the chalk off of the blackboard.'

Lótu expresses 'around' or 'go around':

(25) Dí   dágu   tá   bái   nɔ́ɔ   a   tá   kulé   tá   **lótu**.
    DEF   dog   IMF   bark   then   3S   IMF   run   IMF   go.round
    'The dog is barking and running in circles.'

Dóu 'arrive' marks extent, translating in its serial usage roughly as 'up to':

(26) A   héi   **dóu**   a   mí   hédi.
    3S high   arrive   LOC   1S.POSS   head
    'It came all the way up to my head.'

Túwɛ 'throw' marks that a trajectory of movement ended, conveying what *-to* conveys in *He dropped the keys into the water*:

(27) A   kándi   dí   amána fátu   **túwɛ**   a   dí   bṍɔ̃́.
    3S pour   DEF   Amana fat   throw   LOC   DEF   flour
    'He poured the syrup on the pancakes.'

Note that the meaning here is not that someone "threw" the syrup onto the pancakes, despite the etymological source of *túwɛ*. The core semantics of *túwɛ* are deeply bleached in its serial function, serving only to indicate that the syrup ended up upon the pancakes.

Butá 'put' expresses a concept similar to the serial usage of *túwɛ*, but implying a more deliberate and controlled placement than throwing:

(28) Mi   sáka   dí   búku   **butá**   a   dí   táfa   líba.
    1S   descend   DEF   book   put   LOC   DEF   table   top
    'I placed the book on the table.'

8.3. Serials encoding core grammatical distinctions

8.3.1. *Dá* 'give'

One of Saramaccan's verbs furthest along the grammaticalization pathway, *dá*'s 'give' meaning has created a marker of the dative and the benefactive. A dative example:

(29) *I   músu   háika   andí   dí   máti   fii   táki   dá   i.*
     2S   must   listen what   DEF friend POSS.2S talk   give   2S
     'You have to listen to what your friend says to you.'

It does not require a human agent:

(30) *Andí   súti   dá   i   só?*
     what   sweet   give   2S   so
     'What's so funny?' (i.e. 'What is giving you so much pleasure?')

As such, *dá* + pronominal functions as an equivalent to many languages' indirect object pronouns (cf. 10.2.1. on ditransitive verbs).
   Two benefactive examples:

(31) *A   féni   wã̌   wósu   dá   mi.*
     3S   find   INDF   house   give   1S
     'He found a house for me.'

(32) *Híbi   wã̌   sɛmbɛ   ábi   u   sólúgu   dá   dé   seéi.*
     all   one   person   have   NF   care.for   give   3P   self
     'Everyone has to care for themselves.'

In some cases, its contribution can be interpreted as either dative or benefactive:

(33) *I   sá   tjái   háfu   wáta   kó   dá   mi   nó?*
     2S   can   carry   half   water   come   give   1S   INT
     'Could you please bring me some water?'

The degree to which it has moved in the direction of prepositionhood is indicated by its use even in a grammatically abbreviated declaration with no main serial verb:

(34) *tú   dágu   dá   híbi   wã̌   wómi*
     two   dog   give   all   one   man
     'two dogs for every man'

Dá can also take a clause as an argument (a case in which Veenstra [1996: 101] treats *dá* as a marker of indirect causality):

(35) *A   butá   hɛ̃   seéi   dá   a   fó   ku   schaak.*
     3S   put   3S.POSS   self   give   3S   beat   with   chess
     'He let himself be beaten by her at a game of chess.' (Veenstra 1996: 101)

Dá can occur with arguments that would suggest that it applies also to source arguments, such as here where the "grand manner" is pulled "from" someone:

(36) Mi   ó   púu   gãã̌   fási   **dá**   i.
      1S   FUT   pull   big   manner   give   2S
      'I'll knock you down a few pegs.' (Veenstra 1996: 166)

However, such sentences also lend themselves to the dative (recipient) analysis when viewed separately from what happen to be their European language translations. For example, the pulling in the above sentence is easily conceived of as happening *to* someone or rendered upon them (cf. French *Je te plumerai* 'I will pluck your feathers' rendered with an object clitic), such that the thematic role of *i* 'you' in the above sentence would be recipient. Also possible is an analysis of the role as malefactive, which often develops historically from benefactives, such as:

(37) Mé   tá   pãtá   **dá**   hɛ̌.
      1S.NEG   IMF   fear   give   3SO
      'I am not afraid of her.' (Veenstra 1996: 166)

Yet there is indeed a serial usage of *dá* in which the object of *dá* is an instrument:

(38) Dí   táfa   fíi   boóko   **dá**   mi.
      DEF   table   POSS.2S   break   give   1S
      'Your table broke on my account.'

A way of parsing this usage as dative would be to suppose that the connotation is a dative of interest, or alternately a malefactive, along the lines of English's idiomatic *Your table broke on me*, implying that the breaking was something unexpected and unavoidable that could have happened on anyone's watch.

An indication that *dá* cannot be classified as a preposition in the proper sense is that it strands, whereas prepositions do not:

(39) Ambé   i   bái   dí   báli   **dá**?
      who   2S   buy   DEF   ball   give
      'Who did you buy the ball for?'

(40) Dí   wómi   dí   mi   mandá   dí   biifi   **dá**   kɛé   dí   a
      DEF   man   REL   1S   send   DEF   letter   give   cry   when   3S

      lési   ɛ̃.
      read   3SO
      'The man I sent the letter to cried when he read it.'

(41) Dí   matjáu   dí   mi   tá   kóti   údu   **ku**   *(ɛ̃)   boóko.
      DEF   axe   REL   1S   IMF   cut   wood   with   3SO   break
      'The axe I chop wood with is broken.'

8.3.2. Degree

Pasá expresses the comparative in cases in which passing is literally possible (more often, the comparative is expressed with *mɔ̌ɔ̃* 'more'; cf. 6.5.1.):

(42) I   lánga **pasá** dí   dɔ́ɔ.
     2S   tall   pass   DEF door
     'You are too tall (to pass through the) door.'

Pói 'spoil' is an alternative to adverbial *túmísi* in expressing the excessive (cf. 6.5.6.):

(43) De tá   peé   dí   póku taánga **pói**.
     3P IMF play DEF poku strong too.much
     'They played poku music too loud.'

8.3.3. Repetition

Tooná, from Portuguese's *tornar*, means 'to turn around' independently:

(44) A   **tooná**   sáápi.
     3S   turn.around   slow
     'He turned around slowly.'

But when used as a serial verb it conveys repetition, as in returning:

(45) Dí   a   **tooná** kó,   hɛ̃   a   léi   andí dí   a   bái.
     when 3S return   come   then   3S show what REL 3S buy
     'When he came back, he showed all the things (whatever) he bought.'

8.3.4. Complementation

Táki 'to talk' occurs in serial conjunction with verbs of utterance and cognition to serve as a complementizer. In this function, *táki* occurs in a phonetically abbreviated form *táa*:

(46) De táki   **táa** bé   i   tapá   dí   dɔ́ɔ.
     3P talk   COMP   HORT 2S close DEF door
     'They said for you to close the door.'

(47) Mi sábi   **táa** té   mi gó a   déndu   naandé, nɔ́ɔ de ó
     1S know COMP   when 1S go LOC inside there   NI   3P FUT

     disá   u   woóko.
     leave NF work
     'I know that when I go in there, they will stop working.'

(48) U sí   **táa** á   súti.
     1P see COMP   3S.NEG   sweet
     'We saw that it wasn't nice.'

(49) Mi wái   **táa** i   kó.
     1S happy COMP   2S come
     'I'm glad you came.'

(50) Mi méni **táa** a bi ó kó.
      1S think COMP 3S PAST FUT come
      'I thought she would come.'

Its grammaticalization is quite advanced, such that *táa* can also occur in existential contexts:

(51) Á dé **táa** mi lóbi ẽ seéi.
      3S.NEG be COMP 1S like 3SO even
      'I don't like him anyway.'

The item can be analyzed, in fact, as having completed its morphing into a true complementizer. However, this analysis cannot be based on phonetic form, as *táa* can also be used as a full verb meaning 'to talk':

(52) Mi **táa** i músu heépi mi.
      1S talk 2S must help 1S
      'I insist that you help me.'

8.3.5. Hortative marker

Bé independently means 'to let, permit':

(53) **Bé** mi tapá dí dɔ́ɔ.
      let 1S close DEF door
      'Let me close the door.'

(54) Mbéi a **bé** i gó.
      make 3S let 2S go
      'Make him let you go.'

(55) Dí wómi disá dí dágu **bé** a gó.
      DEF man leave DEF dog let 3S go
      'The man let the dog go.'

It also serves as a hortative marker:

(56) **Bé** i tapá dí dɔ́ɔ.
      HORT 2S close DEF door
      '*You* close the door.'

(57) Dísi ó taánga – **bóo** poobá. (bóo < bé u)
      this FUT strong HORT.1P try
      'This is going to be hard – let's try.'

This hortative reflex of *bé* is used serially as well, in which case it introduces clauses rather than arguments, like *táki* / *táa* (cf. 8.3.4.):

(58) Mi ké **bé** i kondá déẽ andí pasá.
      1S want HORT 2S tell give.3SO what happen
      'I want you to tell him what happened.'

(59) Mé   ké   **bé**   i   kondá déẽ   andí   pasá.
    1S.NEG   want HORT   2S   tell   give.3SO what   happen
    'I don't want you to tell him what happened.'

Note that this is grammaticalized beyond a literal connotation of 'permit':

(60) Méni   **bé**   já   náki   mí   fútu.
    be.careful   HORT   2S.NEG   hit   1S.POSS   foot
    'Be careful that you don't hit my foot.'

(61) Mi púu   de   **bé**   de   á   féti.
    1S pull   3P   HORT   3P   NEG fight
    'I made them not fight.'

In this usage, *bé* has become a "hortative complementizer," in that the general complementizer *táa* is ungrammatical in contexts where this usage of *bé* occurs:

(62) *Mé   ké   **táa**   i   kondá déẽ   andí   pasá.
    1S.NEG   want COMP   2S   tell   give.3SO what   happen
    'I don't want you to tell him what happened.'

More commonly, however, *ké* 'want' is followed by a nonfinite complement (cf. 9.2.2.1.):

(63) Mi bi   ké   u   híi   ũ   tu   kó   akí.
    1S PAST want   NF   all   2P   also   come   here
    'I wanted all of you to come here, too.'

8.4. Serials with moderately grammaticalized meaning

A few verbs, when used serially, have a meaning somewhat removed from their independent meaning, although these new meanings do not correspond to any cross-linguistic grammatical category.
    Lúku, for example, means 'to look (at)' independently:

(64) I   **lúku**   í   seéi   a   dí   sipéi   ó?
    2S   look   2S   self   LOC   DEF   mirror   INT
    'Are you looking at yourself in the mirror?'

but as a serial encodes to 'try to [verb],' conventionalized as such even with verbs semantically incompatible with its independent meaning of 'look':

(65) Tési   dí   pãpú   beɛɛ   **lúku**.
    taste   DEF   pumpkin   bread   look
    'Taste the pumpkin bread.' (Kramer 2001: 135)

(66) Mi ó   gó náki   ẽ   **lúku**.
    1S FUT go hit   3SO   look
    'I'll go try to hit it.'

Léi alone means 'to show,' as in:

(67) *Dí   a   boóko dí   báta   kaa,   hɛ̃́   a   **léi**   mi.*
     when   3S   break DEF   bottle CPLT   then 3S   show   1S
     'When / before he broke the bottle, he showed it to me.'

When used as a second serial verb, however, it means 'to show how to':

(68) *A   boóko dí   báta   **léi**   mi.*
     3S   break DEF   bottle show   1S
     'He showed me how to break the bottle.' (*'He broke the bottle and showed it to me.')

(69) *A   féífi dí   kámba   **léi**   mi.*
     3S   paint DEF   room   show   1S
     'He showed me how to paint the room.' (*'He painted the room and showed it to me.')

However, even in the serial construction, only the core 'to show' meaning is available when the verb is not a change-of-state one (this observation contributed by Marvin Kramer):

(70) *A   hái   dí   góni   **léi**   mi.*
     3S   haul DEF   gun   show   1S
     'He took out the gun and showed it to me.'

Hópo 'stand up' is used serially to indicate that a person or entity performed an action with a high degree of volition and resolve:

(71) *Mi   **hópo**   kumútu   a   dí   wósu.*
     1S   stand.up   exit   LOC   DEF   house
     'I left the house.'

Here, an informant said that one would say this if something made one leave, that the exit would be in response to something. Thus, it can also apply to the pointed efforts of a chick to get out of an egg:

(72) *Dí   ganĩ́ã   **hópo**   kumútu   a   dí   óbo.*
     DEF   chicken stand.up   exit   LOC   DEF   egg
     'The chicken came out of the egg.'

That *hópo* used serially no longer necessarily conveys its literal meaning of 'stand up' is shown in that it can co-occur with a verb for 'stand':

(73) *Mi   **hópo**   tãã́pu,   hɛ̃́   mi   fã   ku   de.*
     1S   stand.up   stand   then   1S   talk   with   3P
     'I stood up and talked to them.'

8.5. Verbs used serially without change in meaning

There are also some verbs that are used serially with no change in their original meaning, lending it in compositional fashion to the sentence.

8.5.1. *Kabá* 'finish'

Kabá 'finish' when used serially indicates that one is finished doing something:

(74)   *Dí   wósu   wɛ   a   mbéi   **kabá**.*
       DEF   house   FOC   3S   make   finish
       'He finished building the *house*.'

It has been treated in this function as a completive marker, but to the extent that we might suppose so, it is a distinctly moderately grammaticalized one. The completive marker as traditionally understood in Saramaccan is a separate item, which *kabá* was the etymological source for: *kaa*. *Kaa* encodes the completive in purely grammatical terms, untranslatable as 'finish' (cf. 7.3.6. for detailed discussion):

(75)   *A   gó   a   dɔ́ɔ   **kaa**   ɔ́?*
       3S   go   LOC   door   CPLT   INT
       'Did he go (and stay) outside?'

8.5.2. Other verbs

Kaí 'fall' and *kíi* 'kill' (the latter used so often here not because the Saramaka are peculiarly violent but because it is germane to discussing hunting) are also commonly used serially, with their core semantics intact:

(76)   *A   lolá   **kaí**   a   gɔ̃ɔ́.*
       3S   roll   fall   LOC   ground
       'It rolled to the ground.'

(77)   *A   súti   dí   dágu   **kíi**   **kaí**   a   gɔ̃ɔ́.*
       3S   shoot   DEF   dog   kill   fall   LOC   ground
       'He shot the dog dead to the ground.'

Disá 'to leave' is used to connote the releasing aspect of actions such as the following:

(78)   *Sáka   dí   dágu   **disá**   bé   a   kulé   gó   a   dɔ́ɔ.*
       descend   DEF   dog   leave   let   3S   run   go   LOC   door
       'Put the dog down and let him go out.'

'Enough' is expressed in Saramaccan with a verb meaning 'to suffice' *tjiká*, used in both shared object serials and in juxtaposed ones:

(79)   *I   ábi   njãnjã́   **tjiká**   ɔ́?*
       2S   have   food   suffice   INT
       'Do you have enough food?'

(80) Mé   ábi   mɔ́ni   **tjiká**.
     1S.NEG have   money suffice
     'I didn't have enough money.'

(81) Déé   óbo akí   á   jasá **tjiká**.
     DEF.PL egg here NEG fry   suffice
     'These eggs aren't fried enough.'

8.5.3. *Téi* 'take' as "instrumental"?

The use of *téi* as a serial verb is anomalous in Saramaccan, in that each verb occurs with its own object and also in that the verbs are not juxtaposed. Instead, it is two verb phrases – each consisting of a verb and its object – that are juxtaposed:

(82) Kobí **téi** dí   matjáu kóti dí   bɛɛ́ɛ.
     Kobi take   DEF axe   cut   DEF bread
     'Kobi took the knife and cut the bread.'

This construction has been analyzed in previous work on Saramaccan as a strategy for expressing the instrumental. However, *téi* has not grammaticalized to the extent of being an instrumental marker per se. The *téi* serial is used only to convey explicit sequences of taking and wielding (such that the translation of the sentence above is not 'Kobi cut the bread with a knife'). Although it does not contain a serial verb construction, the following sentence from running speech exemplifies how the explicit rendering of taking is a strategy of narrative vividness rather than a grammaticalized expression of the instrumental:

(83) Hɛ̃́   a   **téi** dí   páu,   a   tá   náki dí   páu,   gbó!
     then 3S   take   DEF stick 3S   IMF hit   DEF stick IDEO
     'Then he takes the stick, he's banging the stick *bam*!'

Saramaccan uses one of its few prepositions, *ku* 'with,' to convey the instrumental. Informants do not give *téi* serials as translations of instrumental sentences; in our data, in elicitations, folktales, and running speech the instrumental proper is expressed with *ku*, as in:

(84) Dí   mujɛɛ-míi   tá   fɔ́   pindá   **ku**   tatí   a   máta.
     DEF woman-child   IMF beat peanut with   pestle LOC mortar
     'The girl was pounding the peanuts with a mortar and pestle.'

(85) A   náki dí   fɛ̃́sɛ   boóko **ku**   dí   sitónu.
     3S hit   DEF window break with   DEF rock
     'He broke the window with (i.e. holding) the rock.'

The above sentence, for example, was elicited with a narrative buildup designed to elicit a *téi* serial, such that it was emphasized that the person breaking the window picked up a rock and then broke it while holding the rock rather than hurling the rock through the window. Yet though this was the most explicit rendering of the *téi* serial possible, the informant gave a sentence with *ku*.

The sequence of taking and then wielding an object is so entrenched in human experience that, especially in a language in which verb serialization is a feature of the grammar, it is natural that parataxis would develop between clauses with *téi* and following ones describing the subsequent action. In many languages, exactly this has led *take* verbs to devolve into instrumental markers (e.g. the West African languages Nupe [George 1975] and Yatye [Stahlke 1970]).

In Saramaccan, however, this is not the case; there is, rather, a serialized rendering of what we might term "narratively explicit wielding." There is, in fact, little reason to classify this usage of *téi* as a distinct grammaticalized "construction" in the language; Saramaccan happens to express the true instrumental with a different strategy than verb serialization. The *téi* usage is, rather, a typical example of verbal parataxis in Saramaccan, to which all verbs are subject to an extent (see below).

8.6. Verb serialization as *Sprachgefühl*

Finally, verb serialization is, beyond the grammaticalized and conventionalized cases, part of the warp and woof of the grammar overall, applicable to all verbs when used in conjunction with others to convey single actions within which two or more verbal components are involved. That is, coordination in general is not overtly marked in Saramaccan as often as in European languages:

(86) U   tá   **mókisi butá** dí   hédi   a   wã́.
      1P   IMF   mix   put   DEF   head   LOC   one
      'We are putting our heads together.'

(87) A   **vínde** dí   sitónu **boóko** dí   fɛ́sɛ.
      3S   throw   DEF   rock   break   DEF   window
      'He threw the stone and broke the window with it.'

(88) A   **súti**   dí   patupátu **túwɛ gó kaí** a   wáta.
      3S   shoot   DEF   duck   throw go fall   LOC   water
      'He shot the duck and it fell into the water.'

Chapter 9
Coordination and subordination

9.1. Coordination

9.1.1. Conjunction

Between verbs, overt marking of coordination is not as common in Saramaccan as in European languages. For one, to indicate sequential events, Saramaccan can use verb serialization (cf. Chapter 8) to convey what would be marked with coordination markers in European languages:

(1)   *A féni   baáfu   tjá   gó a   wósu.*
        3S find   soup   carry   go LOC   house
        'He found the soup and carried it into the house.'

(2)   *Mi sáka   híi soní   túwɛ   kulé.*
        1S descend   all thing   throw   run
        'I dropped everything and ran.'

The imperfective marker can occur on both verbs in the serial construction:

(3)   *U bi   ó   tá   síngi   tá   bajá.*
        1P PAST   FUT   IMF   sing   IMF   dance
        'We were going to sing and dance.'

One can also use overt sequential markers for greater explicitness. These vary according to the past/non-past distinction that they do in marking new information (cf. 15.2.2.): *hɛ̃́* is used in the past, *nɔ́ɔ* in the non-past:

(4)   *Mi sí dí   awaá   **hɛ̃́**   mi njãmɛ̃.*
        1S see DEF   palm.fruit   then   1S eat.3SO
        'I saw the palm fruit and ate it.'

(5)   *Dí   dágu   tá   bái   **nɔ́ɔ**   a   tá   kulé   tá   lótu.*
        DEF   dog   IMF   bark   now   3S   IMF   run   IMF   go.round
        'The dog is barking and running in circles.'

Verb-phrase ellipsis does not occur in coordinated constructions in Saramaccan. Informants regularly render such sentences as *John went to the store and Amba did too* with the two subjects coordinated as a single noun phrase:

(6)   *John   ku   Ámba   bi   gó a   dí   wɛ̃́kɛ.*
        John   with   Amba   PAST   go LOC   DEF   store
        'John and Amba went to the store.'

9.1.2. Disjunction

'Or' is rendered by (ée) náá (só) 'if it is not that it is so' (cf. 4.6.):

(7) Hɛ̃́   wɛ   a   tjɛ̃́ɛ̃   gó a   dí   písi,
     then   FOC   3S   carry.3SO   go LOC   DEF   home

   náá só ba   ɛ̃   butá   ɛ̃   a   wǎ   bukéti déndu.
   or   carry 3SO   put   3SO   LOC   INDF   bucket inside
   'Then she carried it to her house, or hauled it in and put it into a bucket.' (from a speaker unsure of a detail in a story)

(8) Ná   gó alá   **ée náá só**   mi ó   náki   i.
     NEG   go yonder   or   1S FUT   hit   2S
     'Don't go there or I will beat your butt.'

'Either ... or' is náá ... náá:

(9) I   sá   **náá**   táki   **náá**   duumí.
     2S   can   either   talk   or   sleep
     'You can either talk or sleep.'

9.1.3. Exclusion

'But' is ma:

(10) Mi   súti   dí   píngo,   **ma**   a   dé   a   líbi.
     1S   shoot   DEF   pig   but   3S   be   LOC   live
     'I shot the pig, but he is alive.'

(11) I   bi   sá   kó   éside,   **ma**   ná   tidé.
     2S   PAST   can   come   yesterday   but   NEG   today
     'You could have come yesterday, but not today.'

After concessive adverbial clauses, Saramaccan exhibits what can be termed "expletive exclusion." The exclusionary semantics of the dependent clause ('counterexpectationally to *X*...') bleed into the marking of the matrix, such that *ma* is used in a fashion that would classify as redundant in English (cf. 9.2.3.7. on concessive clauses):

(12) Aluási   fá   mi lóbi   ɛ̃   seéi,   **ma**   tɔ́kúsééi   á
     even.though   how   1S love   3SO   even   but   nevertheless   3S.NEG

   lóbi   mi.
   love   1S
   'Even though I love him, all the same he doesn't love me.'

9.2. Subordination

9.2.1. Finite complements

9.2.1.1. Factive complements

One class of finite complements have been discussed in 8.3.4.: factive sentential complements formed with the serial verb and complementizer *táa*.

This class also includes sentential complements that occur juxtaposed to the matrix with no overt complementizer, such as the usual case when the verb is not one of utterance or cognition:

(13) A   mɔ́ɔ̃   béte   já   wási   dí   wági.
      3S   more   advisable   2S.NEG   wash   DEF   car
      'You'd better not wash the car.'

(14) A   léi   dí   sṹ   tjiká   a   kó   sábi   andí   a   tá   dú.
      3S   learn   DEF   swim   suffice   3S   come   know   what   3S   IMF   do
      'He learned how to swim enough to get the hang of it.'

9.2.1.2. Hortative complements

Bé 'to let' is used as a complementizer carrying hortative meaning (cf. 8.3.5.):

(15) Méni   **bé**   já   náki   mí   fútu.
      be.careful   HORT   2S.NEG   hit   1S.POSS   foot
      'Be careful that you don't hit my foot.'

9.2.1.3. Complements of perception and causation verbs

Verbs of perception and causation take complements whose subjects are not marked as objects as they are in English:

(16) Mi   sí   *a*   tá   kulé   gó.
      1S   see   3S   IMF   run   go
      'I saw him running / run.'

(17) *Mi   sí   ɛ̃   tá   kulé   gó.
      1S   see   3SO   IMF   run   go
      'I saw him running / run.'

(18) Mi   mbéi   *a*   bebé   wáta.
      1S   make   3S   drink   water
      'I made him drink water.'

(19) *Mi   mbéi   ɛ̃   bebé   wáta.
      1S   make   3SO   drink   water
      'I made him drink water.'

The subordinate clause can begin with *fá* 'how' as well:

(20) Mi tá lúku **fá** déé kijɔɔ tá pɛé dí báli.
     1S IMF look how DEF.PL fellow IMF play DEF ball
     'I watch the kids playing ball.'

Thus these complements can be treated as finite, also given that they can be marked for aspect as in the first example above.

However, Veenstra (1996: 57–72) presents an argument that these complements are nonfinite despite the absence of object marking on their subject. Veenstra analyses Saramaccan's subject pronouns as syntactic clitics, such that the complements in the sentences above have null subjects, marked with case by the matrix verb but invisible on the surface; he presents several behavioral features of the complements to support his case. Under his Minimalist analysis, the fact that the complements can be marked with aspect is less important than that they cannot be marked with tense, tense being under generative analysis a diagnostic sign of finiteness:

(21) *Mi sí a **bi** kulé gó.
     1S see 3S PAST run go
     'I saw him run.'

(Note that the ungrammaticality of the above sentence suggests that these sentences do involve a shared argument rather than being matrix clauses with sentential complements. For example, one might suppose that *Mi sí a tá kulé gó* is a rendition of *Mi sí **táa** a tá kulé gó*, but this would leave unexplained the ungrammaticality of the above-glossed sentence with past marker *bi* given that *Mi sí táa a bi kulé gó* is grammatical.)

Verdicts on Veenstra's analysis will depend considerably upon the assessor's orientation towards the Minimalist paradigm. For example, the above sentence is grammatically rendered in the past via marking on the matrix verb:

(22) Mi **bi** sí a kulé gó.
     1S PAST see 3S run go
     'I saw him run.'

such that one might classify marking the dependent verb alone for the past as ruled out by virtue of noniconicity; meanwhile, the possibility of marking *both* the matrix *and* the dependent verb would be ruled out by the fact that double tense marking is ungrammatical in the grammar in general (cf. 8.1.1.).

Meanwhile, causative *mbéi* has been treated as a serial verb in some sources, but we do not include it in that class. There are constructions we have classed as serial verbs that lack one of the prototypical traits of serial verbs: the *téi* serial does not entail a shared object (cf. 8.5.3.), while some serials with directional verbs do not share a subject (cf. 8.1.2.). However, the *mbéi* causative construction lacks both of these traits – and in the meantime is formally identical to sentences with perception verbs taking a complement. The motivation for treating causative *mbéi* as a serial verb, then, is unclear.

9.2.2. Nonfinite complements

9.2.2.1. Control verbs

Control verbs take nonfinite complements, with both subject and object control. The marker of nonfiniteness is (f)u (< *for*), which in this capacity occurs almost always as *u*:

(23) *Mi ké   u   bái   dí   sutúu dí   a   bi   sindó néẽ́*
     1S want NF buy   DEF   chair REL 3S PAST sit   LOC.3S.POSS

   déndu.
   inside
   'I want to buy the chair that he sat in.'

(24) *Mi bi   paamúsi u   wási dí   wági.*
     1S PAST promise NF wash DEF car
     'I promised to wash the car.'

(25) *Mi bi   tá   poobá u   dá   kái   únu.*
     1S PAST IMF   try   NF give call 2PO
     'I was trying to call you.'

(26) *U   hángi   u   sí   únu pói.*
     1P hungry NF see 2PO too.much
     'We were *really* longing to see you.'

(27) *De tá   léi   u   bisí koósu dé seéi.*
     3P IMF learn NF wear clothes 3P self
     'They learn how to dress themselves.'

(28) *Mi sábi táa   té   mi gó a   déndu naandé, nɔ́ɔ de ó*
     1S know COMP when 1S go LOC inside there   NI   3P FUT

   disá u   woóko.
   leave NF work
   'I know that when I go in there, they will stop working.'

(29) *Mi bi   ké   u   híi ũ   tu   kó   akí.*
     1S PAST want NF all 2P also come here
     'I wanted all of you to come here, too.'

(30) *A   hákisi ná   wã́   kódo sɛmbɛ u   heépi ɛ̃.*
     3S   ask   NEG one single person NF help   3SO
     'He hasn't asked a single person to help him.'

(31) *U   hákisi ɛ̃   sábi,   faa   sá   léi u   pási.*   (*faa < fu a*)
     1P ask   3SO knowledge NF.3S UFUT show 1P path
     'We asked him for knowledge, to show us the way.'

High-usage control verbs such as *ké* 'want,' *léi* 'learn to,' and *heépi* 'help' occur variably without *u*:

(32) Naásé i ké gó?
 where 2S want go
 'Where do you want to go?'

(33) Mi ké gó a wósu.
 1S want go LOC house
 'I want to go home.'

(34) Mi heépi ẽ mbéi dí wósu.
 1S help 3SO make DEF house
 'I helped him build the house.'

(35) Tidé u ó gó a lío gó léi wási ú seéi.
 today 1P FUT go LOC river go learn wash 1P self
 'Today we're going to the river to learn to wash ourselves.'

This elision also occurs with sentential complements:

(36) Dí mujée u mi á ké mi bái ẽ.
 DEF woman POSS 1S NEG want 1S buy 3SO
 'My wife doesn't want me to buy it.'

There is no category of raising verbs in Saramaccan (in which the syntactic subject is the semantic subject of the subordinate clause). The verb meaning 'seem,' for example, is used with a pleonastic pronoun and takes an adverbial complement clause:

(37) A géi kumafá a fusutã́ andí mi tá fã́.
 3S seem like 3S understand what 1S IMF talk
 'He seems to understand what I'm saying.'

9.2.2.2. Small clauses

In Saramaccan, small clause complements – i.e. with neither complementizer nor evidence of tense – are possible as noun phrase, adjective phrase, or prepositional phrase:

(38) Mi féni ẽ **wã́ bumbúu dáta**.
 1S find 3SO INDF good.RD doctor
 'I found him (to be) a good doctor.'

(39) Mi féni ẽ **hã́so**.
 1S find 3SO pretty
 'I found her (to be) pretty.'

(40) Mi ké dí pusipúsi **a dí wósu déndu**.
 1S want DEF cat LOC DEF house inside
 'I want the cat (to be) in the house.'

But often elsewhere, where a language like English has small clauses, Saramaccan has a dependent clause marked with *u* and containing an overt verb. This is because Saramaccan grammar is one that tends strongly to express with verbs what is rendered in English with other constituent types.

For example, where English would have a prepositional phrase small clause as in *I want the cat out of the house*, because Saramaccan expresses the concept of 'out' with verbs of leaving or removal and has no preposition meaning 'out,' the Saramaccan translation would be:

(41) Miké   u   dí   pusipúsi gó   disá   a   dí   wosú.
     1S want NF DEF cat   go   leave LOC DEF   house.
     'I want the cat to leave the house.'

Where English has an adjective small clause such as *He painted the house red*, Saramaccan often renders the property item as a verb, such as in conjunction with *kó* 'become':

(42) Mi féífi   dí   wósu   **kó**   bɛ.
     1S paint DEF   house become   red
     'I painted the house red.'

(43) Mi bói   dí   físi   **kó**   tjumá.
     1S cook DEF   fish   become   burn
     'I burned the fish black.'

To be sure, a sentence like this is grammatical without *kó*: *Mi féífi dí wósu bɛ*. Here, however, the sentence is analyzable either as a small clause or as a shared-object serial verb, given that property items in Saramaccan behave as verbs outside of attributive prenominal usage (cf. 6.1.).

Some treatments of small clauses include complements of perception verbs such as in 'I saw him come,' upon which cf. 9.2.1.3. above.

9.2.2.3. Gerund complements

English verbal noun complements are rendered as nonfinite, marked variably with *(f)u*; the subject pronoun is optional in complements containing *(f)u*, but it is not allowed in those without it:

(44) Kobí   wáka   sóndɔ   (f)u   a   kaí.
     Kobi   walk   without NF   3S   fall

     Kobí   wáka   sóndɔ   (f)u   kaí.
     Kobí   wáka   sóndɔ   kaí.
     *Kobí   wáka   sóndɔ   a   kaí.

     'Kobi walked without falling.'

9.2.3. Subordination: Adverbial complement clauses

9.2.3.1. Temporal complements

With temporal complementation, Saramaccan has conditioned variant clause-initial marking of new information on the matrix clause, with both tense and aspect involved in the conditioning.

In the past tense, when the matrix clause is of unbounded semantics, it is introduced by the item *nɔ́ɔ*, which functions in this context as a marker of new information (cf. 15.2.2.):

(45) *Báka dí de gó, **nɔ́ɔ** dí mujée bi tá keé.*
after when 3P go NI DEF woman PAST IMF cry
'After they left, the woman was crying.'

(46) *Bifɔ́ de gó, **nɔ́ɔ** dí mujée bi tá keé.*
before 3P go NI DEF woman PAST IMF cry
'Before they left, the woman was crying.'

(47) *Dí mi bi kó lúku de, **nɔ́ɔ** de bi duumí kaa.*
when 1S PAST come look 3P NI 3P PAST sleep CPLT
'When I came to see them, they were asleep.'

(48) *Dí mi kabá u njã́ a dí sónúati njãnjã́, **nɔ́ɔ** hángi*
when 1S finish NF eat LOC DEF noon food NI hunger

bi kísi mi éti.
PAST catch 1S yet
'After I finished eating lunch, I was still hungry.'

But if the matrix clause has punctual semantics, then the new information marker is *hɛ́* which translates as 'then,' although the Saramaccan rendition of 'then' in an explicitly sequential sense is properly the focus-marked *hɛ́ wɛ* (cf. 15.1.3.2.):

(49) ***Dí** a bi tá duumí, **hɛ́** mi gó kumútu dé.*
when 3S PAST IMF sleep then 1S go exit there
'When he was sleeping, I left.'

(50) ***Dí** mi bi jabí dí dɔ́ɔ, **hɛ́** mi sí dí gṍ ṍ mũnjã́.*
when 1S PAST open DEF door then 1S see DEF ground wet
'When I opened the door, I saw the ground wet.'

In the non-past, for one, the dependent clause is marked not by *dí* but *té*, though both are translatable as 'when':

(51) ***Té** mujée sí Kobí, **nɔ́ɔ** de tá kulé.*
when woman see Kobi NI 3P IMF run
'When women see Kobi, they run.'

(52) ***Té** John fã, **nɔ́ɔ** híi sɛmbɛ tá háika ẽ.*
when John talk NI all person IMF listen 3SO
'When John talks, everybody listens to him.'

In the non-past, *nɔ́ɔ* is neutral to unboundedness and is used with bounded semantics as well, such that *hɛ̃́* is ungrammatical. *Nɔ́ɔ* occurs, for example, in bounded future-marked matrix clauses:

(53) **Té** mi sí Kobí, **nɔ́ɔ** mi ó kulé.
 when 1S see Kobi NI 1S FUT run
 'When I see Kobi, I will run.'

(54) **Té** mi féni dí kámba dí mi lóbi, **nɔ́ɔ** mi ó gó
 when 1S find DEF room REL 1S like NI 1S FUT go

 nɛ̃ɛ̃́ déndu.
 LOC.3S.POSS inside
 'When I find the right room, I will go into it.'

Dí is ungrammatical in marking the dependent clause in the non-past:

(55) Mi ó wái **té** Marv kó. (**Mi ó wái dí Marv kó.*)
 1S FUT happy when Marv come
 'I will be happy when Marv comes.'

This ungrammaticality extends to the conditional:

(56) Mi bi ó wái **té** / *dí Marv kó.
 1S PAST FUT happy when / when Marv come
 'I would be happy when Marv came.'

There are two further remarks on *hɛ̃́* and *nɔ́ɔ* as new information markers. First, as seen above, they are used only when the matrix comes after the subordinate clause, as they mark temporal and/or logical sequence. Second, their absence is grammatical: in running speech they are usually used, but not always. However, the subordinate clause markers *dí* and *té* are obligatory.

The conditioning of these temporal conjunctions and new information markers can be illustrated thus:

Table 25. Co-occurrence patterns of temporal conjunctions and new information markers

	SUBORDINATE	PUNCTUAL MATRIX	UNBOUNDED MATRIX
PAST	dí	hɛ̃́	nɔ́ɔ
NON-PAST	té	nɔ́ɔ	nɔ́ɔ

Té can also connote 'until' (also used: *té fá*):

(57) U láfu **té** u kaí a gõɔ̃́.
 1P laugh until 1P fall LOC ground
 'We laughed till we fell to the floor.'

9.2.3.2. Purpose complements

(F)u conveys 'in order to, so that':

(58) Híi bási dí dá u dí wósu **fuu** sá tã́ akí báka.
 all boss REL give 1P DEF house for.1P UFUT stand here again
 'All the bosses that gave us the house in order that we would stay here again.'

(59) Kulé   u   kulé   **u**   kumútu   kó   a   dɔ́ɔ.
      run   1P   run   for   exit   come   LOC   door
      'We *ran* to come outside.'

With the verbs *gó* 'go' and *kó* 'come,' 'in order to' can be conveyed instead with a second *gó* or *kó* in the complement clause. With these verbs, the use of *(f)u* lends a subjunctive implication that the action may not have been realized:

(60) Mi   bi   gó   a   wósu   **gó**   njã́.
      1S   PAST   go   LOC   house   go   eat
      'I went home to eat.'

(61) Mi   bi   gó   a   wósu   **u**   njã́.
      1S   PAST   go   LOC   house   for   eat
      'I went home to eat (but possibly I didn't get to after all).'

For one informant, the *u* sentence above meant definite failure: "There's no food in the house at all!"

(62) A   gó   a   wɛ́kɛ   **gó**   bái   soní.
      3S   go   LOC   store   go   buy   thing
      'He went to the store to buy things.'

(63) Tidé   u   ó   gó   a   lío   **gó**   léi   wási   ú   seéi.
      today   1P   FUT   go   LOC   river   go   learn   wash   1P   self
      'Today we're going to the river to learn to wash ourselves.'

The subjunctive implication is also lent when *(f)u* is used in conjunction with the second *gó* or *kó* in this construction:

(64) Mi   bi   nángó   a   wɛ́kɛ   **u**   **gó**   bái   wã́   búku,   ma   a   tapá.
      1S   PAST   IMF.go   LOC   store   for   go   buy   INDF   book   but   3S   close
      'I was going to the store to buy a book but it was closed.'

This sentence from Aboikoni and Glock (1997: 15) nicely shows the contrast between the two usages:

(65) Faa   músu   tjá   gó   nɛ̃ɛ̃́   kɔ́ndɛ   **gó**   paatí   dá   déé   gãã́
      for.3S   must   carry   go   LOC.3S.POSS   village   go   divide   give   DEF.PL   big

      wómi   ku   déé   gãã́   mujéɛ,   déé   ná   sá   kó
      man   with   DEF.PL   big   woman   REL.PL   NEG   can   come

      dóu   **fu**   kó   sí   ku   dé   seéi   wójo.
      arrive   for   come   see   with   3P   self   eye
      'It must go into its village to divide (supplies) among those old men and women who cannot (might not be able to) come see with their own eyes.'

9.2.3.3. Locational complements

The marker of locational complements is *ká*, Saramaccan's subordinating conjunction of location distinct from the wh-word *naásé* 'where':

(66) Dísi   da   dí   kamíã **ká**   a   tá   líbi.
     this   be   DEF   place where   3S   IMF   live
     'This is the place where she lived.'

(67) Nɔ́ɔ   máku   bi   tá   njã́   de   **ká**   a   gó   alá.
     now   mosquito PAST   IMF   eat   3P   where   3S   go   yonder
     'So mosquitos were biting them in the place they were travelling in there.'

9.2.3.4. Manner complements

Saramaccan marks clausal complements of manner with *kumafá* or its shorter form *fá* (*kumafá* is derived from *kúma* 'like' + *fá* 'how'):

(68) Dí   ganĩ́ã   á   tá   kandá   **kumafá**   a   bi   kandá   mɔ̃́ɔ̃.
     DEF   chicken NEG   IMF   sing   like   3S   PAST   sing   more
     'The chicken isn't singing like it used to.'

(69) Mé   sá   **fá**   u   táki   ẽ   nɔ́ɔ.
     1S.NEG   know   how   1P   talk   3SO   just
     'I just don't know how we say it …!'

However, the essence of Saramaccan grammar is such that manner is also conveyed with ideophones, to a degree much more than in languages like English, such as this sentence in which leaving suddenly is rendered with an ideophone; cf. 14.7. for further discusssion of ideophones.

(70) U   bi   tá   fã,   hẽ́   a   gó   **djééé**.
     1P   PAST   IMF   talk   then   3S   go   up.and.go
     'We were talking, and then she just up and left.'

9.2.3.5. Causal complements

Causality can be expressed with *bigá* 'because' or *(f)u dí* 'for the thing that':

(71) Dí   bálima   kaí   **bigá**   de   tɔ́tɔ   ẽ.
     DEF   ball.player fall   because   3P   push   3SO
     'The soccer player fell because they pushed him.'

(72) Nɔ́ɔ   **fu dí**   a   paí,   nɔ́ɔ   déé   óto   sɛmbɛ   u   dí   kɔ́ndɛ,
     now   for that   3S   bear   now   DEF.PL   other   person   of   DEF   village

     de   á   tá   sí   ẽ   u   soní.
     3P   NEG   IMF   see   3SO   of   thing
     'Now, because she had a baby, the other village people didn't want to have anything to do with her.'

Another causal marker is *nda*, from *hɛ̃́ da* 'it is':

(73) **Nda** dí wági ná u mi, nɔ́ɔ i ó paká féé.
since DEF car NEG POSS 1S NI 2S FUT pay for.3SO
'Since the car is not mine, you're going to pay for it.'

Another causal construction, with *mbéi* 'make,' entails that the cause is rendered as the matrix clause and the result as the dependent clause, such as this sentence with a sentential nominal subject:

(74) Dí wági u mi boóko **mbéi** mi téi dí bus.
DEF car POSS 1S broken make 1S take DEF bus
'I am taking the bus because my car is broken.'

A more common rendition is *hɛ̃́ mbéi*:

(75) Féé a dí búku akí, **hɛ̃́ mbéi** a ké ɛ̃.
POSS.3SO be DEF book here 3S make 3S want 3SO
'This is his book, that's why he wants it.' (i.e. 'He wants it because it's his book.')

An alternate is *féé mbéi*:

(76) **Féé** **mbéi** mi dé akí.
POSS.3SO make 1S be here
'That's why I'm here.'

9.2.3.6. Conditional complements

'If' is *ée*; notice that *nɔ́ɔ* is available to introduce the matrix sentences, approximating the connotation of English's *then* in the same usage as it does in temporal subordination (but cf. 15.2.2. on the meaning of *nɔ́ɔ*).

(77) Ée mi sí ɛ̃, mi ó kíi ɛ̃.
if 1S see 3SO 1S FUT kill 3SO
'If I see him, I'll kill him.'

(78) Ée dí míi á dú ɛ̃, nɔ́ɔ dí m'má ó náki ɛ̃.
if DEF child NEG do 3SO NI DEF Mom FUT hit 3SO
'If the child doesn't do it, then the Mom will hit him.'

As in English, the hypothetical and the counterfactual are expressed with past marking in the subordinate clause and the conditional (expressed with the pairing of past marker *bi* and future marker *ó*; cf. 7.5.) in the matrix:

(79) Ée ná mi bi síki, mi bi ó gó a wowójo.
if NEG 1S PAST sick 1S PAST FUT go LOC market
'If I weren't sick, I would go to the market.'

(80) Ée mi bi á móni.
if 1S PAST have money
'If only I had money.'

(81) Ée i bi fã dí tuú dá mi, mí háti á
    if 2S PAST talk DEF truth give 1S 1S.POSS heart NEG

bi ó boónu.
PAST FUT burn
'If you'd told me the truth, I wouldn't be angry.'

(82) Ée i bi láfu mi, mi bi ó féti ku i.
    if 2S PAST laugh 1S 1S PAST FUT fight with 2S
'If you'd laughed at me, I'd have fought with you.'

9.2.3.7. Concessive complements

The concessive can be expressed with *híi fá* 'all how,' its shorter form *fá*, *híi dí* 'all that which,' *aluási* 'even though,' or *ée* 'if.' All can co-occur with clause-final *seéi*, derived from *self* (cf. 5.5.) but here used in its pragmatic function which translates as 'even':

(83) **Híi fá** de dé duumí duumí (**seéi**), nɔ́ɔ hɛ̃́ sɛmbɛ kó a
    all how 3P be sleep sleep even NI then person come LOC

dí wósu.
DEF house
'Even though they were sleeping, people came into the house.'

(84) **Fá** u tá dú dísi **seéi**, mi ó tjumá dí wósu akí.
    how 1P IMF do this even 1S FUT burn DEF house here
'Even though we are doing this, I am going to burn down this house.'

(85) **Híi dí** má lóbi ɛ̃ (**seéi**), ma tɔ́kúsééi a
    all that.which 1S.NEG like 3SO even but nevertheless 3S

ó kó akí.
FUT come here
'Even though I don't like him, all the same he will come here.'

(86) **Aluási fá** mi lóbi ɛ̃ (**seéi**), ma tɔ́kúsééi á
    even.though how 1S love 3SO even but nevertheless 3S.NEG

lóbi mi.
love 1S
'Even though I love him, all the same he doesn't love me.'

(87) Ée de á tá féni ɛ̃ ku de **seéi**, ma de tá woóko
    if 3P NEG IMF find 3SO with 3P even but 3P IMF work

a wã̌ seéi kamíã.
LOC one self place
'Though they do not get along, they are working at the same place.'

With *fá* and *ée*, the clause-final *seéi* is obligatory.

In concessive sentences, the subordinate clause is optionally adjoined rather than embedded, with *ma* 'but' and/or *tɔ́kú / tɔ́kúsééi* 'nevertheless' occurring before the main clause.

9.2.3.8. Substitutive complements

'Instead of' is *ká (f)u* (cf. 9.2.3.3 on *ká*):

(88) A   kandá   **ká**   **faa**   bajá.
      3S   sing   place   for.3S   dance
      'He sings instead of dancing.'

Chapter 10
Passive and imperative

10.1. Valence-decreasing operations

10.1.1. Passive voice

In Saramaccan grammar, the promotion of patients to subjecthood and suppression or demotion of agents is relatively marginal compared to the entrenchment of such in European and other languages. Informants strongly tend to give active sentences in the generic third-person plural as translations for passive sentences, and it is in this way that sentences that would be passive in English are usually rendered in Saramaccan discourse:

(1)   *Dí*   *bálima*   *kaí*   *bigá*   ***de tɔ́tɔ***   ***ɛ̃***   ***a***   ***báka***.
     DEF   ball.player   fall   because   3P   push   3SO   LOC   back
     'The soccer player fell because he got hit in the back.'

(2)   *Hɛ̃́*   *da*   *dí*   *fóótóo*   *dí*   *déé*   *sɔ́sútu*   *tjá*   *kó*   *léi*   *mi*   *dí*
     3S   be   DEF   photo   REL   DEF.PL   nurse   carry   come   show   1S   when

     de palí   *i.*
     3P bear   2S
     'This is the picture that the nurses showed me when you were born.'

Note in the previous sentence that the passive is rendered with a third-person plural subject pronoun regardless of literal semantics: the act of bearing a child is, of course, effected by a single person, and yet the passive 'to be born' is rendered in the sentence with *de* 'they.'
     Where passive meaning is expressed, it is only with dynamic transitive verbs:

(3)   *Dí*   *wági*   *akí*   *músu*   *wási*   *híbi*   *wã́*   *wíki*.
     DEF   car   here   must   wash   all   one   week
     'This car has to be washed every week.'

(4)   *Dí   *búku*   *lóbi.*
     DEF   book   love
     'The book is loved.'

Note also that passive semantics are zero-marked, with context determining that the subject is a patient. Thus here is *jasá* 'fry' used in an active meaning:

(5)   *Abíti*   *mɔ́ɔ̃*   *mi*   *ó*   *jasá*   *só*   *óbo.*
     a.little   more   1S   FUT   fry   some   egg
     'I'll be frying some eggs in a minute.'

and then in a passive one:

(6) *Déé óbo akí á jasá tjiká.*
    DEF.PL egg here NEG fry suffice
    'These eggs aren't fried enough.' (*'These eggs do not fry [something] enough.')

As such, verbs used passively are often accompanied by items that disambiguate them from active usage. For example, our informants vastly prefer *sikífi* 'to write' accompanied in the passive by a locational adjunct:

(7) *Dí né sikífi *(nɛ̃ɛ̃).*
    DEF name write LOC.3SO
    'The name is written down *(on it).'

and meanwhile, passive meaning is also often (although not obligatorily) indicated with completive marker *kaa* (cf. 7.3.6.), despite that the passive entails completivity inherently:

(8) *Dí físi kóti **kaa**.*
    DEF fish cut CPLT
    'The fish has been cut.'

For the most part, sentences with passive meaning do not allow expression of the agent. Some sources have posed adjuncts composed of *(f)u* + pronominal (cf. 3.3.1.) as potential *by*-phrases to test with informants, such as:

(9) *Dí wósu dé mbéimbéi **u mi**.*
    DEF house be make.RD 'u' 1S
    'The house has been made by me.' (Bakker 1987: 29)

But even Bakker notes that this sentence is accepted only "at least in certain dialects," i.e. only by some informants. Moreover, informants' acceptance of such a sentence as grammatical does not, in itself, prove that Saramaccan has *by*-phrases. Our informants only accept such sentences as grammatical assuming that, for example, *u mi* is a possessive or benefactive phrase. This is, for example, what Kramer (2001: 122) finds: in his informant work, speakers assume that in *Dí wósu dé mbéimbéi u mi, u mi* means 'my' or 'for me,' such that the sentence means 'My house was made.' Kramer's informant work found the *by*-phrase interpretation ungrammatical, as has our own, and this is also the case when passive meaning is expressed with an unreduplicated verb, e.g.:

(10) **Dí* wósu féífi **u mi**.*
    DEF house paint 'u' 1S
    'The house was painted by me.' (Kramer 2001: 122)

There is in Saramaccan no independent justification for assuming that the semantics of *(f)u*, which encompass possession, association, nonfinite marking, and subjunctive marking with complements of motion verbs, include the agentive connotation of instrumental *by*. Based on *fu*'s semantic and functional domain, our several informants' judgments, and the absence of instrumental usage of *fu* in any oral transcriptions or written sources that we are aware of, we are forced to conclude that the few Saramaccan informants consulted by a small number of analysts who have accepted *fu* as an instrumental marker have been influenced by long-term usage of

European languages such as Dutch. It would appear appropriate to stipulate that *fu* is in fact not an instrumental marker in Saramaccan proper.

While in a language like English, passivized agents are readily and frequently rendered as *by*-phrases, in Saramaccan passivized agents are quite rare. Where they are expressed, it is in the particular context of a usage of *dá* 'to give' in a serial verb construction, in which it means 'on one's account' (cf. 8.3.1.):

(11) Dí   táfa   fii   booko   **dá**   **mi**.
     DEF   table   POSS.2S   break   give   1S
     'Your table broke on my account.'

This can be taken as meaning 'Your table was broken by me.' However, this usage of *dá* occurs only when the object of *dá* is capable of responsibility, and thus human, and only in the particular context in which something inappropriate has occurred for which someone feels a need to apologize. Therefore:

(12) *Dí   pusipúsi   kíi   **dá**   dí   dágu.
     DEF   cat   kill   give   DEF   dog
     'The cat was killed by the dog.'

This usage of *dá* is ungrammatical after reduplicated resultatives (cf. 6.4.); informants interpret *dá* as benefactive in such cases (and also receive the sentence as highly infelicitous):

(13) *Dí   wósu   dé   mbéimbéi   **dá**   **mi**.
     DEF   house   be   make.RD   give   1S
     'The house has been made by me.'

Overall, then, in Saramaccan sentences, passivity less decreases than subtracts valence; almost always, the agent is suppressed rather than demoted, such that passive meaning entails a transitive verb with a single argument instead of two.

Kó 'come' lends Saramaccan's equivalent to English's *get*-passive, in its reflex as 'become' (cf. 8.1.2.), implying that a given state was accomplished counter to some expectation:

(14) Dí   míi   **kó**   wási.
     DEF   child   come   wash
     'The child got washed.' (Kramer 2001: 117)

(15) Dí   bíifi   **kó**   sikífi.
     DEF   letter   come   write
     'The letter got written.' (Kramer 2001: 115)

These constructions are interpretable as resultative, and yet are not reduplicated as they would be after *dé* 'to be':

(16) Dí   né   dé   sikífisikífi   nḛ̃ḛ̃.
     DEF   name   be   write.RD   LOC.3SO
     'The name is written down on it.'

Thus we can either stipulate that the *kó* construction locally suppresses the reduplication of resultatives, or treat this usage of *kó* as Saramaccan's only truly grammaticalized marker of the passive, albeit of only a subset of the total domain of passiveness.

English's *have* [noun] [verb]-*ed* passive construction is rendered as a causative with *mbéi* (cf. 9.2.1.3.):

(17) Djǔsu Djéfi gó mbéi de seeká ɛ̃́ hǔjã dɛ̃́ɛ̃.
just Jeff go make 3P care.for 3S.POSS nail give.3SO
'Jeff just had his nails done.'

In Saramaccan, then, passive meaning – i.e. the promotion of the patient as a subject – is largely interpreted via context, with oblique prepositional phrases and completive marker *kaa* serving as optional strategies to make clear the passive intent of the proposition. The only explicit markers of the passive are usages of *dá* 'to give' and *kó* 'to come,' which express certain pragmatically specific subsets of the passive.

10.1.2. Middle voice

There is no overt marking of middle voice in Saramaccan. Rather, a subset of verbs occur in both active and middle meanings. In the latter, the patient and agent arguments are identical, but only the patient one is expressed. As such, middle voice in Saramaccan is a valence-decreasing construction. Here are *jabí* 'open' and *boóko* 'break' in their active and middle usages:

(18) Dí mi bi **jabí** dí dɔ́ɔ, hɛ̃́ mi sí dí gõɔ̃́ mũnjã́.
when 1S PAST open DEF door then 1S see DEF ground wet
'When I opened the door, I saw the ground wet.'

(19) Dí tjúba kaí u téni dáka, awáa fu dí sónu **jabí**.
DEF rain fall for ten day at.last for DEF sun open
'It rained for ten days and then finally the sun came out.'

(20) Vɛ́tu sá **boóko** ɛ̃ túwɛ ɔ́?
wind can break 3SO throw INT
'Can the wind have broken them (i.e. these branches) down and scattered them around?'

(21) A **boóko** púu a dí páu.
3S break pull LOC DEF tree
'It broke off of the tree.'

There is no equivalent in Saramaccan to the overt expression of the patients of middle verbs as reflexive pronominals, as in Spanish *Se quebró la ventana* 'The window broke (itself).' The reflexive is used only in contexts where the identity of subject and object is concrete and literal:

(22) Mi kóti mí seéi a fútu.
1S cut 1S self LOC foot
'I cut myself on the foot.'

Even in cases that tempt a "middle" analysis along the lines of the use of *-self* in English, the Saramaccan rendition is one whose semantics happen to submit to the literal reflexive interpretation as in the sentence above. For example, albeit the English *behave yourself* is a rare example in that language of a non-literal reflexive (the English speaker knows what it is to "behave," but how one would do such "upon oneself" is compositionally opaque), the equivalent Saramaccan sentence is thoroughly compositional: 'keep a watch upon yourself':

(23) Ũ méni ṹ seéi.
    2P be.careful 2P self
    'You behave yourselves!'

10.1.3. Object omission

Another valence-demoting strategy in Saramaccan is that object pronominals in active sentences can be optionally omitted when context makes the interpretation of the missing object clear. This is by no means as prevalent as in, notoriously, the East/Southeast Asian Sprachbund in languages such as the Chinese ones, but nevertheless occurs to a degree contrasting with European languages:

(24) Dí   a boóko dí   báta   kaa, hẽ́ a léi   mi (ɛ̃).
     when 3S break DEF bottle CPLT then 3S show 1S 3SO
     'When / before he broke the bottle, he showed it to me.'

(25) Mé   sá féni (ɛ̃).
     1S.NEG can find 3SO
     'I can't find it.'

(26) Dí pindá u   mí   mamá. Nɔ́ɔ mé   sá dá
     DEF peanut POSS 1S.POSS mother NI 1S.NEG can give

     sɛmbɛ (de).
     person 3P
     'The peanuts are my mother's. I can't give them to anyone.'

10.2. Valence-increasing operations

10.2.1. Ditransitives

Only a small set of Saramaccan verbs are ditransitive, where the indirect object is promoted as a central one, occurring without overt dative marking, and thus increasing the valence load of the verb. This is the case with *dá* 'to give' itself:

(27) Dá   mi dí matjáu.
     give 1S DEF axe
     'Give me the axe.'

This includes when the indirect object is fronted:

(28) Ambé i dá   dí báli? (*Dá ambé i dá dí báli?)
     who 2S give DEF ball
     'Who did you give the ball (to)?'

Dá also allows this when both direct object and indirect object are pronominals:

(29) *Gádu bi dá **mi i** / **u de** / **únu mi**.*
    God PAST give 1S 2S / 1P 3P / 2P 1S
    'God gave me you / us them / you me.'

The other verbs that occur ditransitively:

(30) *A **léi** mi déé fóótóo.*
    3S show 1S DEF.PL photo
    'He showed me the pictures.'

(31) ***Léni** mi só móni.*
    lend 1S some money
    'Lend me some money.'

(32) *I **paká** mi dií dollar.*
    2S pay 1S three dollar
    'You paid me three dollars.'

With other transfer verbs, indirect objects are rendered as arguments of *dá* in serial verb constructions (cf. 8.3.1.):

(33) *A bái wã́ búku dá mi.* (**A bái mi wã́ búku.*)
    3S buy INDF book give 1S
    'He bought me a book.'

(34) *A séi wã́ búku dá mi.* (**A séi mi wã́ búku.*)
    3S sell INDF book give 1S
    'He sold me a book.'

(35) *Mi mandá dí búku dá i.* (**Mi mandá i dí búku.*)
    1S send DEF book give 2S
    'I sent the book to you.'

(36) *Gádu tjá de kó dá u.* (**Gádu tjá u de.*)
    God carry 3P come give 1P
    'God brought them to us.'

(37) *Téi / kísi / lánga dí matjáu dá mi.*
    take / get / hand DEF axe give 1S
    'Give / get / hand me the axe.'

(38) **Téi / *kísi / *lánga mi dí matjáu.*
    take / get / hand 1S DEF axe
    'Give / get / hand me the axe.'

Ditransitivity, then, is lexically specified upon a closed set of verbs. The use of serial *dá* with these verbs is either ungrammatical, as in the case of *léi* 'show,' or has a benefactive meaning, as with the other two:

(39) **Léni** só móni dá mi.
 lend some money give 1S
 'Lend some money for me.'

(40) I **paká** dií dollar dá mi.
 2S pay three dollar give 1S
 'You paid three dollars for me.'

10.2.2. Causatives

The causative is formed with *mbéi* 'to make' and a finite complement (cf. 9.2.1.3. for an alternate analysis of the complement as nonfinite) of the sort that is also used with verbs of perception and cognition:

(41) Mi **mbéi** a bebé wáta.
 1S make 3S drink water
 'I made him drink water.'

(42) Mi **mbéi** a butá dí údu a wã́ sé.
 1S make 3S put DEF wood LOC one side
 'I made him put the wood on one side.'

Forcing is expressed with *músu* 'must' used as a main verb (cf. 7.4.1.); another expression is *butá ku* 'put with':

(43) Ná wã́ kódo sɛmbɛ **músu** mi u wási dí wági.
 NEG one single person force 1S NF wash DEF car
 'Nobody made me wash the car.'

(44) A **butá ku** mi u woóko.
 3S put with 1S NF work
 'He forced me to work.'

Butá also figures in an indirect causative construction:

(45) A butá hɛ̃́ seéi **dá** a fṍ ku schaak.
 3S put 3S.POSS self give 3S beat with chess
 'He let himself be beaten by her at a game of chess.' (Veenstra 1996: 101)

Saramaccan has lexical causatives to roughly the same extent as English, such as *fáa* 'fell' (cf. *kaí* 'fall'):

(46) A **fáa** dí páu túwɛ **kaí** a wáta.
 3S fell DEF tree throw fall LOC water
 'He chopped the tree down into the water.'

Other pairs of non-causative/causative lexical items include *sí* 'see,' *léi* 'show' and *dέdɛ* 'to be dead,' *kíi* 'kill.' There is also, rarely, zero-marked causativization, such as *léi* 'to learn,' *léi* 'to teach,' inherited from the semantics of Dutch's *leren*.

10.3. The imperative mood

The second-person imperative is expressed with the bare verb:

(47) *Lúku andí i dú!*
 look what 2S do
 'Look at what you did!'

(48) *Hái ɛ̃!*
 haul 3SO
 'Pull him!'

(49) *Sɔ́ tjá gó.*
 thus carry go
 'Go ahead.'

The use of the subject pronominal with the second-person imperative is grammatical, conveying explicitness or emphasis:

(50) *Híbi wã̌ júu té i méni wã̌ soní, nɔ́ɔ i sikífi ɛ̃.*
 all one hour when 2S remember INDF thing NI 2S write 3SO
 'Whenever you remember something, write it down.'

(51) *Ũ méni ṹ seéi.*
 2P be.careful 2P self
 'You behave yourselves!'

The negative imperative is formed with the negator *ná* (cf. 7.1.1.):

(52) *Ná gó alá!*
 NEG go yonder
 'Don't go there!'

(53) *Ná táki ná wã̌ kódo soní.*
 NEG talk NEG one single thing
 'Don't say anything.'

The negative imperative can also be conveyed propositionally with *tapá* 'to prevent, stop,' in which case it conditions expletive negative marking:

(54) *Mi tapá i bé i á gó féti.*
 1S stop 2S HORT 2S NEG go fight
 'I forbid you to go fight.'

To soften a command, *sá* 'to be able' (cf. 7.4.2.2.) is used as in English in a yes/no construction:

(55) *I sá tapá dí dɔ́ɔ ɔ́?*
 2S can close DEF door INT
 'Could you close the door?'

Further softening is accomplished with the sentence-final affective particle *nɔ́* (cf. 15.4.1.):

(56) *I sá tjái háfu wáta kó dá mi **nɔ́**?*
 2S can carry half water come give 1S INT
 'Could you please bring me some water?'

The clause-final use of *sɔ́* 'thus' strengthens a command:

(57) *Kó akí **sɔ́**!*
 come here thus
 'Come here!' (with note of authority)

There is a hortative usage of *bé* 'let' (cf. 8.3.5.):

(58) ***Bé** i tapá dí dɔ́ɔ.*
 HORT 2S close DEF door
 '*You* close the door.'

In the first-person plural, *bé* has combined with pronoun *u* 'we' yielding the portmanteau *bóo*:

(59) *Dísi ó taánga – **bóo** poobá.*
 this FUT strong HORT.1P try
 'This is going to be hard – let's try.'

(60) ***Bóo** u síngi ká fuu bajá.*
 HORT.1P 1P sing where for.1P dance
 'Let's sing instead of dancing.'

Bé also serves as a hortative marker in serial verb constructions (cf. 8.3.5.).

Chapter 11
Questions

11.1. Yes/no questions

Yes/no questions have the same word order as declarative sentences. The interrogative is conveyed by intonation (see section 2.4.5.) and the clause-final interrogative marker *ɔ́*:

(1)   *I wéki kaa ɔ́?*
        2S wake CPLT INT
        'Are you up?'

(2)   *I ábi tjiká ɔ́?*
        2S have suffice INT
        'Do you have enough?'

(3)   *Já gó a New York wã̌ dáka ɔ́?*
        2S.NEG go LOC New York one day INT
        'Have you ever been to New York?'

(4)   *'Táa' ɔ́?*
        táa INT
        'The 'taa' one?' (in reference to a sentence elicited shortly before with complementizer *táa*)

There is an alternate interrogative marker *nɔ́*. *Nɔ́* is not the word for 'no,' which is *nɔ́nɔ*; *nɔ́* is likely derived from the softening pragmatic reflex 'just' of *nɔ́ɔ* (cf. 15.4.1.). *Nɔ́* is almost certainly the source of *ɔ́* via elision of the initial consonant. It often conveys gentler intent:

(5)   *Tío dédɛ **nɔ́**?*
        Uncle dead INT
        'Oh dear, is Uncle dead?'

(6)   *I sá tjái háfu wáta kó dá mi **nɔ́**?*
        2S can carry half water come give 1S INT
        'Could you please bring me some water?'

Nɔ́ retains the explicitly minimizing semantics of its source *nɔ́ɔ* 'just,' whereas its derivant *ɔ́* has bleached into the neutral function of marking interrogation.
     A "minimal pair":

(7)   *I ké baláki ɔ́?*
        2S want vomit INT
        'Do you want to throw up?'

(8)   *I ké baláki **nɔ́**?*
        2S want vomit INT
        'Now, is it that you need to throw up, sweetie?'

The "softening" function of *nɔ́* can be pragmatically implied by context rather than overt, as in this elicited translation of 'Will he ever come?':

(9)   *Á   tá   kó   mɔ̋ɔ̋sɔ   nɔ́?*
       3S.NEG   IMF   come   never   INT
       'Will he ever come?' (lit. 'Will he never come?')

The interrogative markers serve the function of tags in English. Where English would append a tag to a declarative sentence, Saramaccan uses a question marked by an interrogative morpheme that solicits either confirmation or disconfirmation:

(10) *A   tjiká   fii   gó   a   bédi   awáa   ɔ́?*
       3S suffice   for.2S   go LOC   bed   at.last   INT
       'It's about time for you to go to bed, isn't it?'

(11) *Dí   a   kó,   hɛ̋   a   fiká   a   dɔ́ɔ   nɔ́?*
       when 3S   come   then 3S   remain LOC door   INT
       'Since he came, he's just stayed outside, right?'

Yes/no questions are often expressed with negated predicates. In many cases, this lends a note of pragmatic vividness. For example, in:

(12) *Á   tá   kó   mɔ̋ɔ̋sɔ   nɔ́?*
       3S.NEG   IMF   come   never   INT
       'Will he ever come?' (lit. 'Will he never come?')

the phrasing can be taken as calling attention to the explicit possibility of the person's "never" coming. Similarly, in:

(13) *Já   sí?   U   féni   soní   u   njã̋.*
       2S.NEG   see   1P   find   thing   for   eat
       'You see? We got something to eat.' (lit. 'You don't see?')

the sentence is uttered in a folktale in the midst of a famine, when the procurement of food was an accomplishment, and thus the negation connotes the urgency of 'Don't you see?'
   However, in other cases there would seem to be free variation, in which there has been a bleeding of negative polarity into the interrogative realm, as is so common in languages. For example:

(14) *Já   gó   a   New York   wã̋   dáka   ɔ́?*
       2S.NEG   go   LOC   New York   one   day   INT
       'Have you ever been to New York?' (lit. 'You have not ever gone to New York?')

This sentence was not uttered in a context of surprise or urgency, but as a passing sidebar question serving as a scene-setter for a description of life in New York. The same construction is also grammatical and ordinary without negation:

(15) *I   gó alá   wã̋   dáka   ɔ́?*
       2S go yonder   one   day   INT
       'Have you ever been there?'

11.2. Information questions

Saramaccan wh-words are fronted:

(16) **Andí** i tá njã̂ a dí sónúáti?
what 2S IMF eat LOC DEF lunch
'What do you eat for lunch?'

(17) **Ambɛ́** hákísi dí sondí dɛ́?
who ask DEF thing there
'Who asked that (odd question)?'

(*Andí* and *ambɛ́* are borrowings from Fongbe, the African language that had the greatest impact on Saramaccan grammar [the Fongbe forms are *àní* and *mɛ́*]).
  Saramaccan wh-words do not vary for grammatical role:

(18) **Ambɛ́** i bi sí?
who 2S PAST see
'Who did you see?'

Many wh-words are composed from *ǔ* 'which':

(19) **Ǔ** kɔúsu i bisí tidé?
which sock 2S wear today
'Which socks are you wearing today?'

One example is 'which' itself, which also occurs as *ǔndi*:

(20) **Ǔndi** da dí gã̂ã́ fóto a Kirghizstan?
which be DEF big capital LOC Kirghizstan
'What is the capital of Kirghizstan?'

The others are:

(21) **Ǔ méni** déé ápa u tá séi?
how many DEF.PL apple 1P IMF sell
'How many of the apples are we selling?'

(22) **Ǔ sóóti / péi** u físi u ó njã̂ tidé?
which kind / kind of fish 1P FUT eat today
'What kind of fish are we having today?'

(23) **Ǔfá** i mbéi dí ósu? (*fá* < *fási* 'manner')
how 2S make DEF house
'Man, how did you build the house?'

For 'when,' *ǔ* is sandwiched in *naǔtɛ́* between locative marker *na* and *tɛ́* 'time'; *naǔtɛ́* also occurs in the contracted form *ǔtɛ́*:

(24) **Naǔtɛ́ / ǔtɛ́** a dú ɛ̃?
when / when 3S do 3SO
'When did he do it?'

Similar is the locative wh-word, in which the nominal element is *sé* 'side'; it also occurs as *naásé*:

(25) **Naŭ́sé / naásé** a bi dé?
where / where 3S PAST be
'Where was he?'

'Why' is rendered with expressions incorporating *mbéi* 'to make':

(26) **Andí mbéi** fóu tá síngi?
what make bird IMF sing
'Why do birds sing?'

or commonly in concatention with *fá* 'how':

(27) **Faándi mbéi** i dú ẽ?
for.what make 2S do 3SO
'Why did you do it?'

and also:

(28) **Faándi hédi** já tá dá ná wã̌ kódo soní
for.what head 2S.NEG IMF give NEG one single thing

nɔunɔ́u?
now
'Why aren't you giving anything now?'

Saramaccan has no preposition stranding: prepositions are fronted along with the wh-word:

(29) **Na ŭ́** kɔ́ndɛ Jeff kumútu?
LOC which village Jeff exit
'Which village did Jeff come from?'

(30) **Na ŭ́ndi** u déé táfa básu i tá tjubí?
LOC which of DEF.PL table under 2S IMF hide
'Which of the tables did you hide under?'

(31) **Ku ambé** i fã?
with who 2S talk
'Who are you talking to?'

11.3. Indirect questions

Saramaccan uses its battery of wh-words in indirect questions:

(32) Mi sábi **ambé** da i.
1S know who be 2S
'I know who you are.'

(33) *Awáa mi féni **naásɛ́** a bi dé.*
at.last 1S find where 3S PAST be
'I finally found out where he was.'

(34) *Mɛ́ sábi **ũfá** dí pási ó tidé.*
1S.NEG know how DEF road FUT today
'I don't know how the roads will be today.'

Both English's *whether* and *if* (as used in yes/no questions in English) are conveyed with *ée*:

(35) *Mi sá hákísi i, **ée** i bi tɔ́ɔu ɔ́?*
1S can ask 2S if 2S PAST marry INT
'May I ask you whether / if you have ever been married?'

Chapter 12
Nonverbal predication and *be*-verbs

There are two copular morphemes, used to link nonverbal predicates. This is a common division of labor in languages, in which one morpheme is used when the relationship between the subject and predicate is equative (*That boy is my son*) while the other is used when the relationship is locative (*That tree is in my yard*). However, the division of labor between the two copulas is finer than this in Saramaccan.

12.1. Identificational equative predicates: *Da*

12.1.1. Basic traits

Equative predication can indicate *identification* (entailing that subject and predicate refer to the same entity, as in *I am your father*) or *class* (entailing that the predicate is a subclass of the subject, as in *This dog is a Saint Bernard*). Identificational equative predicates in Saramaccan are marked by *da*:

(1)   Mi da Gádu.
        1S be God
        'I am God.'

Its use is not sensitive to definiteness of the predicate:

(2)   Mi da dí   /   wã̌   kabiténi.
        1S be DEF   /   INDF   captain
        'I am the / a captain.'

12.1.2. Irregularities

Da exhibits and conditions more irregularity than perhaps any morpheme in Saramaccan.
   Some of this irregularity suggests that *da* is not a verb as the other copula *dé* (discussed below) is. For example, *da* is negated via replacement with negator *ná*. It cannot occur with predicate negator *á* (cf. 7.1.1.):

(3)   Nɔ́nɔ,   ná   mi.
        no   NEG   1S
        'No, it wasn't me.'

(4)   *Nɔ́nɔ, á   da   mi.
        no   NEG   be   1S
        'No, it wasn't me.'

(5)   Awáa,   dídé   ná   Saamáka   tɔ́ngɔ.
        at.last   that   NEG   Saramaka   language
        'While we're at it, that's not Saramaccan.'

(6) Hɛ̃́   dí   mujée   ná   míi   mɔ́ɔ̃.
    then   DEF   woman   NEG   child   more
    'Then the woman wasn't a child anymore.'

Da cannot be marked for tense; instead, *dé* is used in the equative in such cases:

(7) Dí   fósu   líbisembɛ   bi   dé   (*bi da)   Adám.
    DEF   first   human.being   PAST   be   Adam
    'The first person was Adam.'

(8) Mí   tatá   ó   dé   dí   kabiténi.
    1S.POSS   father   FUT   be   DEF   captain
    'My father will be the captain.'

The third-person singular pronoun *a* is ungrammatical with *da*; instead, the tonic form *hɛ̃́* is used (cf. 5.1.), but in this usage indicating neutral rather than emphatic semantics:

(9) Hɛ̃́   da   dí   mɔ́ɔ̃   lánga   wã̌   a   u   déndu.   (*A da dí mɔ́ɔ̃ lánga ...)
    3S   be   DEF   more   tall   one   LOC   1P   inside
    'He is the tallest one among us.'

(10) Hɛ̃́   da   dí   júu   u   bigí   woóko.   (*A da dí júu ...)
     3S   be   DEF   hour   NF   begin   work
     'It's time for work.'

(11) Ée já   lóbi   ɛ̃   seéi,   ma   hɛ̃́   da   bumbúu   sɛmbɛ.
     if 2S.NEG   like   3SO   even   but   3S   be   good.RD   person
     'Although you don't like him, he is a good person.'

(12) Dísi,   hɛ̃́   da   goólíba.
     this   3S   be   world
     'This is the world.' (i.e. 'This is how the world is.')

'*He* is the one who is the tallest among us' would only be rendered with the enunciation of *hɛ̃́* with special stress (cf. 2.4.4.).

Da is also restricted in terms of word order in a way that *dé* is not, unable to occur sentence-finally as *dé* can:

(13) Mi sá   ambé   da   i.   (*... ambé i da.)
     1S know   who   be   2S
     'I know who you are.'

which contrasts with the usage of *dé* as in:

(14) Awáa   mi féni   naásé   a   bi   dé.
     at.last   1S find   where   3S   PAST   be
     'I finally found out where he was.'

These behaviors can be taken as suggesting that *da* is a presentational marker encoding 'that is' or 'it is.' Under that analysis, there is no expressed copula after *da*, and what occurs before it is a topic. Notably, its etymological source is *dáti* 'that' (still current, for example, in its ancestor

Sranan and sister Ndjuka). A syntactic analysis of example (9) ('He is the tallest one among us') would thus be:

[*Hɛ́*]   [*da*]   ø-copula   [*dí mɔ́ɔ́ lánga wã́ a u déndu*]
topic   subject   predicate

The pronominal analysis would also explain, for example, the requirement that tonic third-person singular pronoun *hɛ́*, the form otherwise used when a third-person pronominal is a topic, occurs before *da* rather than subject pronominal *a*, and furthermore would explain why this pronominal anomaly occurs solely in the third-person singular, inherent to presentational morphemes, rather than with other pronouns (i.e. when occurring with *da*, other subject pronominals do not occur in their high-toned tonic forms).

This would mean that sentences with *da* have their historical source in topic-comment sentences, and that today's *da* sentences are at an intermediate point in a development into true subject-predicate sentences.

Under this analysis, we could say that *da* is not a copula, and that Saramaccan has zero-copula as the regular case with identificational equatives in the present tense, with other morphemes used when tense is expressed, or in locative and other contexts. This is, in fact, a common configuration of copulas in languages around the world.

However, given that sentences with *da* are pronounced under a single intonational contour and that *da* does not occur as a pronominal elsewhere in the grammar, we might also say that *da* is intermediate between deictic pronominal and copula (an analysis that we prefer).

12.1.3. Omission

In Saramaccan's sister creoles of the Caribbean and surrounding regions, cognates of both *da* and the other copula *dé* are frequently omitted, their omissibility and the frequency thereof conditioned by constituent class of the predicate, prosodic factors, and proximity of dialects of the creole to the standard language.

In Saramaccan, however, as in other Surinam creoles, zero-copulas are much less common. For one, only *da* can be omitted, never *dé*; and then, *da* omits only under a few conditions, usually in regular fashion, and where there is variation, it is not sociolinguistically conditioned.

When predicates other than possessive ones are fronted, *da* is omitted:

(15)   *Mí,*   *dísi.*
       1S   this
       'It's me.' (i.e. 'This is me talking to you.')

(16)   *Mí*   *tatá,*   *dísi.*
       1S.POSS   father   this
       'This is my father.'

(17)   *Saaná,*   *mí*   *kɔ́ndɛ.*
       Surinam   1S.POSS   country
       'My country is Surinam.'

Often the fronted item in such sentences takes a marker of focus (*wɛ*) or new information (*nɔ́ɔ*) (cf. sections 15.1.3.2. and 15.2.2., respectively):

(18)   *Wã̌*   *dáta*   *wɛ,*   *dídé!*
        INDF   doctor   FOC   that
        'He's a doctor (and we're proud of him)!'

(19)   *Nɔ́ɔ*   *u*   *nɔ́ɔ*   *dísi*   *kaa.*
        NI   1P   NI   this   CPLT
        'This is the way we are.' (lit. 'This is *us*,' i.e. 'Us is what this is.')

Even if unfronted, if marked by focus marker *wɛ*, a predicate can optionally occur without a copula:

(20)   *Dí*   *wómi*   *dé,*   *dáta*   *wɛ*   *o!*
        DEF   man   there   doctor   FOC   INJ
        'That man is a doctor, now!'

Da is also optionally omissible when the subject is a wh-word (cf. 11.2.):

(21)   *Ǔ*   *búku*   *dídé?*
        which   book   that
        'Which book is that?'

(22)   *Andí*   *dísi?*
        what   this
        'What is this?'

but:

(23)   *Andí*   *da*   *dí*   *búku*   *naandé?*
        what   be   DEF   book   there
        'What is that book there (about)?'

Likely this is due to the fact that the wh-words can be analyzed as having been fronted, in which case cf. the discussion above.
     Da is also regularly omitted when the subject is *tidé* 'today' and the predicate is a day of the week (cf. 16.6.); this anomalous usage qualifies as a happenstance idiom:

(24)   *Tidé*   *dií-dé-woóko.*
        today   three-day-work
        'Today is Wednesday.'

12.1.4. Allomorphy

Da is optionally used when the predicate is a possessive:

(25)   *Dí*   *búku*   *akí*   (*da*)   *u*   *mí.*
        DEF   book   here   be   POSS   1S
        'This book is mine.'

When possessive predicates are fronted for emphasis, *da* obligatorily occurs as the allomorph *a*:

(26) U   mí   a   dí   búku   akí.   (*U mí da dí búku akí.)
      POSS   1S   be DEF   book   here
      'This book is mine.'

(27) U   mí   a   dísi.
      POSS   1S   be this
      'This is mine.'

(28) Fíi   a   dí   búku   akí   ɔ́?
      POSS.2S   be DEF   book   here   INT
      'Is this your book?'

12.1.5. *Da* as sentential presentative

Da is also used pleonastically to introduce a proposition, in the context of highlighting it as an explanation:

(29) Hɛ̃́   wɛ   **da** dí   sukúma   kó   mujɛ́ɛ-míi.
      then   FOC   be   DEF   foam   come   woman-child
      'Then it was (that) the foam became a girl.'

(30) Bigá   **da** mi   sí   kúma   mujɛ́ɛ   a   bi   gó   pidí.
      because   be   1S   see   how   woman   3S   PAST   go   ask
      'Because it was that, I think, the woman went to make a request.'

(31) Ma   **da** i   ló   dí   kijɔ́ɔ   dé   wã̌   dáka   ɔ́?
      but   be   2S   like   DEF   fellow   there   one   day   INT
      'Did you *ever* like that guy?'

12.2. Class equative predicates: *Dé* or *da*

In Saramaccan's sister English-based creoles of the Caribbean and West Africa (e.g. Jamaican, Guyanese, Gullah, Krio, Nigerian "Pidgin," et al.), including its Surinamese closest relatives Sranan and Ndjuka, there is a rigid division of labor in which the equative is expressed with a cognate to *da* while the *dé* cognate is used in the locative and elsewhere. This is not the case in Saramaccan, where instead, *da* is only obligatory in a subset of the equative, the identificational. With class equatives, *da* is only optional, and often can be substituted by *dé*.

For example, when the predicate is a possessive, which is a class predicate (i.e. what is "mine" comprises many entities), *da* occurs, but only optionally (*dé* in this case is ungrammatical):

(32) Dí   búku   akí   (da)   u   mí.   (*Dí búku akí dé u mí.)
      DEF   book   here   be   POSS   1S
      'This book is mine.'

(33) Dí   pindá   (da)   u   mí   mamá.
      DEF   peanut   be   POSS   1S.POSS   mother
      'The (bowl of mashed) peanut is my mother's.'

With other class equative predicates, *da* is grammatical but *dé* is used alternately in free variation (our data suggests that *dé* is in fact the usual choice with class predicates except with possessive ones):

(34) Méiki **dé** / **da** wã̌ soní dí míi tá bebé.
 milk be / be INDF thing REL child IMF drink
 'Milk is something that children drink.'

(35) Dágu **dé** / **da** wã̌ mbéti ku fɔ́ fútu.
 dog be / be INDF animal with four foot
 'A dog is an (one of the) animal(s) with four feet.'

(36) Alísi **dé** / **da** dí soní dí de tá séi.
 rice be / be DEF thing REL 3P IMF sell
 'Rice is the thing that they are selling.'

(37) A **dé** wã̌ súti soní.
 3S be INDF sweet thing
 'It is a good thing.'

(38) Ma dí tɔ́ngɔ akí, a **dé** wã̌ búnu tɔ́ngɔ.
 but DEF language here 3S be INDF good language
 'But this language is a good language.'

12.3. Locative and other predicates: *Dé*

Dé is often described as Saramaccan's "locative" copula along the lines of its cognates in Saramaccan's sister creoles, and it indeed marks locative predicates (note also that it takes tense marking, and as such is prototypically verbal unlike *da*):

(39) Méiki ku wĩ́ bi dé a táfa líba.
 milk with wine PAST be LOC table top
 'Milk and wine were on the table.'

However, in Saramaccan, the "locative" characterization is too narrow: *dé* is, rather, the default *be*-verb in the grammar, occurring in many usages with no locative semantics. It remains behind as a place-filler when a property item is fronted along with a wh-word:

(40) Ũ bígi dí wósu **dé**? (**Dí wósu dé bígi.*)
 how big DEF house be
 'How big is the house?' (Kramer 2001: 36)

It is used with resultative adjectives derived via verbal reduplication (albeit not with unreduplicated property items [cf. 6.1.]):

(41) Dí sutúu dé **boókóbóóko**.
 DEF chair be break.RD
 'The chair is broken.'

and it is used with adverbial clauses:

(42) Dí   kíno   bi   dé   fô   júu   lóngi.
     DEF   film   PAST   be   four   hour   long
     'The film was four hours long.'

(43) Só   a   dé.
     thus   3S   be
     'That's the way it is.'

Dé, then, is Saramaccan's main verb 'to be,' while *da* is an alternate morpheme that occurs in a particular narrow context: sentences that are 1) affirmative, 2) present tense, and 3) non-fronted identificational equative (or class equative only as a statistical alternative) (cf. 12.1.2., 12.2.):

Table 26. Copula morphemes in Saramaccan

	BARE	WITH FRONTING	WITH TENSE MARKING
IDENTIFICATIONAL EQUATIVE	**da**	ø	dé
CLASS EQUATIVE	**da** / dé	**da** / **a** / dé	dé
LOCATIVE	dé	dé	dé
PROPERTY ITEMS	dé	dé	dé
ADVERBIAL	dé	dé	dé

12.4. Existential predicates

Dé, expectedly of a default *be*-verb, is also frequently used to express the existential; Saramaccan often renders English existential sentences with locative phrases:

(44) Ée   hángi   kísi   i,   njãnjã dé   a   dí   éisikási   déndu.
     if   hunger   catch   2S   food   be   LOC   DEF   refrigerator inside
     'If you are hungry, there's food in the refrigerator.'

(45) Híla   pusipúsi   dé   aki.
     many   cat   be   here
     'There are a lot of cats here.'

Where there is no locative adjunct, the pleonastic item is third-person singular subject pronominal *a* (cf. 5.4.):

(46) A   bi   dé   hángi   té.
     3S   PAST   be   hungry   time
     'There was a famine.'

Alternately, the existential is expressed with *ábi* 'to have':

(47) *De á   hía   dágu   a   dí   mátu.*
     3P NEG.have many   dog   LOC   DEF   forest
     'There aren't too many dogs in the woods.'

(48) *dí   soní   dí   ábi   dέ*
     DEF   thing   REL   have   there
     'the things that were there'

Chapter 13
Position, direction, and time

13.1. Spatial indicators

Prepositions carry much less of the functional load of indicating position in Saramaccan than in European languages. Saramaccan has but three common prepositions: *ku* 'with,' *fu* 'of, associational marker,' and *a*, a general locative marker translating roughly as 'at.' The latter preposition figures in spatial marking:

(1) *A   wáka   gó   a   wósu.*
     3S   walk   go   LOC   house
     'He walked home.'

Here, *a* does not have the directional semantics of, for example, Romance languages' [a]. *Gó* conveys the direction in its serial verb function as a marker of such (cf. 8.2.); *a* conveys only location.

For spatial relations more specific than that of the generic *a*, there is a paradigm of nominals that occur postposed to the noun, used with a nominal referent marked by locative marker *a*. This paradigm is:

Table 27. Spatial indicators

	POSITIONAL NOMINAL	TRANSLATION
a dí wósu	líba	'above, on top of the house'
	básu	'under the house'
	báka	'behind the house'
	fési	'in front of the house'
	déndu	'inside the house'
	bandja	'beside the house'

as well as *míndi* which conveys 'in the middle of' or 'between':

(2) *Mi tá   sindó a   Susanne   ku   Marvin   **míndi**.*
     1S IMF   sit   LOC   Susanne   with   Marvin   between
     'I am sitting between Susanne and Marvin.'

Muysken (1987: 97) includes (*h*)*édi* 'head' in this paradigm on the basis of *dí páu édi* 'the top of the tree.' This, however, is an idiomatic usage applied only to trees and mountains, rather than a true grammaticalization.

In an alternate construction, the positional nominal and the referent occur as different prepositional phrase arguments:

(3) *a   dí   líba   u   dí   wósu*
     LOC   DEF   top   of   DEF   house
     'on top of the house'

(4) a   dí   báka / básu / físi u   dí   wósu
     LOC DEF back / under / face of DEF house
     'behind / below / in front of the house'

No semantic difference between these two constructions is evident from our elicitations or data. However, the second construction appears to be used less than the first.

With *wósu* 'house,' a third construction has conventionalized, in which the spatial nominal occurs in a compound relationship with the referent:

(5) a   mí   líba wósu
     LOC 1S.POSS top   house
     'on top of my house'

(6) Nɔ́ɔ mi ó   kándi   a   míndi   wósu.
     NI   1S FUT lie.down LOC middle house
     'So I'll lie down in the middle of the house.'

The construction is grammatical with the whole paradigm of spatial indicators, but is disallowed with other nouns (including *písi* 'home'):

(7) a   mí   báka / bandja wósu   / *písi / *bóto / *sutúu /
     LOC 1S.POSS back / side   house / home   / boat   / chair   /

     *mánda
     basket
     'behind / beside my house / *home / *boat / *chair / *basket'

Déndu wósu has lexicalized into meaning 'room' in a home:

(8) Híni wã̌   sɛmbɛ   ábi   ɛ̃̌   déndu   wósu.
     all   one person have 3S.POSS inside house
     'Each person has his room.'

Nearness and distance are expressed by the stative verbs *zṹtu* 'near' and *lóngi* 'far':

(9) Dí   wósu   zṹtu / lóngi ku   u   mɔ́ɔ̃   dí   óto   wã̌.
     DEF house near / far   with 1P more DEF other one
     'The house is closer to / further from us than the other one.'

However, both items also occur as adverbs:

(10) Dí   pen dé zṹtu ku   dí   telephone.
     DEF pen be near with DEF telephone
     'The pen is near the telephone.'

(11) A   líbi lóngi ku   mi.
     3S live far   with 1S
     'He lives far from me.'

13.2. Deictic adverbials

There is a three-grade proximity distinction in deictic adverbials: *akí* 'here,' *dé* 'there,' and *alá* 'over there, yonder' (these three grades all exist in the marking of demonstratives; cf. 4.2.):

(12) Mi sá   dú soní   **akí**.
     1S can   do thing   here
     'I can do things here.'

(13) Mi sindó **dé**   tá   mbéi   hóha.
     1S sit   there   IMF   make   yawn
     'I sat there yawning.'

(14) Ná   gó   **alá**!
     NEG   go   yonder
     'Don't go (over) there!'

Dé can extend optionally to the domain of *alá*, used alternately to express locations at a considerable remove:

(15) I   gó alá   wã̌   dáka   ó?
     2S   go yonder   one   day   INT
     'Have you ever been there?'

(16) Mé   bi   sái dé   seéi.
     1S.NEG   PAST   be there   even
     'I've never been there anyway.'

Alá is typical when extreme distance is pragmatically salient, translating as 'way over there' or 'in that faraway place.'
    Dé is also used to connote distance in an abstract discourse sense, as a pragmatic strategy for foregrounding (cf. 4.2.):

(17) Dí   wíki   dí   bi   pasá   **dé**,   mé   bi   sá   peé.
     DEF   week   REL   PAST   pass   there   1S.NEG   PAST   can   play
     'Last week I couldn't play.'

All three forms can occur with locative marker *a*'s allomorph (and source etymon) *na: na akí, naandé, na alá*. The forms *na akí* and *na alá* are used when a more explicit deixis is desired than simple placement of the referent in space. For example, in this sentence *na akí* connotes what English might express as *I have money on me*, highlighting that the physical cash is upon one's person:

(18) Mi á   móni   na   akí.
     1S have   money   LOC   here
     'I have money here (on me).'

In the following example, *na alá* is used in a discussion about exactly where Jeff's book might be found (an informant says that *na alá* conveys that one knows that the book is there):

(19) Dí   búku dé a   Jeff kámba na   alá.
      DEF   book be LOC Jeff room   LOC yonder
      'The book is in Jeff's office over there.'

With *dé* the *na*-marked form has become especially entrenched, used in free variation with *dé* alone, the narrowing function of *na* bleached away:

(20) Vínde ɛ̃   túwɛ   gó naandé.
      throw 3SO throw go there
      'Throw it over (onto) there.' (with a table top pointed out as the intended place of landing)

(21) Naandé dí   wóto   kabá.
      there   DEF story finish
      'The story ends there.' (after a pause during which it wasn't clear whether the story was over; i.e. 'That is where the story ends.')

(22) Mi ké   dí   mɔ́ni   a   sáku   naandé.
      1S want DEF money LOC pocket there
      'I want the money in your pocket there.' (in which 'there' has the same adjunct, highlighting force that it would in the English version)

That *naandé* has no highlighting function is usefully obvious in the conventionalized expression *léti naandé* 'right there,' in which *léti* 'right, exactly' serves a reinforcement function that *na* alone performs in *na akí* and *na alá*.

Where in cases of positional deixis alone, *dé* encroaches upon the domain of *alá*, *alá* encroaches upon that of *dé* when direction or movement are also indicated:

(23) A   wáka té   alá   / *naandé sɔ́.
      3S walk until yonder / there   thus
      'He walked way off that way.'

Our data also suggest that *gó alá* is more frequent than *gó naandé*.

The deictic adverbials can combine with the positional nominals (cf. 13.1.):

(24) a   básu   akí
      LOC under here
      'down here'

In this case as well, *alá* is preferred over *dé* (although the latter is grammatical):

(25) a   líba / básu   alá
      LOC top   / under yonder
      'up / down there'

(26) té   a   líba / básu   alá
      until LOC top   / under yonder
      'way up / down there'

13.3. Direction

Saramaccan conveys with verbs many of the directional concepts conveyed by prepositions and adverbs in European languages (cf. also section 8.2.).

13.3.1. Some directional verbs

For example, 'across' is conveyed with with the verb *ába* (< *over*) 'to cross over':

(27) Mi tá **ába** dí sitááti.
 1S IMF cross DEF street
 'I'm crossing the street.'

(28) Mi wáka **ába** dí pási.
 1S walk cross DEF path
 'I walked across the path.'

When used positionally rather than directionally, *ába* is used in the compound *ába sé*:

(29) Mi lóbi dí wósu a ába sé.
 1S like DEF house LOC cross side
 'I like the house across the street.'

'Through' is rendered by *pasá* 'pass':

(30) Vínde ẽ **pasá** a dí wall.
 throw 3SO pass LOC DEF wall
 'Throw him through the wall.'

and 'around' by *lṍtu* 'to go around':

(31) Dí dágu tá bái nɔ́ɔ a tá kulé tá **lṍtu**.
 DEF dog IMF bark then 3S IMF run IMF go.round
 'The dog is barking and running in circles.'

13.3.2. Allative and ablative movement

The domain of the allative (movement towards) and ablative (movement away) is expressed by serial verb constructions, and more specifically, different serial verb constructions according to whether the action is transitive or intransitive.

13.3.2.1. Ablative

In transitive sentences, the ablative is expressed with a serial verb usage of *púu* (< *pull*):

(32) A gó féki dí keéti púu a dí bóutu.
 3S go dust.off DEF chalk pull LOC DEF blackboard
 'He's going to wash the chalk off of the blackboard.'

(33) A   hái   ɛ̃   fínga   púu   a   dí   baáku   déndu.
      3S   haul 3S.POSS finger pull LOC DEF   hole   inside
      'He pulled his finger out of the hole.'

Púu's status as purely ablative in this usage is demonstrated in that it can refer to an action effected by an agent who pushes rather than pulls:

(34) A   pusá   dí   míi   púu   a   dí   nési.
      3S   push   DEF   child pull LOC DEF   nest
      'It pushed the child out of the nest.'

(35) A   tɔ́tɔ   ɛ̃   púu   a   dí   sípi.
      3S   push   3SO pull LOC DEF   ship
      'He pushed him off the ship.'

Ablative *púu* does not occur when the main verb is *púu*:

(36) De   bi   tá   púu   wáta   (*púu)   nɛ̃ɛ̃.
      3P   PAST IMF   pull   water pull   LOC.3SO
      'They were hauling water out of it (i.e. a boat).'

but does occur when the main verb is a synonym to *púu*:

(37) Hái   ɛ̃   púu!
      haul   3SO   pull
      'Pull him out!'

In the intransitive, the ablative is expressed with *kumútu* 'to come out, exit':

(38) A   wáka   kumútu /   *púu   a   dí   wósu.
      3S   walk   exit   /   pull   LOC DEF   house
      'He walked out of the house.'

(39) A   fusí   kumútu   a   sitááfu   wósu.
      3S   sneak   exit   LOC punishment   house
      'He escaped from jail.'

To express a place of origin, *kumútu* can optionally occur with *u* ([ʃ]*u* in its 'of' meaning) rather than *a*:

(40) Hɛ̃́   da   u   Boston Jeff   kumútu.
      3S   be   of   Boston Jeff   exit
      'Jeff comes from *Boston*.'

The prepositional phrase can occur as a nonverbal predicate; here *fu* is altered morphophonemically by assimilation with following *alá* (cf. 3.3.2.):

(41) Mi   ná   fa   alá.
      1S   NEG   of   yonder
      'I'm not from there.'

13.3.2.2. Allative

In transitive allative sentences expressing a concluded projectile motion, *túwɛ* 'to throw' is grammaticalized to mark the trajectory having been completed. For example, in the sentences below, the core semantics of 'throw' would be highly awkward or nonsensical; the function of *túwɛ* is purely grammatical:

(42) Kobí tɔ́tɔ dí wómi túwɛ.
Kobi push DEF man throw
'Kobi pushed the man down.'

(43) A kóti dí páu túwɛ.
3S cut DEF tree throw
'He cut the tree down.'

(44) A kándi dí amána fátu túwɛ a dí bɔ̃ɔ̃́.
3S pour DEF Amana fat throw LOC DEF flour
'He poured the syrup on the pancakes.'

(45) A jáka déé ganĩ́ã túwɛ gó a dɔ́ɔ.
3S chase DEF.PL chicken throw go LOC door
'He chased the chickens outside.'

Butá 'to put' is used in a similar construction, to mark the end of a movement trajectory that is more carefully directed physically than free movement through the air:

(46) Mi tá tjá wáta gó butá a dí bóto déndu.
1S IMF carry water go put LOC DEF boat inside
'I am carrying water into the boat.'

(47) Mi sáka dí búku butá a dí táfa líba.
1S descend DEF book put LOC DEF table top
'I placed the book on the table.'

There is no such marking of end-of-pathway with intransitive verbs:

(48) Dí sikífi-papái tómbi kaí a dí táfa líba.   (*tómbi [kaí] túwɛ)
DEF write-paper spill fall LOC DEF table top
'The pen rolled off of the table.'

Púu 'to pull' is used to express the ablative in the intransitive in one idiomatic construction, as the first serial verb in conjunction with *kaí* to express accidental falling (i.e. dropping):

(49) A púu kaí a mã́ũ.
3S pull fall LOC hand
'It fell out of my hand.'

(50) Mi púu kaí lási ɛ̃.
1S pull fall lose 3SO
'I lost it (it fell off of / out of my hand).'

In this usage, *púu* connotes 'to move away from,' as especially evident in this fuller sentence:

(51) A   bi   púu   a   líba   kaí kó   a   gṍṍ.
      3S   PAST pull   LOC top   fall come   LOC ground
      'He fell off of the roof.' (DeGroot 1977: 16)

However, this usage qualifies as an isolated idiom; *púu* does not convey, for example, the accidental with any other verbs but *kaí*:

(52) *Dí   wági   púu   náki   a   dí   wall.
       DEF   car   pull   hit   LOC   DEF   wall
       'The car smashed into the wall.'

The intransitive verbs *gó* 'go' and *kó* 'come' are used in serial constructions (cf. 8.2.) to mark movement towards:

(53) A   sikópu   dí   báli   **gó**   a   wósu.
      3S   kick   DEF   ball   go   LOC   house
      'He kicked the ball into the house.' (away from the speaker)

(54) A   sikópu   dí   báli   **kó**   a   John.
      3S   kick   DEF   ball   come   LOC   John
      'He kicked the ball to John.' (towards John)

Table 28. Directional verbs

	TRANSITIVE	INTRANSITIVE
ALLATIVE	*butá* (deliberate placement) *túwɛ* (projection)	*gó* (towards speaker) *kó* (away from speaker)
ABLATIVE	*púu*	*kumútu* (*púu* in idiom with *kaí*)

13.4. Time expressions

13.4.1. Units of time

yesterday	éside
today	tidé
tomorrow	amã́jã́

minute	miníti
hour	júu
day	dáka
week	wíki, sába
month	líba
year	jáa

Júu 'hour' is conventionalized to connote 'time' in a general sense, as in:

(55) Á toóbi, i sá njã̌ na ũ̌ **júu** i ké é.
    3S.NEG trouble 2S can eat LOC which hour 2S want INJ
    'It's no big deal – you can eat at whatever time you want.'

However, 'time' as in 'sequential occurrence' is conveyed by *pási*, such as in:

(56) Mi sí sindéu a wã̌ pási.
    1S see snow LOC one time
    'I saw snow once (i.e. one time).'

13.4.2. Timeline placement of events

Simple duration is marked with *lóngi*:

(57) dií dáka lóngi
    three day long
    'for three days'

However, specification of the length of time that an accomplishment required is marked with zero, rather than an adposition like English's *in*:

(58) Mi sikífi dí búku dií líba.
    1S write DEF book three month
    'I wrote the book in three months.'

Specification of a duration extending from the present to a particular future point at which an event will occur is marked with *báka* 'after':

(59) Mi ó sí i báka dií sába.
    1S FUT see 2S after three Saturday
    'I will see you in three weeks.'

To specify a point in time regardless of duration requires general locative *a*:

(60) Mi tá woóko a dií-dé-woóko wɛ.
    1S IMF work LOC three-day-work FOC
    'I work on *Wednesday*.'

'Ago' is expressed with *pasá* 'pass':

(61) tú dáka pasá
    two day pass
    'two days ago'

'Last' and 'next' (e.g. week) are expressed as subject relative clauses (cf. 4.4.) with *pasá* and *kó* respectively:

(62) *Dí wíki dí bi pasá dé, mé bi sá pɛɛ́.*
DEF week REL PAST pass there 1S.NEG PAST can play
'Last week I couldn't play.'

(63) *Mi sí kúma a ó gó dí líba dí tá kó.*
1S see how 3S FUT go DEF month REL IMF come
'It looks like he will leave next month.'

Óto 'other' displaces an event one step in the past or future: *óto éside* 'the day before yesterday'; *óto amã́jã́* 'the day after tomorrow'; *dí óto sónde* 'Sunday after next.'

Chapter 14
Adverbial modification

Adverbial modification in Saramaccan is accomplished with a range of forms, including conventionalized adverbial complements, serial verb constructions, and ideophones.

14.1. Intensifiers

There is no English- or Portuguese-modelled word for 'very' in Saramaccan. Intensification can be conveyed by the ideophone *tééé*:

(1) A hãso tééé.
     3S handsome very
     'He's very handsome.'

Tééé is sometimes analyzed as an extended reflex of *té* 'until,' an analysis reinforced by the fact that *té* 'until' does figure in other adverbial expressions of intensification and extent (as seen below in this section). However, this may be a case of convergent influence, given that Kikongo, one of Saramaccan's two principal substrate languages, has an identical item with identical meaning (*tééé*) (cf. Daeleman 1972: 17).

The expression *té ámbúnu* 'until it wasn't good' is conventionalized as a common intensifier:

(2) Dí   mbéti tá wái   té   ámbúnu.
     DEF animal IMF happy until 3S.NEG.good
     'The animals were incredibly happy.'

Similar in meaning is an echo construction with *té*:

(3) Mi njã́ té   mi njã́.
     1S eat until 1S eat
     'I really ate a lot.'

(4) Mi bebé té   mi bebé!
     1S drink until 1S drink
     'I really drank a lot.'

The expression *té a bígi* is conventionalized to indicate that an activity was pursued to a heightened, memorable degree of intensity:

(5) De peé / bajá / kandá té   a bígi.
     3P play / dance / sing until 3S big
     'They really *played / danced / sang*.'

and thus it is ungrammatical with verbs denoting activities not amenable to engagement to a telic degree:

(6)   *Dí   míi   peé   /   kulé   té   a   bígi.
       DEF child play /   run   until   3S   big
       'The child really *played / ran*.'

An equivalent expression is *té* + pronominal + *kabá*:

(7)   Mi   bi   tá   bajá   té   mi kabá,   síngi   té   mi   kabá.
       1S PAST IMF dance until   1S finish   sing   until   1S   finish
       'I danced my ass off and sang myself hoarse.'

14.2. Time adverbials

'Now' is a frozen reduplicated form (cf. 3.1.1.2.), the inherent explicitness and deictic quality of its semantics having led naturally to reduplication occurring more often than it did not:

(8)   Ma   nɔ́unɔ́u á   tá   baláki   mɔ́ɔ̃.
       but   now   3S.NEG IMF   vomit   more
       'But now he doesn't throw up anymore.'

'Just' (as in 'recently') can be expressed with *djǔsu*, which can also connote 'very soon' depending on context – i.e. it refers to an event that is suspensefully proximate either in the past or the future:

(9)   Djǔsu mi   kó.
       just   1S   come
       'I just got here.' / 'I'm about to get there.'

Otherwise, another rendition of 'soon' is with *abíti mɔ́ɔ̃*:

(10) Mi   ó   bigí   woóko   abíti   mɔ́ɔ̃.
       1S   FUT begin   work   a.little   more
       'I'm starting work soon.'

Bifɔ́ means 'before' in adverbial complement clauses (cf. 9.2.3.1.), but in matrix clauses, despite its etymology its meaning is 'for now':

(11) Mi   nángó   bifɔ́.
       1S   IMF.go   for.now
       'I'm going for now.' (*'I'm going before.')

(12) U   tapéẽ   akí   bifɔ́.
       1P   stop.3SO here for.now
       'We're done for now.' (on ending a phone call)

(13) Té   a   kabá u   mbéi dí   ósu,   bifɔ́   u   ó   gó
     when 3S   finish NF   make DEF house for.now 1P   FUT go

    nɛ̃ɛ̃́   déndu.
    LOC.3S.POSS inside
    'When he finishes building the house, that's when we will go into it.'

The source of this reanalysis of the English word's meaning possibly is sentences such as this one, in which the meaning of *bifɔ́* could have begun as the English word's (i.e. 'You apologize to me; before that, I will not talk to you'):

(14) Té   i   dá   mi   piimísi, bifɔ́   mi á   ó   fã   ku   i.
     until 2S   give 1S   pardon   for.now 1S NEG FUT talk with 2S
     'Until you apologize to me, I will not talk to you.'

The sentential adverb with the meaning of English's *beforehand* or *formerly* is *fósúfósu*.
  'Again' is expressed usually with *báka* (< *back*):

(15) De súti   alá   báka.
     3P shoot yonder   back
     'They're shooting down there again.'

(16) Bisí ɛ̃   báka.
     wear 3SO back
     'Put it back on.'

It can also be expressed with a serial verb usage of *tooná* 'return' (cf. 8.3.3.):

(17) Dí   a   tooná   kó,   hɛ̃́   a   léi   andí dí   a   bái.
     when 3S   return come   then 3S   show what REL 3S   buy
     'When he came back, he showed all the things (whatever) he bought.'

'First':

(18) Méni   naásé i   bi   sí   ɛ̃   fósu.
     remember where 2S   PAST see 3SO first
     'Remember where you first saw it.'

'Once':

(19) Mi sí   sindéu a   wã́   pási.
     1S see snow   LOC one time
     'I saw snow once.'

'Still':

(20) U   tá   lúku éti.   (*U éti tá lúku.)
     1P   IMF   wait yet
     'We're still waiting.'

'Then' ('at that time'):

(21) A   dí   tɛ́   naandé de kabá soní.
      LOC DEF   time   there   3P finish thing
      'Then they ruined things.'

14.3. Adverbs of quantity

'Also' is expressed with *tu*:

(22) Mi bi   ké   u   híi ũ   **tu**   kó   akí.
      1S PAST want NF all 2P also   come here
      'I wanted all of you to come here too.'

The excessive (cf. 6.5.6.) is expressed either with *túmísi*:

(23) I   lánga **túmísi**,   báa.
      2S tall   too.much   brother
      'You're too tall, brother.'

or with a serial usage of *pói* 'to spoil' (cf. 8.3.2.):

(24) De tá   peé   dí   póku taánga **pói**.
      3P IMF   play DEF poku strong too.much
      'They played poku music too loud.'

'Enough' is expressed with a serial verb usage of *tjiká* 'to suffice' (cf. 8.5.2.):

(25) I   ábi   njãnjã́ **tjiká** ɔ́?
      2S have food   suffice INT
      'Do you have enough food?'

'Only' in the adverbial sense is expressed with *nɔ́ɔ*, which is a homonym of the new information marker *nɔ́ɔ* but which occurs strictly at the end of independent clauses (cf. 15.4.1.):

(26) Mi lési téni baáti u   dí   búku **nɔ́ɔ**.
      1S read ten   page   of DEF book just
      'I've only read ten pages of the book.'

'About' (as in 'approximately') is conveyed with *sɔ́*:

(27) A   téi   u   (kúma) dií   dáka **sɔ́**   fu kabá   ɛ̃.
      3S take 1P like   three day   such   NF finish 3SO
      'It took us about three days to finish it.'

A related concept, 'not quite / not exactly,' is also conveyed by *sɔ́*:

(28) Mé   sábi   ɛ̃   **sɔ́**   dí   né   fɛ̃ɛ̃.
      1S.NEG know   3SO   such   DEF name POSS.3S
      'I don't quite know what her name is.'

14.4. Adverbs of manner

'Suddenly' is the conventionalized *té wã́ písi*:

(29) *Té   wã́   písi,   dí   pɛndɛ́mbéti   hópo.*
     until   INDF   while   DEF   jaguar   stand.up
     'Suddenly the jaguar got up.'

'Fast' and 'slow' are expressed by *hési* and *sáápi*, both of which are quite often used in reduplicated form, especially when referring to an extreme degree of the quality (but not always) (cf. 3.1.1.2.):

(30) *A   tooká   gó   a   dé   sé   hésíhési.*
     3S   switch   go   LOC   3P.POSS   side   fast.RD
     'He switched to their side as quickly as possible.'

(31) *hópo   sáápísáápi*
     stand.up   slow.RD
     'arise slowly'

'Thus, like so, in this way' is expressed as *só*:

(32) *A   sá   dé   só,   ma   áá   fu   dé   só.*
     3S   can   be   thus   but   3S.NEG.have NF   be   thus
     'It can be that way, but it doesn't have to be.'

(33) *Hɛ́   mbéi   mi   bisí   só.*
     3S   make   1S   dress   thus
     'That's why I dress like this.'

'Like' as in 'seems like' is expressed via the verb *géi* 'seem,' which can be interpreted as 'looks like':

(34) *A   géi   wã́   dágu.*
     3S   seem   INDF   dog
     'He looks like a dog.'

Géi kúma is 'sounds like':

(35) *A   géi   kúma   páu   hɛ́   kaí.*
     3S   seem   like   tree   3ST   fall
     'It sounds like a tree is falling.'

Beyond the concepts of 'look' and 'sound,' 'like' is *kúma*; cf.:

(36) *A   sumɛ́ɛ   /   tési   /   fii   kúma   wã́   dágu.*
     3S   smell   /   taste   /   feel   like   INDF   dog
     'He smells like / tastes like / feels like a dog.'

14.5. Adverbs of frequency

'Usually' is conveyed most literally by habitual marker *ló* (cf. 7.3.3.):

(37) *Mé   ló   u   gó a   sitááti té   tjúba tá   kaí.*
      1S.NEG HAB NF go LOC street   until rain   IMF fall
      'I don't usually go into the street when it rains.'

The adverb *náa* can convey the past habitual (cf. 7.3.4.):

(38) *Mi bi   náa   gó a   San Francisco.*
      1S PAST HAB   go LOC San Francisco
      'I used to go to San Francisco.'

'Always' is alternately abbreviated variants of *híbi wã́ júu* 'every hour':

(39) *A   ló   njã́ híbi wã́   júu   / híbi júu   / híi wã́   júu*
      3S HAB   eat   all   one hour / all   hour / all one hour

      / *híi júu.*
      / all hour
      'He always eats.'

(40) *Híi júu   a   tá   peé   basketball.*
      all hour 3S IMF   play basketball
      'He's always playing basketball.'

'A lot' (also 'often') can be expressed with *híla* (cf. 4.5.):

(41) *Mi lési híla.*
      1S read a.lot
      'I read a lot.'

or with a serial verb usage of *pói* 'spoil' (cf. 8.3.2.), which in this usage covers a semantic domain from the excessive down to the remarkable, and as such, 'a lot':

(42) *Mi woóko taánga pói.*
      1S work   strong too.much
      'I work hard a lot.'

'Sometimes':

(43) *Só   júu   mi tá   fã   ku   mí seéi.*
      some hour 1S IMF talk with 1S self
      'Sometimes I talk to myself.'

202   *Adverbial modification*

14.6. The evidential adverbial construction

The expression *sí kúma* 'see how' indicates that someone has reason to believe something but is not certain:

(44)   I   sí   kúma   de   wíni   ɔ́?
       2S   see how   3P   win   INT
       'Do you think they will win?'

(45)   Mi   sí   kúma   de   tá   peé   báli   nɔ́unɔ́u.
       1S   see how   3P   IMF   play ball   now
       'It looks like they are just playing ball.'

Sí kúma, then, serves the role of propositional adverbial in specifying its complement clause as unconfirmed.

The expression can occur clause-finally with no complement to *kúma*, suggesting that *sí kúma* has moved along a pathway to becoming a single verb:

(46)   Aái,   mi   sí   kúma.
       yes   1S   see how
       'Yes, I think so.'

14.7. Ideophones

In Saramaccan, much of the functional load of semantically modifying verbs is carried by onomatopoeic expressions that occur after the verb. (Cf. 1.2.3. and 2.2.3.5. for discussion of distinguishing phonetic traits of these ideophones.) These items are the equivalent of English's *Pow!*, conventionalized as indicating the sound of a gunshot. However, unlike in English, in Saramaccan there are hundreds of conventionalized expressions of this kind, and they are central to full expression in the language. Following are some examples from our data; importantly, these are just a few of a great many ideophones in the language:

(47)   Dí   wági   dé   límbo   **tééé**.
       DEF   car   be   clean   very
       'The car is really clean.'

(48)   U   bi   tá   fã,   hẽ́   a   gó   **djééé**.
       1P   PAST   IMF   talk   then   3S   go   up.and.go
       'We were talking, and then she just up and left.'

(49)   Dí   dí   bóto   kó,   nɔ́ɔ   a   tapá   ku   wẽ́wẽ   **gbìtìì**.
       when   DEF   boat   come   NI   3S   cover   with   fly   IDEO
       'When the boat came, it was covered with flies.'

(50)   Mi   ké   u   déé   biífi   woóko   músu   dé   kabákábá   **kééé**.
       1S   want   NF   DEF.PL   letter   work   must   be   finish.RD   completely
       'I want my papers to be clean.'

(51)　Dí　　bundji　tá　　tapá　**pìtììì**.
　　　DEF　fog　　IMF　cover　IDEO
　　　'The fog keeps coming in.'

(52)　A　tá　　téi　　mi　**tjàtjàtjàtjà**!
　　　3S　IMF　take　1S　IDEO
　　　'It made me so angry I was almost shaking.'

(53)　Wómi, dú **páápáá**!
　　　man　do　IDEO
　　　'Man, hurry up!'

(54)　I　mú　　dέ　**píí**.
　　　2S　must　be　IDEO
　　　'You have to be completely quiet.'

Here is a passage from a vividly delivered narration of a folktale, rich with ideophones:

(55)　Hέ　　a　téi　　dí　　páu,　a　tá　　náki　dí　　páu,　**gbò**!
　　　then　3S　take　DEF　stick　3S　IMF　hit　　DEF　stick　IDEO

　　　Déé　　　mbéti　　tá　　kó　　　**gbìtìì**,　dí　　wósu　fúu　　**pɔ́ɔ́ɔ́**!　Ma té
　　　DEF.PL　animal　IMF　come　IDEO　　DEF　house　full　IDEO　but until

　　　wã́　　písi,　ma,　hélipe,　a　lúku　dí　　dédɛ　　dέ　**píí**,　a　táa　　'Hέ!
　　　INDF　while　but　monkey　3S　look　DEF　corpse　be　IDEO　3S　talk　3ST

　　　Dí　　soní　　akí,　u　　táa　　dédɛ　o,　　mi　sí,　　táa　　a　tá　　　bɔɔ́!'
　　　DEF　thing　here　1P　talk　dead　INJ　1S　see　COMP　3S　IMF　breathe

　　　A　pikí　　**sììì**,　a　toná　　　　sáápi,　gó　dé　　a　　dɔɔ　búka.
　　　3S　little　IDEO　3S　turn.around　slow　　go　there　LOC　door　mouth
　　　'Then he took the stick and banged it, pow! The animals were in swarms, the house was full to bursting. But all of a sudden, Monkey looked at the corpse laying there so quietly, and said 'Look at him! We're saying he's dead, but I see him *breathing*!' Hunched all up, he turned away slowly and went over to the doorway.'

Each color term (cf. 6.6.) is specified to be modified by a particular ideophone to indicate intensification:

(56)　A　bɛ　　/　ros　　**njàâ**.
　　　3S　red　/　pink　IDEO
　　　'It's really red / pink.' (This ideophone is the one to indicate shining.)

(57)　A　wéti　　**fáã́**.
　　　3S　white　IDEO
　　　'It's really white.'

(58)　A　oranje　　/　paars　　**njɛ̀ɛ̂ɛ̀**.
　　　3S　orange　/　purple　IDEO
　　　'It's really orange / purple.'

(59) A gũűũ / baáka / baáu **píí**.
      3S green / black / blue IDEO
      'It's really green / black / blue.' (This ideophone indicates, elsewhere, quietness.)

14.8. Placement of adverbs

Typically adverbs can occur either clause-intially or clause-finally:

(60) A   ló   njã̌   **híi júu**.
      3S HAB   eat   all hour
      'He always eats.'

(61) **Híi júu**   a   tá   peé   basketball.
      all hour   3S   IMF   play   basketball
      'He's always playing basketball.'

However, it is quite rare for adverbs to occur between the subject and the verb as in *George often goes to the movies after work*. Only one adverb regularly occurs in this slot in our data, *tu* 'also':

(62) Mi   bi   ké   u   híi ũ   **tu**   kó   akí.
      1S   PAST want   NF   all 2P also   come   here
      'I wanted all of you to come here too.'

(Contrary to Veenstra [1996: 26], we analyze past habitual marker *náa* [cf. 7.3.4.] as an auxiliary clitic rather than as an adverb meaning 'usually.')

Chapter 15
Information structure

15.1. Contrastive focus

15.1.1. Impressionistic prominence

One strategy for contrastive focusing in Saramaccan is stressing the focused item (cf. 2.4.4.):

(1) Mi ábi wǎ **dágu**, ná wǎ pusipúsi!
    1S have INDF dog NEG INDF cat
    'I have a dog, not a cat!'

With pronouns, focusing entails both stressing and high tone:

(2) **Mí** hákísi dí soní.
    1S ask DEF thing
    'I asked it (i.e. the question).'

except in the third-person singular, in which there is a distinct tonic form *hɛ̌* (cf. 5.1.):

(3) Mɔ́ni **hɛ̌** mi ké.
    money 3ST 1S want
    'It's money I want.' (lit. 'Money, *it* I want.')

15.1.2. Contrastive focus on verbs

Verbs are contrastively focused via clefting, with a copy left behind:

(4) Nɔ́nɔ, ná tapá dí sípi tá tapá, síngi a tá síngi.
    no NEG stop DEF ship IMF stop sink 3S IMF sink
    'No, the ship isn't *stopping*, it's *sinking*.'

The construction is often used to express contrast with an implied alternative action rather than an overtly expressed one:

(5) Kulé u músu kulé kumútu a dí wósu.
    run 1P must run exit LOC DEF house
    'We had to *run* out of the house.'

In such usages, an apt translation may not entail contrastive focus at all:

(6) Léi nɔ́ɔ de ké léi dí soní.
    learn NI 3P want learn DEF thing
    'What they want (their whole purpose) is to learn the thing (i.e. here, a language).'

Second verbs in serial verb constructions (cf. Chapter 8) can be clefted and copied when their usage as a serial verb is only moderately grammaticalized, such that a lexical residue remains:

(7) Gó Kobí kulé gó a dí wósu.
go Kobi run go LOC DEF house
'Kobi ran *to* the house.'

but not when their serial usage is deeply grammaticalized such that the lexical meaning is no longer compatible with the semantics of the proposition. For example, *túwɛ* 'throw' as a second serial verb connotes the end of a pathway of movement (cf. 13.3.2.2.), a thoroughly grammatical connotation too removed from the lexical one of throwing to submit to focus:

(8) *Túwɛ Kobí fáa dí páu túwɛ.
throw Kobi fell DEF tree throw
'Kobi cut the tree *down*.'

15.1.3. Contrastive focus on arguments and adjuncts

15.1.3.1. Fronting

One strategy in Saramaccan for focusing an argument or adjunct is fronting:

(9) A dí éside dí wági u mi boóko.
LOC DEF yesterday DEF car POSS 1S break
'It was yesterday that my car broke down.'

(10) Alísi de tá séi.
rice 3P IMF sell
'They're selling *rice*.' (i.e. 'It's rice that they're selling.')

In the following example, copula *da* is absent, an absence generally grammatical only when the predicate is fronted (cf. 12.1.3.), which reveals this sentence as one in which the predicate has been fronted for focus:

(11) Saaná, mí kɔ́ndɛ.
Surinam 1S.POSS country
'My country is *Surinam*.'

15.1.3.2. Contrastive focus marker wɛ

On arguments and adjuncts, contrastive focus can also be marked with *wɛ*. This is a borrowing from Saramaccan's main substrate language Fongbe, whose cognate item serves a similar function. Despite its phonetic similarity to English's *well*, *wɛ* is not derived from *well* and is untranslatable into any English lexical or grammatical item.

In the two following sentences, *wɛ* marks subjects:

(12) Mí **wɛ** hákísi dí soní.
1S FOC ask DEF thing
'*I* am asking the question.'

(13) Sääná **wɛ** da mí kɔ́ndɛ.
 Surinam FOC be 1S.POSS country
 '*Surinam* is my country.'

Here it marks an adjunct:

(14) Mi tá wóoko a díí-dé-wóoko **wɛ**.
 1S IMF work LOC three-day-work FOC
 'I work on *Tuesday*.'

With internal arguments, *wɛ* often co-occurs with fronting:

(15) Dí wósu **wɛ** a mbéi kabá.
 DEF house FOC 3S make finish
 'He built the *house*.'

(16) Dí wósu u mí **wɛ** a mbéi kabá.
 DEF house POSS 1S FOC 3S make finish
 'He built *my* house.'

(17) A Boston **wɛ** Jeff kumútu é?
 LOC Boston FOC Jeff exit INJ
 'Does Jeff come from *Boston*?'

With objects, *wɛ* can only occur with fronting:

(18) *Hákísi mí **wɛ** dí soní.
 ask 1S FOC DEF thing
 'Ask *me* the question.'

(19) Mí **wɛ** i músu hákísi dí soní.
 1S FOC 2S must ask DEF thing
 '(You must) ask *me* the question.'

(20) *Mi léi dí búku **wɛ** éside.
 1S read DEF book FOC yesterday
 'I read the *book* yesterday.'

(Therefore, *in situ* objects are contrastively focused via intonational prominence, fronting [see above], or strategies described below.)
 Wɛ can also apply to entire propositions, occurring in both initial and final position, to encode sentential focus:

(21) **Wɛ** a dé ku líbi.
 FOC 3S be with life
 '(After all, the fact is that) he lives.'

(22) Nɔ́ɔ   hɛ̃́   wɛ   a   tá   kondá   dá   de   tá   táki   táa   **wɛ**,
    NI   then   FOC   3S   IMF   tell   give 3P   IMF   talk   COMP   FOC

   sɔ́   dí   soní   dí   mbéti   pɛndé.
   such   DEF   thing   DEF   animal   colored.
   'So then he was telling them that, it's like this, the animals were colored.'

Wɛ also occurs frequently with *hɛ̃́* 'then' to express explicit sequentiality:

(23) **Hɛ̃́**   **wɛ**   a   ó   táki   a   dí   bígi.
     then   FOC   3S   FUT   talk   LOC   DEF   big
     'Then he'll talk to The Big One.'

or consequence:

(24) **Hɛ̃́**   **wɛ**   nɔ́nɔ,   u   sí   táa   á   súti.
     then   FOC   no   1P   see   COMP   3S.NEG   sweet
     'Then (i.e. for that reason), no – we saw that it wasn't nice.'

15.1.3.3. Contrastive focus marking with hɛ̃́

Another focus strategy for arguments and adjuncts, functionally equivalent to the usage of *wɛ*, is the use of tonic third-person singular *hɛ̃́* with left-dislocation of the focused constituent (i.e. the constituent leaves behind *hɛ̃́* as a resumptive pronominal). With subjects:

(25) Dí   u   mí wági   **hɛ̃́**   boóko,   ná   dí   fíí.
     DEF   POSS   1S car   3ST   break   NEG   DEF   POSS.2S
     '*My* car broke down, not yours.'

(26) A   géi   kúma   páu   **hɛ̃́**   kaí.
     3S   seem   like   tree   3ST   fall
     'It sounds like a *tree* is falling.'

With objects:

(27) Mɔ́ni   **hɛ̃́**   mi   ké.
     money   3ST   1S   want
     'It's *money* I want.'

When prepositional phrase adjuncts encoding spatial relations (or metaphorically related ones indicating time) are left-dislocated for focus, the referent occurs first, followed by a prepositional phrase treating the spatial relation as its possessum, with locative preposition *a* 'at, in' fused with oblique third-person pronoun *ɛ̃́* to yield the portmanteau morpheme *nɛ̃ɛ̃́* (this is a regular morphophonemic rule in the grammar [cf. 3.3.4.2.]: /a ɛ̃́ wósu/ 'LOC 3S.POSS house' > *nɛ̃ɛ̃́ wósu*):

(28) De   bi   tá   bósi   **a**   dí   wósu   báka.
     3P   PAST   IMF   kiss   LOC   DEF   house   back
     'They kissed in back of the house.'

becomes:

(29) Dí wósu dé **nɛ̃ɛ̃** báka de bi tá bósi.
 DEF house there LOC.3S.POSS back 3P PAST IMF kiss
 'That's the house they kissed in back of.'

Similarly:

(30) Éside **nɛ̃ɛ̃**, dí wági u mi boóko.
 yesterday LOC.3S.POSS DEF car POSS 1S break
 'It was yesterday that my car broke down.'

cf.:

(31) **A** dí éside dí wági u mi boóko.
 LOC DEF yesterday DEF car POSS 1S break
 'It was yesterday that my car broke down.'

15.1.3.4. Focus marker hɛ̃ da

Another focusing strategy for arguments and adjuncts is a presentative one with *hɛ̃ da* 'it is':

(32) **Hɛ̃ da** u Boston Jeff kumútu.
 3S be of Boston Jeff exit
 'Jeff comes from *Boston*.'

15.1.3.5. Reduplicated pronouns?

Voorhoeve's (1961) description of the Upper River Saramaccan dialect proposes that Saramaccan has a paradigm of "reduplicated" pronouns used for emphasis, such as *mí-i wáka* '*I* walk,' *dé-e wáka* '*they* walk.' One might consider that this "reduplication" is actually simply a matter of marking the pronoun with high tone and stress, such as occurs in the Lower River dialect spoken by our principal informants. We have encountered nothing indicating a separate paradigm of reduplicated pronouns per se.

15.2. Pragmatic markers

15.2.1. Given-information marking

Saramaccan, as a primarily oral language, makes frequent use of topic-comment constructions over ones with just a subject and a predicate. Topicalization (i.e. usually entailing a sentence-initial constituent coreferent with the subject) serves often as a marker of given information:

(33) Nɔ́ɔ hɛ̃ we wã́ mujɛ́ɛ bi dé a dí kɔ́ndɛ naandɛ́.
 NI then FOC INDF woman PAST be LOC DEF village there

 Nɔ́ɔ **dí mujɛ́ɛ**, a palí dí míi wã́ dáka.
 NI DEF woman 3S bear DEF child one day
 'So, then: there was a woman in the village there. The woman, she bore a child one day.'

(34) **Dísi, hɛ̃́** da goólíba,   aái.
this   3S be world   yes
'The world, this is – yes.' (said after a description of various aspects of living on earth; i.e. 'this,' *dísi*)

(35) **Dí**   woóko u   **mi**, a nángó   dóu.
DEF   work   POSS   1S   3S IMF.go   arrive
'My work is keeping on going.' (the work in question having been discussed on an earlier occasion)

(36) **Déé**   sɛmbɛ   u   kɔ́nde   alá,   de   ó   fii   ɛ̃   tu.
DEF.PL   person of   village yonder 3P   FUT   feel   3SO   also
'The people of the village down there, they will feel it as well.'

(In the above sentence, the location of the people as "there" indicates that they are a familiar referent to the conversants, even though they had not been discussed in the conversation until this point.)
When the topic occurs to the right of the clause, it also conveys given information:

(37) Mɛ́   sábi   ɛ̃   só,   dí   né   fɛ̃ɛ̃.
1S.NEG   know   3SO   such   DEF   name   POSS.3S
'(You know,) I don't quite *know* what her name is.' (lit. 'I don't quite know it, her name.')

15.2.2. New-information marking: *Nɔ́ɔ* and *hɛ̃́*

Nɔ́ɔ is sometimes translated as 'then.' However, its overall usage does not submit to translation as any English item. A unified analysis of its usage is that of a pragmatic marker of new information.
The 'then' translation is most apt in its usage as a sequential marker, in which it occurs quite frequently in narration, often marking each clause as *and so* and *then* do in spoken English narrations. This can be treated as a type of new-information marking that retains a heavy degree of lexical content:

(38) **Nɔ́ɔ**   mi   ó   kándi   a   míndi   wósu. **Nɔ́ɔ**   i   butá   wã́
NI   1S   FUT   lie.down   LOC   middle house   NI   2S   put   INDF

kódjo, wã́   kódjo   a   bandja.   **Nɔ́ɔ**   i   kái   woló   kɛɛ́! ...
cudgel INDF   cudgel LOC   side   NI   2S   call   alas   cry
'I'm going to lay down in the middle of the house. Then you put a stick, a stick off to the side. Then you wail out 'Alas!' ...'

Nɔ́ɔ occurs in this usage only in the non-past; in the past, *hɛ̃́* is used as a sequential marker:

(39) **Hɛ̃́**   wɛ   a   sí,   a   kái,   táa   'Jejéta, Jejéta, dá   mi   só
then   FOC   3S   see 3S   call   talk   Jejeta   Jejeta   give   1S   some

pindá   o!'
peanut INJ
'Then he sees her and calls out 'Jejeta, Jejeta, why don't you give me some peanut?!''

(40) **Hɛ́**   a   táa   'Nɔ́nɔ, Anási.'
      then 3S   talk   no   Anancy
      'And she said "No, Anancy."'

(41) Mi sí   awaá   **hɛ́**   mi   njǎmɛ̃.
      1S see palm.fruit then   1S   eat.3SO
      'I saw the palm fruit and ate it.'

(42) Mi sí   dí   fuúta **hɛ́**   Kobí kó   njǎmɛ̃.
      1S see DEF fruit then   Kobi come   eat.3SO
      'I saw the fruit and Kobi ate it.'

However, *nɔ́ɔ* is used more generally in more pragmaticized fashion, as a default new-information marker. Here, from a spontaneous utterance, *a búnu* 'so okay' concludes a discussion, and then *nɔ́ɔ* introduces a new issue:

(43) A   búnu. **Nɔ́ɔ** mi ó   tá   háika   i.
      3S good   NI   1S FUT IMF listen 2S
      'Good. So I'll be listening for you (i.e. waiting for your answer).'

This sentence was uttered in reference to arranging an elicitation session. The following day, in an exchange reiterating the arrangement, the same informant produced a sentence much like the previous one, but without *nɔ́ɔ*, because the relevant information was no longer new information, having already been established:

(44) A   búnu, mi ó   tá   háika   dí   kái   fii   tidé   néti.
      3S good   1S FUT IMF listen DEF call POSS.2S today night
      'Good, I'll be listening (i.e. waiting) for your call tonight.'

The status of *nɔ́ɔ* as a new-information marker rather than simply an equivalent to English *then* is clear, however, in cases in which the *then* translation would be impossible. Here, *nɔ́ɔ* marks the person's return to playing as new information:

(45) Dí   wíki dí   bi   pasá dé,   mé   bi   sá   pɛɛ́,
      DEF week REL PAST pass there 1S.NEG PAST can play

      ma   **nɔ́ɔ** mi kó   tá   pɛɛ́   báka.
      but NI   1S come IMF play again
      'Last week I couldn't play, but now I'm playing again.'

15.2.2.1. Position of nɔ́ɔ

Only with independent clauses does *nɔ́ɔ* as a new-information marker occur initially. Otherwise, it is postposed, such as on dependent clauses:

(46) Té   wǎ   óto   pási báka   **nɔ́ɔ**, i   tǎ   búnu.
      until INDF other time again NI   2S stand good
      'Till another time, be well.'

(The subordinate clause constitutes a shift of topic from discussion to leave-taking, and as such is marked as new information.)

This postposing also occurs with clefted items:

(47) Híi fá   de tá   dú dé   léi   **nɔ́ɔ** de ké   léi   dí   soní.
     all how   3P IMF do there learn NI   3P want   learn DEF   thing
     'The whole thing they are doing there is that they want to *learn* the thing.' (i.e. 'The whole purpose is that they want to *learn* it.')

and when *nɔ́ɔ* marks arguments and adjuncts:

(48) Ũ   kái   bakúba   **nɔ́ɔ**   baána.
     2P call   banana   NI   banana
     'You call (what we call) the bakuba a banana.' (Aboikoni and Glock 1997: 12)

(49) A   búnu   é   –   amǎjǎ   **nɔ́ɔ**   mi ó   jéi   fii.
     3S   good   INJ   tomorrow NI   1S FUT   hear   for.2S
     'So very good – tomorrow I'll listen for you (i.e. wait for your call).'

In this passage of running speech, *nɔ́ɔ* is postposed to two clauses that echo a preceding dependent one, such that they are underlyingly dependent despite not being overtly marked as such. Then, when a new independent clause begins, it is marked as new information clause-initially, as is the independent clause afterwards:

(50) Wε   i   sí, fá   wó   bigí   alá ... (fá)   u   kó   akí   **nɔ́ɔ**,
     FOC   2S   see how   1P.FUT   begin   yonder   1P   come   here   NI

     (fá)   u   wéki   alá   **nɔ́ɔ**.   Nɔ́ɔ   u   dé alá,   **nɔ́ɔ**   híi soni
            1P   do.fine yonder NI   NI   1P   be yonder   NI   all thing

     nángó   búnu.
     IMF.go   good
     'So now, so you see how we'll kick it off – how we came here, how we were surviving up there. So, there we were, and everything was going fine.'

15.2.2.2. Nɔ́ɔ and adverbial complements

Nɔ́ɔ is especially conventionalized in marking matrix clauses that occur after preceding adverbial complements, the matrix clause containing the new information. This is the case with temporal complements:

(51) Báka   dí   de gó,   **nɔ́ɔ**   dí   mujéε   bi   tá   kεέ.
     after   when   3P go   NI   DEF   woman   PAST   IMF   cry
     'After they left, the woman was crying.'

(52) Té   mujéε   sí   Kobí,   **nɔ́ɔ**   de tá   kulé.
     when   woman   see   Kobi   NI   3P IMF   run
     'When women see Kobi, they run.'

(53) Té   mi féni dí   kámba dí   mi lóbi, **nɔ́ɔ** mi ó   gó
     when   1S find DEF room REL 1S like NI   1S FUT go

     nɛ̃ɛ́   déndu.
     LOC.3S.POSS inside
     'When I find the right room, I will go into it.'

as well as causal and concessive ones:

(54) Nda   dí   wági ná   u   mi, **nɔ́ɔ** i   ó   paká fɛ̃ɛ́.
     since DEF car   NEG POSS 1S   NI   2S FUT pay   for.3SO
     'You're going to pay for the car, since it is not mine.'

(55) Ée dí   míi   á   dú ɛ̃,   **nɔ́ɔ** dí   m'má ó   náki ɛ̃.
     if DEF child NEG do 3SO NI   DEF Mom   FUT hit   3SO
     'If the child doesn't do it, then the Mom will hit him.'

(56) Híi fá   de dé duumí duumí, **nɔ́ɔ** hɛ̃́   sɛmbɛ   kó   a   dí
     all how 3P be sleep sleep   NI   then person come LOC DEF

     wósu.
     house
     'Even though they were sleeping, people came into the house.'

In this usage with matrix clauses with preceding adverbial complements, *nɔ́ɔ* is conventionalized but not obligatory, as seen in grammatical sentences such as:

(57) Ée i   bi   láfu   mi, mi bi   ó   féti   ku   i.
     if 2S PAST laugh 1S   1S PAST FUT fight with 2S
     'If you'd laughed at me, I'd have fought with you.'

(58) Fá   u   tá   dú dísi seéi, mi ó   tjumá dí   wósu   akí.
     how 1P IMF do this even   1S FUT burn   DEF house here
     'Even though we are doing this, I am going to burn down this house.'

15.2.2.3. New information versus focus-marking

Given the close correlation between focus and new information, naturally *nɔ́ɔ* and focus marker *wɛ* (cf. 15.1.3.2.) can occur interchangeably in some contexts. Take the following sentence:

(59) Nɔ́ɔ u   **nɔ́ɔ** / wɛ,   dísi kaa.
     NI   1P NI   / FOC   this CPLT
     'This is *us*.' (i.e. 'This is the way we are.')

First, *nɔ́ɔ* occurs sentence-initially to mark the proposition as new information. But then, *nɔ́ɔ* can occur redundantly as marking the fronted nonverbal predicate as new information (the fronting revealed in that zero-copula is only grammatical when the predicate is fronted [cf. 12.1.3.]), and it occurs after the (fronted) predicate since it is not a full sentence (cf. 15.2.2.1). However, equally grammatical is that the fronted predicate is marked for contrastive focus with *wɛ*.

As the result of this pragmatic intersection in the denotation of *nɔ́ɔ* and *wɛ*, the items can occur together to connote the marking of both focus and new information. They occur thus in both orders:

(60) **Nɔ́ɔ wɛ,** *nɔ́ɔ déé máku tá njã̌mɛ̃.*
NI   FOC   NI   DEF.PL   mosquito   IMF   eat.3SO
'So, the mosquitos were biting him.'

(61) **Wɛ nɔ́ɔ,** *wɛ i sí, fá wó bigí alá ...*
FOC   NI   FOC   2S   see   how   1P.FUT   begin   yonder
'So now, so you see how we'll kick this thing off ...'

15.2.2.4. *Hɛ̌* as new-information marker in the bounded past

In matrix clauses occurring after temporal adverbial complements, in the past tense, *nɔ́ɔ* is superseded as a new-information marker by *hɛ̌* 'then,' in line with its usage as a sequential marker in the past (cf. 15.2.2.):

(62) *Dí a bi tá duumí,* **hɛ̌** *mi gó kumútu dé.*
when   3S   PAST   IMF   sleep   then   1S   go   exit   there
'When he was sleeping, I left.'

However, this is only when the matrix clause semantics are bounded; otherwise, *nɔ́ɔ* is required:

(63) *Dí mi bi kó lúku de,* **nɔ́ɔ** *de bi duumí kaa.*
when   1S   PAST   come   look   3P   NI   3P   PAST   sleep   CPLT
'When I came to see them, they were asleep.'

(Cf. 15.2.2. for more discussion of the division of labor in new-information marking between *nɔ́ɔ* and *hɛ̌*.)

But often *nɔ́ɔ* "asserts itself" as the default indicator of new information in co-occurring with *hɛ̌* as *nɔ́ɔ hɛ̌* even with matrix clauses of bounded semantics:

(64) *Mi dé a dí wósu báka,* **nɔ́ɔ hɛ̌** *mi sí wã̌ mujéɛ,*
1S   be   LOC   DEF   house   back   NI   then   1S   see   INDF   woman

hɛ̌ mi sí dí wómi náki dí mujéɛ.
then   1S   see   DEF   man   hit   DEF   woman
'I was behind the house, then I saw a woman and saw the man hit the woman.'

(65) *Dí a bóoko dí báta kaa,* **nɔ́ɔ hɛ̌** *a léi mi.*
when   3S   break   DEF   bottle   CPLT   NI   then   3S   show   1S
'When he broke the bottle, he showed it to me.'

15.3. Combinations of focus and pragmatic markers

The reinforcement of *hɛ̌* in its sequential usage with preposed *nɔ́ɔ* and postposed *wɛ* can result in the tri-morphemic marker of sequential new information *nɔ́ɔ hɛ̌ wɛ*:

(66) Nɔ́ɔ   hɛ́ ... wɛ   a   kó   dú   ɛ̃,   hɛ́   wɛ   da   dí   sukúma
      NI   then   FOC   3S   come do   3SO   then   FOC   be   DEF   foam

      kó   mujɛ́ɛ-míi.
      come   woman-child
      'So then he came and did it; then it was that the foam became a girl.'

In this extract from a folktale narrative, we see how the three morphemes are used in variable combination:

(67) Nɔ́ɔ   hɛ́ ... hɛ́   wɛ   a   gó   ku   dí   míi   nɛ̃ɛ́   písi.
      NI   then   then   FOC   3S   go   with   DEF   child LOC.3S.POSS home

      A   kó   a   míi.
      3S   come   LOC   child
      'So then ... then he went into the child's home. He came to the child ...'

      Nɔ́ɔ   hɛ́   wɛ   wã́   dáka   tééé   dí   mujɛ́ɛ-míi   fɛ̃ɛ̃,
      NI   then   FOC   one   day   very   DEF   woman-child   POSS.3SO
      'So then once upon a time, the woman's daughter'

      de   bi   tá   kái   ɛ̃   Jejéta.
      3P   PAST   IMF   call   3SO   Jejeta
      'was called Jejeta.'

      Nɔ́ɔ   hɛ́   wɛ   wã́   dáka,   dí   mujɛ́ɛ-míi   tá   fṍ
      pindá,
      NI   then   FOC   one   day   DEF   woman-child   IMF   beat   peanut
      'So one day, the girl was beating peanuts'

      tá   fṍ   pindá   ku   tatí   a   máta.
      IMF   beat   peanut   with   pestle   LOC   mortar
      'beating peanuts with a mortar and pestle.'

      Hɛ́   wɛ   Anási   wáka   dóu   dé.   Hɛ́   wɛ   a   sí,
      then   FOC   Anancy   walk   arrive   there   then   FOC   3S   see

      a   kái,   táa
      3S   call   talk
      'Then Anancy goes in there, then he sees her and calls out:'

      'Jejéta,   Jejéta,   dá   mi   só   pindá   o!'
      Jejeta   Jejeta   give   1S   some   peanut   INJ
      'Jejeta, Jejeta, why don't you give me some peanut?!'

      Hɛ́   a   táa   'Nɔ́nɔ,   Anási.   Mi   á   ó   dá   i.
      then   3S   talk   no   Anancy   1S   NEG   FUT   give   2S

      Dí   pindá   ná   u   mi.'
      DEF   peanut   NEG   POSS   1S
      'And she said 'No, Anancy. I won't give any to you. The peanut isn't mine.''

      'U   mi   mamá.   Nɔ́ɔ   mi   á   músu   dá   sɛmbɛ.'
      POSS   1S   mother   NI   1S   NEG   must   give   person
      'It's my mother's. So I mustn't give it to anybody.'

15.4. Pragmatic-marking adverbs

There are various words in Saramaccan whose meaning serves to indicate a speaker's attitude towards a proposition. Most of them would traditionally be described as adverbs. However, their meanings have become so abstractly pragmaticized that they are the equivalent of, for example, German's modal "particles" or the proliferation of such particles typical of languages in Southeast Asia.

15.4.1. Nɔ́ɔ 'just, only'

New-information marker *nɔ́ɔ* has a homonym, which translates as 'just' or 'only':

(68) Mi   lési   téni   baáti   u   dí   búku   **nɔ́ɔ**.
      1S   read   ten   page   of   DEF   book   just
      'I've only read ten pages of the book.'

but whose meaning also extends to softening a request or observation (rather like German's modal particle *mal* as in *Willst du mal abbeissen?* 'Would you like to take a little bite?'):

(69) Bóo   gó   **nɔ́ɔ**   wã́   u   déé   dáka   akí.
      HORT.1P   go   just   one   of   DEF.PL   day   here
      '(So ...) why don't we go one of these days?'

This homonym is derived from the still living item *nɔ́ɔmɔ*, whose etymology is *no more*. This is clear first in that *nɔ́ɔmɔ* has a different but related meaning to this homonym of *nɔ́ɔ* (cf. 15.4.2.), and in that in Saramaccan's progenitor creole Sranan, the less phonetically evolved *nomo* is cognate to Saramaccan's "softening" homonym of *nɔ́ɔ*.

Note that this homonym of *nɔ́ɔ* does occur sentence-finally on independent clauses, unlike the new-information marking homonym (cf. 15.2.2.1.). This means that the Saramaccan speaker interprets the meaning of *nɔ́ɔ* according to a particular positioning rule: only when *nɔ́ɔ* occurs at the end of an independent clause is it interpreted as 'only.' That is, when:

a) beginning an independent clause
b) occurring after an external or internal argument in an independent clause
c) occurring after a dependent clause

nɔ́ɔ is interpreted as a new-information marker. Note that in the sentences above in 15.2.2.1. in which *nɔ́ɔ* occurs after arguments or dependent clauses, its interpretation as 'just' or 'only' would be impossible.

15.4.2. Nɔ́ɔmɔ 'indeed'

Nɔ́ɔmɔ is derived from *no more*. One of its meanings is 'definitely,' conveying conviction on the part of the speaker:

(70) Mi   ó   dú   ẽ   **nɔ́ɔmɔ**.
      1S   FUT   do   3SO   definitely
      'I'm definitely going to do it.'

(71) Mi ó gó téi ɛ̃ **nɔ́ɔmɔ**.
    1S FUT go take 3SO definitely
    'I'm definitely going to get her (romantically).'

Nɔ́ɔmɔ is used, then, in the sense of 'that's all there is to it,' and also connotes, as an interjection, 'indeed.' An additional meaning of *nɔ́ɔmɔ* extends this meaning to duration, conveying 'always' or 'continuously':

(72) Nɔ́ɔ léti fuu u mú súku **nɔ́ɔmɔ**.
    NI right POSS.1P 1P must look.for always
    'We must always look for the right way for us to be.'

15.4.3. *Seéi*

Seéi is the reflexive marker (cf. 5.5.) and is derived from *self*. However, elsewhere in the grammar it is used as a highly versatile pragmatic marker. The core meaning that all of its occurrences share is an indication of counterexpectation.

This meaning is inherent even in the reflexive use of *seéi* when the reflexive is used to highlight agency:

(73) Ú **seéi**, u ábi dí kaakíti dé.
    1P self 1P have DEF power there
    'We ourselves have that power.'
(74) Mí **seéi** ó bói ɛ̃.
    1S self FUT cook 3SO
    'I will cook it myself.'

For example, *seéi* in this sentence connotes 'The person who cooks it will be, counter to your expectation, me.' Likely, this was the source of *seéi*'s usage elsewhere as a pragmatic marker.

Seéi, for example, can connote 'even':

(75) Mi ó bái ɛ̃, ée já lóbi ɛ̃ **seéi**.
    1S FUT buy 3SO if 2S.NEG like 3SO self
    'I'm buying it even if you don't like it.'

(76) Ná beɛ́ɛ **seéi** i sá bái!
    NEG bread self 2S can buy
    'You couldn't even buy bread.'

The above sentence means, for example, that while one might not be surprised that supplies were low, things were in fact counterexpectationally bad: even bread was unavailable.

Seéi can mean 'the same':

(77) De tá woóko a wã́ **seéi** kamíã.
    3P IMF work LOC one self place
    'They are working at the same place.'

(78) Mé   sábi ée jó   sá   kái   mi amájá   a   dí
    1S.NEG know if 2S.FUT can call 1S tomorrow LOC DEF

    seéi júu.
    same hour
    'I don't know if you can call me tomorrow at the same time.'

'at all':

(79) Mi áá   móni   seéi.
    1S NEG.have money self
    'I don't have any money at all.'

and serve as an intensifier, in cases in which one is expressing surprise:

(80) Tjúba seéi tá   kaí!
    rain   self IMF fall
    'Boy, it's really raining, isn't it?'

'In any case' is also conveyed with seéi, again a concept entailing the counterexpectational:

(81) Mé   lóbi ɛ̃   seéi.
    1S.NEG like 3SO self
    'I don't like him anyway.'

Contextually, the assertion that one does not like the person is presented as a negation to a supposition amidst the preceding dialogue that one did like the person.

A reduplicated form connotes precision, in contexts in which the preciseness is foregrounded (a counterexpectational situation):

(82) Mi ábi   wã̂   dágu seéisééi.
    1S have one dog   self.RD
    'I have only one dog.'

15.4.4. *Awáa* 'at last'

In the semantic sense, *awáa* can convey what *finally* and *at last* do in English:

(83) Awáa   mi féni naásé a   bi   dé.
    at.last 1S find where 3S PAST be
    'I finally found out where he was.'

(84) Awáa   de kó   lóbi dé seéi.
    at.last 3P come like 3P self
    'They came to like one another.'

In this meaning, *awáa* can also be followed by *fu*:

(85) Dí   tjúba kaí u   téni dáka, awáa   fu   dí   sóni jabí.
    DEF rain   fall for ten   day   at.last for DEF sun   open
    'It rained for ten days and then finally the sun came out.'

However, it also extends into a pragmatic function: indicating that something has occurred after an extended period during which it did not. In this sentence, for example, *awáa* translates roughly as 'by now'; i.e. the evening has passed and now we are at the point when you should go to bed:

(86) A   tjiká   fíi   gó   a   bédi   **awáa**   ɔ́?
      3S   suffice   for.2S   go   LOC   bed   at.last   INT
      'Isn't it about time for you to go to bed?'

Similarly, this sentence highlights the fact that the event occurs after much time during which it could not:

(87) Mi   gó   a   Djuúmu   te   mi   kó,   nɔ́ɔ   **awáa**   mi   féni   pási
      1S   go   LOC   Djuumu   until   1S   come   NI   at.last   1S   find   time

      kó   lúku   i   **awáa**.
      come   look   2S   at.last
      'I went to Djuumu and came back, and now here I am with a chance to come to take care of you.'

Note also that *awáa* is very flexible in terms of positional occurrence: it occurs both clause-initially and clause-finally and can occur more than once in a sentence.

Other sentences:

(88) **Awáa**   i   tá   hã́so.
      at.last   2S   IMF   pretty
      'You're getting prettier.'

(89) **Awáa**   á   tá   woóko   taánga   sɔ́   mɔ̃́ɔ̃.
      at.last   3S.NEG   IMF   work   strong   such   more
      'Now he's not working that hard.'

The following sentence was uttered by one speaker to another one in the middle of a conversation being taped; the implication was that a Sranan word had interceded amidst what had, over a long period until then, been a conversation in Saramaccan only:

(90) **Awáa**   dídé   ná   Saamáka   tɔ́ngɔ.
      at.last   that   NEG   Saramaka   language
      'Wait a minute, (here we've been speaking in Saramaccan but suddenly now) that's not Saramaccan.'

Awáa can also be used as an interjection:

(91) **Awáa**   –   bédi   júu   dóu.
      at.last   bed   hour   arrive
      'So – it's getting time for bed.'

15.4.5. Interjection *é*

É occurs clause-finally and lends vigor to an assertion:

(92) Dí   wómi   dé bumbúu   **é**.
      DEF   man   be good.RD INJ
      'The man is a good guy.'

(93) A   táku   **é**!
      3S   ugly   INJ
      'He's *ugly*!'

(94) Máku   tá   njã̌   mi éti **é**!
      mosquito   IMF   eat   1S yet INJ
      'But mosquitos are still biting me (whatever else you say)!'

15.4.6. Interjection *o*

O (to be distinguished from the interrogative marker *ɔ́* [cf. 11.1.]) conveys a note of affirmation with a socially intimate coloring. For example, in this sentence *o* conveys something along the lines of English's *You know what I mean?*:

(95) A   dí   fósu   dáka   mi   bi   wéi,   ma   a   dí   u
      LOC   DEF   first   day   1S   PAST   tired   but   LOC   DEF   for

      tũě̌ti-a-síkísi   dáka   mi   bi   mɔ́ɔ̃   wéi   **o**.
      twenty-LOC-six   day   1S   PAST   more   tired   INJ
      'On the first day I was tired, but on the 26ᵗʰ day I was more tired, you know?!'

This sentence would be uttered in reference to a local person who has returned after achieving the status of being a doctor:

(96) Dí   wómi   dé,   dáta   wɛ   **o**!
      DEF   man   there   doctor   FOC   INJ
      'That man is a doctor, now!'

This exchange is a conventionalized greeting sequence:

(97) a. I   wéki   nɔ́?
          2S   wake   INT

      b. Mi   wéki   **o**.
          1S   wake   INJ

      a: 'Good morning.' b: 'Good morning.'

Chapter 16
Numerals and other time expressions

16.1. Cardinal numbers

1   -   wã́
2   -   tú
3   -   dií
4   -   fɔ́
5   -   féífi
6   -   síkísi
7   -   séibi, sébɛn
8   -   áiti
9   -   néigi, néni
10 -   téni
11 -   élúfu
12 -   tuwálúfu
13 -   téni-a-dií
14 -   téni-a-fɔ́
20 -   tűẽti, tú téni
21 -   tűẽti-a-wã́
22 -   tűẽti-a-tú
30 -   dií téni
40 -   fɔ́ téni
50 -   féífi téni
100 -   hɔ́ndɔ
1000 - dúsu

16.2. Ordinal numbers

Ordinals are constructed with (f)u 'for':

(1)   u   tú   /   u   dií   búku
        for two   /   for three   book
        'second / third book'

Also possible:

(2)   dí   búku   dí   (f)u   mbéi   dií
        DEF   book   REL   for   make   three
        'the third book'

16.3. Distribution

(3) *Dí mbéti wáka gó a dí sípi déndu bandja ku bandja*
DEF animal walk go LOC DEF ship inside side with side

tú ku tú.
two with two
'The animals walked into the ship side by side two by two.'

16.4. Fraction

Háfu, although derived from *half*, denotes 'portion' (cf. 4.5.), and thus can refer to a literal half:

(4) *Mi njã̌ wã̌ háfu fóu ku pikí sɔ́ batáta.*
1S eat INDF half bird with little so sweet.potato
'I ate half of a bird with some sweet potatoes.'

or an unspecified portion:

(5) *I sá tjái háfu wáta kó dá mi nɔ́?*
2S can carry half water come give 1S INT
'Could you please bring me some water?'

16.5. Time by the clock

(6) *dí síkisi júu tɛ̌*
DEF six hour time
'six o'clock'

(7) *Síkisi júu kísi.*
six hour catch
'It is six o'clock.'

(8) *téni-a-féífi miníti pasá síkisi júu*
ten-LOC-five minute pass six hour
'quarter after six'

(9) *A fiká téni-a-féífi miníti u síkisi júu.*
3S remain ten-LOC-five minute of six hour
'It is a quarter to six.'

(10) *hálufu síkisi*
half six
'five thirty'

(11) *sónúáti* 'noon' (lit. 'sun hot')
tuwálúfú júu ndéti 'midnight'

16.6. Days of the week

Monday	-	fɔ́dáka (lit. 'four day') / múnde
Tuesday	-	féífidáka (lit. 'five day') / tú-dé-woóko (lit. 'two-day-work')
Wednesday	-	pikísaba (lit. 'little rest') / dií-dé-woóko (lit. 'three-day-work')
Thursday	-	gã́ã́saba (lit. 'big rest') / fɔ́-dé-woóko (lit. 'four-day-work')
Friday	-	dímíngo / fééda
Saturday	-	sáta
Sunday	-	sónde

The words in the first set of alternates are older than the second, which are more associated with Christianity.

16.7. Months

January	-	jái-líba (lit. 'New.Year's.Day-month')
February	-	báka-jái-líba (lit. 'after-New.Year's.Day-month')
March	-	gã́ã́-líba (lit. 'big-month')
April	-	pikí-deé-wéi-líba (lit. 'little-dry-weather-month')
May	-	sébítáá-líba (lit. 'leech-month')
June	-	hóndima-líba (lit. 'hunter-month')
July	-	baí-mátú-líba (lit. 'clear-forest-month')
August	-	tanvú-wátá-líba (lit. 'crazy-water-month')
September	-	wajamáká-líba (lit. 'iguana-month')
October	-	tínímú-líba / tímu (lit. 'tenth-[month]—month')
November	-	élúfúmú-líba / élúfúmu (lit. 'eleventh-[month]—month')
December	-	tuwálúfúmú-líba (lit. 'twelfth-[month]—month')

Chapter 17
Lexical variation

17.1. Dialects

Detailed study of the traits of the Lower River (*básusɛ*) and Upper River (*líbasɛ*) dialects remains to be done. However, there are two known features that sharply distinguish the two:

a) The predicate negator (cf. 7.1.1.) in the Upper River dialect is *ã́*, while the Lower River form is the less phonetically conservative *á*.

(Also, the pronoun-negator portmanteau in the third-person singular [cf. 7.1.2.], in both dialects identical to the predicate negator alone, is therefore *ã́* in Upper River and *á* in Lower River: *ã́ / á wáka* 'He doesn't walk.')

b) The first-person singular pronoun and this negator combine morphophonemically to yield *má* in the Upper River dialect, but the less phonetically predictable *mé* in the Lower River dialect.

17.2. Free variation

There are many words in Saramaccan that occur in two or more variations. The variation does not correspond to the two abovementioned dialects, nor is it determined by sociological factors or rapidity of speech. Rather, for a given word, some informants use only one variant while others alternate between the two, usually using one more than the other. Future research will determine whether there are systematic conditionings determining these usages (such as perhaps regional isoglosses). See Chapter 1 for discussion of this variation with reference to particular segment pairs.
  Most of these variations are documented as early as the late 1700s in the first transcriptions of Saramaccan (cf. Schuchardt 1914), and thus apparently originated within the first century of the language's existence and have persisted for two centuries-plus since.
  In many cases, etymology allows us to designate one form (here, the second-cited ones) as more conservative than the other:

seéi / seépi 'self' (cf. Sranan *srefi*)
hía / híla 'many' (cf. Dutch *helemaal* 'entirely')
paí / palí 'to give birth' (cf. Portuguese *parir*)
tjína / kína 'taboo' (cf. Kikongo *kíina*)
híni wã́ / híbi wã́ 'each' (< *every*, with English [v] > [b] regularly in Saramaccan)
sɛmbɛ / sɔmbɛ 'person' (< *somebody*; *sɛmbɛ* by regressive assimilation)
soní / sondí 'thing' (< *something*)
naásé / naṹsé 'where' (*naásé* via assimilation)
né / nẽ́ 'name' (the nasality is presumably a remnant of the [m]; nasality often erodes in high-
  usage Saramaccan words, such as past marker *bi* [< *been*; cf. Sranan *ben*] and imperfective
  marker *tá* [< *stand*; cf. Sranan *tan*])

In other cases, it is less obvious which form was preliminary if either was:

bifɔ́ / ufɔ́ 'before'
hǎso / hǎse 'handsome, pretty'

The following case constitutes alternate items entirely:

hɔ́jo / kódo 'single'

Words beginning with [o] often also occur with a [w]-initial variant (cf. discussion of the consonant *w* in section 1.1.2.4.); this list is non-exhaustive:

wósu / ósu 'house'
wójo / ójo 'eye'
wóto / óto 'story'
wómi / ómi 'man'
wódi / ódi 'greeting'
wóbo / óbo 'egg'

The [o]-initial forms are the more conservative. This is clear first from the fact that the etymological sources have no source for a [w] (e.g. *house*, or Portuguese *ôlho* 'eye' and *homem* [[omẽ]] 'man'). Moreover, in cases where the etymological source is itself *w*-initial, there is no variant *w*-less form: *woóko* 'work' (*oóko), showing that the process was not a matter of erosion of an initial [w]. Finally, Sranan and Ndjuka's cognates do not occur with alternate *w*-initial variants, showing that this is an innovation in Saramaccan.

Finally, two *o*-initial words have an innovated variant with initial [h]:

hópo / ópo 'stand up' (< *up*)

The word *ógi* 'evil' has both an *h*-initial and a *w*-initial variant:

hógi / wógi / ógi (< *ugly*)

In earlier Saramaccan, there were also *h*-initial variants of *ódi* 'greeting' and *óbo* 'egg,' as recorded in C. L. Schumann's dictionary of 1778 (Schuchardt 1914: 70). Apparently, the intrusion of [w] was a successful change-in-progress that regularized in favor of the intrusion of [h], given that Schumann, for 'egg,' recorded *wóbo* as "better" than the now-extinct *hóbo*. (See 1.1.2.4. for further discussion.)

The above examples are a symptom of a general alternation in a class of words between variants with initial [h] and without, such as *hákísi / ákísi* 'ask' and *hédi / édi* 'head.' Most vowel-initial words do not have [h]-initial variants, however, and some (although not most) [h]-initial words do not occur without the [h], such as *hǎso* 'handsome' (*ǎso).

There is a smaller class of words, beginning with [e], with alternate [j]-initial renditions, such as *éti / jéti* 'yet' and *éside / jéside* 'yesterday.' This encompasses words with [j]-initial etymological sources (e.g. *yesterday*), in contrast to words with [w]-initial variants in the above-discussed case. Many words beginning with [je], however, cannot occur as [j]-less, such as *jési* 'ear,' while some [e]-initial words do not occur in a [j]-initial variant.

(See 1.1.2.3. and 1.1.2.4. for further discussion of these alternations.)

Word list

English	Saramaccan	Source
I	mi	*me*
you	i	*you*
we	u	*we*
this	dísi	*this*
that	dídɛ́	*this-there*
who?	ambɛ́	Gbe *mĕ*
what?	andí	Gbe *aní*
not	ná	*no*
many	hía	(unknown)
one	wã́	*one*
two	tú	*two*
big	bígi, gã́ã́	*big*, P. *grande*
long	lánga	*long*
small	pikí	P. *pequeno*
woman	mujɛ́ɛ	P. *mulher*
man	wómi	P. *homem*
person	sɛmbɛ	*somebody*
fish	físi	*fish*
bird	fóu	*fowl*
dog	dágu	*dog*
louse	lósu	*louse*
tree	páu	P. *pau*
seed	síi	*seed*
leaf	uwíi	*weed*
root	lútu	*root*
bark	kákísa	P. *casca*
skin	búba	possibly Kikongo *búuba* 'small piece of clothing'
flesh	mbéti	*meat*
blood	buúu	*blood*
bone	bónu	*bone*
grease	fátu	*fat*
egg	óbo	P. *ovo*
horn	tutú	K. *túutu*
tail	lábu	P. *rabo*
feather	puúma	P. *pluma*
hair	uwíi	*weed* (likely from reduplicated *wíwíi*)
head	hédi	*head*
ear	jési	*ears*
eye	wójo	P. *olho*
nose	núsu	*nose*
mouth	búka	P. *bôca*
tooth	tánda	D. *tand*
tongue	tɔ́ngɔ	*tongue*
claw	hṹjã	P. *unha*
foot	fútu	*foot*
knee	kiní	*knee*

hand	máũ	P. *mão*
belly	bɛ́ɛ	*belly*
neck	gangáa	P. *garganta*
breasts	bóbi	prob. earlier English *bubby*
heart	háti	*heart*
liver	lɛ́bɛ̃	D. *lever*
drink	bebé	P. *beber*
eat	njã́	Wolof *njam*
bite	njã́	Wolof *njam*
see	sí	*see*
hear	jéi	*hear*
know	sábi	P. *saber*
sleep	duumí	P. *dormir*
die	dɛ́dɛ	*dead*
kill	kíi	*kill*
swim	sṹ	*swim*
fly	buwá	P. *voar*
walk	wáka	*walk*
come	kó	*come*
lie	kándi	D. *kantelen*
sit	sindó	*sit down*
stand	tãã́pu	*stand up*
give	dá	P. *dar*
say	táki	*talk*
sun	sónu	*sun*
moon	líba	P. *above, over*
star	teéja	P. *estrela*
water	wáta	*water*
rain	tjúba	P. *chuva*
stone	sitónu	*stone*
sand	sándu	*sand*
earth	goṍlíba	compound *ground-top*
cloud	wɔlúku	D. *wolk*
smoke	sumúku	*smoke*
fire	fája	*fire*
ash	síndja	P. *cinza*
burn	tjumá	P. *queimar*
path	pási	*path*
mountain	kúnunu	(unknown)
red	bɛ	Gbe *vè*
green	gṹṹ	D. *groen*
yellow	kóóko	P. *coró-coró* (type of bird)
white	wéti	*white*
black	baáka	*black*
night	ndéti	*night*
hot	kéndi	P. *quente*
cold	kɔ́tɔ	*cold*
full	fúu	*full*
new	njṹnjũ	*new*
good	búnu	P. *bom*
round	lótúlótu	*round*
dry	dɛɛ́	*dry*
name	né	*name*

Folktale transcription

A	bi	dé	hángi	té,	hángi	té.	Hángi	tá	kíi	híi	sɔmbɛ.[1]
3S	PAST	be	hunger	time	hunger	time	hunger	IMF	kill	all	person

Hɛ́	wɛ	pendémbéti,
then	FOC	jaguar

'There was a famine. The famine was killing people. So Jaguar,'

Tatá	Djaíni,	táki	déé		mujée,	táa	'A	kamíã	akí,
father	Djaini	talk	give.3SO.POSS		woman	COMP	LOC	place	here

tía,	mi	ó	peé	wã́	kɔ́ni.'
woman	1S	FUT	play	INDF	trick

'Father Djaini, said to his wife 'On this spot, woman, I'm going to play a trick.''

Já	sí	hángi	dé	ku	u?	Wá	sondí[2]	u	njã́.
2S.NEG	see	hunger	be	with	1P	1P.NEG.have	thing	for	eat

Mi	ó	peé	wã́	kɔ́ni,	mi	ó	peé ...
1S	FUT	play	INDF	trick	1S	FUT	play

'You see the hunger we are suffering from? We don't have anything to eat. I'm going to play a trick, I'm going to play ...'

mi	ó	gãjã́	déde.	Nɔ́ɔ	mi	ó	kándi	a	míndi	wósu.
1S	FUT	pretend	dead	NI	1S	FUT	lie.down	LOC	middle	house

'I'm going to pretend I'm dead. I'll lay down in the middle of the house.'

Nɔ́ɔ	i	butá	wã́	kódjo,	wã́	kódjo	a	bandja,[3]	wã́	kódjo
NI	2S	put	INDF	cudgel	INDF	cudgel	LOC	side	INDF	cudgel

a	bandja.	Nɔ́ɔ	i	kái	woló,	kɛɛ́	'Má'néngé,'[4]
LOC	side	NI	2S	call	alas	cry	Oh.my.God

'You put a stick, a stick to the side, a stick to the side. Then you call 'Alas!', you cry 'Oh my God,''

'gã́ã́	wóto,	mí	mánu	déde,	hí̃! hí̃! hí̃! hí̃! hí̃! hí̃! hí̃!'	Nɔ́ɔ
big	story	1S.POSS	husband	dead	IDEO	NI

dí	sɛmbɛ	ó	kulé	kó,
DEF	person	FUT	run	come

''big news, my husband is dead, boo hoo hoo!' Then the people will run in,'

déé	mbéti	ó	kulé	'Andí	pasá?	Andí	pasá?'
DEF.PL	animal	FUT	run	what	happen	what	happen

'the animals will run in, 'What happened? What happened?''

De	sí	mánu	déde,	a	déde,	gã́ã́	wóto!
3P	see	husband	dead	3S	dead	big	story

'They'll see your husband dead, he's dead: big news!'

'Tío	déde	nɔ́?	Aái!	Hǎ!	Gãã́	wóto	–	Má'néngé,	ũfá	wó
uncle	dead	INT	yes	INJ	big	story		Oh.my.God	how	1P.FUT

dú	dí	soní	akí?'
do	DEF	thing	here

"Aw, is Uncle dead? Yeah – hey! Big news – Oh my God, how will we do the thing here?"

'Déde	kíi	tío,	hó!	Aái,	báa.'	Ma	déé	mbéti	ó	kó,
death	kill	uncle	INJ	yes	brother	but	DEF.PL	animal	FUT	come

"Death got Uncle, ha! (Yeah, man!).' But – the animals will come,'

dí	wósu	ó	fúu.	Dí	wósu	ó	fúu!	Déé	mbéti
DEF	house	FUT	full	DEF	house	FUT	full	DEF.PL	animal

tá	wái	té	ámbúnu.
IMF	happy	until	3S.NEG.good

'the house will be full to bursting. The house will be full! The animals will be happy to no end.'

Já	sí?	'Tatá	pendémbéti	déde.	Já	sí	ú
2S.NEG	see	father	jaguar	dead	2S.NEG	see	1P.POSS

bɔɔ́?'
breath

'Don't you see? 'Father Jaguar is dead. You see how we can relax?''

'Hɛ̌	tá	kíi	u	gãã́	kíi.	U	bɔɔ́	fẽẽ́.	A	déde.'
3ST	IMF	kill	1P	big	kill	1P	breath	POSS.3SO	3S	dead

"He was really *killing* us. We can relax now. He's dead."

De	ó	tá	kó	háika.	Kɔkɔ́ni	tá	kó,	djangafútu	tá	kó ...
3P	FUT	IMF	come	listen	rabbit	IMF	come	deer	IMF	come

ee ...	ee ...	pakía	tá	kó,	píngo	tá	kó,
um	um	peccary	IMF	come	pig	IMF	come

'They'll be coming to listen. Rabbit will be coming, Deer will be coming ... um ... um ... Peccary will be coming, Pig will be coming,'

hélipe	tá	kó,	déé	mbéti	tá	kó	gbìtìì,	dí	wósu
monkey	IMF	come	DEF.PL	animal	IMF	come	IDEO	DEF	house

fúu	pɔ́ɔ́ɔ́!
full	IDEO

'Monkey will be coming, the animals will come in swarms, the house will be bursting with them.'

Ma	té	wǎ	písi,	ma,	hélipe,	a	lúku	dí	déde	dé
but	until	INDF	while	but	monkey	3S	look	DEF	dead	be

píí,	a	táa	'Hɛ̌!	Dí	soní	akí,'
IDEO	3S	talk	3ST	DEF	thing	here

'But all of a sudden, but, Monkey, he looks at the dead man laying there quietly, and he says 'Look at him! The thing is,''

'u	táa	'Dédɛ	ɔ́?'	Mi	sí,	táa	a	tá	bɔɔ́!'	A
1P	talk	dead	INT	1S	see	COMP	3S	IMF	breathe	3S

pikí	sììì,	a	tooná	sáá-á-á-pi,
small	IDEO	3S	turn.around	slow

"we're saying 'Is he dead?', but I see that he's *breathing!*" He hunches all up and turns very slowly'

gó	dé	a	dɔ́ɔ	búka.	Hã́!	De	tá	keé	té	ámbúnu.
go	there	LOC	door	mouth	INJ	3P	IMF	cry	until	3S.NEG.good

'Má'néngé,	tío	dédɛ!'
Oh.my.God	uncle	dead

'and goes to the doorway. So there! They're crying to high heaven. 'Oh my God, Uncle is dead!''

'Já	sí	tío	dédɛ,	tío	dédɛ?	Ma	ũfá	u	ó	dú ...
2S.NEG	see	uncle	dead	uncle	dead	but	how	1P	FUT	do

fu	seeká	soní?'
for	arrange	thing

"Don't you see, Uncle is dead, Uncle is dead! But how will we manage to take care of things?"

Dí	wósu	fúú-ú ...	té	wã́	písi,	hélipe	tá	síngi
DEF	house	full	until	INDF	while	monkey	IMF	sing

wã́	síngi	fẽẽ.	A	táa
INDF	song	POSS.3SO	3S	talk

'The house is *full* ... all of a sudden, Monkey is singing a song of his. He says:'

'Wan	suma	e	sribi	ma	a	n'e	sriiiibi!⁵ ...	Hã́!'
INDF	person	IMF	sleep	but	3S	NEG.IMF	sleep	INJ

"Someone is sleeping but he isn't slee-e-e-ping! Ha!"

A	tá	síngi,	déé	sɛmbɛ	á	tá	háika	ḯ	seéi,
3S	IMF	sing	DEF.PL	person	NEG	IMF	listen	3SO	even

de	tá	keé	té	ámbúnu.
3P	IMF	cry	until	3S.NEG.good

'He's singing, the people aren't even listening to him; they're crying to high heaven.'

'Wan	suma	e	sribi	ma	a	n'e	sriiiibi!'	De	á
INDF	person	IMF	sleep	but	3S	NEG.IMF	sleep	3P	NEG

tá	háika	ḯ	seéi.
IMF	listen	3SO	even

"Someone is sleeping but he's not slee-e-e-ping!" They aren't even listening to him.

Té	wã́	písi,	dí	pɛndémbéti	hópo,	hḯ	a	téi	dí
until	INDF	while	DEF	jaguar	stand.up	then	3S	take	DEF

páu,	a	tá	náki	dí	páu,	gbó!	–		
stick	3S	IMF	hit	DEF	stick	IDEO			

'All of a sudden, Jaguar gets up, then he takes the stick and bangs the stick pow!'

gã́ã́	wóto,	Má'néngé!	–	gbó! gbó! gbó! gbó!	De	á	sá
big	story	Oh.my.God		IDEO	3P	NEG	can

kulé	gó	a	dóɔ	mɔ́ɔ̃ ...
run	go	LOC	door	more

'big news, Oh my God – pow, pow, pow, pow! They can't run to the door anymore ...'

Té	fá	i	méni,	akí	sóméni	mbéti	píí...
until	how	2S	think	here	so.many	animal	IDEO

Hɛ̃́	a	wéki	ɛ̃,⁶	hɛ̃́	wɛ	a	táa
then	3S	awake	3SO	then	FOC	3S	talk

'Until you think, there are so many animals laid out dead here ... then she/he wakes him/her up, then he says:'

'Já	sí?	U	féni	soní	u	njã́.'
2S.NEG	see	1P	find	thing	for	eat

"'You see? We got something to eat.''

---

1. The speaker here uses the variant *sɔmbɛ* for 'person,' although elsewhere he uses *sɛmbɛ*.

2. The speaker here uses the variant *sondí* for 'thing,' although elsewhere he uses *soní*.

3. The speaker's phonetic rendition of the /b/ here is implosive ([ɓ]) (on all utterances of the word).

4. This term is a shortened form of *Mása nénge* 'Master Negro.'

5. This song is in Sranan Creole (cf. the Introduction). (Thanks as always to Rohit Paulus for illuminating a passage that was maddeningly opaque to me for years no matter how many times I played the tape.) In folktales, Sranan is often used as the "high" language of the oppressor. Here, Monkey sings in Sranan to mock the high status of Father Jaguar as the feared predator.

6. Just why the wife awakens Jaguar here does not cohere within the narrative. Two informants presented with it draw a blank on its meaning, such that it would appear to be a passing hair out of place in the telling, rather as if someone said in telling the Goldilocks tale that when she got to the *fourth* bowl of porridge it was "just right," even though there had only been two previous bowls. It would seem that the teller, briefly and unwittingly, distorted Jaguar's feigning sleep into his flailing the other animals in a kind of "sleepwalking" state, out of which he would have to be awakened by his wife. It might be relevant that the informant was excitedly engaged in the tale as he told it, including taking the part of Jaguar and miming the physical movements while moving around the room, such that it was perhaps not unusual that a small degree of narrative fluidity briefly entered his rendition.

Conversational passage

A	lóngi	wá	sí	únu	nɔ́ɔ.	Mi	seeká	únu,	u	hángi
3S	long	1P.NEG	see	2PO	NI	1S	care.for	2PO	1P	hungry

u	sí	únu	pói.
NF	see	2PO	too.much

'So, we hadn't seen you for a long time. I cared about you, we were just aching to see you.'

Mi	bi	tá	poobá	u	dá	kái	únu.	Mi	bi	ké	u	híi
1S	PAST	IMF	try	NF	give	call	2PO	1S	PAST	want	NF	all

únu	tú	kó	akí.
2P	two	come	here

'I was trying to call you. I wanted both of you to come here.'

U	músu	kumútu	a	dí	wósu	déndu,	kulé	u	kulé	u	kumútu
1P	must	exit	LOC	DEF	house	inside	run	1P	run	1P	exit

kulé	kó	a	dɔ́ɔ.
run	come	LOC	door

'We (had) had to come out of the house, we *ran* from out of the house outside.'

Fá	a	dí	dáka	sái	dé,[1]	a	bi	dé	wã̌	soní	u	wái,
how	3S	DEF	day	be	be	3S	PAST	be	INDF	thing	for	happy

ma	á		dé	u	wái.
but	3S.NEG		be	for	happy

'The way it was that day – there had been things to be happy about, but (now) there wasn't.'

Nɔ́ɔ	dí	soní,	a	háti	mi	sɔ́	taánga	táa	kúma ...	fá
NI	DEF	thing	3S	hurt	1S	so	strong	COMP	as	how

mi	bi	sábi	Ameeká̌,
1S	PAST	know	America

'So, things were hurting me so much that, like … how I had known America,'

de	wáiwái	a	New York.	Já	gó	a	New York	wã̌
3P	happy.RD	LOC	New York	2S.NEG	go	LOC	New York	one

dáka	ɔ́?
day	INT

'they're super-happy in New York. Have you ever been to New York?'

Mi	ó	tá,	nee,[2]	mé	ó	gó	alá,	faándi	mbéi
1S	FUT	talk	no	1S.NEG	FUT	go	yonder	for.what	make

mi	gó	a	New York?
1S	go	LOC	New York

'I would say 'No, I'm not going there, why would I go to New York?''

Mi	sábi,	New York	hɛ̃	da	dí	goǒlíba,	híi	sembɛ
1S	know,	New York	3S	be	DEF	world	all	person

a	goǒlíba.
LOC	world

'I knew, New York, it is the world, all the people in the world.'

A	bi	dé	súti,	wáiwái	soní,	fá	déé	zangers[3]
3S	PAST	be	sweet	happy.RD	thing	how	DEF.PL	singers

'It was a great, super-happy thing, how those singers'

Frank Sinatra,	a	ó	kó	a	TV,	a	ó	tá	kandá
Frank Sinatra	3S	FUT	come	LOC	TV	3S	FUT	IMF	sing

déé	kandá,	tá	kandá	"It's My Way."
DEF.PL	song	IMF	sing	"It's My Way"

'Frank Sinatra, would come on TV, he'd be singing those songs, singing "It's My Way".'

A	dé	wǎ	súti	soní,	u	kó	a	dí	kɔ́ndɛ	akí.
3S	be	INDF	sweet	thing	1P	come	LOC	DEF	country	here

'It was a great thing, us coming to this country.'

Hɛ̃	wɛ,	nɔ́nɔ,	u	sí	táa	á	súti.	A	háti	mi.	A
then	FOC	no	1P	see	COMP	3S.NEG	sweet	3S	hurt	1S	3S

háti	mi	túmísi.	Mi	tá	feɛ́ɛ	té	ámbúnu.
hurt	1S	too.much	1S	IMF	afraid	until	3S.NEG.good

'Then, though, no, we saw that it isn't great. It hurt me. It really hurt me. I was scared to death.'

Wá	sá	fá	u	dú,	u	tá	bégi	Mása	Gãã́ngádu,
1P.NEG	know	how	1P	do	1P	IMF	pray	master	big.God

heépi	u.
help	1P

'We didn't know how to go about things, we were praying to God, to help us.'

Ú	seéi,	u	ábi	dí	kaakíti dɛ́,	a	músu	dá	u	mɔ̃́ɔ̃
1P	self	1P	have	DEF	power there	3S	must	give	1P	more

sábi	tu.
knowledge	also

'Ourselves, we have that power, it must give us more knowledge too.'

U	hákísi	ẽ	sábi,	fá	a	sá	léi	u	pási,	pási
1P	ask	3SO	knowledge	how	3S	can	teach	1P	road	road

tapá	dí	soní	akí,	kandé	déé	sɛmbɛ	sá	háika.
protect	DEF	thing	here	may.be	DEF.PL	person	can	listen

'We ask him for knowledge, how he can teach us the way, the way protects the things here, maybe people can listen.'

---

1. *Fá a sái dé* 'the way it is,' 'the way things are' is an expression of disapproval.

2. Dutch loan.

3. Dutch loan.

References

Aboikoni, Laurens, and Naomi Glock
    1997   *Di Duumi u Gaama Aboikoni*. Paramaribo: Summer Institute of Linguistics.

Aceto, Michael
    1996   Early Saramaccan syllable structure: An analysis of complex onsets from Schumann's 1778 manuscript. *Journal of Pidgin and Creole Languages* 11: 23–44.

Arends, Jacques, and Matthias Perl (eds.)
    1995   *Early Suriname Creole Texts: A Collection of 18th-Century Sranan and Saramaccan Documents*. Frankfurt: Vervuert.

Bakker, Peter
    1987   Reduplications in Saramaccan. *Studies in Saramaccan Language Structure*, ed. by Mervyn C. Alleyne, 17–40. Amsterdam: Instituut voor Algemene Taalwetenschap.

Bakker, Peter, Norval Smith, and Tonjes Veenstra
    1995   Saramaccan. *Pidgins and Creoles: An Introduction*, ed. by Jacques Arends, Pieter Muysken, and Norval Smith, 165–178. Amsterdam: John Benjamins.

Berlin, Brent, and Paul Kay
    1969   *Basic Color Terms: Their Universality and Evolution*. Berkeley, CA: University of California Press.

Boersma, Paul, and David Weenink
    2009   Praat: Doing phonetics by computer [Computer program]. http://www.praat.org/.

Byrne, Francis
    1987   *Grammatical Relations in a Radical Creole*. Amsterdam: John Benjamins.

Casali, Roderic F.
    2008   ATR harmony in African languages. *Language and Linguistics Compass* 2: 496–549.

Daeleman, Jan
    1972   Kongo elements in Saramacca Tongo. *Journal of African Languages* 11: 1–44.

DeGroot, Anton
    1977   *Woordregister met Context en Idioom: Nederlands–Saramakaans*. Paramaribo.

    1981   *Woordregister Saramakaans–Nederlands*. Paramaribo.

Donicie, Antoon, and Jan Voorhoeve
    1963   *De Saramakaanse Woordenschat*. Amsterdam: Bureau voor Taalonderzoek in Suriname van de Universiteit van Amsterdam.

Dryer, Matthew S.
    2009   Verb-object-negative order in central Africa. *Negation Patterns in West African Languages and Beyond*, ed. by Norbert Cyffer, Erwin Ebermann, and Georg Ziegelmeyer, 307–362. Amsterdam: Benjamins.

George, Isaac
: 1975 A grammar of Kwa-type verb serialization: Its nature and significance in current generative theory. University of California, Los Angeles PhD dissertation.

Glock, Naomi, and S. Catherine Rountree
: 2003 Nederlands–Saramaccaans–English woordenboek. http://www.sil.org/americas/suriname/Saramaccan/National/SaramNLDictIndex.html.

Good, Jeff
: 2003 Tonal morphology in a creole: High-tone raising in Saramaccan serial verb constructions. *Yearbook of Morphology 2002*, ed. by Geert Booij and Jaap van Marle, 105–134. London: Kluwer.

: 2004 Tone and accent in Saramaccan: Charting a deep split in the phonology of a language. *Lingua* 114: 575–619.

: 2006 The phonetics of tone in Saramaccan. *Structure and Variation in Language Contact*, ed. by Ana Deumert and Stephanie Durrleman, 9–28. Amsterdam and Philadelphia: Benjamins.

: 2009a Loanwords in Saramaccan. *Loanwords in the World's Languages: A Comparative Handbook*, ed. by Martin Haspelmath and Uri Tadmor, 918–943. Berlin: Mouton de Gruyter.

: 2009b Saramaccan vocabulary. World Loanword Database, ed. by Martin Haspelmath and Uri Tadmor. Munich: Max Planck Digital Library. http://wold.livingsources.org/vocabulary/36.

Goodman, Morris F.
: 1987 The Portuguese element in the American creoles. *Pidgin and Creole Languages*, ed. by Glenn G. Gilbert, 361–405. Honolulu: University of Hawaii Press.

Hancock, Ian
: 1987 A preliminary classification of the Anglophone Atlantic creoles with syntactic data from thirty-three representative dialects. *Pidgin and Creole Languages*, ed. by Glenn G. Gilbert, 264–333. Honolulu: University of Hawaii Press.

: 1994 Componentiality and the creole matrix: The Southwest English contribution. *The Crucible of Carolina: Essays in the Development of Gullah Language and Culture*, ed. by Michael Montgomery, 95–114. Athens, GA: The University of Georgia Press.

Kouwenberg, Silvia
: 1987 Morphophonemic change in Saramaccan pronominal forms. *Studies in Saramaccan Language Structure*, ed. by Mervyn C. Alleyne, 1–15. Amsterdam: Folklore Studies Project.

Kramer, Marvin
: 2001 Substrate transfer in Saramaccan Creole. University of California, Berkeley PhD dissertation.

: 2004 High tone spread in Saramaccan serial verb constructions. *Journal of Portuguese Linguistics* 3: 31–53.

: 2007 Tone on quantifiers in Saramaccan as a transferred feature from Kikongo. *Synchronic and Diachronic Perspectives on Contact Languages*, ed. by Magnus Huber and Viveka Velupillai, 43–66. Amsterdam: Benjamins.

Muysken, Pieter
　　1987　　Prepositions and postpositions in Saramaccan. *Studies in Saramaccan Language Structure*, ed. by Mervyn C. Alleyne, 89–101. Amsterdam: Instituut voor Algemene Taalwetenschap.

Narrog, Heiko
　　2005　　Mood and the modal system in Saramaccan. *Gengo Kenkyu* 128: 33–72.

Price, Richard
　　1976　　*The Guiana Maroons*. Baltimore: Johns Hopkins University Press.

　　1983　　*First-Time: The Historical Vision of an African American People*. Baltimore: Johns Hopkins University Press.

Price, Richard, and Sally Price
　　1991　　*Two Evenings in Saramaka*. Chicago: University of Chicago Press.

Rountree, S. Catherine
　　1972a　　Saramaccan tone in relation to intonation and grammar. *Lingua* 29: 308–325.

　　1972b　　The phonological structure of stems in Saramaccan. *Languages of the Guianas*, ed. by Joseph E. Grimes, 22–27. Norman, OK: Summer Institute of Linguistics.

　　1992　　*Saramaccan Grammar Sketch*. Paramaribo: Summer Institute of Linguistics.

Rountree, S. Catherine, and Naomi Glock
　　1977　　*Saramaccan for Beginners: A Pedagogical Grammar of the Saramaccan Language*. Paramaribo: Summer Institute of Linguistics.

Rountree, S. Catherine, J. Asodanoe, and Naomi Glock
　　2000　　Saramaccan–English word list. Paramaribo: Summer Institute of Linguistics. http://www.sil.org/americas/suriname/Saramaccan/English/SaramEngDictIndex.html.

Schuchardt, Hugo
　　1914　　*Die Sprache der Saramakkaneger in Surinam*. Amsterdam: Johannes Müller.

Schumann, Christian Ludwig
　　1914　　Saramakkanish–Deutsches Wörterbuch (1778). Schuchardt (1914), 44–116.

Smith, Norval
　　1975　　Vowel harmony in two languages of Surinam. *Spektator* 4: 315–320.

　　1987a　　Gbe words in the creole languages of Surinam. Paper presented at the Workshop on Creoles, University of Amsterdam.

　　1987b　　The genesis of the creole languages of Surinam. University of Amsterdam PhD dissertation.

　　2003　　New evidence from the past: To epenthesize or not to epenthesize? That is the question. *Phonology and Morphology of Creole Languages*, ed. by Ingo Plag, 91–107. Tübingen: Niemeyer.

Smith, Norval, and Vinije Haabo
　　2004　　Suriname creoles: Phonology. *Handbook of Varieties of English: Volume I: Phonology*, ed. by E. W. Schneider, K. Burridge, B. Kortmann, R. Mesthrie, and C. Upton, 525–564. Berlin: Mouton de Gruyter.

2007 The Saramaccan implosives: Tools for linguistic archaeology? *Journal of Pidgin and Creole Languages* 22: 101–122.

Stahlke, Herbert F.
1970 Serial verbs. *Studies in African Linguistics* 1: 60–99.

Veenstra, Tonjes
1996 *Serial Verbs in Saramaccan*. The Hague: Holland Academic Graphics.

Voorhoeve, Jan
1959 An orthography for Saramaccan. *Word* 15: 436–445.

1961 Le ton et le grammaire en Saramaccan. *Word* 17: 146–163.

1973 Historical and linguistic evidence in favor of the relexification theory in the formation of creoles. *Language in Society* 2: 133–145.

Zwicky, Arnold M., and Geoffrey K. Pullum
1983 Cliticization vs. inflection: English *n't*. *Language* 59: 502–513.

Index

ability expressions, 7.4.2.2.
ablative , 13.3.2.1.
accent, Ch. 2.2.2.
accusative → pronouns (oblique)
adjectives, 2.3.1.2., 3.4. (second para), 4.8., Ch. 6, 9.2.2.2.
   and reduplication, 6.2., 6.3., 14.4. (second para)
   resultative, 3.1.1.1., 6.4., 10.1.1., 12.3. (sentence before example (41))
adjuncts, 10.1.1., 15.1.3.
adpositions, 2.3.1.3.
   → prepositions, spatial indicators
adverbial expressions, 2.3.1.6., Ch. 14
   adverbial complements → complements (adverbial)
   deictic adverbials, 3.3.5., 3.5. (sentence before example (42)), 4.2., 13.2.
   of degree, 6.5.6., 8.3.2.
   of frequency, 14.5.
   of manner, 14.4.
   of quantity, 14.3.
   time adverbials, 14.2.
affixes → prefixes, suffixes
agentive markers, 2.2.3.3., 3.1.2., 3.4. (last para)
aggregate plural, 3.1.1.4., 4.1. (para before example (18))
Aktionsart, 6.2. (first para), 6.4., 7.2.1.
alienability → possession (alienable and inalienable)
allative, 13.3.2.2.
Amerindian languages, Intro, 1.3. (first para), 3.1.1.6. (first para of section '4')
articles → determiners
aspect, 6.1. (beginning to example (6)), 7.3., 8.1.1., 9.2.1.3.
Atlantic English-based Creole, Intro, 7.4.1. (last para)
ATR, 1.1.3.1., 1.2.2. (section on 'upper mid and lower mid vowels')
auxiliary verbs → verbs (auxiliary)

Bantu languages, Intro, 1.3. (first para)
benefactive, 6.1. (para before example (9)), 8.3.1., 10.1.1. (paras before examples (10) and (13)), 10.2.1. (last para)
be-verbs → copulas
bilingualism, Intro, 4.4.1. (para before example (83)), 5.3., 10.1.1. (para after example (10))
boundedness, 7.3.1. (sentence before example (61)), 9.2.3.1., 15.2.2.4.

Cameroonian Pidgin English, Intro
cardinal numerals → numerals (cardinal)
Carib, 3.1.1.6. (para beginning with '4')
case → pronouns (oblique, possessive, subject, tonic)
causation, 8.3.1. (sentence before example (35)), 9.2.1.3., 9.2.3.5., 10.1.1. (sentence before example (17)), 10.2.2., 15.2.2.2.
Central African languages, 2.4.1. (second para), 2.4.3. (first para), 2.4.4. (first para)
Chinese → Sinitic languages
clauses
   and intonation → utterance-level phonological processes
   complement → complements
   nonfinite, 7.4.1. (last para)
   small → small clauses
   subordinate → subordination
clefting, 6.1. (para before example (7)), 15.1.2., 15.2.2.1.
   → fronting
clitics, 3.5., 7.3.2., 7.4.2.2. (last sentence), 14.8.
   pronominal → pronouns (and cliticization)
coda consonants, 1.1.3.2., 1.2.1., 1.2.3. (second para)
color terms, 6.6., 14.7. (from last sentence to end)
comitative, 2.3.1.3. (first para)
commands → imperatives
comparison, 6.5., 8.3.2.
   equal, 6.5.3.
   negative, 6.5.4.
   → degree expressions (of comparison), excessives, superlatives
complementizers, 8.3.4., 8.3.5., 9.2.1.1., 9.2.1.2.
complements
   adverbial, 7.2.1. (sentence before example (49)), 9.2.2.1. (last para), 9.2.3., 14.2. (sentence before example (11)), 15.2.2.2., 15.2.2.4.
   factive, 8.3.4., 9.2.1.1.
   finite, 9.2.1., 10.2.2. (first para)
   nonfinite, 8.3.5. (last sentence), 9.2.1.3., 9.2.2., 10.2.2.
   temporal, 7.2.1. (para before example (49)), 9.2.3.1, 15.2.2.2., 15.2.2.4.

completive, 7.3.6., 7.3.7., 8.5.1., 10.1.1. (para before example (8), and last para)
complexity, Intro
compounding, 1.1.2.2. (section on 'm'), 1.1.3.3. (para after table 9), 1.2.2. (section on 'prenasalized stops in a single morpheme'), 2.2.2.2. (first para), 2.2.2.3. (second para after table 12), 2.2.4., 2.3.1.1., 3.4.
concessives, 9.1.3., 9.2.3.7., 15.2.2.2.
conditionals, 7.5., 9.2.3.1. (sentence before example (56)), 9.2.3.6.
conjunction → coordination (conjunction)
consonants, 1.1.1., 1.1.2.
 → coda consonants, implosive consonants, nasals, syllabic consonants
content questions → information questions
continuative, 7.3.8., 15.4.2.
contrastive focus → focus marking
control verbs → verbs (control verbs)
coordination, 4.6., 9.1.
 conjunction, 4.6., 5.1. (sentence before example (8)), 9.1.1.
 disjunction, 4.6., 9.1.2.
 exclusion, 9.1.2., 9.1.3.
 → serial verbs
copulas, 3.3.4.4., 5.3. (last para), 6.3., 7.1.1. (sentence before example (8)), Ch. 12
 omission → zero-marking (of copular clauses)
Cornwall English, 7.3.4.
counterfactual marking → hypothetical marking
count nouns → mass/count distinction
cranberry morphemes, 3.4.
creole studies, Intro

dative, 4.4.1. (from beginning to example (78)), 8.3.1., 10.2.1. (first para)
days of the week, 12.1.3. (last para), 16.6.
definite markers, 3.5., 4.1., 4.2. (sentence before example (31)), 4.3. (sentence before example (69)), 4.7., 6.5.5.
degree expressions
 adverbial → adverbial expressions (of degree)
 and serial verbs → serial verbs (degree)
 of comparison, 6.5.2.
deictic forms → adverbial expressions (deictic adverbials), demonstratives, pronouns
demonstratives, 4.2., 4.8.
deontic modality, 6.5.1. (para before example (65)), 7.4.1., 8.3.5.
derivational morphology, 3.1., 3.4. (last two paras)
 → agentive markers, reduplication

determiners, 3.5., 4.1., 4.2., 4.3.
deverbal nouns, 3.1.1.5.
 → gerunds
deverbal resultatives → adjectives (resultative)
devoicing, 1.1.3.2. (third para), 2.4.2. (last sentence)
dialects, Intro, 1.1.1. (first para), 1.1.2.1. (sections on 'b,' 'd,' and 'kp'), 1.1.2.2. (section on 'mb'), 1.1.2.4. (sections on 'l' and 'j'), 1.4., 2.1. (second para), 10.1.1. (para after example (9)), 12.1.3. (first para), 17.1.
 → Lower River dialect, Matawai dialect, Upper River dialect
diphthongs → vowels (combinations)
directional expressions → serial verbs (directional)
direct objects, 5.1. (sentence before example (5)), 10.2.1. (sentence before example (29))
discontinuous constituents → demonstratives
disjunction → coordination (disjunction)
dislocation → fronting
distributive expressions, 16.3.
 → aggregate plural
ditransitive verbs, 4.4.1. (first para), 10.2.1.
double negation → negation (double)
downdrift, 2.4.1.
downstep → downdrift
dual → plural
dummy subject → pronouns (pleonastic)
durative expressions, 7.3.5., 13.4.2., 15.4.2.
Dutch, Intro, 1.1.2.1. (section on consonant 'kp'), 1.3. (first para), 4.4.1. (para after example (82)), 6.6., 10.1.1. (para after example (10)), 10.2.2. (last para), 17.2. (first list of words)
dynamic verbs, 3.1.1.1., 6.4., 7.2., 7.5., 10.1.1. (sentence before example (3)), 10.1.2. (first para)

East Asian languages, 3.4. (first para), 10.1.3.
elision → rapid speech phenomena
ellipsis → verbs (ellipsis)
emphasis
 and stress → stress
 intonational → utterance-level phonological processes (emphasis within a clause)
 of imperatives, 10.3.
 of negation, 7.1.1. (sentence before example (12)), 7.1.2. (sentence before example (21))
 of possession, 4.3. (para before example (66)), 12.1.4.

emphatic pronouns → pronouns (emphatic)
epenthesis, 1.2.1. (last two paras), 3.3.4.5.
    → nasals (epenthetic nasal consonants), vowels (epenthetic)
epistemic modality, 7.4.2.
equal comparison → comparison (equal)
equative predicates, 5.3. (last para), 7.1.1. (para before example (8)), Ch. 12
    class equative predicates, 12.2.
    identificational equative predicates, 12.1.
evidentiality, 14.6.
excessives, 6.5.6., 8.3.2., 14.3.
exclusion → coordination (exclusion)
existential constructions, 8.3.4. (line before example (51)), 12.4.
experiential, 7.1.3. (paras preceding examples (33) and (34))
expletive negation → negation (expletive)
extraposition → fronting

factive complements → complements (factive)
feet → metrical feet
finite complements → complements (finite)
focusing intonation → utterance-level phonological processes (emphasis within a clause)
focus marking, 5.5. (sentence before example (28)), 6.1. (para before example (7)), 12.1.3., 15.1., 15.2.2.3.
Fongbe, Intro, 3.2.3., 11.2. (para after example (17)), 15.1.3.2. (first para)
formality → politeness
fractions → quantification (fractional)
French, 1.1.1. (second to last para), 1.1.3.2. (first para), 1.2.1. (second para), 8.3.1. (para after example (36))
frequency effects, 3.3.4.1. (from para preceding example (19) to end), 5.2.2. (last para)
    → rapid speech phenomena
frequency expressions → adverbial expressions (of frequency)
fronting, 4.4.1. (last para), 6.1. (from para before example (10) to end), 7.3.6. (para before example (96)), 10.2.1. (sentence before example (28)), 11.2. (first and last sentences), 12.1.3., 12.1.4., 12.3., 15.1.3.1., 15.1.3.2., 15.2.2.3.
    → clefting
fusional morphology, 3.2.1.
    → morphophonemic processes, rapid speech phenomena
future tense, 7.2.2., 7.5., 9.2.3.1. (para before example (53))

future time reference, 7.4.2.3. (first three paras), 13.4.2., 14.2. (paras before and after example (9))
    → future tense

Gbe languages, 1.3. (first para)
gender → nominal prefix
generic referents, 4.1. (para before example (20))
genitive → possession
German, 15.4. (first para), 15.4.1. (para before example (69))
gerunds, 4.7., 9.2.2.3.
given-information marking, 15.2.1.
glossing conventions, (Abbreviations page), 5.1. (last para)
grammaticalization, 3.1.2., 3.1.3., 6.5.1. (para before example (59)), 7.3.3., 7.3.6., 7.3.7., 7.3.8., Ch. 8, 10.1.1. (para after example (16)), 13.1. (para after example (2)), 13.3.2., 15.1.2. (last two paras)
grammatical relations → subjects, objects, obliques
Gullah, Intro, 12.2. (first para)
Guyanese, Intro, 12.2. (first para)

habitual, 7.3.1., 7.3.3., 7.3.4., 14.5. (first two sentences), 14.8. (last sentence)
harmony
    ATR, 1.2.2. (section on 'Upper mid and lower mid vowels')
    nasal, 1.1.2.2. (section on *nj*), 1.1.2.4. (section on *w*), 1.2.2. (section on 'Nasal harmony')
    vowel, 1.2.3.
headless relative clauses → relative clauses (headless relative clauses)
heavy syllables → syllables (and weight)
Hindi, 3.2.3.
honorific → politeness
hortative, 3.3.6., 8.3.5., 9.2.1.2., 10.3. (last 3 sentences)
human/non-human distinction, 10.1.1. (para preceding example (12))
hypothetical marking, 7.4.2.3. (para after example (146)), 9.2.3.6.

ideophones, 1.1.2.1. (section on 'gb~gw'), 1.2.1. (second para), 1.2.3., 2.2.3.5., 3.1.1.6. (para beginning with '1'), 9.2.3.4., 14.1., 14.7.
imperatives, 7.1.1. (sentence after example (12)), 10.3.
imperfective, 3.2.1., 6.1. (sentences before examples (5) and (6)), 7.3.1., 7.3.4., 8.1.1.
impersonal constructions, 7.4.2.3. (last para)

implosive consonants, 1.1.2.1. (sections on 'b', 'd', 'g', and 'kp~kw')
inalienability → possession (alienable and inalienable)
inceptive, 7.3.1., 7.3.6.
inchoative, 6.1. (sentences before examples (5) and (6))
indefinite markers, 4.1.
indirect objects, 4.4.1. (first para), 5.1. (sentence before example (5)), 8.3.1. (sentence after example (30)), 10.2.1.
indirect questions, 11.3.
inflectional morphology, 3.2., 7.3.1. (para before example (68)), 7.3.4.
information questions, 2.4.4., 11.2.
information structure, Ch. 15
instrumental, 8.5.3., 10.1.1. (para after example (10))
intensification, 3.1.1.2, 14.1., 14.7. (last sentence and following examples), 15.4.3. (sentence before example (80))
interjections, 15.4.2., 15.4.4. (last sentence), 15.4.5., 15.4.6.
interrogative expressions → questions
   interrogative intonation → utterance-level phonological processes (question intonation)
   interrogative particles → question particles
   interrogative pronouns → wh-words
intonation → utterance-level phonological processes
intransitive verbs, 6.1., 13.3.2.
inversive, 3.4. (last two paras)
Italian, 4.3. (para before example (63))

Jamaican, Intro, 7.4.1. (last para), 12.2.
Japanese, 2.2.1.
juxtaposition
   of nouns → compounding
   of sentential complements, 9.2.1.1., 9.2.1.3., 9.2.2.1.
   of verbs → serial verbs

Kikongo, Intro, 3.2.3., 14.1., 17.2.
Krio, Intro, 12.2.
Kwa languages, Intro

Latin, 2.2.1. (first para)
lax vowels → vowels (tense and lax)
left-dislocation → fronting
length → vowels (length)
lexical strata, 1.3., 2.2.1., 2.2.2.1. (second to last para), 2.5.
lexical variation, 5.3., 17.2.

lexicon, Intro
   → lexical strata, lexical variation
light syllables → syllables (and weight)
locative expressions, 2.3.1.3., 3.3.4.2., 3.3.5., 4.4.2. (sentence before example (99)), 11.2. (sentence before example (25)), 12.3., 12.4., 13.1., 13.2., 15.1.3.3.
Lower River dialect, Intro, 1.1.3.1., 7.1.2., 15.1.3.5., 17.1.

malefactive, 8.3.1. (from para before example (37) to para after example (38))
mass/count distinction, 4.5. (sentences before examples (105) and (119))
Matawai dialect, Intro
metrical feet, 2.2.2.4.
middle voice, 10.1.2.
Minimalism, 9.2.1.3.
modality → deontic modality, epistemic modality
Monogenesis Hypothesis, Intro
mood → imperatives
moras, 2.2.1. (second to last para), 2.2.2.3. (sentence after table (12)), 2.2.2.4. (para after example (7))
morphology, Ch. 3
   → cranberry morphemes, derivational morphology, fusional morphology, inflectional morphology, nominal prefix, serial verbs (and tone)
morphophonemic processes, 3.3., 4.3. (para before table (20)), 5.2.1., 15.1.3.3. (para before example (28)), 17.1. (last sentence)
motion expressions → serial verbs (directional)

nasals
   and co-occurrence restrictions, 1.2.2.
   epenthetic nasal consonants, 3.3.4.5.
   harmony → harmony (nasal)
   nasal codas, 1.1.3.2., 1.2.1., 1.2.3. (second para)
   nasal consonants, 1.1.2.2.
   nasal vowels, 1.1.3.2., 1.1.3.3.
Ndjuka, Intro, 1.1.2.3. (section on consonant 's'), 12.1.2. (para after example (14)), 12.2. (first para), 17.2. (para after 'egg')
negation, 7.1., 11.1., 12.1.2. (from second para to example (6))
   and intonation → utterance-level phonological processes (negative lowering)
   double, 7.1.3.
   emphatic → emphasis (of negation)

expletive, 7.1.4., 7.4.2.3. (sentence before example (153)), 10.3. (sentence before example (54))
negative comparison → comparison (negative)
negative pronouns → pronouns (and negation)
negative quantifiers → quantification (negative)
new-information marking, 9.2.3.1., 12.1.3. (sentence before example (18)), 15.2.2., 15.3., 15.4.1.
Niger-Congo languages, Intro, 1.3. (second para), 3.2.3.
Nigerian "Pidgin," Intro, 12.2. (first para)
nominalization, 3.1.1.5., 4.8.
   → agentive markers, gerunds
nominal prefix, 1.3. (second para), 3.2.3.
nominative → pronouns (subject)
nonfinite
   clauses → clauses (nonfinite)
   complements → complements (nonfinite)
nonverbal predication, 4.4.1. (para before example (88)), 6.1. (sentence after example (11)), 7.1.1., Ch. 12, 13.3.2.1. (sentence before example (41))
noun class → nominal prefix
noun phrases, 2.3.1.2., 2.3.1.3., Ch. 4
number → aggregate plural, plural
numerals, Ch. 16
   cardinal, 16.1.
   fractions → quantification (fractional)
   ordinal, 16.2.
Nupe, 8.5.3. (second to last para)

objects → direct objects, indirect objects
   and tone, 2.3.1.5., 2.3.2., 3.2.2.
   focus marking, 15.1.3.2., 15.1.3.3.
   in serial verb constructions, 8.1.2., 8.5.3.
   omission, 10.1.3.
   pronominal, 3.3.4., 5.1., 5.2.1., 10.1.3.
obligation → deontic modality, imperatives
obliques, 2.3.1.3., 3.1.2., 4.4., 8.3.1., 10.1.1., 13.1., 13.2., 15.1.3.2., 15.1.3.3.
   oblique pronouns → pronouns (oblique)
onomatopoeia, 3.1.1.4., 3.1.1.6. (para beginning with '3')
   → ideophones
ordinal numerals → numerals (ordinal)
origins of Saramaccan, Intro
orthography, Ch. 1, 2.1., 2.2.1., 2.2.2.3. (first para), 2.2.2.4. (para after example (6))

parataxis → juxtaposition
participles, 6.4., 7.3.1. (sentence before example (66)), 8.1.1. (sentence before example (5))
particles → question particles

partitive, 4.1. (para before example (16)), 4.5. (sentence before example (119))
   → quantification (fractional)
passive voice, 6.4., 7.1.1. (para before example (15)), 7.3.6. (para before example (96)), 10.1.1.
past tense, 7.2.1., 7.5., 9.1.1. (para before example (4)), 9.2.1.3., 9.2.3.1., 9.2.3.6., 15.2.2. (sentence before example (39)), 15.2.2.4.
past time reference, 7.3.4., 13.4.2., 14.2., 14.8. (last sentence)
   → past tense
personal pronouns → pronouns
person marking → morphophonemic processes
phonology, Ch. 1, Ch. 2
phonotactics, 1.2.
phrases → noun phrases, verb phrases
pidgins, Intro
pitch accent → accent
plateauing → tone (tonal plateauing)
pleonastic pronouns → pronouns (pleonastic)
pluperfect, 7.2.1.
plural, 4.1., 4.2. (sentence before example (29)), 4.3. (sentence before example (72)), 4.4. (first para)
   → aggregate plural, pronouns
polar questions → yes/no questions
politeness, 5.1. (para after example (9)), 7.4.2.2. (sentence preceding example (136))
Portuguese, Intro, 1.1.2.1. (section on 'kp~kw'), 1.3. (first para), 2.2.2.2. (first para), 2.2.2.5. (first para), 3.4. (second para after 'interlocutor'), 5.3., 8.3.3., 14.1. (first sentence), 17.2.
positional nominals → spatial indicators
possession, 2.3.1.3., 3.3.1., 4.2. (sentence before example (31)), 4.3., 4.4.1., 10.1.1. (paras before and after example (10)), 15.1.3.3.
   alienable and inalienable, 3.3.1., 4.3.
   emphatic → emphasis (of possession)
   external possessor marking, 4.3. (para before example (64)),
   possessive pronouns → pronouns (possessive)
   predicative, 4.3., 7.1.1. (sentence before example (10)), 12.1.4., 12.2.
possibility expressions, 7.4.2.3.
postpositions → spatial indicators
pragmatic markers, Ch. 15
prefixes, 2.3.1.3. (para after example (20)), 3.2.1., 7.3.1. (para before example (68)), 7.3.4.
   → nominal prefix

prepositions, 2.3.1.3., 3.1.2., 3.3.1., 4.3. (para before table (20)), 5.1. (sentence before example (5)), 8.3.1. (sentences before examples (34) and (39)), 8.5.3. (para before example (84)), 9.2.2.2., 10.1.1. (last para), 11.2. (sentence before example (29)), 13.1., 13.3. (first sentence), 13.3.2.1. (last sentence), 15.1.3.3.
presentational expressions, 7.1.1. (para before example (3)), 12.1.2., 12.1.5., 15.1.3.4.
present tense → tense
probability expressions, 7.4.2.1.
progressive, 7.3.1., 7.3.4., 7.5.
pronouns, Ch. 5
    and cliticization, 2.3.1.5. (para before example (25)), 3.3.4., 5.2., 9.2.1.3. (para before example (21))
    and negation, 3.3.3., 7.1.2., 17.1.
    and reduplication, 15.1.3.5.
    emphatic, 15.1.3.5.
    interrogative → wh-words
    oblique, 3.3.4., 3.3.5., 4.3. (beginning to table (20)), 5.1., 5.2.1., 5.5. (first para), 15.1.3.3.
    pleonastic, 5.4., 7.4.2.3. (sentence before example (150)), 9.2.2.1. (last para), 12.4.
    possessive, 3.3.5. (last sentence), 4.3., 5.1., 7.1.1. (sentence before example (10))
    reflexive → reflexive expressions
    resumptive, 4.4.1., 15.1.3.3. (first para)
    subject, 2.2.3.3., 3.3.2., 5.1., 5.4., 9.2.1.3., 9.2.2.3., 10.1.1. (first two paras), 10.3. (sentence before example (50)), 12.1.2. (from example (14) to end), 12.4. (sentence before example (46))
    tonic, 1.1.2.2. (section on 'm'), 2.2.3.3., 4.3. (beginning to example (44)), 5.1., 5.3., 5.5., 5.6., 12.1.2., 15.1.1., 15.1.3.3.
property items → adjectives
prosodic phonology, Ch. 2
purpose expressions, 9.2.3.2.

quantification, Ch. 16
    adverbial → adverbial expressions (of quantity)
    fractional, 4.5. (example (123) and sentence preceding it), 16.4.
    negative, 7.1.3.
    numeric → numerals
    predicative, 4.5. (example (104) and sentence preceding it)
    within the noun phrase, 4.5.
question particles, 2.4.5., 11.1.

questions, 2.4.4., 2.4.5., Ch. 11
    → indirect questions, information questions, question particles, tag questions, utterance-level phonological processes (question intonation), wh-words, yes/no questions
question words → wh-words
quotative, 8.3.4.

raising verbs → verbs (raising verbs)
rapid speech phenomena, 3.5., 5.2.2.
reciprocal expressions, 5.6.
reduplication, 1.2.3. (second to last para), 3.1.1., 6.2., 6.3., 6.4., 10.1.1., 15.4.3. (last sentence)
    and plurality → aggregate plural
    and tone, 2.2.4. (last para), 2.3.1.1., 3.1.1.6.
    → adjectives (and reduplication), adjectives (resultative), pronouns (and reduplication), verbs (and reduplication)
referentiality, 4.1. (from beginning until sentence after example (10))
reflexive expressions, 5.1. (last para), 5.5., 10.1.2., 15.4.3.
relative clauses, 3.5. (sentence after example (38)), 4.4., 13.4.2. (sentence before example (62))
    headless relative clauses, 4.4.2.
resultative adjectives → adjectives (resultative)
Romance languages, 8.2. (first para), 13.1. (para after example (1))

segmental co-occurrence restrictions, 1.2.2.
segmental phonology, Ch. 1
    → consonants, vowels
serial verbs, 3.1.2., 4.4.1. (sentence before example (78)), 4.5. (last sentence), 6.1. (para before example (9)), 7.3.1. (sentence before example (66)), 7.3.6. (last two paras), 7.3.8., 9.1.1., 9.2.1.3. (last para), 9.2.2.2. (para after example (43)), 10.1.1. (para before example (11)), 10.2.1., 10.3. (last sentence), 14.2. (sentence before example (17)), 15.1.2.
    and tone, 2.3.2., 3.2.2
    degree, 6.5.1., 6.5.6., 8.3.2., 14.3., 14.5. (sentence before example (42))
    directional, 8.2., 13.3.
Sinitic languages, 2.2.1. (first para), 10.1.3.
small clauses, 9.2.2.2., 8.1.2. (last para)
sociolinguistics, Intro, 1.1.2.1. (sections on 'kp~kw'), 1.1.2.4. (section on 'l'), 3.5. (last para), 12.1.3. (second para), 17.2. (first para)
Southeast Asian languages, 3.4. (first para), 10.1.3., 15.4.
Spanish, 5.3., 10.1.2.

spatial indicators, 2.3.1.3., 13.1., 15.1.3.3.
specificity, 4.1.
Sprachbund, 10.1.3.
Sranan, Intro, 1.1.2.1. (sections on 'tj,' 'kp~kw,' and 's'), 1.2.1. (last para), 1.3. (first para), 1.4. (last para), 2.2.2.4. (last para), 2.3.1.6., 3.1.1.6., 5.3., 12.1.2. (para after example (14)), 12.2., 15.4.1. (para after example (69)), 15.4.4. (second to last para), 17.2.
stative verbs, 3.1.1.1., Ch. 6, 7.2., 7.3.1. (sentence before example (62)), 7.3.5., 13.1. (sentence before example (9))
stress, 2.2.1., 2.2.2.4., 2.2.3.4., 2.4.1., 3.1.1.6. (second to last para), 12.1.2. (sentence after example (12)), 15.1.1., 15.1.3.5.
  → syllables (and stress)
subjects, 7.1.1. (between examples (14) and (15)), 7.4.1. (para before example (128)), 8.1.1., 9.2.1.3., 9.2.2.3., 10.1.1., 12.1., 15.2.1.
  → pronouns (subject)
subjunctive, 9.2.3.2., 10.1.1. (para after example (10))
subordination, 8.1.1., 9.2.
substitutive expressions, 9.2.3.8
substrate languages, Intro, 1.1.2.1. (section on 'kp~kw'), 14.1., 15.1.3.2. (first para)
suffixes, 3.1.2., 3.1.3.
  → agentive markers
superlatives, 6.5.5.
suppletion, 6.1. (last para), 6.3. (sentence before example (36)), 6.5.1.
suprasegmental phonology, 1.2., Ch. 2
syllabic consonants, 1.1.2.2. (section on *m*), 1.2.1. (second para)
syllables, 1.1.3.3., 1.2.1., 2.2.1., 2.2.2.2., 2.2.2.3., 2.2.2.4.
  and stress, 2.2.2.4., 2.2.3.4., 2.3.2. (last para)
  and weight, 2.2.2.3., 2.2.2.4. (para after example (6))
  structure, 1.2.1.
  → coda consonants, syllabic consonants

tag questions, 11.1. (examples (10) and (11))
temporal expressions → time expressions
tense, 2.3.1.4., 6.1. (beginning until example (4)), 7.2., 8.1.1., 9.2.1.3., 9.2.3.1., 12.1.2. (sentence before example (7)), 12.3.
  → future tense, past tense
tense vowels → vowels (tense and lax)
time expressions, 13.4., 14.2., 16.5.
  → complements (temporal)
Tirió, Intro
tone, Ch. 2
  and objects → objects (and tone)
  and reduplication → reduplication (and tone)
  and serial verbs → serial verbs (and tone)
  super-high tones, 2.2.3.5.
  tonal morphology → serial verbs (and tone)
  tonal plateauing, Ch. 2, 3.1.1.6., 3.2.2.
topic-comment constructions, 4.4.1. (paras immediately before and after example (87)), 12.1.2. (from para after example (14) to end), 15.2.1.
transitive verbs, 3.1.1.1. (first sentence), 10.1.1., 13.3.2.
Twi, Intro
typology, Intro

unboundedness → boundedness
uncertain future marker, 7.4.2.3. (from beginning to para after example (146))
unergative verbs, 6.4. (para after example (42))
Universal Grammar, Intro
unstressed syllables → syllables (and stress)
Upper River dialect, Intro, 1.1.3.1. (in sections on *e*, *ɛ*, and *o*), 3.3.3., 7.1.1. (first para), 7.1.2. (first para), 15.1.3.5., 17.1.
utterance-level phonological processes, 2.4., 2.5.
  emphasis within a clause, 2.4.1., 2.4.4.
  negative lowering, 2.4.1., 2.4.3.
  question intonation, 2.4.1., 2.4.4. (second para), 2.4.5.
  utterance-final lowering, 2.2.2.4. (before example (8)), 2.3.1.7. (last para), 2.4.1., 2.4.2.

valency, Ch. 10
  valency-decreasing operations, 10.1.
  valency-increasing operations, 10.2.
verbal nouns → gerunds
verb phrases, 2.3.2. (para before example (33)), 2.5., 8.1.1. (para after example (5)), 8.1.2. (last para), 8.5.3. (first para)
verbs
  and nominalization → nominalization
  and reduplication, 3.1.1., 6.4., 7.3.5., 7.3.6. (sentence before example (96))
  and transitivity → ditransitive verbs, intransitive verbs, transitive verbs
  auxiliary, 7.3.2., 7.4.2.2. (last para), 14.8.
  compounding → serial verbs
  control verbs, 9.2.2.1
  copular → copulas
  ellipsis, 7.1.1. (sentence before example (7)), 9.1.1. (last para)

inflection, 3.2.1., 3.2.2., 7.3.1. (para before example (68)), 7.3.4.
raising verbs, 9.2.2.1. (last para)
serialization → serial verbs
vocabulary → lexicon
voice → middle voice, passive voice
vowels, 1.1.1., 1.1.3.
   and ATR → ATR
   combinations, 1.1.2.4. (section on 'j'), 1.1.3.3., 1.2.2. (section on 'nasal consonants and nasalized vowels'), 1.4., 2.2.1. (para after example (1))
   epenthetic, 1.1.3.3. (para after table (6)), 1.2.1. (last two paras), 2.2.2.5. (first para)
   harmony → harmony (vowel)
   length, 1.1.2.4. (section on 'j'), 1.1.3.3., 1.2.2. (section on 'nasal consonants and nasalized vowels'), 1.2.3., 1.4., 2.2.1., 2.2.2.4.
   nasal → nasals (nasal vowels)
   tense and lax, 1.1.3.1., 3.4. (para after 'interlocutor')

weight → moras, syllables (and weight)

West African languages, Intro, 1.1.2.1. (section on 'kp~kw'), 1.1.3.1 (second para), 1.2.2. (section on 'upper mid and lower mid vowels'), 2.2.4. (second para), 2.3.1.2. (first para), 2.4.1. (second para), 2.4.4. (first para), 8.5.3. (second to last para), 12.2. (first para)
wh-questions → information questions
wh-words, 3.3.5., 4.4.2., 11.2., 11.3., 12.1.3., 12.3. (second para)
word formation → morphology
word order, Intro, 3.4. (sentence before 'boat carrier'), Ch. 4 (first para), 7.5., 11.1. (first para), 12.1.2. (sentence before example (13))
writing system → orthography

Yatye, 8.5.3. (second to last para)
yes/no questions, 2.4.5., 11.1.

zero-marking
   of causative, 10.2.2. (last para)
   of copular clauses, 7.3.6. (para after example (95)), 12.1.3., 15.1.3.1., 15.2.2.3.
   of passive, 6.4. (from sentence before example (48) to end), 10.1.1. (examples (5) and (6))
   of past tense, 7.2.1. (second para)

www.ingramcontent.com/pod-product-compliance
Lightning Source LLC
Chambersburg PA
CBHW080637170426
43200CB00015B/2864